OTHER BOOKS BY THE BROTHERS MEDVED

The Fifty Worst Films of All Time (1978)

The Golden Turkey Awards (1980)

*The Hollywood Hall of Shame:
The Most Expensive Flops
in Movie History* (1984)

BY MICHAEL MEDVED

What Really Happened to the Class of '65?
(with David Wallechinsky, 1976)

*The Shadow Presidents: The Secret History of the
Chief Executives and Their Top Aides* (1979)

*Hospital: The Hidden Lives of a
Medical Center Staff* (1983)

SON OF GOLDEN TURKEY AWARDS

SON OF
GOLDEN TURKEY
AWARDS

by
HARRY and MICHAEL
MEDVED

VILLARD BOOKS   NEW YORK   1986

All rights reserved under International
and Pan-American Copyright Conventions. Published in
the United States by Villard Books,
a division of Random House, Inc., New York, and
simultaneously in Canada by
Random House of Canada Limited, Toronto.

Library of Congress Cataloging-in-Publication Data
Medved, Harry.
    Son of golden turkey awards.
    Includes index.
    1. Moving-pictures—Anecdotes, facetiae, satire,
etc.   I. Medved, Michael.   II. Title.
PN1994.9.M44   1986   791.43′75   85–40717
ISBN 0–394–74341–5

Photograph sources and copyrights: Orion Pictures, New World Pictures, Tri-Star Pictures, Filmways International, Associated Film Distribution, Hammer Films, Fanfare Films, Crown International, Toho International, Fairway-International, Howco-International, Film Ventures International, Europix International, Merrick International, Independent International, Monogram Pictures, Mascot Pictures, Sonney Amusement Corporation, Sack Amusement Enterprise, Ellman Enterprises, Emereson Film Enterprises, New American Enterprises, Hemispher Productions, Cambist Films, Topaz Films, The Wrather Corporation, Sunn Classics, World Northal Pictures, Jensen-Farley Pictures, U.P.A., G.G. Communications, ABKCO Film, Cineworld Corporation, Morgan-Steckler Productions, Carter Film Production, Tropical Pictures Inc., Realart Pictures, Unusual Pictures Inc., Museum of Modern Art Film Stills Archives, Academy of Motion Picture Arts and Sciences.

Grateful acknowledgment is made to the following for permission to reprint previously published material:

ABKCO Music, Inc.: Excerpt of lyrics to "That's the Way It's Got to Be" written by Tony Myles, George Gallacher, Hume Payton. From the motion picture *Mars Invades Puerto Rico*. Published by ABKCO Music, Inc. © 1965. Used by permission.

Buttermilk Sky Associates, Inc.: Excerpts of lyrics to "How to Stuff a Wild Bikini. © 1965 OPC Music Publishing, Inc. (administered by Buttermilk Sky Associates, Inc.). Used by permission.

Peer Southern Productions: Excerpt of lyrics to "Down on the Sunset Trail" by Lew Porter from the motion picture *The Terror of Tiny Town*. Copyright 1938 by L. Wolfe Gilbert Music Co. Copyright renewed and assigned to La Salle Music Publishers, Inc. International copyright secured. All rights reserved. Used by permission.

Designed by Beth Tondreau

Manufactured in the United States of America
9 8 7 6 5 4 3 2
First Edition

For our agents, Arthur and Richard Pine,
with appreciation for a full decade of
support and friendship.

Of human work none but what is bad can be perfect
in its own bad way.

—John Ruskin
(1819–1900)
The Stones of Venice

CONTENTS

THE LAST WORD

Why, you may ask, does the world need a second volume of
Golden Turkey Awards?
It's a reasonable question and it deserves an honest answer.

When the original book appeared six years ago, we never expected it to spawn a sequel. We tried to tell our readers everything we knew about bad movies, and hoped that our work would satisfy the public's curiosity about this important field.

It soon became clear, however, that we had greatly underestimated the scope and complexity of our subject. Letters poured in from around the world, most of them taking us to task for having neglected some particularly beloved turkey. "How dare you guys put out a book on terrible movies," began one typical dispatch from the trenches, "without even mentioning my personal favorite, *The Beach Girls and the Monster*!"

The omission of this worthy film, and of many other notable contenders, reflected gaps in our research rather than disagreement on matters of taste. Though we made every effort to investigate all the most celebrated bad films, and considered some two thousand titles in the process, we had only begun to scale the mountain of wretched celluloid that Hollywood had built up over the years.

This new project gave us the chance to climb higher, and to discover literally hundreds of fresh films that had previously remained hidden from view. Many of them—particularly low budget gems of the forties, fifties, and sixties—had fallen into well-deserved obscurity immediately following their release, and for us to locate them, determined detective work was required. In this ongoing "strange pursuit" (see: THE WORST ROCK 'N' ROLL LYRICS IN MOVIE HISTORY) correspondence from bad movie fans around the world provided invaluable assistance. This book includes descriptions of more than two hundred films we have never discussed before; more than fifty of those titles appear here thanks to canny and valuable recommendations from our readers.

Another rich source of new material is Hollywood itself, which, though the pace of production has slowed somewhat in recent years, continues to turn out dozens of turkey titles every season. These late arrivals—including fabled fiascos such as *Sheena* and *Rhinestone*—have enriched many of the categories in this book.

Finally, we have been significantly assisted in our research by the advent of the age of video. When researching the original *Golden Turkey Awards* we had to rely on screenings—at theaters, film libraries, or on television. The welcome proliferation of home video recorders has made an enormous difference. Bad movie buffs throughout North America shared rare and precious tapes with us and gave us a chance to marvel at some long-forgotten films recorded from broadcast on the late, late shows of obscure television stations in Buffalo, New York, El Paso, Texas, or other centers of American culture. The development of the VCR also enhanced our ability to record every priceless detail of these films and made it much easier to report on some of the immortal dialogue in these films. Instead of furiously scribbling notes in darkened screening rooms, we could now go back, rewind, reconsider, and so savor every golden moment —an ability that has also contributed to the surprising worldwide popularity of cinematic stinkers on videocassette.

This popularity provides powerful evidence of the growing public fascination with Hollywood's most embarrassing products, and cynics will suggest that we have undertaken this latest book in order to capitalize on an international fad we helped to start. According to this hardheaded view, we are in the bad movie business primarily for the money, having discovered the secret so long sought by the ancient alchemists who craved a means for turning dross into gold.

Though we are of course flattered by these generous estimates of our business acumen, we must point out that they unfortunately ignore the very substantial cost of research, photographs, old pressbooks, film rental, taping, interviews with filmmakers, memorabilia, and frequent travel as part of our continuing turkey hunt. On the first *Golden Turkey* book, these costs easily consumed the bulk of our personal proceeds. While we would hardly suggest ourselves as the objects of pity, it is fair to point out that Harry earned more working as a theater usher during his senior year in high school than he did, after expenses, as co-author of a lengthy tome on ridiculous movies.

Nevertheless, we pushed forward with this project, and we will admit that our motivation remained primarily selfish. The bald fact is that we enjoy what we're doing. We find bad movies almost endlessly amusing, and we want our readers to share our peculiar passion. The sincere stupidity of an egregiously inept motion picture is far more entertaining than the contrived silliness of most intentional comedies —and it is also far more endearing. As we hope our writing makes clear, we not only enjoy the examples of human frailty and incompetence chronicled in this volume; we also cherish them.

The format for *Son of Golden Turkey Awards* follows the familiar pattern of show business award presentations, with a listing of the nominees in each category, and then the eagerly awaited announcement of the winner. We take sole responsibility for these often subjective choices and try to provide a brief explanation of why we selected the winner in each case. In many of the book's twenty-three categories, we present five nominees for the coveted prize, but in others—such as THE MOST IDIOTIC AD LINES OR THE MOST PRIMITIVE MALE CHAUVINIST FANTASY—the serious contenders proved so plentiful that we couldn't limit ourselves to an arbitrary number. In all cases, we list the nominees in chronological order (as opposed to the Academy Awards, which lists its choices alphabetically) so that the reader can follow the historical development of, say, bad beach party movies or tasteless biker sagas. At the conclusion of the book we offer a Who's Who of the most important names in the exotic history of bad movies, honoring the often unheralded directors, producers, writers, stars, and oddly assorted others who crafted many of the most beloved Golden Turkey films. This "Rogues' Gallery" provides brief biographical notes on a collection of colorful characters who, for the most part, will never find their way into standard film encyclopedias.

As we proceeded with the two years of intermittent effort behind this book, we began to feel a deepening sense of identification with these crackpots and visionaries. The viewing of bad movies became with us not just a hobby but an addiction, erasing the normal dividing line between eccentricity and obsession. We happen to live in separate homes on the same piece of property near the Pacific Ocean, and the long sleepless nights of crossing back and forth over the patio between our premises, talking, arguing, punching notes into the word processor, and checking pieces of videotape puzzled even our long-suffering Norwegian elkhound. By the end of the project, the guest house, which Harry shares with an enormous collection of books, files, tapes, posters, film reels, projectors, catalogues, Godzilla toys, and other creative clutter, became sort of a living shrine to Golden Turkeydom. Fortunately, none of the Hollywood tours have yet discovered this particular museum.

As we write these words we have, at long last, begun to emerge from this insanity and reorganize our lives. Harry, having delayed his graduation from the film department at UCLA for more than three years while he pursued his fascination with bad movies, has finally completed his slow, stately progress toward a seven-year BA. He will now attempt to find honest employment in the film industry, with the hope of discovering at least a few producers whom he hasn't offended with his writing. Michael, meanwhile, is already hard at work on his latest nonfiction project (which is not at all connected to the world of Hollywood) while each week he reviews the new movies, the good as well as the bad and ugly, on national television.

Son of Golden Turkey Awards may not be the last word on bad movies, but it is *our* last word. Though no one can tell with certainty what the future may bring, we hereby solemnly pledge that the years ahead will produce no further Golden Turkey publications by the Medved brothers. This hardly means that the field has been exhausted, but it does mean that we now pass the torch to whichever brave souls feel ready to take up the challenge.

Santa Monica
October, 1985

SON OF GOLDEN TURKEY AWARDS

LET'S TALK TURKEY.

THE MOST IDIOTIC AD LINES IN HOLLYWOOD HISTORY

C atchy and well-crafted advertisements have always played an important role in the movie business. A particularly cunning slogan—such as "Pray for Rosemary's Baby" (1968) or "Just When You Thought It Was Safe to Go Back in the Water" (Jaws II, 1978)—can generate extra millions at the box office while leaving a lasting impression on the moviegoing public.

But just when you thought it was safe to go back in the theater, Hollywood hucksters assault you with another sort of ad campaign: commercial approaches so squalid and ill-conceived that they encourage potential patrons to stay home and save their money. These examples of superheated hyperbole may be offensive, but they often display more imagination than the movies they attempted to sell.

AND THE NOMINEES ARE...

★ *A Giggle Gurgling Gulp of Glee—*
   With Pretty Girls, Peppy Scenes and Gorgeous Revues—plus a good story.
   —*Tea with a Kick (1924)*

★ *Whoopee! Let's go! . . . Hand-picked beauties doing cute tricks!*
   GET IN THE KNOW FOR THE HEY-HEY WHOOPEE!
   —*The Wild Party (1929)*

★ *YOU HEAR HIM MAKE LOVE!*
   DIX—the dashing soldier!
   DIX—the bold adventurer!
   DIX—the throbbing lover!
   —*The Wheel of Life*
   (No, this is not an early porno talkie, but rather the first sound outing of silent-screen matinee idol Richard Dix.)
   (1929)

★ *SEE CHARLES BUTTERWORTH DRIVE A STREETCAR AND SING LOVE SONGS TO HIS MARE "MITZIE"!*
   —*The Night Is Young (1934)*

★ KATHARINE HEPBURN as the lying, stealing, singing, preying witch girl of the Ozarks . . . "Low down white trash!"? Maybe so—but let her hear you say it and she'll break your head to prove herself a lady!
—*Spitfire* (1934)

"She'll break your head to prove herself a lady!":
Katharine Hepburn amazes moviegoers (and her co-stars)
in Spitfire.

★ Do Native Women Live with Apes?
—*Love Life of a Gorilla* (1937)

★ JUNGLE KISS!!
When she looked into his eyes, felt his arms around her—she was no longer Tura, mysterious white goddess of the jungle tribes—she was no longer the frozen-hearted high priestess under whose hypnotic spell the worshippers of the great crocodile god meekly bowed—she was a girl in love!
SEE the ravening charge of the hundred sacred CROCODILES!
—*Her Jungle Love* (1938)

★ LOVE! HATE! JOY! FEAR! TORMENT! PANIC! SHAME! RAGE!
—*Intermezzo* (1939)

★ She's got the biggest six-shooters in the West!
—*The Beautiful Blonde from Bashful Bend* (1949)

★ CAST OF 3,000!
    4 WRITERS,
    2 DIRECTORS,
    3 CAMERAMEN,
    3 PRODUCERS!
    1 YEAR TO MAKE THIS FILM—
    24 YEARS TO REHEARSE—
    20 YEARS TO DISTRIBUTE!
        BEAUTIFUL BEYOND WORDS!
        AWE-INSPIRING! VITAL!
    THE PRINCE OF PEACE *PROVIDES THE ANSWER TO OUR EVERY PROBLEM!*
        Be Brave—bring your troubles and your family to HISTORY'S MOST SUBLIME EVENT! YOU'LL FIND GOD —RIGHT IN THERE!
—*The Prince of Peace* (Starring members of the Wichita Mountain Pageant and featuring Millard Coody as Jesus) (1948)

★ The Miracle of the Age!!! A LION *in your lap!* A LOVER *in your arms!*
—*Bwana Devil* (A pioneering, sleep-inducing 3-D extravaganza about railway construction crews in darkest Africa) (1952)

"The miracle of the age!!! A LION in your lap!":
Barbara Britton and Robert Stack take aim at 3-D big
game in Bwana Devil.

★ **OVERWHELMING!**
  ELECTRIFYING!
  BAFFLING!
  Fire Can't Burn Them! Bullets Can't Kill Them! See the Unfolding of the Mysteries of the Moon as Murderous Robot Monsters Descend Upon the Earth! You've Never Seen Anything Like It! Neither Has the World!
      SEE . . . Robots from Space in All Their Glory!!!
                      —*Robot Monster* (1953)

★ *1,965 pyramids, 5,337 dancing girls, one million swaying bullrushes, 802 sacred bulls!*
                      —*The Egyptian* (1954)

★ *They hungered for her treasure! And died for her pleasure! SEE Man-Fish Battle Shark-Man-Killer!*
                  —*The Golden Mistress* (1954)

★ *See Jane Russell in 3-D; She'll Knock* Both *Your Eyes Out!*
                      —*The French Line* (1954)

★ *See Jane Russell Shake Her Tambourines . . . and Drive Cornel* WILDE*!*
                      —*Hot Blood* (1956)

Viewers of Hot Blood *watched Gypsy girl Jane Russell "Shake Her Tambourines and Drive Cornel WILDE!"*

★ *The nightmare terror of the slithering eye that unleashed agonizing horror on a screaming world!*
                  —*The Crawling Eye* (1958)

★ *SEE a female colossus . . . her mountainous torso, skyscraper limbs, giant desires!*
                      —*Attack of the*
                      Fifty-Foot Woman (1958)

★ *Here is Your Chance to Know More About Sex.*
  What Should a Movie Do? Hide Its Head in the Sand Like an Ostrich? Or Face the JOLTING TRUTH as does . . .
                  —*The Desperate Women*
                      (1958)

★ **HOODLUMS FROM ANOTHER WORLD ON A RAY-GUN RAMPAGE!**
                  —*Teenagers from Outer Space*
                      (1959)

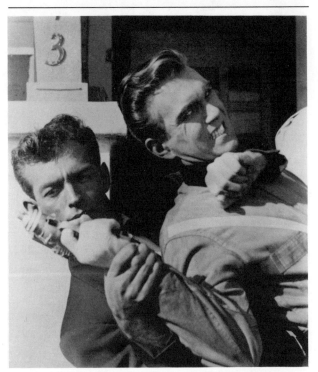

David Love and Bryan Grant star as "HOODLUMS FROM ANOTHER WORLD ON A RAY-GUN RAMPAGE!" in Teenagers from Outer Space.

★ *Which will be Her Mate . . . MAN OR BEAST?*
  Meet Velda—the Kind of Woman—Man or Gorilla Would Kill . . . to Keep.
                  —*Untamed Mistress* (1960)

★ NOW AN ALL-MIGHTY ALL-NEW MOTION PICTURE BRINGS THEM TOGETHER FOR THE FIRST TIME. . . . HISTORY'S MOST GIGANTIC MONSTERS IN COMBAT ATOP MOUNT FUJI!

—*King Kong vs. Godzilla*
(1963)

"*TOGETHER FOR THE FIRST TIME*": *The two battling stars of* King Kong vs. Godzilla.

★ POWERFUL! SHOCKING! RAW! ROUGH! CHALLENGING! SEE *A LITTLE GIRL MOLESTED!*

—*Never Take Candy from a Stranger* (1963)

★ She Sins in Mobile—
Marries in Houston—
Loses Her Baby in Dallas—
Leaves Her Husband in Tucson—
MEETS HARRY IN SAN DIEGO! . . . .
FIRST—HARLOW!
THEN—MONROE!
NOW—McCLANAHAN!!!

—*The Rotten Apple*
(Starring the irresistible
Rue McClanahan)
(1963)

★ NOT FOR SISSIES! DON'T COME IF YOU'RE CHICKEN! A Horrifying Movie of Weird Beauties and Shocking Monsters. . . . 1001 WEIRDEST SCENES EVER!! MOST SHOCKING THRILLER OF THE CENTURY!

—*Teenage Psycho Meets
Bloody Mary* (Alternate Title:
*The Incredibly Strange
Creatures Who Stopped
Living and Became Mixed-Up
Zombies*) (1964)

★ SCENES THAT WILL STAGGER YOUR SIGHT!
—DANCING CALLED GO-GO
—MUSIC CALLED JU-JU
—NARCOTICS CALLED BANGI!
—FIRES OF PUBERTY!
SEE *the burning of a virgin!*
SEE *power of witch doctor over women!*
SEE *pygmies with fantastic* Physical Endowments!!!

—*Kwaheri* (1965)

★ The Big Comedy of Nineteen-Sexty-Sex!

—*Boeing Boeing* (1965)

★ AN ASTRONAUT WENT UP—
A "GUESS WHAT" CAME DOWN!
The picture that comes complete with a 10-foot tall monster to give you the wim-wams!

—Herschell Gordon Lewis's
Monster a Go-Go (1965)

★ When You're Six Tons—And They Call You Killer—It's Hard to Make Friends. . . .

—*Namu, the Killer Whale*
(1966)

★ Meet the Girls with the Thermo-Nuclear Navels!

—*Dr. Goldfoot and the
Girl Bombs* (1966)

Vincent Price inspects the "Girls with the Thermo-Nuclear Navels" in Dr. Goldfoot and the Girl Bombs.

★ A GHASTLY TALE DRENCHED WITH GOUTS OF
BLOOD SPURTING FROM THE VICTIMS OF A CRAZED
MADMAN'S LUST.
—*A Taste of Blood*
(1967)

★ A mis-spawned murderous abomination from the
nether reaches of an unimaginable hell.
—*The Killer of Castle Brood*
(1968)

★ NEW—SICKENING HORROR to make your STOMACH
TURN and FLESH CRAWL!
—*Frankenstein's Bloody Terror*
(1968)

★ LUST-MAD MEN AND LAWLESS WOMEN IN A VICIOUS
AND SENSUOUS ORGY OF SLAUGHTER!
—*Five Bloody Graves* (1969)

★ The family that slays together stays together.
—*Bloody Mama* (1970)

★ HOT STEEL BETWEEN THEIR LEGS!
—*The Cycle Savages* (1969)

★ The Hand that Rocks the Cradle . . .
    Has no Flesh on It!
—*Who Slew Auntie Roo?*
(1971)

★ TWO GREAT BLOOD HORRORS TO RIP OUT YOUR
GUTS!
—For the memorable 1971
double bill of Del Tenney's
I Eat Your Skin and *I Drink
Your Blood.*

★ They Went In People and Came Out Hamburger!
—*The Corpse Grinders* (1971)

★ SHE TOOK ON THE WHOLE GANG! A howling hellcat
humping a hot steel hog on a roaring rampage of
revenge!
—*Bury Me an Angel* (1972)

★ WHAT'S THE SECRET INGREDIENT USED BY THE
MAD BUTCHER FOR HIS SUPERB SAUSAGES?
—*Meat Is Meat* (1972)

★ TODAY the Pond!
TOMORROW the World!
—*Frogs* (1972)

★ Different! Daring! Dynamic! Defying! Dumbfounding!
    SEE Uncle Tom lead the Negroes to FREEDOM!
    . . . Now, all the SENSUAL and VIOLENT passions
Roots couldn't show on TV!
—*Uncle Tom's Cabin* (1972)

★ An appalling amalgam of carnage and carnality!
—*Flesh and Blood Show* (1973)

★ WHEN THE CATS ARE HUNGRY . . .
RUN FOR YOUR LIVES!
Alone, only a harmless pet . . .
    One Thousand Strong, They Become a Man-Eating
    Machine!
—*The Night of a Thousand Cats*
(1972)

★ They're Over-Exposed
But Not Under-Developed!
—*Cover Girl Models* (1975)

★ An AVALANCHE of KILLER WORMS!
—*Squirm* (1976)

★ Most Movies Live Less Than Two Hours.
This Is One of Everlasting Torment!
—*The New House on the Left*
(1977)

★ WE ARE GOING TO EAT YOU!
—*Zombie* (1980)

★ It's not human and it's got an axe.
—*The Prey* (1981)

★ SEE rebel guerrillas torn apart by trucks!
    SEE corpses cut to pieces and fed to dogs and
vultures!
    SEE the monkey trained to perform nursing duties for
her paralyzed owner!
—*Sweet and Savage* (1983)

★ **What a Guy! What a Gal! What a Pair!**
—*Stroker Ace* (Starring
Loni Anderson and
Burt Reynolds) (1983)

*Loni Anderson congratulates co-star Burt Reynolds on a
particularly appropriate costume for his role in the 1983
turkey* Stroker Ace. *"What a Guy! What a Gal! . . ."
What a Bomb.*

★ **It's always better when you come again!**
—*Porky's II: The Next Day*
(1983)

★ **You Don't Have to Go to Texas for a Chainsaw
Massacre!**
—*Pieces* (1983)

AND THE WINNER IS . . .

. . . KWAHERI

This 1965 pseudodocumentary compilation of ama-
teurishly photographed jungle oddities featured not
only the most idiotic, but the most mercilessly ver-
bose print advertisements in the history of movies.
One such layout promised gullible filmgoers:

A LAND OF WITCH DOCTORS!
A NATION OF TRANQUILIZERS!

SEE THE FORBIDDEN!
SEE THE UNSEEN!
SEE THE IMPOSSIBLE!
*FORGET ANYTHING AND EVERYTHING EVER SEEN ON
FILM! . . .*
DEFIES DEBATE!
DEFIES DESCRIPTION!
DEFIES DEATH!
  BETTER THAN A $10,000 VACATION!!!
A FILM THAT SWALLOWS ENTIRE CENTURIES WHOLE!
GIANT SNAKES SWALLOW ANIMALS WHOLE!

*SEE FRANTIC VIRGINS DANCE IN THE FIRES OF
PUBERTY!*
*SEE An African Witch Doctor perform brain surgery
without Anesthetic, Drugs or Hypnotism. See "KWAHERI."*
*SEE Wild Beasts! Giraffes! Zebras! Beautiful Birds!
Elephants! Antelope! Cape Buffalo! Hyenas! Rhinoceros!
[sic] See "KWAHERI."*
*SEE Gabon Vipers! Pythons! Lizards! Puff Adders! Dung
Beetles! Leopards! Dwarfs! Gazelles! Albinos!
See "KWAHERI."*
*SEE Ankole Monkeys! Mambas! Okapi! Giant Spiders!
Jungle Beasts of Great Muscle and Great Power!
See "KWAHERI."*
*SEE 400 Elephants slaughtered for their 800 Tusks!
Unequaled brutality! The land of thatched huts and
hatched nuts. See "KWAHERI."*
*SEE Caves in the jungles as yet unexplored by man! Soil
red with the blood of white animals! See "KWAHERI."*
*SEE Dazzling Dwarfs who wanta be tall—Gigantic Giants
who wanta be small. Witness a man's arm turned around.
See "KWAHERI."*
*SEE The Suks—a people who must walk a hundred miles
for a pale [sic] of water. A people who drink blood.
See "KWAHERI."*

*THE UNIVERSE HOLDS IT'S [sic] BREATH AT THE
AUDACITY OF MAN!"*

Hollywood held its breath, in any event, at the
audacity of the imaginative—and all but illiterate—
hucksters who devised this astonishing campaign.

Their text, quoted above, raises several intriguing
questions. In a single line it promises to treat the
public to visions of "dung beetles" and "dwarfs"—it
is well known, of course, that these particular creatures offer a potent box office draw. What's more, in

One of the many imaginative (and illiterate) newspaper layouts for Kwaheri, *featuring a model who appears to be well beyond the "FIRES OF PUBERTY!"*

a subsequent line these dwarves are described as "dazzling," which seems to suggest that they have been fitted in appropriately miniaturized gold lamé suits. On the other hand, the giants in *Kwaheri* are no ordinary giants—no way! These big fellas, we are told, are "*gigantic* giants"—always the best kind.

This use of telling, perfectly chosen adjectives characterizes the entire ad. One of the thrills offered by this film is, of course, "soil red with the blood of white animals," which is ever so much more horrifying than soil red with the blood of ordinary brown, gray or black animals.

But even if the copywriter makes idiosyncratic decisions about his choice of words, or spelling (he should *pail* with embarrassment for having written about a "pale" of water), we can rest assured that he is a veritable whiz at arithmetic. After all, no sooner do we read of the tasty slaughter of "400 elephants" than, quick as a wink, we see the calculation that the poor beasts have been killed "for their 800 tusks." How many tusks were they supposed to have? 300? 620? 940? You can never tell with this movie. After all, a film that promises the ultimate thrill of "witnessing a man's arm turned around" is capable of delivering on any mind-boggling marvel.

The chief marvel associated with this project, however, is the fact that it did as well as it did at the box office. The lurid newspaper and magazine ads helped to generate large crowds, eager to enjoy the breathtaking spectacle of "beautiful birds," "puff adders," "lizards," "dung beetles," and "dazzling dwarfs" cavorting together on the big screen.

The fun actually begins with an attention-getting scene of a 250-pound snake slowly swallowing a terrified calf. From there, this out-of-focus-but-in-color travelogue proceeds up and down the continent of Africa, accompanied by pretentious and stentorian narration by Les Tremayne, erstwhile star of *The Slime People* and *Creature of Destruction.* Along the way we meet "the world's foremost husband": a tired-looking jungle denizen with 49 wives and 212 children; a cowboy named Bill Daniel (from Liberty, Texas) who successfully lassos a two-ton rhino; witch doctors who file off portions of villagers' teeth every time they commit a sin; "the world's foremost snake hunter," Alan Tarlton; tribal good ol' boys who "prefer blood to beer"; and, most memorably, the "world famous trephination scene, an unforgettable three minutes on screen," which, according to the press book, "became the talk of the medical profession in this country." Brain surgery with banana leaf sutures? You got it. As the official publicity describes the proceedings: "The operation is performed in the open air with flys [sic] and bugs everywhere. Pig fat is used to pack the cranial cavity afterwards. The incision is pulled together by tying jungle leaves around the woman's head."

The public relations genius behind the triumphantly tacky advertising campaign for *Kwaheri* was H. Kroger Babb, one of Hollywood's most celebrated salesmen and a deserving winner of the Golden Turkey Award in this category. Working on behalf of the movie's aptly named distributor, Unusual Films, Mr. Babb (or "Krog," as he was known by his friends) personally wrote all ads for *Kwaheri*, as he did for each of the movies he promoted in the course of his long career. As one of his colleagues admiringly recalled, "He was the greatest showman this business ever saw. Krog could take any piece of junk and sell it."

THE HIGH PRIEST OF HYPE: Former carnival barker H. Kroger Babb, who personally prepared the ads for Kwaheri *and many other Hollywood "spectaculars."*

And how did Mr. Babb prepare for his chosen role?

Go ahead, take a guess.

Looking at the text of his ads, one might assume that he took a literature degree at Yale or Cambridge, but in fact, Mr. Babb worked for years as a barker—for various carnivals, sideshows, and Broadway attractions. In this capacity he developed his personal motto: "You've Got to Tell 'Em to Sell 'Em." He put this principle into practice in promoting more than

a hundred films, including the twenty memorable pictures he produced himself before his death in 1973.

Particularly notable in this body of work was *The Prince of Peace* (1948), featuring an ad campaign that earned its own nomination for the Golden Turkey in this category. Inspired by a $10,000 subsidy from an altruistic oil company, Krog filmed the Wichita Mountain Pageant in Lawton, Oklahoma. With most of the biblical dialogue delivered in a thick, twangy southwestern drawl ("Which one o' y'all is gonna be the one who's gonna betray me?"), the picture was aptly described by film historian Kenneth Turan as "the only film in history that should have been dubbed from English to English." Mr. Babb worried about another problem: With power lines clearly visible in the background during the procession to Calvary, the producer feared that "when people see that, they'll think they're going to *electrocute* Him." Despite these drawbacks, the producer's aggressive sales techniques (including the heavy sale of "inspirational pamphlets" at the theaters) insured that *The Prince of Peace* became a substantial hit, like nearly all of his other projects.

Among his few fiascoes were a mini-epic called *The Secrets of Beauty* (1938), which told the inspiring story of a homely girl who transforms herself into a Hollywood glamor puss through the wonders of a remarkable new line of makeup, conveniently made available for sale in the theaters screening the film; and *One Too Many* (1950), a solemn, cautionary tale about the dangers of drunk driving. Shortly after the film's release, Mr. Babb himself was arrested for driving under the influence as he ran a red light near his home in West Los Angeles. The officers remained unimpressed by his fanciful claims that he was the producer of TV's *Your Show of Shows* and Bob Hope specials; Babb obviously felt, under the circumstances, that it would have been a breach of taste to mention his public-spirited work on *One Too Many*.

The press nonetheless found out about his arrest and made the connection for the public between the inebriated producer and his preachy film. A lesser man might have been powerfully embarrassed, but Mr. Babb's friends naturally assumed that he had staged the arrest as yet another imaginative publicity stunt.

In any event, his humiliation remained less profound than that of the major stars who were caught quite literally with their pants down as the nominees in our next category. . . .

THE MOST EMBARRASSING NUDE SCENE IN HOLLYWOOD HISTORY

S ince motion pictures began, they have, on innumerable occasions, revealed the glory of the unadorned human form.

Some of the earliest experiments with moving images, conducted by Eadweard Muybridge in the 1870s, showed nude figures running and jumping. By the turn of the century, artistic visions of dancers in all their natural splendor had become fairly common, and during the silent era occasional nudity even played a role in mainstream Hollywood films.

The production codes of the 1930s changed all that, but European "art films" still reached these shores and, with their far less restrictive standards, helped several aspiring stars make the most of their natural assets. Hedy Lamarr's celebrated skinny-dip in the Czech film Ecstasy *(1933) made her a household name, while Sophia Loren's brief part as a naked slave girl in the eminently forgettable Italian epic* It's Him—Yes! Yes! *(1951) helped convince audiences, and producers, that she was one spicy meatball.*

In more recent years nude scenes have become so common that they attract little notice except under extraordinary circumstances—such as Brooke Shields baring her all as a 12-year-old prostitute in Pretty Baby *(1978), or Bo Derek displaying herself as Bo Derek in* 10 *(1979). Nevertheless, many aspiring actors and actresses still feel that the best way to get exposure is through exposure. As a 26-year-old starlet, Jacqueline Bisset appeared in the buff in a dreary and pretentious British melodrama called* Secrets *(1971); the role came back to haunt her when the producers rereleased the film after its lead actress had achieved international stardom. More humiliating still was an early star turn by a starving young actor named Sylvester Stallone who, in 1970, went the distance to play one of the title roles (guess which one) in a crudely shot hardcore porno romp entitled* A Party at Kitty and Stud's. *After* Rocky *won the Oscar as Best Picture of the Year for 1976, this grainy exercise became a smash hit at the naughtier neighborhood theaters and then later as a videocassette. With its provocative new title* The Italian Stallion, *it gave millions of movie fans the thrill of watching Sly Stallone pumping something a bit more challenging than mere iron.*

These established "body beautiful" stars might feel uncomfortable when caught with their pants down in these youthful indiscretions, but they had less reason for public embarrassment than did some of the aging, lumpish, or out-of-shape performers who, for various reasons, felt the need to disrobe before the cameras. Surely we could have been spared those revealing moments spent with Liz Taylor (Ash Wednesday, *1973), Abbott and Costello (*Ride 'Em,

Cowboy, *1942*), *Adam ("Batman") West (*The Happy Hooker Goes to Hollywood, *1980*), *Buck Henry (*Taking Off, *1971*), *Diana Dors (*The Amorous Milkman, *1972*), *and Albert Finney (*Under the Volcano, *1984*). In each of these cases, however unpleasant the resulting spectacle, it could still be explained, for reasons comic or otherwise, in the context of the film. Our unfortunate nominees, however, played nude scenes that proved to be not only unwelcome but unnecessary; they stood blushing before the eyes of the world without even a fig leaf of artistic justification. In burlesque houses of old, enthusiastic audience members used to encourage the performers by cheering for them to "Take it off! Take it all off!" The actors and actresses listed below have, on the other hand, caused outraged crowds to yell, "Put it on! Put it all back on!" Their embarrassing achievements stand as a concise and eloquent argument for the return to the days of the Hays Office and the rigorous censorship of Hollywood productions.*

AND THE NOMINEES ARE...

BURGESS MEREDITH IN
SUCH GOOD FRIENDS (1971)

Even as a young man, Burgess Meredith never exactly qualified as a beefcake star; his slight frame and mobile, expressive face made him better suited for comic or character roles than for romantic leads.

Why, then, at the age of 62, did this distinguished American actor feel a sudden urge to reveal his withered physique to a moviegoing public that had demonstrated neither curiosity nor appetite for the appalling spectacle?

While a superficial examination of the situation might lead one to suspect a perverse streak of exhibitionism, or perhaps premature senility, Mr. Meredith insisted that his decision to disrobe in public arose out of a profound commitment to artistic integrity. "The new freedom will make film so much more valuable," he told an interviewer in 1971. "The kids are way ahead of us. To be ashamed of sex or the human body is against art. It's stupid. . . . It has been suppressed for so long—and anything natural which is blocked up will eventually explode."

Meredith himself exploded—onto the screen, at least—wearing only a hardcover book dangling from his waist on a sagging chain, in a vehicle described by Richard Schickel as "the most repellent movie of that repellent year 1971 . . . disgusting. . . . The only question posed by *Such Good Friends* is which is the most vulgar in its endless succession of vulgar im-

Burgess Meredith bravely preparing to disrobe for his long-awaited nude debut in Such Good Friends.

ages?" Meredith tried his best to answer that question by dancing in the buff, with his belly drooping and jiggling, his thighs shivering, and his spindly arms waving expressively in an obscene parody of the latest go-go moves. In a part that made his recurring role as the Penguin on the *Batman* TV series look like a model of dignity and decorum, he played Bernard Kalman, a pompous novelist who is encountered at a cocktail party by the film's feminist heroine, Julie Messenger (Dyan Cannon). As Kalman offers an insufferably windy speech about a recent meeting with the President of the United States, Julie fantasizes that his clothes disappear—except for the strategically placed copy of his latest novel. As the respected man of letters bumps and grinds, or at least grinds his bumps, he reaches into Ms. Cannon's vest to tweak one of her breasts and poses the suave and subtle question, "How about a little nookie?"

The filmmaker who persuaded Meredith to expose his talents in this distinctly unflattering light was Otto Preminger. In addition to their work together on this lamentable project, Otto and Burgess combined forces on such other stinkers as *Hurry Sundown* (1967) and *Skidoo* (1968), not to mention their joint participation in the *Batman* series, where Preminger played the bald and monocled meanie Mr. Freeze.

Preminger's original plans for *Such Good Friends* called for Dyan Cannon to strip down for action in a steamy nude scene, but when she absolutely refused to shed her clothes the director gallantly informed the press that "perhaps she does not like her own body" and settled for Meredith, who had no such problems. The rare opportunity of working in close proximity to the Penguin's privates unfortunately failed to inspire the film's female star with the proper sort of enthusiasm. "The discord and mayhem on that set sent me reeling," Dyan Cannon recalls. "I would never make another film rather than work with Preminger again. I don't think he could direct his little nephew to the bathroom."

Most critics wholeheartedly agreed. Donald J. Mayerson in *Cue* called *Friends* a "gloriously bad movie," and Peter Buckley in *Films and Filming* proudly declared that "never in the history of Otto Preminger has he, or anybody else for that matter, been responsible for such a disgusting pile of trash as this. It's offensive on every level I can think of (and some that even I can't think of). . . . No, it's not particularly dirty or sexy or anything fun like that, it's merely totally, thoroughly disagreeable, like a closet full of smelly underwear." All viewers agreed meanwhile that Meredith would have been better off had he kept his underwear on, smelly or not.

When he spoke to the press after the debacle, he expressed surprise at the public's reaction. "I thought people would accept nudity as a thing of beauty," he idealistically declared, "but there was some shock over it. . . . It caused a lot of distress and pain."

The only prospect we can imagine that might cause more distress and pain than Burgess Meredith's naked twists and turns in *Such Good Friends* would have been the sight of Preminger himself, stripped to the buff (except for his monocle, of course) and offering his own Teutonic version of the watusi. We will look forward to that scene in one of the veteran director's future projects.

ANGIE DICKINSON IN *BIG BAD MAMA* (1974)

Angie Dickinson, with co-stars Susan Sennett and Robbie Lee, in one of her less embarrassing moments in Big Bad Mama.

She's bad, but she's not that big.

With this cheapie feature for the legendary "B" movie maven Roger Corman, Angie Dickinson hoped to provide a quick lift for her sadly sagging career. She had not yet hit it big as Sergeant Pepper Anderson on the popular TV series *Police Woman* so she had few qualms about walking on the wrong side of the law to play this matriarch of mayhem. The movie tells the story of a hard-bitten Texas widow during the dark days of the Depression who turns to a life of crime in order to save her daughters from a life of poverty (and to indulge her own penchant for suspiciously 1970s-looking dresses). She begins as a bootlegger but soon moves on to more piquant delights, such as armed robbery, bank busting, and kidnapping. Mama and the girls also spend an inordinate amount of time hopping in and out of the sack with Tom Skerritt and William Shatner (who comes across like Captain Kirk on Quaaludes) and various and sundry pseudo-incestuous combinations. Naturally, all this free-spirited family fun finally attracts the attention of the law enforcement authorities, who terminate the film none too soon with a bloody slo-mo shootout lifted straight from *Bonnie and Clyde.*

During all the action Angie Dickinson struts from scene to scene with hairstyles and outfits never dreamed of in the Depression; she looks more like Nancy Sinatra than Ma Joad. Her attitude toward these threads proves her to be a thoroughly modern mama as she flamboyantly flashes her 43-year-old form. The ads for the film tried to make the most of this Bad Ol' Girl with slogans such as "IN VICE, MAMA KNOWS BEST" and "HOT LEAD, HOT CARS, HOT DAMN!" By the time the film reached theaters around the country, Dickinson had premiered in *Police Woman,* and the box office swelled when curious TV viewers turned out to see what their favorite lady cop was packing under her shoulder holster.

In a sense Angie Dickinson is out of place as a nominee in this category. It's true that her performance in *Big Bad Mama* is inept, and that her thick-as-molasses honey-chile drawl is outrageously and obviously bogus, but as far as her nude scenes are concerned, we will faithfully report that she has no reason to be ashamed of her trim, athletic body. In fact, her talents as exhibited in this film, and her much-heralded television comeback, helped her to win a lucrative contract as official spokesperson for California avocados ("The Sexy Fruit"), in which capacity her charismatic corpus served as eloquent evidence of the preservative power of the gooshy green. This particular Golden Turkey, however, is for the most *embarrassing* nude scene, and in light of her subsequent amnesia on the subject, *Big Bad Mama* has proven particularly humiliating to our Angie. By 1980 she had apparently forgotten about her earlier escapades and refused to disrobe for director Brian De Palma on the set of *Dressed to Kill*—he had to bring in a former *Penthouse* Pet of the Year to body-double her celebrated shower scene.

Then in 1984 came an astonishing interview with the *Los Angeles Herald Examiner* in which Ms. Dickinson intimated that she had never appeared in anything more revealing than a police woman's uni-

form. She stated that she had no objection whatever to the abdication of Miss America Vanessa Williams following the publication of long-forgotten nude photographs of the beauty queen, stating: "I think that the pageant officials had to call for her resignation because Miss America is more than a beauty contest—it is a role model."

When asked if she herself would ever consider posing in the nude, she responded indignantly, "I'm not that kind of a person. There are certain things that I won't do. . . . I've posed semi-nude—it was for my guy and *not* for everybody."

Oh, really? Then for about $2.99 any one of you lonely fellas out there can become Angie Dickinson's "guy," since that's the average cost of renting the videocassette of *Big Bad Mama.* The only problem is that once you've rented it you may actually be tempted to sit through the movie.

LILY TOMLIN IN
MOMENT BY MOMENT (1978)

Perhaps the only two people in Hollywood who look more alike than Lee Marvin and James Coburn are Lily Tomlin and John Travolta. The same dark hair, unisex haircuts, long noses, and fleshy faces—when they appear together on screen in *Moment by Moment,* lounging in a hot tub, it appears to be a special effect, a split-screen trick like the TV twins on *The Patty Duke Show.* This is supposed to be a torrid, sensual encounter, but despite the leisurely display of wet and glistening flesh the scene communicates ennui rather than passion. Apparently it took considerable effort behind the scenes to work the stars up even to this level of indifference. As Sally Ogle Davis reported from the set for *Los Angeles* magazine: "The chemistry between Tomlin and Travolta began to rival that between Yassar Arafat and Menachem Begin."

The project originated with producer Robert Stigwood, who had put together Travolta's prior blockbusters *Saturday Night Fever* and *Grease.* After watching Tomlin's smash hit one-woman show on Broadway, he decided that a generation gap romance featuring the 24-year-old Travolta and the 42-year-old "Queen of Comedy" would provide the last word in kinky and trendy entertainment. The chief obstacle to this plan was Tomlin's intimate friendship with one Jane Wagner, a television comedy writer from Morristown, Tennessee. Despite the fact that Wagner had never before worked on a feature film, Tomlin felt her pal would be perfect as writer-director of the new project and she refused to participate unless she got her way. Stigwood and Travolta reluctantly agreed, and the fun began.

BUBBLE, BUBBLE, THEY'RE IN TROUBLE: John Travolta (right) *wonders what that naughty nude Lily Tomlin is doing in his hot tub in their romantic travesty* Moment by Moment.

Wagner's painfully earnest script tells the story of Trish, a Beverly Hills housewife who tries to buy Seconals but is refused because her prescription has run out. Strip (yes, that's the name of Travolta's character) takes pity on her and leaves his job as a part-time parking lot attendant and a full-time panhandler to bring her a "love gift" of the red pills. "Oh . . . *Strip!*" Trish/Tomlin mumbles, touched by his thoughtfulness, and the rest of the film focuses on their treks from the beach to the hot tub, from the hot tub to the bed, and from the bed back to the beach.

In the hands of a gifted comedienne such as Tomlin, the insipid story might have served as the basis for a hip parody, but unfortunately both the star and the director treated the material as if they were filming *War and Peace.* Wagner told reporters that her screenplay offered "both a romance and something that might be seen as political: wealth and the Third World." Tomlin, meanwhile, saw herself as making a similarly profound statement. "With a person, a male who is younger and is still more an-

drogynous in a way, the Trish character can explore her sexuality/sensuality," she mused. "In *Moment by Moment* we're saying something important about women in the culture."

With these high ambitions in mind, the cast and crew treated the two stars' "intimate scenes" with reverence. Wagner, in fact, felt so awed by the responsibility of bringing all this profundity to the public that she apparently couldn't make up her mind whether to shoot some of the beach sequences dressed, partially dressed, or in bathing suits. Eventually she filmed them all three ways, spending several days on each approach.

She could not, however, film her stars fully clothed during the infamous hot tub scene, so instead she labored to protect what remained of Lily Tomlin's modesty with a few strategically placed bubbles. Despite these noble efforts, the resulting footage still showed the giggling and jeering audiences that Travolta in his birthday suit looked considerably more shapely than his hapless tubmate. The press reported that in screenings around the country, the moment that Tomlin stepped out of her bathrobe, angry patrons headed for the doors, while those who remained in the theaters howled in derision.

Jane Wagner may have been the only one associated with the production who felt surprised when American moviegoers failed to share her enthusiasm for eyeing Edith Ann in the altogether; others expected trouble from the beginning. "Two weeks into the shooting on location in Malibu there was nobody on that set that didn't know we were in the middle of a turkey," recalled one member of the crew. "It was like being on the voyage of the damned."

By the time the ghost ship finally went down in a whirlpool of hostile reviews and audience giggles, Lily Tomlin had already moved on to her next project, *The Incredible Shrinking Woman.* After considering the response to *Moment by Moment,* Tomlin began to worry about her incredible shrinking career, and so gave in to the executives at Universal who insisted that she accept a director other than the redoubtable Jane Wagner. Joel *(St. Elmo's Fire)* Schumacher came in to take over, but his efforts to defuse the Jane Wagner script could not prevent the detonation of yet another box office bomb. Miss Tomlin had to wait for a full-fledged comeback until 1984 and her much praised role in *All of Me.* Significantly enough, she played her scenes in this film in flowing robes or as a disembodied voice, and ventured nowhere near either Jane Wagner or a hot tub.

TATUM O'NEAL IN
A CIRCLE OF TWO (1980)

Tatum O'Neal reassures a badly shaken Richard Burton that she'll never strip for him again in A Circle of Two.

After Elizabeth Taylor left him for the last time in 1976, Richard Burton searched the world for a co-star to replace her—someone so charismatic, so alluring, so fabulously beautiful and gifted that she could make him forget those fabled violet eyes.

At last he found this divine creature in the unlikely person of Tatum O'Neal.

Tatum O'Neal?

Yes, *that* Tatum O'Neal, and in *A Circle of Two* she joins Burton in a putrid tearjerker that makes the romantic pairing of Tomlin and Travolta seem absolutely inspired by comparison.

Having already played a summer camper out to lose her virginity in *Little Darlings* (also 1980), the 16-year-old Tatum leaves childhood even further behind with her efforts here. To make it seem plausible that she would involve herself in a touching affair with a world-famous painter in his sixties, screenwriter Tom Hedley (who later won fame for *Flashdance*) strained to give the two lovers the proverbial "cute meet." In fact, it is hard to imagine anything cuter than this one: O'Neal, playing an adventurous prep school girl, first encounters the dozing Burton in a porno theater and wakes him up by bopping the dirty old man over the head with her purse, so naturally he falls instantly in love with her. After all, the

two of them have so much in common—particularly their taste for abysmal dialogue. When Tatum asks her new beau what he does for a living, he announces: "I spend a lot of time on a boat worrying about why I haven't painted for ten years." Later she begs him to "go all the way" and to enable her to lose her virginity. In one of their emotional scenes together, Tatum looks straight toward the camera and pleads, "You've *got* to help me with this *burden!*"—apparently mispronouncing the name of her somnolent co-star. He, in turn, assumes that no one's scripting skills could be worse than those of the geniuses behind this film, and bellows at his pubescent paramour: "You have a *responsibility* to write! You have an absolutely *natural* talent!"

In its 105 minutes, this hopelessly contrived Canadian concoction includes so many incongruous elements that it is difficult to know where to begin. In the audience in the sleaze house where the two stars enjoy their first sentimental encounter are Tatum's off-screen dad, Ryan O'Neal (in a cameo appearance), and the Six Million Dollar Man himself, Lee Majors—perhaps meeting in the darkened theater to discuss their common problems with Farrah Fawcett. The promotional material released with the movie actually boasted of the unique fact that it was created by a blind producer (Milton Zysman), though after watching the finished film it would be as easy to believe it was the work of a blind director. In reality, the film's director, Jules Dassin, had two perfectly good eyes and a respectable track record in motion pictures *(Never on Sunday, The Naked City)*, so he naturally asked that his name be removed from the credits once he had the chance to look over his handiwork.

Amidst the confusion, Tatum O'Neal's brief display of her paper moons stands out as the film's most hilarious moment. Feeling frustrated over the fact that Burton has stubbornly spurned her advances and refused to consummate their affair, she travels to his studio in the woods for a confrontation. After looking over his canvases—including some provocative nudes—she hits upon the idea of melting his resolve by revealing her glorious body in all its 16-year-old splendor. As he unsuspectingly leaves the room to fetch tea, she steps out of her clothes and stands before us, defiantly smoking one of Burton's cigars, with a cunningly placed chair barely concealing her crotch. This frank view of a painfully ordinary teenage girl, whose build, to put it charitably, runs toward stockiness, makes it abundantly clear that Ms. O'Neal's motion picture career has been based on family connections and her acting ability as a juvenile star, and not on physical beauty. When Burton returns to find "his muse" fully revealed in front of the easel, he seems no more interested than we are. "Get dressed!" he howls, and kicks his paint box in frustration. "Get—*dressed!*" The audience, without question, shares his sentiments.

KIRK DOUGLAS IN
SATURN 3 (1980)

"The best and perhaps only way to enjoy *Saturn 3,*" began *Newsweek*'s review, "is to pretend that you're watching a 'Saturday Night Live' parody of *Saturn 3.*" The sappy plot pretentiously combines elements of *Silent Running, Last Tango in Paris,* and the biblical Garden of Eden story. Kirk Douglas plays Adam (get it?), an aging space jockey who inhabits a remote scientific outpost on Saturn's third moon along with his lab assistant and playmate, Farrah Fawcett. The exact nature of their research is never revealed, though it appears to involve an investigation into how much trendy California living two human beings (and a movie audience) can endure. We watch Kirk and Farrah jogging together endlessly, tending

Unabashed exhibitionist Kirk Douglas reacts impulsively to Harvey Keitel's perfectly sensible observation that he might be too old for Farrah Fawcett as part of the sci-fi stupidity in Saturn 3.

their houseplants, sipping drinks on patio furniture, going through aerobics workouts, taking showers together, imbibing recreational drugs called blue dreamers, and modeling innumerable changes of stylish Gucci space wear. To show that they have left all unpleasant "guilt trips" (along with reruns of *Charlie's Angels*) back on earth, our two lovebirds stumble through several scenes au naturel and strike poses that would be more suitable for *Sun Worshipper* magazine than for *Playboy.* Douglas, at the ripe age of 63, flexes his muscles and throws out his chest with understandable pride at the way his physique has resisted the ravages of time; his strutting peacock display, in fact, recalls his early, pre-movie days as a sometime professional wrestler. He further expresses his cheeky attitude toward the audience by shooting the moon, straight at the camera, in one memorable scene; aging fan-club presidents and discerning cinéastes must have been fascinated to discover that the trademark Douglas cleft is not confined to Kirk's celebrated chin.

Fortunately, a visitor from earth arrives in the midst of these revels and forces our two dedicated scientists to put on their clothes. We know this guest is a psychopath because he is played by Harvey Keitel, and he travels in the company of an eight-foot-tall "demigod" robot conveniently stored in his suitcase. Keitel decides that Farrah is just too lovely to be left to an over-the-hill actor who booms out his lines as fatuously as Kirk Douglas does, so he decides to turn on the charm and steal the movie's only available female. Sidling up to everyone's favorite poster girl, he declaims with a straight face: "You have a beautiful body. May I use it?" When she decides to pass on this opportunity, Keitel transfers his frustrated lust to his throbbing, blinking robot, Hector. This malevolent machine then wreaks havoc on Kirk's fashionably decorated condominium, trying to kill everyone in sight so he can have his blonde cheesecake and eat it too. To overcome this challenge to his manhood, and to save the houseplants and Farrah's little dog, Mr. Douglas spends the last half of this space oddity gritting his teeth, snarling at danger, and overacting in the old familiar style, but it was the novel sight of his bare bottom that left the deepest impression on the critics. "It's less a performance than a strip tease," declared *The Hollywood Reporter.* In summing up the sorry situation, *Variety* scolded: "She shows a T and he shows an A and they both should have behaved themselves."

LINDA BLAIR IN
CHAINED HEAT (1983)

In Chained Heat, *savvy prison gang leader Sybil Danning advises Linda Blair (as the new kid on the cell block) that a nude scene might be the only way to revive her failing movie career.*

The course of Linda Blair's career since she won international fame, and an Oscar nomination, for her performance in *The Exorcist* at age 14 might lead one to believe that she is still cursed by evil spirits. First she drew blame from Warner Brothers when their attempt to repossess her in *Exorcist II: The Heretic* (1977) emerged as a hilarious and expensive failure. Then came a succession of tawdry and exploitative films, including *Roller Boogie* (1979), *Hard Ride to Rantan* (1979) and *Hell Night* (1981). In the midst of these embarrassments, the teenage star endured two well-publicized arrests for cocaine and amphetamine abuse and was sentenced to a total of nine months of closely supervised rehabilitation. This program may have helped her drug problems but it did nothing to improve her acting. Since winning fame as the much-abused Regan (the girl, not the president) in *The Exorcist*, she has, in her screen and television portrayals, played the passive and innocent victim of every imaginable malevolent force. With her steadily expanding girth her only defense against a cruel world, she has been raped (by crucifix, broomstick, and drooling human scum), kidnapped, attacked by grasshoppers, hijacked, turned into an alcoholic, and tortured by disco music. These atrocities served to prepare her for the ultimate degradation: a starring role in the motion picture *Chained Heat*.

This sleazeball project bore the distinctive stamp of producer Billy Fine, president of Ideal Pictures

and creator of such other Fine films as *New Year's Evil, The Concrete Jungle,* and the projected *Ordeal: The Story of Linda Lovelace.* Skeptics might classify him as a specialist in exploitation films, but Fine himself has another word for it. They are "action films," he claims. "We are not exploiting women. I'm not making sex films." Apparently the twenty-odd instances of frontal female nudity in *Chained Heat* have nothing to do with sex or exploitation; instead Fine is offering a useful anatomy lesson to all the eager physiology students in the moviegoing audience. "I'm more proud of this film than any film I have personally made," he solemnly intoned. "There's tears in this picture. . . . I can't help it if lesbianism happens in a women's prison."

And happen it does, with Sybil Danning and Tamara Dobson as the leaders of rival prison gangs, fighting over the fresh young flesh that occasionally comes their way. You know that these silicone-packing, braless prison mamas must be sex-starved to the point of insanity, ready for any unspeakable perversion, since they all go gaga for Linda Blair. As the new kid on the cell block, Ms. Blair is supposed to be a sweet-tempered virgin who has been sent to prison through some awful mistake, and won't do anything to escape her predicament because she doesn't want her parents to know what's happened to her. This premise is no less plausible than the assumption that in this combination prison and health spa, inhabited exclusively by statuesque models and starlets, the one female who proves absolutely irresistible to the lecherous warden is the chunky, awkwardly waddling Linda Blair. The warden (played by John Vernon, Dean Wormer in *Animal House*) invites her to his office and offers to videotape her if she will climb into the hot tub conveniently installed beside his desk. As he stares at her wide-set, bovine eyes, this prurient penologist eloquently purrs, "Come here, my pretty little Lolita!" When she spurns his advances, he beats and rapes her—only one of more than a dozen assaults in the course of a movie that might have been horrifying had it not been so incompetently executed. It is difficult to be shocked by even the most violent scene when the actors are obviously reading their lines from cue cards, and when the microphone boom bobs noticeably in and out of the frame throughout most of the picture.

Despite these obvious shortcomings, producer Billy Fine and director Lutz Schaarwaechter (a West German schlockmeister hiding for this film behind the pseudonym "Paul Nicolas") try to please their audience with one show-stopping production number at the center of the movie: a spectacular shower scene in which all of the movie's two dozen principal players have a chance to display the results of the prison's exercise program. As Schaarwaechter's fluid and poetic camera pans lovingly from one glistening body to another, showing each of the characters sinuously twisting under the water jets, it finally comes to rest, by way of climax, on the decidedly anticlimactic sight of Linda Blair. She stands there flatfooted and embarrassed, baring her chest and staring off camera, obviously trying to pretend she is somewhere else. Writers will sometimes compliment an

Linda Blair blows a torrid kiss to those devoted fans (whoever and wherever they are) who have supported her preposterous bid for international sex stardom.

older woman by saying she has the firm, taut body of a young girl; perhaps the best way to compliment poor Ms. Blair under these humiliating circumstances would be to say she puts us in mind of, shall we say, a much more *experienced* actress. Even the heartless filmmakers appear to have taken pity on this unfortunate star, or at least on the audience: While every other actress is shown from head to toe, the lower two thirds of Ms. Blair's body is conveniently concealed by a shower wall that mercifully intrudes itself in front of the camera.

If nothing else, Linda Blair deserves credit for a sensible attitude toward her role. "I am not doing this as an art piece, I'm not doing it from my heart,

as a statement of my beliefs or my philosophy," she confided to the *Los Angeles Times*. "I'm working." After *Chained Heat* she continued her career as a working girl by taking the lead in the astonishingly tasteless "police comedy" *Night Patrol*, and playing a gun-toting "vigilante mama" in those charming companion pieces *Savage Streets* and *Savage Island* (all three released in 1985).

Despite these temporary setbacks, Linda Blair continues to pursue a lofty and inspiring ambition. "What I'd really like to be seen as," she confided in 1983, "is a young female version of Burt Reynolds." Considering the recent direction of Mr. Reynolds' career, someday her dream might just come true.

AND THE WINNER IS . . .

. . . BURGESS MEREDITH IN *SUCH GOOD FRIENDS*

Rather than attempt a lengthy explanation of why Burgess Meredith deserves the Golden Turkey in this category, we will resort to the well-known Chinese proverb: One picture—or, in this case, one production still—is worth 10,000 words.

THE MOST LUDICROUS PROFESSIONAL NAME IN MOVIE HISTORY

*W*ho *would have ever gone to see macho hits like* True Grit *and* The Sands of Iwo Jima *if the star's name, listed above the titles, had been Marion Morrison? Fortunately for the course of American history, a young actor from Iowa had the good sense to trade in that sissified moniker for the far more appropriate handle "John Wayne"; otherwise, the West might never have been won, or the U.S. could have even lost the war to the Japanese.*

Hollywood has always understood the magic in names. Betty Perske, Archie Leach, and Mary Collins, for instance, don't sound like sex symbols; but Lauren Bacall, Cary Grant, and Bo Derek do.

Occasionally an aspiring star picks a nom de cinema *that hinders rather than helps a struggling career. When Lucille Le Sueur first tried to break into show business and found that most people misspelled her name "Le Sewer," she adopted the "zippy" new designation "Billie Cassin." The switch never worked—"Billie Cassin" not only lacked romantic flair, but led many producers to assume she was a man. So poor Lucille tried again, this time with a nationwide publicity contest conducted on her behalf by MGM, and came up with the promising new name "Joan Crawford."*

The would-be stars honored in this category should have followed her example by trying a second name change. None of them possessed conspicuous acting ability, but even if they had, the inane aliases they initially selected would have blocked all chance of success. After all, it's difficult to imagine an Oscar presenter ripping open the famous envelope on Hollywood's "night of nights" and announcing to all the world: " . . . And the winner, for Best Actress of the Year . . . Bermuda Schwartz!"

AND THE NOMINEES ARE . . .

ACQUANETTA

It's a great name for a hair spray, but for an aspiring actress . . . ?

The studio bosses at Universal no doubt had the right idea when they decided that the hot young property they hoped to develop as the new Maria Montez needed an appropriately exotic tag. After all, with ads promoting her as "The Glamour Queen of the Beast-Claw Men!" and "The Venezuelan Volcano," her real name, Mildred Davenport, simply wouldn't do. Instead, the studio wanted something mysterious, alluring, and dangerous that would obscure the hopeful star's corn-fed midwestern origins. When the name they invented, "Burnu Acquanetta," proved too difficult for most people to pronounce, she quickly shortened it to the musical, elegant "Acquanetta," and so she is known to the ages.

Acquanetta as "Queen of the Beast-Claw Men" leads calisthenics for her bored co-stars in Tarzan and the Leopard Woman.

In the course of her brief career, Acquanetta specialized in playing primitive temptresses who were "half girl and half beast." She first clawed her way into pictures as "Paula the Ape Girl"—an orangutan who had been changed into a beautiful woman by a mad scientist played by John Carradine. She played the part twice (in *Captive Wild Woman* [1943] and *Jungle Woman* [1944]), then went on to land the coveted co-title role in *Tarzan and the Leopard Woman* (1946). These parts may have been demeaning, but they allowed her to walk through her pictures without delivering lines of dialogue—an important advantage for the "Venezuelan Volcano," who otherwise might have been forced to fake an accent. Judging from her performances, in which she changes her leopard-skin outfits far more frequently than she does her facial expressions, this sort of verbal versatility may well have been beyond her capacities. In 1949 Acquanetta tried to revive her bid for stardom with a well-publicized ceremony installing her as an official Sioux Indian chief. The press releases issued on this solemn occasion emphasized her

"Arapaho Indian blood" (Arapaho Indians in Venezuela?) and explained that her unusual name actually meant "Burning Fire and Deep Water."

Her career was certainly in deep water by that time, and her final film, *The Lost Continent,* came two years later. In it she plays a cave girl who helps a group of twentieth-century scientists—including Cesar Romero, John Hoyt (from *Attack of the Puppet People*), and Hugh Beaumont (of *Leave It to Beaver* fame)—to recover a misplaced rocket ship on a prehistoric mountaintop. Her director and producer on this last-gasp project, the brothers Sam Newfield and Sig Neufeld, had racked up plenty of experience handling novelty acts, including the creation of memorable motion pictures with all-chimpanzee and all-midget casts (*see:* THE MOST RIDICULOUS COWBOY HERO IN HOLLYWOOD HISTORY). Nevertheless, not even the sure guidance of these experienced exploiters could return the misnamed starlet to the good graces of an increasingly bored and skeptical public.

AUNT JEMIMA

In comparison to the insulting antics of Aunt Jemima, the work of the much-maligned Stepin Fetchit stands as a sensitive and realistic depiction of the black experience in America. That "big, tuneful gal" with an identity borrowed from the face on a box of pancake mix was, in reality, a white vaudeville comedienne named Lois Gedelia with a heavy layer of burnt-cork makeup and an even heavier layer of artificial stuffing inside her dress. Gedelia/Jemima made her only screen appearance in *Stand Up and Cheer* (1934), a "chase the blues" variety show released at the height of the Depression. She plays a washerwoman with a sunny disposition who, in a big production number, while flashing her teeth and shaking her padded behind, tells America, "I'se laffin'—so's can you!"

Though Stepin Fetchit himself co-stars in the film, the producers resisted the temptation to script a love scene between their two stereotypical stars. Mr. Fetchit actually appears in a relatively distinguished capacity as a character identified as "George Bernard Shaw," setting up the supposedly hilarious line, "Why, G. B. Shaw—you're a little sunburned!" The plot of the film concerns a Broadway producer (Warner Baxter) who wins appointment to a new

Cabinet post as "Secretary of Amusement," though it appears that Washington (and this picture) would have benefited far more from a Civil Rights Commission. Aside from marking the beginning (and end) of Aunt Jemima's blessedly brief career in Hollywood, *Stand Up and Cheer* is remembered today as the debut vehicle for 5-year-old Shirley Temple, who stole the picture with a brief singing-and-dancing number called "Baby, Take a Bow."

JOY BANG

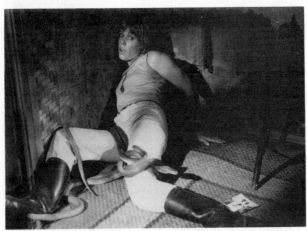

Accomplished Method actress Joy Bang brings the full range of human emotion to her challenging role in Night of the Cobra Woman.

Despite a name that seemed more appropriate for an aspiring porno queen, this ambitious actress tried for success in mainstream motion pictures. Amazingly enough, she won parts in a number of respectable productions before her immodest name combined with her modest acting ability to put an end to her career.

Born in Kansas City, Missouri, she was adopted by a New York City couple and studied drama at Boston University. She appeared in two Broadway productions and participated in the prestigious company of the Café La Mama before making her screen debut in the experimental film *Separation* (1968). Appropriately enough, she played "Joy," the uninhibited girlfriend of a Greenwich Village director. The name she used in the credits—"Joy Wener"—left it up to the discretion of the audience whether to pronounce it *Wenner*, *Wayner*, or, more suggestively, *Weener*, but the new designation she acquired for her next picture (*Sky Pirate*, 1970) left nothing to the imagination.

The moniker "Joy Bang" at least succeeded in attracting attention: those who read movie credits carefully got a good chuckle and invariably remembered her name. The young thespian's big break came in 1971 when she won a part as a sensuous high school girl in Roger Vadim's *Pretty Maids All in a Row,* appearing alongside such big-name stars as Rock Hudson, Angie Dickinson, Telly Savalas, and Roddy McDowall. She also played featured roles in two 1972 countercultural drug trade sagas: *Cisco Pike* (with Gene Hackman, Karen Black, Kris Kristofferson, and Harry Dean Stanton) and *Dealing: Or the Berkeley-to-Boston-Forty-Brick-Lost-Bag Blues* (with John Lithgow, Charles Durning, and Barbara Hershey). The year 1972, in fact, proved a very big one for Miss Bang, because in addition to these formidable credits, she played one of Woody Allen's dates during his après-divorce adjustment in *Play It Again, Sam.* It's easy to imagine that Mr. Allen cast her in that role as much for the pleasure of seeing her name in the credits as for her unique screen presence.

That presence, despite the suggestive pseudonym, never brought her a role as an out-and-out sexpot; instead, she played various "bimbos," "airheads," and "space cadets" who seemed lovable because of their abject helplessness. The hallmark of her mature acting style involved the impressive trick of opening her mouth to react with astonishment at even the most ordinary developments around her.

Joy Bang had plenty of chance to act astonished in her most celebrated film, *Night of the Cobra Woman* (1973). As a gee-whiz field researcher for UNICEF in the jungles of the Philippines, she essentially plays straight woman to the Cobra Queen (Marlene Clark), who kidnaps her boyfriend and uses him for unceasing sex in order to maintain eternal youth. Advertised as the world's only feature shot entirely in "Slitherama," the picture also featured a rugged young actor named Slash Marks as "Sergeant Merkle." Not surprisingly, Miss Bang's featured role in this wretched mess sent her career into severe decline and she soon slithered away from feature films.

CASH FLAGG

In Hollywood, great stars often develop enduring and fruitful associations with great directors: Marlene Dietrich teamed again and again with Josef Von

Sternberg; John Wayne with John Ford; and Robert De Niro with Martin Scorsese. In this noble tradition Cash Flagg, a long-nosed, slope-browed leading man of the sixties, starred in five different feature films for the versatile director Ray Dennis Steckler. In fact, no other director ever gave Flagg a chance to work in a motion picture. This is easy to understand if you've seen his performances, but it leaves a question as to why Steckler proved so peculiarly partial to this bug-eyed star's monochromatic acting style.

Cash Flagg (center) *shows the sophisticated comic style that failed to make him famous in the children's classic* The Lemon Grove Kids Meet the Green Grasshopper and the Vampire Lady from Outer Space.

The answer, of course, is that Cash Flagg and Ray Dennis Steckler enjoyed an intense and intimate relationship; in fact, they occupied the same body. Steckler, embarrassed that his name already appeared in the credits to his films as producer, director, writer, and cinematographer, invented the alias "Cash Flagg" to cover his achievements as an actor. He chose the name to express the forlorn hope that his unconventional movies might bring home big bucks, and to protest one of the built-in hazards of the world of ultra-low-budget exploitation flicks in which he worked. Steckler recalls that in the early days of his career, whenever he received checks from his associates they most often bounced; his insistence on *cash* payments soon became a standing joke and led to his distinctive screen name.

One might have expected a more imaginative moniker from Steckler, the man who invented such marquee-stretching titles for his films as *The Incredibly Strange Creatures Who Stopped Living and Became

Mixed-Up Zombies (1964), *Rat Pfink a Boo Boo* (1964), *The Lemon Grove Kids Meet the Green Grasshopper and the Vampire Lady from Outer Space* (1965), and his most recent creation, *The Hollywood Strangler Meets the Skid-row Slasher* (1980).

As an actor, Steckler/Flagg played one of two basic roles: either a bloodthirsty, maniacal killer (*Zombies, The Thrill Killers* [both 1964]) or a slobbering, slow-witted clown (*The Lemon Grove Kids* series). In 1966 he made a brief but brave attempt to promote himself as a horror star. He offered free autographed pictures to all fans who wrote in to his production company and took out an ad in the Hollywood trade papers that read "Karloff . . . Lugosi . . . Chaney . . . Price . . . Lorre . . . Carradine . . . *and now* . . . CASH FLAGG!" Whatever his shortcomings as an actor, Mr. Flagg always enjoyed the luxury of being able to blame his director.

Disheartened by the tepid public response to his performances, Cash Flagg retired from the screen in 1972. Ray Dennis Steckler, on the other hand, continues to work on exciting new projects (including a forthcoming police drama tentatively titled *Bloody Jack*) in the time he can spare from his prestigious position as Professor of Film Production at the University of Nevada, Las Vegas.

BEVERLY HILLS

The beauteous Beverly Hills energetically declines her opportunity to become one of the Brides of Blood *in a movie alternately titled* Island of Living Horror.

The stripper in question achieved popularity of such staggering proportions that, according to a legend promulgated by her hyperactive press agent, a sleepy southern California village decided to borrow *her* professional name, and only thereafter won world fame as a center for overpriced imported merchandise and a vacation home for Eddie Murphy.

Whether or not you accept this version of events, there is no doubt that the energetic ecdysiast Beverly Hills eventually managed to bump and grind her way onto the big screen. She made her movie debut as a nightclub dancer in Blake Edwards' *Breakfast at Tiffany's* (1961), following up this triumph with brief appearances on the *Thriller* and *Perry Mason* television series.

The statuesque beauty went on to appear in scores of important motion pictures, playing alongside some of the greatest male sex symbols of our time, including Elvis Presley, Frankie Avalon, and Bob Hope. Her screen credits include *Comedy of Terrors* (1964), *Kissin' Cousins* (1964), *Young Dillinger* (1965), *I'll Take Sweden* (1965), *The Loved One* (1965), *Brides of Blood* (1968), *Angel in My Pocket* (1969), and *More Dead Than Alive* (1969). In each of these films she played purely decorative roles as a gun moll, saloon hostess, or "orgy dancer" and displayed considerably more cleavage than talent. She tried to expand her horizons by playing a courageous agent of the Atomic Energy Commission in *Brides of Blood* (aka *Island of Living Horror*) whose uncontrollable sexual appetite leads her to her doom as she attempts to make love to a melting-mess radioactive monster.

Miss Hills concluded her career in the 1970s when, after years of gracious living, the rest of her anatomy caught up with her celebrated advance guard.

LASH LA RUE

This rough-tough western hero galloped through thirty-six feature films in the 1940s and '50s and even inspired a popular line of cowboy comic books. His screen name, however, always seemed better suited to his original occupation—that of a perfectionist Hollywood hairdresser.

Born Alfred La Rue in 1917, he first broke into pictures at age 28 with a role in a low-budget oater called *Song of Old Wyoming*. "The director said to me,

'Gee, I'd like to use you in the picture, but I wanted somebody who could use a whip,'" La Rue recalls. "So I went out and got a couple of whips and nearly beat myself to death." Nevertheless, on screen he minded his P's and Q's (or at least his S's and M's) and swished the lethal leather with enough aplomb so that the young actor Al La Rue thereafter became known as *Lash* La Rue, King of the Bullwhip.

Former hairdresser Lash La Rue can barely conceal his contempt for the carelessly styled beard of his sidekick, Fuzzy St. John.

"The King of the Bullwhip" demonstrates the incredible mastery of his chosen weapon that made him a he-man star to millions of American youngsters.

By applying himself diligently to his chosen discipline, La Rue soon became as proficient with the whip as he had once been with the curling iron. At the peak of his fame he boasted to the press that he was the only man in Hollywood who could "handle a sixteen-footer." Along with his scruffy, bearded sidekick, Fuzzy St. John (a bargain basement Gabby Hayes), La Rue starred in *Law of the Lash* (1947), *Mark of the Lash* (1948), *Return of the Lash* (1949), and many others. He won favorable reviews for his splendid outfits (billing himself as "the first cowboy hero to dress entirely in black"), but with his furrowed brow and perpetually puzzled expression he never seemed entirely at home on the range. Behind the scenes, he became notorious for his binges, fits of temperament, and a rocky personal life as he whipped through ten marriages and divorces in surprisingly short order.

When the western movie stagecoach finally reached the end of the line in the 1950s, La Rue tried to make the transition to mainstream stardom. Unfortunately his bad reputation preceded him and made it impossible for him to find work. In 1956 he was arrested along with a shapely female accomplice and accused of fencing stolen property; in 1958 the despondent western hero attempted suicide. His career seemed miraculously resurrected in 1959, when he won the role of "Sheriff John Behan" on the hit *Wyatt Earp* TV series, but the more dependable cowboy Steve Brodie replaced him within a year.

La Rue then invested his remaining funds in a small motel in Reno, Nevada, where the King of the Bullwhip became the King of the Desk Register. To promote this latest venture, he devised a billboard that suggestively announced TRUCKERS AND DIVORCEES WELCOME!, but when Lash himself went through his latest divorce, his wife took the motel as part of the settlement.

By this time he no doubt felt like the world's whipping boy and, on September 28, 1964, took out a humbling but attention-getting ad in *The Hollywood Reporter*:

When this novel public relations approach failed to generate jobs, La Rue settled down as a water-conditioner salesman in Los Angeles, but, as he later confided, "The Lord hadn't finished with me yet." In the early seventies he discovered the Bible and began dispensing religious pronouncements strangely tinged with the wisdom of the East. "Everything you think I am, you are," he told the press. "You can't be me, but he who is with me will be instantly you." By 1973 the former cowboy hero had launched a new venture in St. Petersburg, Florida, founding a traveling revival show called the Hollywood Western Revue for the Lord. His new-found career, however, did nothing to prevent his arrest on charges of vagrancy and public drunkenness in 1974, nor did it deter a Jonesboro, Georgia, judge from convicting him of marijuana possession in 1975. The skeptical magistrate refused to believe La Rue's claim that he had only accepted the evil weed temporarily as part of a selfless effort to "save the souls" of two teenage hitchhikers; after considerable discussion he had persuaded them to give up their stash in exchange for a new Bible. The district attorney admiringly observed that La Rue's forceful presentation of this story constituted "one of his better performances."

As he entered the 1980s, the one-time whip-cracking idol tried yet another comeback with a series of personal appearances and small roles in the low-budget horror films *The Dark Power* (1984) and *Alien Outlaw* (1985). When asked about his future plans, he expressed a desire to "just live, man. Be me. Maybe go fishin' on Jupiter. And watch the rest of the baseball season on TV." Looking back on his colorful career, he can only laugh out loud. "You gotta have a sense of humor," he says, "or you couldn't understand God at all."

—MAN—

Ready to work. Was boxoffice when an irresponsible jerk. Now adult, worthy and well-qualified. Good health, small waistline, and a full head of hair. A better man makes a better actor. Let me prove it!

LASH LA RUE
221 W. Caliente
Reno, Nevada

BERMUDA SCHWARTZ

Though her screen name might be more readily associated with a Coney Island beach party movie, this plump and pleasing property made her one and only appearance in a costume drama set in seventeenth-century Italy. *Head Lady* (1968), based on a tale from Giovanni Boccaccio's bawdy classic *Il decamerone*, tells the story of a lesbian headmistress in charge of a school for young noblewomen. Miss Schwartz plays one of these noblewomen who falls in love with Mario (Mike Cosim), the newly hired school gardener, who pretends to be mute in order to win sympathy from the girls and to take advantage of his position. When the jealous headmistress discovers the two lovebirds bathing together, she flies into a rage and viciously beats and abuses poor Bermuda. After a good deal more unpleasantness—including several additional beatings and a suicide—producer-director B. Ron Elliot provides a surprise ending: The lascivious gardener and the dominatrix schoolmarm, recognizing all they have in common, run off together to begin a new life.

The best that can be said for Miss Schwartz's performance is that she maintains a sweet smile in the midst of all this softcore silliness, and that the filmmakers avoided lewd and humiliating references to her Bermuda triangle. At the time of the movie's release the producers provided no information whatever as to the background of their star, obviously hoping to fudge the fact that this budding ingenue seemed to be at least twice the age of the 16-year-old character she portrayed. In any event, Miss Schwartz, along with the other absolutely unknown actors associated with this addlebrained adventure in exploitation, disappeared from view shortly after the picture's world premiere in Minneapolis. Director B. Ron Elliot, on the other hand, went on—without his erstwhile star—to direct such notable cinematic triumphs as *The Acid Eaters* (1968), *Space Thing* (1969), and the inspirational *Love Thy Neighbor and His Wife* (1970).

SLEEP 'N EAT

Hollywood's shameful treatment of black Americans in the first fifty years of this century offers one of the most embarrassing chapters in the history of movies. Nearly all the black actors and actresses (as well as various blackface impersonators) of the 1930s worked under degrading pseudonyms; the one authentic black superstar of the period, Lincoln Theodore Perry, used the infamous alias "Stepin Fetchit." Others came and went, including Aunt Jemima (see above), the Two Black Crows, Buckwheat, and Snowflake, but none of these clowns of the early talkie era assumed an identity as insulting as that of the unfortunate Sleep 'n Eat.

Born Willie Best in rural Mississippi in 1916, the future star came to California as a teenage chauffeur

Proudly billed as "the screen's slowest-moving, slowest-talking human," the ethnic comedian Sleep 'n Eat made his movie debut in 1931 as a laundry boy (here seen with William Haines) in Up Pops the Devil.

for what his official biography later described as "a nice white man." When his boss returned to the Deep South, young Willie remained in Los Angeles and tried to support himself washing dishes at hash houses, but, as the studio publicists chortled, "he was too slow to make a good living at that."

His fateful "discovery" by two Hollywood talent scouts came one afternoon as he sat on a fireplug in downtown L.A., broke and hungry. "My gosh, what a type!" one of the movie men enthused to the other. "Another sleepy Stepin Fetchit!" Willie's less than energetic response to their offers only increased their conviction that they had made a major find. "Actin'?" he reportedly drawled. "Ain't never done dat kin' o' work. Kain't do dat kind o' work."

Nevertheless, he was soon earning $25 a week toiling long days in the studios, appearing under his new name, "Sleep 'n Eat." In his debut role (*Up Pops the Devil*, 1931) he plays the part of a foot-shuffling, eye-popping laundryman who steals a chicken leg from Carole Lombard's kitchen. His next picture, *The Monster Walks* (1932), offered a far more substantial role, with Sleep 'n Eat co-starring, alongside "Yogi the Gorilla," as a frightened chauffeur in a haunted house. At one point he looks the monkey in the eye and comments, "Well, I dunno, I had a gran'pappy dat looked like him—'cept he wasn't as active!"

And so it went through twelve featured roles, playing slow-witted porters and servants with names such as "Exodus," "Wellington," "Catfish," "Drowsy," and, inevitably, "Sambo." When he reached the height of his career in the mid-thirties, Warner Brothers proudly described Mr. Eat as "the man who replaced Stepin Fetchit as the screen's slowest-moving, slowest-talking human!" In movies such as *The Nitwits, Kentucky Kernels,* and *Thank You, Mr. Jeeves,* he worked endless variations on the same themes, talking to himself, running in terror from various spooks, and delivering lines of dialogue like "Ah jus' love to take off mah shoes an' play in de raindrops!"

By 1936 he had accumulated enough clout with the studios to drop the demeaning "Sleep 'n Eat" designation and begin acting under his own name, though the nature of his roles remained entirely unchanged. In fifty-five more films as Willie Best, from *Two in Revolt* (1936, in which he co-starred with a dog and a horse) to *South of Caliente* (1951, with Roy Rogers, Dale Evans, and Pinky Lee), the veteran performer never departed from the persona of "that lazy, easygoing colored comedian."

In 1951 an embarrassing arrest for possession of heroin combined with the public's declining interest in "ethnic humor" to put an end to his long career. Even the smallest roles proved beyond his reach after the drug charges, and the former Sleep 'n Eat died in 1962 after a decade of difficult living. His passing received only the briefest mention in the Hollywood trade press.

TWINKLE WATTS

This little lady's high-voltage presence graced only a handful of films before the lights went out on her career and she retired from show business, at age 8, in 1946. A Shirley Temple look-alike with plump pink cheeks and a mass of blonde curls, she made her movie debut in Republic Studios' $1.5-million extravaganza *Lake Placid Serenade* (1944), strutting her stuff along with such dubious luminaries as the Merry Meisters, the glamorous Vera Vague, cowboy stalwart Bob Livingston, the immortal Roy Rogers, the Royal Hawaiians, and the indefatigable Vera Hruba Ralston, who just happened to be the mistress of studio head Herbert J. Yates. Since Miss Ralston was a world-class Czechoslovakian figure skater whose command of English equaled Fernando Valenzuela's, the moviemakers confined most of the action to elaborately staged production numbers in a gaudy skating rink. This gave tiny Twinkle, an accomplished skater since age 3, the chance to dis-

play her most formidable skill as she sails over the ice on her plump little legs while the adoring spectators shown on screen applaud her uproariously.

Unfortunately her final screen roles (as "Twinkle, a Girl of the Old West" in a Civil War melodrama called *California Joe,* and as the plucky daughter of tragic widower Allan "Rocky" Lane in *A Guy Could Change*) forced her to act rather than skate. American moviegoers found little difficulty in resisting her charms in these roles, which made Twinkle seem as gooey and insubstantial as a Twinkie. *The New York*

The high-voltage presence of Twinkle Watts did nothing to illuminate California Joe *or any of her other low-budget tearjerkers of the 1940s.*

Times summed up her appeal after *Lake Placid Serenade* by describing her as "a diminutive performer who shows promise as the Vera Hruba Ralston of 1955." Miss Watts sank from sight long before the accuracy of this glorious prediction could possibly be tested. Presumably she changed her name somewhere along the way, giving rise to the question:

Twinkle, Twinkle,
Kiddie Star,
Now we wonder
Where you are?

AND THE WINNER IS . . .

. . . SLEEP 'N EAT

The Golden Turkey here goes not to Sleep 'n Eat himself, but to those studio publicists who made such relentless attempts over the years to promote him to moviegoers as a comical subhuman. The various press releases designed to advance his career could have served as the basis for either libel suits or race riots had they been issued today.

They describe the star as "coal bin ebony" with "kinky black hair on a perfectly round dome. . . . He is six feet tall when he straightens up. . . . He thinks he is about 22 years old but is not quite sure. . . . When he is not in a scene he is usually found curled up in a corner sleeping."

Most insulting of all, the press hacks boasted that Sleep 'n Eat "gets a nice salary but the studio only gives him five dollars a week and puts the rest in a trust fund so he will have some of it left, as he spends every cent of it as fast as he gets it, and doesn't care."

It's ironic that the victim of this abuse invariably impressed his co-stars as a sensitive and capable professional. Bob Hope, who worked with him on *The Ghost Breakers* (1940), once described him as "the best actor I know." In 1934, while still wearing the label of Sleep 'n Eat, Willie Best sadly confided to a black journalist: "I often think about these roles I have to play. Most of them are pretty broad. Sometimes I tell the director and he cuts out the real bad parts. . . . But what's an actor going to do? Either you do it or get out."

One actor who *did* get out, leaving the pressure cooker of Hollywood for a far less difficult and demanding career, is celebrated in our next category. . . .

THE WORST PERFORMANCE BY RONALD REAGAN

O ne of the most common misconceptions about the fortieth President of the United States is that he disgraced himself as the star of Bedtime for Bonzo. *In reality, his role in that 1951 screwball comedy stands today as one of Ronald Reagan's finest achievements on the big screen. Nor does Mr. Reagan, in this or any other film, play the part of a chimpanzee, as his political adversaries have snidely suggested. In* Bonzo *he plays the college professor—straight man to a chimpanzee, and it must be acknowledged that he does a convincing job of it.*

The other highlights of his long movie career can be summarized briefly—very briefly. In Knute Rockne—All American *(1940) he played a doomed college football star; in* Kings Row *(1942) he won praise for his moving portrayal of a double amputee; in* The Hasty Heart *(1949) he was touching as a devoted friend attempting to comfort a soldier with a terminal disease; and he offered a chilling performance as a ruthless crime boss in* The Killers *(1964).*

Having dutifully enumerated his best roles, that leaves sixty-one other films to sort through in selecting the Worst *Performance by Ronald Reagan. We can assure you it has not been an easy task. The problem is not that the future president was such a terrible actor, or even that he made so many bad films; the problem is that his affable acting proved so consummately predictable and bland. While none of Reagan's films emerge from the dull gray pack as overwhelming or spectacular embarrassments, the performances listed below stand out as notably less competent than the rest.*

AND THE NOMINEES ARE ...

CODE OF THE SECRET SERVICE (1939)

Long before he got to know the Secret Service in its celebrated capacity as protector of the president, Ronald Reagan became familiar with the lesser-known function of this gallant group of government agents: as crime-busting counterfeit-fighters for the Department of the Treasury. These activities inspired four terrible movies in the 1930s in which Reagan portrays an intrepid investigator and daring pilot named Brass Bancroft. While gritting his teeth, glowering at the camera, and swinging his arms backward and forward in meaningless gestures, the determined hero defends American civilization from the dire threat posed by purveyors of "funny money" from South of the Border.

In *Code of the Secret Service,* the second of the Brass Bancroft films and by all accounts the worst of the bunch, our hero stalks the cunning crooks to their hideaway headquarters in a Mexican mission. The bad guys try to stop him by shooting him in the chest, but the bullet hits a Spanish language dictionary he conveniently carries in his jacket pocket. As he removes the book and stares, with wide eyes and open mouth, at the bullet imbedded in its pages, Reagan declares with gee-whiz intensity, "Boy! If you ever need an endorsement, call on me!"

Young Ronald Reagan is ready to take on all challengers as Lieutenant Brass Bancroft of the Secret Service.

The arch villain of the piece is a corrupt cleric known as Friar Parker (Moroni Olsen), who directs the counterfeiting ring from the cardboard belfry of his church. Brass Bancroft defeats his dastardly plans with his fists rather than his wits, which was only appropriate for the one-dimensional beefcake image Warner Brothers wanted for the young Reagan. The studio billed him as "The New Answer to a Maiden's Prayers" and assigned him to work with director Noel Smith, who had earned his previous reputation as a specialist in handling animal stars. Since Smith had successfully guided recalcitrant canines through films such as *Fangs of Justice* and *Fangs of Fate,* he seemed the ideal director to put the inexperienced contract player through his paces.

Reagan himself hated the entire series and felt particularly uncomfortable about *Code of the Secret Ser-*

vice. He complained repeatedly to producer Bryan "Briney" Foy, head of the Warner Brothers assembly line for low-budget productions known as "The B Hive."

"Briney, take me off this picture!" he begged. "It will ruin me."

Foy expressed sympathy but urged Reagan to keep working. "Ronnie, I tell you this picture can't possibly hurt you," he said. "Because, my boy, *nobody* goes to see a bad picture. Nobody."

Code, however, turned out to be embarrassing beyond the producer's wildest dreams. Desperate attempts to reedit the picture proved so unproductive that Foy eventually changed his mind and joined Reagan in urging Warner Brothers to shelve the finished film. He may have been motivated in part by concern for the reputation of his brother, Eddie Foy, Jr., who plays Brass Bancroft's supposedly comical sidekick, "Gabby," in this pathetic picture.

The studio brass gave serious consideration to the idea of writing off the entire movie, but in the end decided that the humiliation of Ronald Reagan was a small price to pay for the prospect of making a few dollars on the project. Nevertheless, in deference to the feelings of the principals, the Warner executives agreed to withhold the picture from the Los Angeles area; had it played in Hollywood, Reagan commented, "it could have destroyed all of us." He claims today that it is the only one of his movies that he has never seen.

In his 1965 autobiography, *Where's the Rest of Me?,* the future President described the chagrin he felt at the time of the picture's release. During a publicity tour of the Pacific Northwest he happened to pass a neighborhood movie house where, as he put it, "this turkey was on display." As he slowed down to glance at the stills in front of the theater, he noticed that the ticket taker had recognized him. "He was just standing there, shaking his head," Reagan recalled. "I said, 'Now wait a minute, I didn't even want to make this picture in the first place,' and all he would say in reply was, 'You should be ashamed.' "

NIGHT UNTO NIGHT (1949)

Ronald Reagan never felt satisfied with his position as the likable, lightweight star of Warner Brothers "B" pictures; for years he yearned for acceptance as a serious actor and a first-string romantic lead.

Perhaps Warner Brothers assumed that the miscasting of Broderick Crawford (left) as a sensitive painter would complement their similarly silly decision to feature Ronald Reagan as a brooding, suicidal biochemist in Night unto Night.

In 1942, following his much-praised supporting part in *Kings Row,* the studio offered him the sort of breakthrough role he craved: as an expatriate American café owner in an atmospheric tale of international intrigue tentatively entitled *Everybody Comes to Rick's.* Before he had a chance to pick out a trench coat or to practice the line "Here's looking at *you,* kid," the plans for the picture changed abruptly. Ingrid Bergman became available for the female lead, replacing Ann Sheridan, so Warner Brothers increased the budget and gave Reagan's part to Humphrey Bogart in the project that became known as *Casablanca.* Though he never discussed the episode in public, Reagan remained haunted by a sense of his missed opportunity: five years later, as he lay in delirium in a Santa Monica hospital, sweating and shivering with viral pneumonia, he dreamed "he was playing opposite Humphrey Bogart in a trench coat."

By 1947, after three frustrating wartime years on the Hollywood front lines as part of the Army's film production unit, our rapidly aging hero felt desperate enough to gamble with an oddball love story called *Night unto Night.* Though he had often begged the studio for a change of pace, this preposterous script gave him more than he bargained for: The robust, perpetually smiling outdoorsman got the chance to play a bookish, profoundly depressed biochemist with an "incurable disease." To demonstrate his depth as an actor, Reagan indulged himself on screen in an epileptic seizure and a suicide attempt in the midst of a howling storm. Watching the affable star engaging in these unaccustomed antics, Holly-

wood insiders wondered why he had consented to a role that his biographer, Laurence Leamer, aptly described as "a bit of miscasting on a par with Doris Day playing Mary, Queen of Scots."

The action of the film begins when Reagan, informed by a doctor of his tragic condition, retires to a remote town on the Florida coast to ponder the meaning of life. He rents a haunted house from a neurotic young widow (played by Swedish bombshell Viveca Lindfors) who spends most of her time in ghostly conversations with her dead husband. The widow's nymphomaniac sister (Osa Massen) makes a play for Reagan, but Miss Lindfors stops her seductive maneuvers by punching her in the nose. Eventually our heroine wins the heart of the stricken scientist by stopping him from taking his own life and demonstrating an amazing tolerance for his pseudo-philosophical rambling about love, God, and the-purpose-of-it-all. Their long conversations about "The Big Issues" convey the depth and intensity of a Woody Allen parody, as Reagan emits more hot air than in even the most misleading presidential press conference. Small wonder that *Time* magazine judged that he played his tragic role "with the abstracted air of a man who has just forgotten an important phone number."

Though he tried to focus all his energies on this extraordinary thespian challenge, Reagan's off-screen activities offered plenty of distractions. He had recently secured his first political office as president of the Screen Actors Guild, and he spent every spare moment on union business. Rosemary DeCamp, who played one of his neighbors in the film, recalled that "he worked eighteen to twenty hours a day—at night, trying to resolve an ugly industry strike . . . then all day on that baffling film. . . . But he remained cheerful and loquacious with three or four hours of sleep a night. This went on for months and may have been the cause of his divorce from Jane Wyman."

The press, meanwhile, wrote mercilessly about his marital problems and even suggested that he had become romantically involved with his Swedish co-star. In reality, Miss Lindfors considered Reagan "distant and bland," while concentrating her attention on the film's director, Don Siegel, whom she later married. Their passionate love affair brought new problems to an already troubled production; Siegel later admitted that his direction suffered as a result.

In the midst of the chaos Reagan decided that the

script required major rewrites, and for the first time in his career he attempted to make the changes himself. One key issue involved Miss Lindfors' on-screen description of her husband's tragic death. In the original screenplay she says he was sleeping on the beach, waiting for her, when two horses happened by and accidentally stepped on his face. As an experienced horseman, Reagan knew that no self-respecting horse would ever dirty his hoofs on a human being if he could possibly avoid it, so he changed the script to provide death by drowning. He also rewrote some of his own lines, while director Siegel, preoccupied with his personal passions, gave him his way. When producer Owen Crump screened the results, he gave Siegel a severe reprimand. "My God," he bellowed, "don't *ever* let an actor get a pencil in his hand!"

Despite Reagan's best efforts as actor and script doctor, *Night unto Night* proved such a dismal disappointment that Warner Brothers held up its release for a full two years; when they finally tried to foist a sloppily reedited version on an unsuspecting public in 1949, the critics concluded that they should have waited another two hundred. *Cue* pronounced it "a badly muddled, ineptly written drama," while *The New Republic* described it simply and directly as "the poorest entertainment imaginable."

HONG KONG (ALTERNATE TITLE: *BOMBS OVER CHINA*) (1951)

The promotional material released with this film made it sound far more topical and exciting than it was. "Ronald Reagan, an ex-GI, returns to China to earn a fast buck, but instead runs right into Commie aggression!" panted one Paramount press release. An apocalyptic action adventure, in which two-fisted Ronnie single-handedly defends the Free World against hundreds of millions of rampaging Reds? That's the sort of picture that might have provided uplifting entertainment for our time, but *Hong Kong* never delivers on its promises. The only "Commies" in the film appear in distant stock footage, which seems to have been tacked on as an afterthought in order to capitalize on the recent headlines about Mao's revolution. Reagan never lifts a finger (or even an eyebrow) to stop the advancing Marxist hordes,

Ronald Reagan warns the "yellow peril" bad guy (Marvin Miller) that he's picking on the wrong American in Hong Kong, *while Rhonda Fleming and war orphan Danny Chang appreciate his manly defense of Our Way of Life.*

but spends much of his time on screen battling an overweight Oriental capitalist.

As the cynical adventurer "Jeff Williams," Reagan gets to wear a leather jacket and an Indiana Jones hat while pitching woo to ravishing redhead Rhonda Fleming. She plays a prim and proper teacher from a mission school who, while fleeing the Communists, meets both Reagan and a 4-year-old war orphan (Danny Chang). After they all arrive in Hong Kong, Ronnie does a W. C. Fields imitation and steals the helpless child's only possessions in the world: a pet cricket on a leash and a precious jeweled idol. Before he sells the stolen goods, Miss Fleming helps him understand why it's not polite to rob widows and orphans, and the leading man is instantly transformed from a heel to a hero. For the rest of the picture he struggles to keep the gaudy gold Buddha out of the hands of an unscrupulous antiques dealer, played by Marvin Miller (of the TV series *The Millionaire*) in several layers of yellow-peril makeup.

To try to intensify his aging star's sex appeal, director Lewis R. Foster persuaded Reagan to deliver his opening narration in his underwear. It didn't help, nor did the unbelievably stilted dialogue in his love scenes with his co-star. Screenwriters for cheapie adventures like this one will often present background details about their characters in doughy, undigestible lumps, but information has never been advanced more awkwardly than it is here. To the sound of swelling violins, while they hug, smooch, and blink, the two lovers patiently review each other's resumés:

RHONDA FLEMING: You're not just a man I met on the plane trip from Lu-Chow—now I can look at you and say: that's Jeff Williams. Born in a white adobe ranch house near Douglas, Arizona. Cut his first tooth on a saddle horn. Spoke his first cuss words in Spanish. And spent the rest of his life looking for the right woman—or so he said.

RONALD REAGAN: Now I can look at *you* and say, that isn't just a schoolteacher I happened to fall in love with. That's Victoria Evans. Raised in a two-story house in Evansville, Indiana. Her father was principal of the high school. Mother played the harp. She got that little scar on her forehead by falling out of a tree when she was very little.

Rhonda and Ronald had so much fun with this sort of scene that they worked together on three other Technicolor action-adventures in the early fifties. Miss Fleming considered him a "thoughtful, considerate, ladies-first type of guy" and appreciated the way he soothed her frequently bruised feelings on the high-pressure, low-budget set. The shooting of *Hong Kong* proved particularly problematical because of the participation of little Danny Chang, whom Reagan remembers as an even worse scene stealer than his previous co-star Bonzo the Chimp. On several occasions the temperamental child halted difficult scenes with demands for a glass of water, then took twenty minutes of everyone's time, smiling sadistically at the aggravated adults as he slowly drank his fill.

The exploitation of this cuddly cub helped make *Hong Kong* a box office hit despite dismal reviews and its leading man's sleepy, half-hearted performance. It's painfully obvious in many of Reagan's big scenes that he's making not the slightest attempt to listen to the other actors, but concentrating instead on remembering his own lines. To display his thespian subtlety, his character reacts to every emotional situation with the same expressive gesture: reaching up and rubbing the back of his neck with one hand.

The picture's main entertainment value lies today in some of the ironic overtones it unexpectedly acquired in light of its star's subsequent activities. For its rerelease in 1953, Paramount used the zippy new title *Bombs over China*, and in the course of the film Reagan delivers several suggestive lines that are sure to delight dyed-in-the-wool Democrats.

- "Get yourself a solid fellow with a job," he tells Rhonda Fleming, "and don't get mixed up with a tramp like me."
- He also hints at his politics when he declares, "Looks like I'm playing *right* field on this club."
- Most pleasing of all to Reagan's political opponents is a scene where his co-star tries to arouse his social conscience. "The homeless, the old, the children—they'll need more help than ever!" Miss Fleming pleads.

"They've always been kicked around," the future president shrugs. "They're used to it."

With one eye closed, Ronald Reagan is almost convinced by Marvin Miller's Oriental makeup in a movie that was also released with the provocative, wishful-thinking title Bombs over China.

CATTLE QUEEN OF MONTANA (1954)

No, Ronald Reagan didn't play the title role in this one; that honor fell to Barbara Stanwyck, who said of this film years later: "Awful! Dreadful! You might wonder how such a thing could happen. The answer is simply that you make a horrible mistake."

For Reagan the horrible mistake of *Cattle Queen* was only the latest in a series of blunders that had already crippled his once promising career. Since leaving his exclusive contract at Warner Brothers in 1950, he wandered from one production company to another, looking for projects that might stretch his acting abilities. He particularly wanted to do westerns ("It's like getting paid to play cowboy and Indian," he observed) and felt jealous of those stars who regularly got a chance to ride the range. After fourteen years in Hollywood he starred in a western for the very first time in *The Last Outpost* (1951) and enjoyed it so much that he subsequently accepted even the most ridiculous parts so long as they allowed him to get back in the saddle again.

In *Cattle Queen*, Ronnie plays a rent-a-thug who goes to work for the evil McCord (Gene Evans), a greedy land baron who wants to steal Miss Stanwyck's ranch. The bad guys ply murderous redskins with "firewater" to accomplish their nefarious ends, and, even worse, they invade the Cattle Queen's privacy. We first encounter Reagan as a Peeping Ron, spying on his 47-year-old co-star as she skinny-dips in a mountain lake. "You're a mighty fine swimmer, lady," he gallantly comments as he exposes himself (from behind the trees). "The men in your outfit must be plumb loco letting you sashay around like this. This is Montana, remember! White women's scalps are mighty valuable—especially red ones."

Ronnie makes the American West safe for Barbara Stanwyck, otherwise known as the Cattle Queen of Montana.

For the rest of the picture this hired he-man is torn between love for the virtuous Stanwyck and loyalty to his vicious employer. At the very end of the movie we suddenly discover he's been a good guy all along: Reagan patiently explains he's an undercover agent for the U.S. Army, sent to gather evidence on McCord's whiskey-pollution of the local Indians. Just when we expect him to propose to the beauteous "Sierra Nevada Jones" (Miss Stanwyck), he suggests instead that she should serve her country. "Jonesy, I don't know whether you're lucky or just plain talented, but the Army sure could use you."

And Reagan sure could have used some help from his director: unsure whether to play his character as hero or heavy, he compromises by acting consistently confused. Nothing about the picture worked out the way he had planned it, not even his cherished scenes on horseback. In one sequence he was supposed to gallop toward the camera, pull to a sudden halt, and deliver a line. As director Allan Dwan recalled the experience, "We got him on an Indian horse that wasn't broken . . . and as he started up, the horse began to dance sideways and he wound up way over there. And all the time Reagan is hollering, 'Whoa! Whoa! Whoa!' As he went by the camera, he yelled out to me, mad as hell, 'I'm not one of those Hollywood riders who says he can ride and can't ride! This goddamn horse won't do what I tell him!' He's explaining himself to me as he flies by the camera. Of course, we're howling with laughter."

Observers also howled with laughter at the time of the movie's release, when RKO unveiled its Montana masterpiece with a memorably lurid ad campaign:

SHE STRIPS OFF THE PETTICOATS AND STRAPS ON THE GUNS!
Barbara Stanwyck: Woman of Fire—In a Land of Flame!
Ronald Reagan: Dangerous Friend—Deadly Foe!

Walter Mondale and others can attest that Reagan, even without his six-guns, is still a deadly foe, while movie fans will confirm that this picture, in revival houses or on videocassette, is still a deadly bore. As "Woman of Fire" Barbara Stanwyck fondly recalls, "Within one week after the start of shooting, everybody on the set knew that the thing was just not jelling. But by that time you're hooked. So you do the best you can—and you privately hope that nobody goes to see it."

HELLCATS OF THE NAVY (1957)

"I understand there are only two reasons to wake up President Reagan in the middle of the night," quipped Johnny Carson on *The Tonight Show*. "One is World War III. The other is if *Hellcats of the Navy* turns up on the Late Show."

Hellcats remains a special picture for our Chief Executive: Not only is it his last theatrical feature (at least to date), but it is also the only movie in which

The future President of the United States clearly believes that his co-star, Arthur Franz, should show greater respect for a photograph of the future First Lady—all part of the fast and furious action in the stirring wartime drama Hellcats of the Navy.

he appears alongside the First Lady—former starlet Nancy Davis. In their efforts to promote Ronald Reagan as a plausible romantic hero, producers over the years tried teaming him with various leading ladies, including Jane Wyman (five films and an eight-year marriage), Ann Sheridan (five films), Rhonda Fleming (four films), Patricia Neal, Virginia Mayo and Doris Day (two films each), and even the adolescent Shirley Temple (*That Hagen Girl—see:* THE MOST PREPOSTEROUS ROMANTIC PAIRING IN HOLLYWOOD HISTORY). None of these on-screen partnerships worked particularly well, so it seemed only logical that at the end of his movie career Reagan should turn, in desperation, to the same leading lady who had begun to fill his private life with a full measure of domestic bliss.

At the time they made the film, the Reagans had been married for five years and had already produced Patti, the first of their two children. Their desire to work together on a film was easy to understand, but it's difficult to imagine a less romantic project than this one. The picture focuses on submarine warfare in World War II—on mines, torpedoes, and male bonding beneath the waves. When Reagan huskily murmurs "What a temptation!" he's not talking about his co-star, but about the chance to blow up a Japanese destroyer.

Nancy, as a Navy nurse, is little more than a glassy-eyed, walking plot device. Her main contribution to the action is an eight-by-ten photo of her smiling face which she presents to a junior officer

(Harry Lauter) on Commander Ronnie's sub. This shocking indiscretion ("I wanted to prove I could still circulate . . . but it certainly wasn't love") causes problems between the skipper and his crew. Rightly concerned about the reputation of a future First Lady, Reagan sends his potential rival swimming out of the sub on a dangerous errand, then promptly abandons him to the Japanese. After this controversial command decision, he spends the rest of the movie cleaning off the fan. A court of inquiry investigates his actions; his second-in-command (Arthur Franz) taunts him with the fatal photo of Nancy; an emotional sailor expresses his contempt by heaving his gooey birthday cake at Reagan's head.

The star endures these on-screen indignities in the same stoic spirit with which he accepted his discomforts on the set. After twenty years of ups and downs his movie career had come full circle, returning him to the sort of pathetically low-budget black and white action pictures he had made in the thirties as part of the Brass Bancroft/Secret Service series. *Hellcats* saved money by avoiding sets altogether; the entire production was shot in and around real submarines, provided free of charge by the United States Navy. This arrangement may have made sound financial sense, but it forced the director to cram cast, crew, cameras, lights, cables, and sound equipment into ridiculously confined quarters. For many scenes, boom microphones had no room to maneuver, so the various actors hid portable mikes in their armpits.

Reagan's self-described "lifelong tendency toward claustrophobia" made the situation a special nightmare for him; in his memoirs he recalled that whenever he began to feel uncomfortable, he used to peer through the periscope for a quick but reassuring glimpse of the outside world. This habit has been preserved on screen, as the skipper reacts to even the most innocuous comments from his colleagues by running suddenly to his periscope for no apparent reason. Never noted for his dramatic range as an actor, Reagan is reduced here to a single earnest expression: He registers fear, love, anger, remorse, and exultation with the same pursed lips and furrowed brow—as if trying out for future parts in laxative commercials. This troubled pose is absurdly accompanied by a ponderous, intense, minor-key score by Mischa Bakaleinikoff. If the music sounds more appropriate to a horror film than to a wartime drama, it's no accident: Columbia Studios saved still more money by using these same themes as background for another 1957 release, *The Giant Claw* (*see:* THE MOST LAUGHABLE CONCEPT FOR AN OUTER SPACE INVADER).

In later years Reagan blamed the failure of *Hellcats* on studio bosses who were "more in love with the budget than the script," but considering the low quality of this Navy-surplus screenplay their preference is perfectly understandable. The picture begins with some supposedly patriotic narration about "one of the most daring and formidable operations in the history of naval warfare" as delivered by the venerable war hero Admiral Chester Nimitz. This old salt may have won the War in the Pacific, but he goes down to defeat when faced with a movie camera: he blinks his eyes, fidgets, and stumbles over his words in a style designed to make Ronnie and Nancy look good.

As for the two lovebirds, they play their big moment of South Pacific romance like *Dumb Enchanted Evening,* standing on a dock in front of a stack of explosive mines:

> NANCY: What are you going to do after the war?
>
> RONNIE: I told you a hundred times.
>
> NANCY: I want to hear it once more.
>
> RONNIE: I'm going into the surplus business. I'm gonna buy up all the old mines and sell 'em to the man in the moon.
>
> NANCY: But there's no water on the moon!
>
> RONNIE: How do you know so much about the moon?
>
> NANCY: I know a lot about it. I spend all my time looking at it when you're away. That's how it still is with me.
>
> RONNIE: It's time for me to go now.

This dialogue may leave most viewers cold, but it had the power to move poor Nancy Reagan to tears. When she tried to deliver her lines, she lost all control and delayed the production for several hours. "I was sending him off to risk his life and I couldn't stand it," she recently recalled. "The idea got to me. I kept breaking up in tears, and we had to reshoot and reshoot." Reagan himself remembers her "giggling between sobs, laughing at herself for having gotten so carried away." He suffered patiently with

his emotional missus, but his experience on *Hellcats* helped persuade him to bring his movie career to an end. His only subsequent screen appearance came in Don Siegel's *The Killers,* a 1964 TV movie deemed too violent for home viewing and instead released to theaters.

With his motion picture adventures behind him, Ronnie began to focus all his energies on a job he had held since 1954 as host of the popular weekly television show *General Electric Theater.* This position (and a later slot as host of the western adventure series *Death Valley Days*) never offered him the dramatic challenges of *Night unto Night* or *Hong Kong,* but it did bring his warm and genial personality into living rooms throughout America. What's more, it left him plenty of free time to pursue his rapidly developing political interests.

Nancy, meanwhile, knew it would be impossible to top the peak emotional experience of *Hellcats of the Navy,* and so, following the public's tepid response to the picture, she retired permanently to her chosen starring role as wife and mother. For old times' sake she occasionally ventured forth to make television appearances with Ronnie. Most memorable of these was her co-starring role beside her beloved husband in a November 1960 presentation of *G.E. Theater* called "A Turkey for the President"—a touching Thanksgiving tale, and a subtle forecast of the coveted award we are about to bestow. . . .

AND THE WINNER IS . . .

. . . HELLCATS OF THE NAVY

This picture takes the Golden Gobbler because it gives us two Reagans for the price of one, and they both do a remarkably poor job in front of the cameras. For Nancy in particular, it's a sub-par performance: in her previous ten films (*The Frogmen, Donovan's Brain*, etc.) she projected a natural and sympathetic screen presence that is sadly missing in her final appearance.

Before she met Ronnie, Nancy Davis had been known—if at all—as a vaguely promising MGM contract player who had been lucky enough to date Clark Gable for a few months. Then came a 1949 introduction to the charismatic president of the Screen Actors Guild and a slow, sweet courtship. As her character tells the daring sub commander in the course of *Hellcats of the Navy*: "I played it safe until I knew you were Mr. Right."

Her devotion to Mr. Right only increased as their marriage progressed, and by the time she finally got the chance to star with him on screen, her attitude had developed into breathless adoration. That is precisely the problem with her performance: When standing beside her husband she seems to be hypnotized by his presence, transfixed by his sheer magnificence. In her starched nurse's uniform, with her shoulders straight and her hands clasped prayerfully in front of her, it's as if she is too thrilled to breathe. Her staring eyes speak volumes: "Oh, Ronnie! It's so wonderful the way you wear that navy costume! Oh, Ronnie! It's so wonderful the way you remember your lines!" Her worshipful gaze is certainly out of place in this picture, but it is no doubt utterly sincere; it is, in fact, the same gaze the First Lady turns on Him today.

As bad as this movie may be (and it is, certainly, an insipid and slovenly piece of work) there is something terribly endearing about it, and about the almost adolescent vulnerability of its two stars. Watching them on screen, even in their embarrassment, it's difficult not to like them. The same, of course, is true of all of Reagan's other worst performances—in politics as well as in movies. Reviewing *Hong Kong* for the *Los Angeles Times* in 1952, Philip K. Scheuer wrote: "There's a clean-cut something about Ronald Reagan which just saves him from looking foolish, time and again"—a line that might stand as an eloquent summary of our President's surprisingly durable career.

Nancy Reagan looks adoringly at her personal commander-in-chief, who in turn tries to persuade some skeptical extras that his wife is actually a better actress than she appears to be.

THE MOST AWKWARD ON-SCREEN MARRIAGE PROPOSAL

AND THE NOMINEES ARE...

SALOME, WHERE SHE DANCED (1945)

DAVID BRUCE: You've seen enough trouble—you've probably *caused* enough trouble.

YVONNE DE CARLO: Oh, Cleve!

DAVID: Oh, I don' wanna hurt you, Sah-low-mee! Ah've had trouble too. But the theater's no place to start life again! You don' belong here! . . . You were sayin' that you'd do anythin' if'n ah'd go straight!

YVONNE: Yes, anything.

DAVID: Then come home with me—to Virginny! I wanna take you out of all this. None of it is any good. None of it! An' you know it!

YVONNE: Oh, Cleve!

THE JOLSON STORY (1946)

(After meeting at a party at a Manhattan penthouse, Larry Parks [as Al Jolson] and Evelyn Keyes [as Ruby Keeler] escape to a balcony for a private conversation.)

LARRY: I've gotta tell you how I feel! And it's gonna take me hours! 'Course I shouldn't be rushin' it like this, you'll think I'm kiddin'. But look. You see, I've been waitin' for something for a long time. I didn't know what it was. My manager's been tellin' me it was about—well, about gettin' everything and nothing out of life! I didn't know what he was talkin' about. Then I saw you! Yes, sir—then I saw *you!* Look. I gotta great idea: suppose you and I got married and went to California together? How about it?

EVELYN: Of course, I'm rehearsing "Show Girl" and we open in two weeks.

LARRY: Oh, yeah. That's too bad. If it just wasn't for that, huh?

BIRD OF PARADISE (1951)

Debra Paget considers Louis Jourdan's sly suggestion that they exchange sarongs before their marriage in Bird of Paradise.

(Debra Paget, as a Polynesian princess named Kahlua, has just finished walking barefoot over hot coals to prove her undying love for a visiting Princeton student [with a distracting French accent] played by Louis Jourdan.)

LOUIS: Why, you're not burned!

DEBRA: No. I did not feel the fire.

LOUIS: But I stood there—I saw the fire in the stones! This is incredible!

DEBRA: We have the answer. The gods have smiled on us. Now we can be one. You can buy me.

LOUIS: Buy you?

DEBRA: Yes, from my father. It is the custom. I will be very expensive.

LOUIS: You will be worth it.

VALENTINO (1951)

ANTHONY DEXTER: You know how to use a woman's most powerful weapon—her mystery!

ELEANOR PARKER: But Rudy . . . we only met six days ago!

ANTHONY: The world was created in six days.

ELEANOR: Please . . . you know we should wait . . .

ANTHONY: Tomorrow is a poor excuse for people who are afraid to live today!

Anthony Dexter tries to hold up Eleanor Parker long enough to allow her the chance to deliver her romantic lines in Valentino.

CAT WOMEN OF THE MOON (1953)

VICTOR JORY: You can't turn love on and off like a faucet! Believe me, baby, I could chase you across the world, around the moon, and all the way stations in between! [He shakes her shoulders.] If it hadn't been for Laird [Sonny Tufts], I would have tried to make it "you and me" a long time ago!

MARIE WINDSOR: Flattery will get you noplace. Take your big hands off me!

VICTOR: Not until you level with me. Come on, now, I'm not hurting you that much.

MESA OF LOST WOMEN (1953)

(Robert Knapp and Mary Hill huddle around a campfire by their downed plane.)

ROBERT: I think I understand you.

MARY: Oh no you don't. You can't.

ROBERT: Oh yes I can! I've had my hard knocks too. I've had to work ever since I was a kid. Some of it wasn't very much fun. Well, I guess it all boils down to what you want out of life.

MARY: What is it for you?

On the eve of their climactic confrontation with the mad doctor who dominates the Mesa of Lost Women, *Robert Knapp and Mary Hill pause to discuss their romance.*

ROBERT: Well, I want a girl who's sincere. Real. Someone who would stick by me when the chips are down. One who wants me for only what I *am*, and not what I *have*. It's a big order, huh? [They kiss.]

ROBERT: Now wait a minute . . .

MARY: Yes. Yes. Of course. That was a foolish thing to do.

JUBILEE TRAIL (1954)

JOAN LESLIE: I've got to get away from this country, John. Some way I've got to get my son to New York. He'll be safe there.

FORREST TUCKER: He's too young to take overland. I'll see if there're any clipper ships when I get up to "San Francisco"—that's what they call the old port of Yerba Buena now.

JOAN: Are you—are you—going away again?

FORREST: Tonight.

JOAN: John—don't you ever get tired of the trail?

FORREST: Guess I was meant to keep movin'. It's all right for some folks to stay in one place, I guess, but . . .

JOAN: What about your land grant? Won't you someday want to settle down and have a ranch?

FORREST: I don't know. Bein' a rancher or farmer seems kinda quiet to me. Someday I s'pose. Maybe.

JOAN: Someday? Maybe?

FORREST: Garnet!

JOAN: Yes!

Joan Leslie wants cowboy Forrest Tucker to settle down (and try to find a new clothing designer) as a precondition to marriage in Jubilee Trail.

FORREST: Before I came out here I lived on a plantation in Virginia. I didn't own it. I was an orphan. Livin' with rich kinfolks. Livin' in that same house. With just those same people. People I had to be grateful to. Say "thanks" for everything I had. For what I ate. And for my room. And my clothes. I guess that filled me *up* with livin' in one place. With the same people.

JOAN: Is that why you never want anybody to *mean* anything to you?

FORREST: I guess so. I'm not one that anybody should figure on settlin' down on. I'm sorry.

JOAN: I'm sorry too, John. . . .

FORREST: But I did miss you this time, Garnet! I don't want to travel alone anymore. [They embrace.] Every turn of the trail I came to I hoped you'd be around the next bend. I love you, Garnet.

JOAN: Oh, John!

THE TEN COMMANDMENTS (1956)

Egyptian princess Anne Baxter can't resist the charms of Charlton Heston in The Ten Commandments. *"Oh, Moses! Moses!" she murmurs. "You stubborn, splendid, adorable fool!"*

(Anne Baxter [as the Egyptian princess Nefretiri] summons Charlton Heston [as Moses] to her barge to try to persuade him to forsake his people and become her husband.)

ANNE: Is that what you want? To be a *slave?* Then why aren't you kneeling to the feet of a princess?

CHARLTON: I'm afraid the mud pits have stiffened my knees, Royal One.

ANNE: Shall I call back the guards?

CHARLTON: Do you think they could bend them?

ANNE: *Oh, Moses! Moses! You stubborn, splendid adorable fool!!* [They embrace.]

CHARLTON: I'm not kneeling to a princess.

ANNE: No. You're kneeling to a woman! . . . If you want to help your people, come back to the palace. Oh, Moses! The gods have fashioned you for greatness. . . . When you are Pharaoh, you can free your people, worship whatever gods you please, so long as *I* can worship *you!* [They kiss.]

THE LIFE, LOVES AND ADVENTURES OF OMAR KHAYYAM (1957)

(Cornel Wilde plays the eleventh-century Persian poet and mathematician, who surprises his "first and only love," Sharain [Debra Paget], in a courtyard of the palace of the shah.)

CORNEL: Have you . . . forgotten me?

DEBRA: My love, I must . . . I must!

CORNEL: Tell me why.

DEBRA: Yet I cannot forget you. I weep for you.

The shah's daughter (Debra Paget) falls in love with Cornel Wilde's left nostril in The Life, Loves and Adventures of Omar Khayyam.

CORNEL: And I see your tears now . . . silent tears—the saddest of all! [He kisses her hand.] They say—when love does not give all you wish, be grateful for the happiness you have received. I am grateful, but—could you and I—could you and I—

Could you and I with Fate conspire
To grasp this sorry scheme of things entire . . .

DEBRA (Whispering): Go on!

CORNEL: There is no more.

DEBRA: Oh, Omar! The best verses always come suddenly to you!

QUEEN OF OUTER SPACE (1958)

Eric Fleming and Zsa Zsa Gabor develop a love that is strong enough to overcome the difference in their planets of origin in Queen of Outer Space.

(Venusian scientist Zsa Zsa Gabor and Earthman astronaut Eric Fleming huddle around a campfire in a cave on the surface of Venus, "The Female Planet.")

ERIC: You know, under other circumstances, this would be so wonderful. You beside me; watching the fire; the two of us planning the future.

ZSA ZSA: I must admit I vuz thinking about the same thing. But then again, ve might haff no future at all! Tell me, Captain: are you happy on your planet?

ERIC: Oh, I was doing work that I liked. I would say I was pretty content.

ZSA ZSA: Vere you really?

ERIC: No, I hadn't found the girl I wanted.

ZSA ZSA: I'm glad you said that. I vould be *terribly* jealous!

ERIC: Talleah! You're amazing! Why, you know, on Earth a girl would rather die than show her real feelings. We have an old saying, "A man chases a girl until *she* catches him."

ZSA ZSA: How silly! Vot a silly vaste of time! I think if a girl vants a man she should tell him so!

ERIC: You're very beautiful, Talleah! . . . I just want to say, while I have the chance: I love you!

ZSA ZSA: Luff? I had almost forgotten. But if it is that varm feelink that makes my heart sing, then I do luff you!

WATUSI (1959)

DAVID FARRAR: Look, Erika. I'm pretty beat up, and I haven't got too much hair, and I'm not too young anymore. What I mean to say is, well, I'd like you to marry me.

TAINA ELG: It's so difficult to think with so much danger around!

DAVID: Not for me, it isn't! [pause] . . . Oh well. I'd have made a lousy husband anyway.

David Farrar takes time from his pursuit of diamonds in darkest Africa to measure the upper-arm width of Swedish sensation Taina Elg in Watusi.

THE OSCAR (1966)

(Stephen Boyd drives Elke Sommer back to Hollywood after a day watching the bullfights in Tijuana.)

ELKE: It's been a lovely day, Frankie.

STEPHEN: Pretty good for me, too. I can't relax this much around most people.

ELKE: Sometimes we do go well together, don't we?

STEPHEN: I go better with you than any other girl I know . . . *woman* I know. Which are you, Kay? Girl or woman?

ELKE: I'd like to think that I'm a woman, Frankie.

STEPHEN: *Woman!* Spend the night with me at Rosarita Beach! I think I'm in love with you!

ELKE: Oh, Frankie, I want to go with you to Rosarita. I want to—I do.

STEPHEN: Marry me, Kay. Marry me—tonight!

RED TOMAHAWK (1967)

JOAN CAULFIELD: I don't know who I am—what I am—what life is all about. Just an endless game! I keep coming up with the wrong combination!

HOWARD KEEL: Could be that's all over.

JOAN: 'Cause you say so?

HOWARD: Is there anyone else to say so?

JOAN: I'm tired of coming up with the wrong combination! I'm tired of pretending I'm a hard case.

HOWARD: You're not a hard-case anything, believe me.

JOAN: Then who am I?

HOWARD: You're Lil! [They embrace.]

CLAWS (1977)

JASON EVERS: Are you happy?

CARLA LAYTON: A little.

JASON: Just a little?

CARLA: A whole lot. And then a *heap* more.

JASON: You and me, baby! Forever and overtime! [They embrace.]

SHEENA (1984)

TANYA ROBERTS: I am not a foolish young girl. The Shaman taught me that brave tales do not always have happy endings. I know what guns can do. I know that you and I may not live to see another sunset.

TED WASS (He kisses her.): Mmmmm!

TANYA (Pulling away): You are an enemy!

TED: I'm what?

Ted Wass grits his teeth at the prospect of a lifetime spent listening to his jungle-queen lover, Tanya Roberts, delivering inane lines as Sheena.

TANYA: The Shaman taught me—an enemy is someone who takes without asking.

TED: I'll ask then—may I?

TANYA: Yes! [They kiss.] . . . You will be welcome in Zukuru! The head man's locust bean cakes—they'll be your locust bean cakes! His fermented buffalo milk will be your fermented buffalo milk . . .

AND THE WINNER IS . . .

. . . BIRD OF PARADISE

Those culture-crossed lovers, Debra Paget and Louis Jourdan, take the turkey for the only scene in screen history to combine firewalking with a proposal of marriage.

After this red-hot beginning, their relationship proceeds to an elaborately staged "native" wedding ceremony (filmed in handsome Technicolor on location in the Hawaiian Islands) and a few weeks of connubial bliss. This idyll is interrupted by that hoary staple of South Seas romances, an exploding volcano—a development that leads the nasty old local witch doctor (hilariously portrayed by that stalwart of the Yiddish Art Theater, Maurice Schwartz) to conclude that the entire tribe has been punished for Princess Kahlua's marriage to a French *shaygetz.* To appease the angry gods, Miss Paget sacrifices herself by leaping into the volcano, leaving her heartbroken hubby to return to his studies (in comparative religion?) at Princeton.

In addition to its thoroughly silly and sentimental script (based on a stage play of 1912), the picture boasts some of the most peculiar casting east of Pago Pago. Miss Paget, according to *Time* magazine, "never resembles anything but a cute trick in a bathing beauty contest at Hollywood High," while the script makes a feeble attempt to explain her blue eyes and fair skin by describing her as "the descendant of an English sea captain."

How, then, can we explain the presence of the inimitable Maurice Schwartz, in bare chest and a low-slung sarong, as the scowling "Big Kahuna"? The great Lower East Side tragedian, best known for his extravagant performance in the popular Yiddish language version of *King Lear,* appears to have made a dreadfully wrong turn somewhere around Second Avenue. It is difficult to know whether he found his role as the malevolent Polynesian priest as amusing as the audience does.

Witch doctor Maurice Schwartz scowls at native prince Jeff Chandler (left) for bringing a stranger (Louis Jourdan) home with him for summer vacation. "Zis vhite one brinks evil mit him," quoth Schwartz. "He must get out fun zis place."

Bosley Crowther of *The New York Times* described *Bird of Paradise* as "a rambling mishmosh of South Seas romance and travesty, of solemn high-priesting and low clowning, of never-never spectacle and sport. . . . Even the volcano in this instance has the look of a pyrotechnic fake."

As transparent as this fakery may be, it is no more blatantly bogus than the "volcanic passions" and "explosive violence" perpetrated by the antisocial sickos who roar through the films in our next category. . . .

THE WORST BIKER MOVIE OF ALL TIME

*A*ccording to most social historians, America's notorious motorcycle gangs got their start in California (where else?) shortly after World War II. Returning veterans who had a difficult time adjusting to peacetime routine joined motorcycle clubs as an outlet for their frustrations and to re-create some semblance of battlefield camaraderie. These budding organizations first made headlines in 1947, when a group of rough-tough bikers virtually took over the sleepy village of Hollister, California, successfully defying all law enforcement authorities for several days. This celebrated incident helped to inspire Marlon Brando's hit film The Wild One (1953), which in turn generated eager new recruits for the motorcycle gangs. By 1965 these biker bands—in particular, the ever-popular Hell's Angels—had established a clear-cut image in the public mind. Their members represented the dark side of the sixties counterculture: black leather in place of paisley; swastikas instead of peace signs; tire chains and brute force as opposed to peace and love. To most middle-class Americans the cycle outlaws became synonymous with pointless violence, mind-bending drugs, the degradation of women, foul language, sadism, and intolerable body odor—in other words, a perfect subject for exploitation by Hollywood.

The most remarkable fact about the string of biker films churned out during this era is that a few of them actually proved to be cult classics: Roger Corman's The Wild Angels (1966), Richard Rush's Hell's Angels on Wheels (1967), and Dennis Hopper's Easy Rider (1969) come immediately to mind. A large number of future movie luminaries got their start working on such low-budget cycle sagas, including Jack Nicholson, Bruce Dern, Diane Ladd, Harry Dean Stanton, Peter Fonda, Peter Bogdanovich, and Karen Black. With these gifted professionals on hand, even the most dreary and predictable formula films in this genre could occasionally boast a good performance, or else a few lyrical shots of shiny "hogs" roaring down sun-baked country roads. The five films nominated for the Golden Turkey, however, lack any such redeeming characteristics. Despite the fact that some of them achieved considerable commercial success, the creators of these horrendously tacky entertainments would still be entitled to quote Easy Rider's famous line: "We blew it."

AND THE NOMINEES ARE . . .

THE BORN LOSERS (1967)

Remember the character Billy Jack—a blue-eyed Native American and Vietnam vet who fought for tolerance, holistic healing, and universal brotherhood by beating his opponents into a bloody pulp? He emerged as a significant cult hero of the 1970s, delivering New Left platitudes along with karate chops, and Method-mumbling his way through three major films (*Billy Jack* [1971], *The Trial of Billy Jack* [1974], and *Billy Jack Goes to Washington* [1977]) that appealed to 12-year-olds of all ages. But before achieving cinematic notoriety, before causing millions of prepubescent Americans to waste an entire summer whistling "One Tin Soldier" through their braces, before taking on the court system, the political establishment, imagined White House conspiracies, and movie reviewers (with an astonishing series of "Billy Jack vs. The Critics" newspaper ads), our boy B.J.—and his alter ego, actor-director-producer Tom Laughlin—did battle with a band of sleazy and sadistic bikers in *The Born Losers*—a cockeyed exploitation flick hailed by one of Hollywood's trade papers as "the most depraved, demoralizing and degrading film ever packaged for American consumption" and by the *Los Angeles Times* as "unrelieved trash."

The project began auspiciously enough when Tom Laughlin met and "made friends" with an attractive stewardess named Elizabeth James during a cross-country flight. At the time, Mr. Laughlin, who

American folk hero Billy Jack (Tom Laughlin) makes his screen debut as a karate-chopping, biker-stomping, guitar-strumming, mystical Native American medicine man in The Born Losers.

had played juvenile bit parts in a number of big-screen productions before going to work as director of a Montessori school in Santa Monica, had already begun his controversial career as an independent producer-director. His first efforts included a primitive comedy about sexual initiation (*The Proper Time*, 1960) and a religious picture (*The Young Sinner*, 1965), intended as the first segment of a projected trilogy known as *We Are All Christ*. Since his religious scruples (not to mention his marriage to Delores Taylor, who later served as executive producer on *The Born Losers* and most of his other films) prevented him from making the customary approaches to a shapely stewardess, he made a suggestion of a different sort when he met Miss James in midair: How would she like to write a feature film? As it happened, the friendly flight attendant had long nursed ambitions as a writer, and so shortly after her fateful meeting with Laughlin, she spun out a story line to serve as the basis for his next project. The resulting tale, originally entitled *The Contrary*, so thrilled the struggling producer that he asked the obviously multitalented but untried Elizabeth James to play the female lead in the production. This proved a wise decision, since, according to one of her co-stars in the finished film, her grateful (and well-to-do) family in Colorado helped to finance the entire enterprise.

And what an enterprise it was, with plenty of wildly emoting actors trying to impersonate a band of filthy, vicious motorcycle thugs who terrorize a small California town. Their main victims are, conveniently enough, a group of voluptuous teenyboppers dressed invariably in bikinis and go-go boots. Elizabeth James plays Vicky, a visiting college girl, and you can tell she's the heroine because she has the smallest bikini and the shiniest white go-go boots in town. The bikers, in fact, are so impressed by her sartorial splendor that they rape her several times, hold her prisoner, and torture her by making her watch this entire movie to its bitter end. These fun-loving cyclists all bear cute and cuddly names such as "Gangrene," "Speechless," "Cue Ball," and "Crabs" and display the endearing habit of boasting of their venereal diseases after committing one of their countless rapes.

What the poor, persecuted townspeople really need is a truckload of penicillin, but what they get is Billy Jack—a sullen Indian mystery man and martial arts expert who descends from his mountain hideaway to restore law and order. Blinded by ethnic prejudice, the local officials show their appreciation by throwing Billy into jail, but he gets out in time to give sensitive rape counseling to Vicky and to shoot the chief bad guy through the head. On the way to this satisfying conclusion, Laughlin has decorated his turgid mess with all sorts of extraneous and totally anomalous elements, including a loving shot of a dead walrus on the beach, which not only makes a statement against environmental pollution, but also helps to prepare us for a later cameo appearance by Jane Russell. That "Full-Figured Gal," still one of Hollywood's biggest stars long after her career had faded, makes an enormous contribution as the distraught mother of one of the cyclists' victims. The filmmakers suggest, however, that Ms. Russell's on-screen daughter (Janice Miller) deserves everything she gets, because moments before she is taken prisoner by the thugs we watch her perform a highly suggestive striptease in front of a mirror while making lewd comments to her stuffed toy doggie.

In the final analysis, what makes this movie so much worse than an ordinary, run-of-the-mill exercise in ultraviolent exploitation is the laughable solemnity with which it attempts to deliver various sociopolitical messages. Executive producer Delores Taylor, Tom Laughlin's off-screen wife and long-term partner-in-schlock, insisted to the press that *The Born Losers* was "a very serious, very personal picture." How else could she explain its ham-handed and irrelevant digressions concerning the corruption of the judiciary, the need to preserve Native American folklore, police racism, the callousness of health care professionals, corporate abuse of the environment, the need to bridge the generation gap, and the danger of rampant social diseases? All of this is served up with awkward, preachy, tin-eared dialogue that makes it abundantly clear that screenwriter Elizabeth James bears not even the most distant relation to Henry James. In one particularly memorable scene, Vicky (as portrayed by Miss James herself) huddles beside a mountain campfire with her enigmatic protector, Billy Jack. As she looks up at the stars overhead, she poetically ponders her own cruel fate and the eternal vulnerability of the female:

> You know, I feel like those stars up there are inside of me . . . just glowing softly. I've always felt that I had a light bulb–like thing inside of me and all my seeds were in it. If I ever let the wrong person in, the little light bulb would be jabbed . . . and broken! And all of me would pour out . . . and be gone! Forever! Oh, Billy, Billy, Billy . . . what am I going to do?

One would hardly expect such a tender soliloquy in the midst of a bloody biker saga, but then *The Born Losers* is full of surprises. One of the biggest was the picture's respectable performance at the box office, generating enough profit to encourage Billy Jack's return, four years later, in the next picture in the insufferable series. Tom Laughlin's cinematic achievements have been featured in all our prior books on bad movies—with *The Trial of Billy Jack* included as one of *The Fifty Worst Films of All Time*, *Billy Jack Goes to Washington* winning a trophy in the original *Golden Turkey Awards*, and the disastrous *Master Gunfighter* briefly described in *The Hollywood Hall of Shame*. In view of our long and intimate association with Mr. Laughlin's work, we could hardly complete this latest book without giving appropriate recognition to *The Born Losers*—the first fully realized expression of his mature artistic vision. Though Laughlin's ambitious and egomaniacal mini-empire collapsed in the late seventies after the costly failure of *The Master Gunfighter*, we can only hope that he will succeed in his plans for a comeback. In 1985, he announced to a press conference that he had begun work on *The Return of Billy Jack*, in which our righteous hero turns his wrath on a cabal of insidious child molesters at a California nursery school. Go get 'em, B.J.!

Real-life stewardess Elizabeth James roars into motion pictures as the glamorous star and brilliant writer of her friend Tom Laughlin's sensitive biker saga, The Born Losers.

SATAN'S SADISTS (1969)

**WILD BEYOND BELIEF! HUMAN GARBAGE—IN THE
SICKEST LOVE PARTIES!
WHEN THEY SOCK IT TO A GIRL—SHE FEELS IT!
DEPRAVED BEYOND DESCRIPTION—A NEW KIND OF
ABNORMAL LOVE!
WARPED WOMEN! MOTORCYCLE MANIACS! FANTASTIC
FIGHTS!**

With subtle advertising lines such as these, it was safe to assume that moviegoers who paid their hard-earned cash to see *Satan's Sadists* weren't expecting, say, an Oscar Wilde comedy. They therefore must have been thoroughly surprised to discover the unintentional laugh riot of the year—a movie that offered 90 nonstop minutes of outrageously entertaining trash deluxe, featuring some of the decade's worst acting, most ill-conceived script ideas, shabbiest editing, and most hilariously inept rock 'n' roll.

The star of this extravaganza of bad taste was none other than Russ Tamblyn, the sprightly actor and dancer well known for his roles in *Seven Brides for Seven Brothers* (1954), *Peyton Place* (1957), *West Side Story* (1961), and *How the West Was Won* (1962). Though he had once played Tom Thumb (in the 1958 movie of the same name), by the time he was ready for *Satan's Sadists* he might more appropriately have been cast as Gargantua. (The bulky and bloated star had, in fact, played a leading role in the 1967 Japanese classic *War of the Gargantuas*—but he portrayed an American reporter rather than one of the title creatures.) In any event, Mr. Tamblyn had, at age 35, come a long, long way from his days as an adorable child star and a nimble-footed teenage hoofer. In this film he plays Anchor, the redoubtable leader of a band of motorcycle brigand thugs known as (you guessed it) Satan's Sadists. Mr. Tamblyn wears round pink sunglasses through the entire course of the movie, but these specs do nothing to hide his bleary-eyed and listless approach to his part. In place of Brando's celebrated portrayal of *The Wild One*, Tamblyn offers us a gang chieftain who, despite all his scripted brutality, might still be described as the Mild One.

His ill-disguised ennui, however, is supposed to be fatally attractive to women; in particular, it inspires the gang's Main Mama, billed in the ads for the film as "The Freak-Out Girl," to an all-consuming romantic obsession with the Leader of the Pack. The lovesick floozy is portrayed by Regina Carrol, off-screen wife of the film's director, Al Adamson. With her bleached white dustmop hair, mauve lipstick, and a pair of false eyelashes that look to weigh several pounds, this romantic heroine actually resembles a plump transvestite hooker. Ms. Carrol (whose first name is properly pronounced Re-GY-na, to rhyme with . . . oh, never mind) had previously played bit parts in notable productions such as *The Beat Generation* (1959) and *Viva Las Vegas!* (1964), and worked as a singer-dancer at various nightclubs. At the time of *Sadists'* release she was hosting her own TV variety show (*The Regina Carrol Show—Direct from Las Vegas!*) but despite claims in the promotional material distributed with the film that this daring venture had established itself as "a BIG hit coast to coast," the project proved short-lived. Ms. Carrol nevertheless went on to plum movie roles in many more of hubby Al Adamson's productions, including *Dracula vs. Frankenstein, Blood of Ghastly Horror, Angels' Wild Women, The Female Bunch, The Creature's Revenge*, and, of course, the sensitive art film *Blazing Stewardesses*, but in *Satan's Sadists*, her very first starring vehicle, her acting style had already matured. As the Freak-Out Girl, she is called upon to perform a "wild, suggestive dance" designed to arouse the interest of her beloved Anchor, but the boss biker remains decidedly more interested in raping and murdering strangers than in giving his girl even a moment from his busy schedule. In the course of the film he rejects her advances a half dozen times, but she finally gets the point after he punches her in the stomach and tells her, "You ain't nothing but a piece of dead meat." With tears streaking her caked-on mascara, the poor Freak-Out Girl mounts her motorcycle (it's better than nothing) and rides off into the sunset, driving herself over a cliff and whispering the sweet name "Anchor!" while the soundtrack offers the snappy musical number "Is It Better to Have Loved and Lost?":

> Is it better to have loved and lost
> Than never to have loved at all?
> To pay the price at any cost
> For a moment of pleasure?

This touching song is the handiwork of the well-known hitmakers Harley Hatcher and the Nightriders, who prepared all six of the original numbers used in the film.

But along with romantic and musical interludes, *Satan's Sadists* also provides the requisite smorgasbord of mayhem and molestation. In most biker movies the gang members take over an entire town, but since this is a *very* low-budget enterprise the fun-loving Sadists must content themselves with the capture of a small diner. The scale of their conquest, however, does nothing to dampen their natural high spirits, as they manage to slaughter a pair of young lovers, a retired cop and his wife, the diner's owner, and three pert and pudgy college coeds who happened to be gathering geology samples in the desert. Before they are murdered each of the victims is, of course, humiliated, subjected to a strong dose of LSD, raped (if they happen to be female), tortured, or, perhaps worst of all, force-fed spaghetti and meatballs. But just when it seems that nothing can stop the brutish bikers in their homicidal (not to mention their culinary) excesses, a heroic Vietnam veteran (shades of Billy Jack?) who managed to escape the "diner of death" returns to the fray to battle the gang to a standstill. Actually, our hero (Gary Kent) deserves the title "sadist" at least as much as the bikers, since he murders them with such inventive little ploys as strangulation by rattlesnake, smashing a face with a medicine cabinet mirror, impaling an Adam's apple with a hurled dagger, and drowning a suitably ugly thug in a toilet bowl.

The actors who stagger through this fast and furious action are either aging has-beens or youthful never-will-be's, and their thespian approaches range all the way from mere wooden incompetence to woozy, stumbling "Where's my paycheck?" recklessness. Among the down-on-their-luck character actors vaguely recognizable in their cameo roles are Scott Brady (who went on to play the gravelly voiced sheriff in *Gremlins*) and Kent Taylor, best known as Boston Blackie from the old-time TV series of the same name. But *Satan's Sadists* not only served as a temporary refuge for some worn-out Hollywood veterans, it also provided inspiration and training for promising newcomers who went on to become big-league bad movie directors in their own right. Greydon Clark (who portrays the drug-crazed "Acid") later took charge of such worthy projects as *Satan's Cheerleaders* and *Joysticks,* while John "Bud" Cardos (who played the vicious half-breed, "Firewater") eventually directed William Shatner in *Kingdom of the Spiders,* Cathy Lee Crosby in *The Dark,* and guided the dynamic duo of Rafer Johnson and Cesar Romero (Cesar Romero?) through *Soul Soldier.* In short, the role of this movie as a fertile breeding ground for the bad cinema of the future has been, so far, insuffi-

William Bonner (with beard) *and Greydon Clark pause for a philosophical interlude in the midst of the murder and mayhem of* Satan's Sadists.

ciently appreciated by film scholars. We hope that some enterprising graduate student will set out to remedy this lamentable situation by attempting an overdue exploration of the influence of Al Adamson (and of his consort, the Freak-Out Girl, Regina Carrol) on a new generation of filmmakers.

BLACK ANGELS (1970)

In the decade of the 1970s, black Americans made great strides toward equality: thanks to a wave of popular exploitation films they got their very own vampire (*Blacula*), hard-boiled detective (*Shaft*), murderous schizophrenic (*Dr. Black and Mr. Hyde*), Mafia warlord (*Black Godfather*), karate champ (*Black Belt Jones*), lab-created monster (*Blackenstein*), reborn Nazi (*Black Gestapo*), amorous hairdresser (*Black Shampoo*), exorcist (*Abby*), and, with *Black Angels,* a down-home gang of soulful cyclists. According to the ads for this film, these mean motorcycle mothers "*Exploded* Out of the Slums, *Slamming* into the Establishment, Brutally Clashing—Head-On—in a Fury of *Blood* and Burning *Rubber*!!!"

If the aroma of blood and burning rubber (mmmm!) proved insufficiently tantalizing to lure audiences into the theaters, producer-director-writer Laurence Merrick offered an additional selling point: Instead of hiring professional actors, he ensured the film's realism (and no doubt saved money) by asking a real-life band of down-and-dirty bikers to play themselves. Unfortunately the featured gang did not call itself the Black Angels but rather the Choppers — which seems to suggest a group of dentists (or butchers) on wheels, rather than a bunch of baaaad biker brothers. Nevertheless, in order to maintain the "integrity" of this ambitious social protest movie, that is the name used to designate the boys on screen. Whatever you call them, this crew looks formidable. We soon discover that this is a group that "ain't 'fraid of nuffin' "—except, perhaps, the camera, since many of its members stare directly into it during their big scenes like doomed, frightened rabbits hypnotized by the headlights of an oncoming car.

The plot concerns two rival gangs who have developed ethnic antagonism to a rivalry that is as bloody as it is predictable. The Serpents, deadly enemies of the Choppers, are a collection of hate-filled Harley honkies who make Archie Bunker look like Mother Teresa. Unbeknownst to them, their gang's newest member, Johnny Reb (played by that dynamic biker-actor, King John III), is actually a light-skinned black and a member of the Choppers, who is passing as white in order to make the Serpents unwitting Equal Opportunity Destroyers. This infiltration pays off when he slips Mickey Finns to his new-found friends and enables the Choppers to kick their lily-white behinds while they are still groggy. Eventually the Serpents wake up (though most of the audience doesn't) and seek revenge. In a final showdown all members of both gangs are killed, providing the

SOULFUL CYCLISTS: The Black Angels *strike a powerful blow for equality in bad movies.*

story with its uplifting moral: We must live together as brothers, or we will die together as ketchup-soaked nonactors in bad biker movies.

Laurence Merrick, who created this motorbike morality play, pursued a varied career during his years in Hollywood. Using many of the same sleazy riders who roared their way through *Black Angels,* he also directed *Guess What Happened to Count Dracula?* (1970), starring the versatile Des Roberts, former gang leader of the Serpents, in the title role. In addition to these cinematic achievements, Merrick ran the Merrick Studios Academy of Dramatic Arts on Vine Street, where aspiring actors could learn from his expertise and share in what he described as his "dream for a better world through art." He further advanced that dream by directing a sensationalist cinematic "exposé" called *Manson* which, like *Black Angels,* attempted the awkward but all too familiar Hollywood trick of condemning violence at the same time it exploited it. Nevertheless, *Manson* received an Academy Award nomination as Best Documentary of the Year and won its creator new respect in the motion picture industry. Unfortunately the 50-year-old Merrick had scant opportunity to enjoy his success. On January 26, 1977, while on his way to the men's room of his dramatic academy, he was shot and killed by an unemployed cannery worker named Dennis Mignano. The press speculated on a connection between the lone assassin and the Manson family, which had been angered by Merrick's film, but it soon became clear that Mignano was an unaffiliated free-lance psychotic. He had once auditioned at Merrick's acting school and came to believe that the producer had cast black magic spells which caused him to "shrink physically in size." The court judged the killer not guilty by reason of insanity and remanded him to a state mental hospital.

Merrick's colleagues, meanwhile, placed in the Hollywood trade papers a large "In Memoriam" ad which deserves a Golden Turkey all its own for its lugubrious prose and syntactical originality. "We are like seeds in the winter snow, yearning for eternal spring," the ad began. "A season has passed and you are nearer the sun. . . . Above all, you have taught us determination and self-pride and that failure is nonexistent, for mutability is the only evitability [sic]. . . . Your life here on earth is over, but your work will live on."

It is in that spirit that we recall, and honor, *Black Angels.*

WEREWOLVES ON WHEELS (1971)

The Motorcycle Gang thought it was tough . . . until it found a new type of hell . . . THE BRIDE OF SATAN!

The title suggests an excursion in high-camp hilarity, with a snarling squad of freewheeling wolfmen tearing down the highway in frightening formation and giving the song "Leader of the Pack" a whole new dimension. Unfortunately this dreary film never delivers on that promising premise: the producers apparently could not afford monster makeup for an entire motorcycle gang, so only two members of the group actually become werewolves. What's more, the audience is regularly cheated out of the chance to witness even this limited transformation. In most werewolf films, seemingly ordinary people are turned into killer creatures only when the full moon comes out; in *Werewolves on Wheels* the two principals become monsters only when they are off camera. To be fair, it should be noted that the grand climax does offer nearly a minute of pathetic close-ups of latex hair and Halloween fangs, but for the most part we must satisfy ourselves by viewing the bloodied victims of the ravening beasts promised by the title. By the end of this torturously boring muddle we are all, in a sense, their victims.

The biker gang that provides the focus of what passes for the film's action is known as the Devil's Advocates. You know that this is supposed to be a group of lovable and refined thugs because they have the sort of polysyllabic name that most motorcyclists couldn't even pronounce. They also boast a thoughtful member known as Tarot (Deuce Berry), who is interested in the occult and who persuades them to pay a visit to a group of devil-worshipping monks. This arcane order practices an intense brand of mumbo jumbo that is about as menacing as the ritual at a Shriners convention, so it is hardly surprising that they succeed, with the help of some drugged wine, in putting the visiting bikers to sleep. The monks take advantage of the situation by leading Helen (D. J. Anderson), winsome mama of the boss biker, to their insidious altar. There, after chanting and gyrations reminiscent of the classic *Wild Women of Wongo*, she becomes, quicker than you can say *Rosemary's Baby*, "the bride of Satan."

Unfortunately the honeymoon is interrupted when the somnolent cyclists suddenly awake, begin beating on the monks, rescue the girl, and ride off to the desert. There Helen is romantically reunited with her main man, Adam (Stephen Oliver), and is so excited by the experience that she gives him a bloody hickey. This token of her esteem transforms him magically (and unobtrusively) into a werewolf, which conveniently enables him to join her in murdering their fellow gang members one by one. By the time the surviving cycle men catch on to what's happening they are plenty burned up, and so put both their former leader and his gal to the torch. They also plan to teach the evil monks a lesson for all the distasteful monk-ey business to which they have been subjected, but when they invade the monastery, swinging chains, they are overcome by the mystic power of their opponents.

The audience by this time will be overcome by the mystic power of nausea, and the certainty that they have seen it all before. As *Variety* wrote of this film: "If one can imagine 'Macbeth,' 'The Wolf Man,' 'The Addams Family' and 'Easy Rider' in one stew, this is it." Some of the actors may also look vaguely familiar: Billy Gray, sadly aged since his days as Bud on TV's *Father Knows Best*, plays one of the gang members. Former pop star Barry ("Eve of Destruction") McGuire is likewise along for the ride, but apparently (and most unfortunately) Wolfman Jack was not available.

As producer Joe Solomon, self-proclaimed "lone ranger of the motion picture industry of the 1970s," proudly described the secret of his success: "I'm always looking for a new angle on a motorcycle picture." In that same spirit he had previously crafted *The Losers* (1970)—which is not to be confused with Tom Laughlin's *Born Losers*, cited above. Originally entitled *'Nam's Angels, The Losers* told the inspiring tale of a filthy, vicious, sadistic motorcycle gang that is employed by the CIA and imported to Southeast Asia to help the good ol' U.S.A. clean out hordes of murderous Commie gooks. The picture became a runaway hit, so producer Solomon felt confident about duplicating its success. Having successfully popularized a band of CIA cyclists, he naturally assumed it would be an easy matter to build similar public support for a gang of Werewolves on Wheels, but America's fickle film fans sadly disappointed him. Despite its show of fur and fangs, when it came to box office receipts this film proved not so much a wolf as an ordinary flea-ridden dog.

THE PINK ANGELS (1972)

Having advanced the affirmative-action agenda to cover blacks, women (*The Mini-Skirt Mob*, 1968), and werewolves, the makers of motorcycle films took the next logical step in 1972: *The Pink Angels* offered its specialized audiences a gang of the meanest, toughest, scruffiest San Francisco hairdressers who ever humped a Harley. As these six beautician-bikers make their way down the coast to attend a drag queen ball in Hollywood, no cliché—and no stomach—is left unturned. Die-hard fans of the late Edward D. Wood, Jr. (*see:* THE ROGUES' GALLERY), may be disappointed to see that the dirty half-dozen have left their angora sweaters at home, but black leather is definitely the style here. An unsuspecting hitchhiker who thumbs a ride with the mincing motorcyclists soon finds himself the object of their amorous attentions. To decide which one of them will have the opportunity to enjoy the hunky hitchhiker as his new scooter mama, the guys in the gang engage in a hotdog-throwing competition in a roadside café. While your basic all-American, wholesomely heterosexual movie motorcycle gang will most often leave out-of-the-way diners soaked in ketchup-blood, the Queens on Machines in this film do nothing worse

than make a mess with mustard. Even the inevitable confrontation with the authorities is given a rather lame (or should we say limp) comedic twist in this film: When a highway patrolman stops the boys to search their belongings, he is appalled to find frilly gowns, lacy underthings, and setting gel.

No amount of costuming or special effects magic, however, could enable these gentlemen to rival a statuesque topless waitress (Melanie Sintangelo) whom they meet along the way and who is baffled by her inability to get a rise out of these seemingly macho marauders. A coven of back-country call girls is similarly perplexed when the Pinks ignore their tender charms in order to proceed to their own wine-and-cheese party deep in the woods. This elegant social event is lit by several candelabra—in a touching homage to Liberace—but the carefully nurtured ambience is suddenly spoiled by the appearance of "real" Hell's Angels spoiling for a fight. Our heroes, of course, would rather swish than fight—especially when the nasty newcomers issue their bottom-line demand that they "hand over" their women. Sending an emissary racing back to town for the call girls, the Pinks proudly present these beefy beauties as a "piece" offering to their colleagues. The two gangs then proceed to a night of drunken revelry, but the next morning, long after the Pink Angels have departed, the Hell's Angels stagger awake to find themselves wearing delicate new hairdos, lavender ribbons, and lipstick.

In view of the campy capers in the script, one might have expected an appropriately vivid and ex-

A stunned state trooper discovers that The Pink Angels *are the world's only motorcycle gang with an extensive collection of lacy underthings.*

aggerated acting approach by the members of the cast. Director Lawrence Brown, however, inexplicably decided to play this material straight; most of the actors deliver their lines in an earnest monotone, as if trying to piece together the words phonetically from cue cards. The only recognizable professional in the midst of the silly stereotypes is TV's "Grizzly Adams," Dan Haggerty, here playing one of the "real men" in the Hell's Angels and doing a convincing job of looking drunk on camera.

Though a few critics sardonically suggested that the release of *The Pink Angels* marked a milestone, of sorts, in the march toward gay rights, most activists —and movie audiences—happily ignored it. The national publicity campaign, featuring the slogan "Think Pink" and tie-ins with local motorcycle dealers who were supposed to drape new models with pink streamers, managed to alienate even the hard-core macho audience for most biker films. Nevertheless, *The Pink Angels* deserves recognition for its prophetic elements; within six years of its release a well-publicized group of cycle-riding lesbians began turning up in San Francisco Gay Pride parades, proudly billing themselves as Dykes on Bikes.

AND THE WINNER IS...

... SATAN'S SADISTS

This picture deserves the prize not only for its incompetent execution and loathsome content, but also for the revolting manner in which the producers hawked their product to the gullible public. Within weeks of *Sadists'* release, the bloody and senseless murders of actress Sharon Tate and a half dozen others by Charles Manson and his followers made front-page headlines around the world. Independent-International, the distribution group in charge of the film, seized upon this grisly story as an unprecedented public relations "break" and began gleefully pointing out "haunting parallels" between the Manson Family and the Satan's Sadists in the film. After all, both gangs lived in the desert and killed people, didn't they? What's more, it was rumored that on more than one occasion cult leader Charlie M. may have even ridden a motorcycle. Duly noting these startling coincidences, the distributors used *Boxoffice* magazine to urge theater owners to exploit the death of Sharon Tate as a selling point. They suggested that the exhibitors bill *Sadists* as "The REAL Story of California's Sadistic Tate-Murder Hippie Cult!!!" and "get original Tate murder clippings and compare with information provided by Independent-International." Sorry to say, this unspeakably sleazy sales strategy paid off handsomely for its perpetrators: fascination with the entire Manson story proved to be so intense that audiences rushed, helter-skelter, into the theaters. *Satan's Sadists,* which cost only $50,000 to make, grossed more than $10,000,000 during its worldwide release.

Naturally, this sort of success inspired plans for a sequel, but *Sadists'* creator, Al Adamson, faced one small problem: He had killed off every last one of his fictional gang members by the end of the first film. Undeterred by this minor inconvenience, Adamson called for his two stars, Russ Tamblyn as "Anchor" and his off-screen amorata, Regina Carrol, as "The Freak-Out Girl," to experience miraculous resurrections. What's more, Regina's character has apparently benefited from her brief visit to the Great Beyond, because in the sequel, originally entitled *Satan's Blood Freaks,* she expands her on-screen persona to include a stirring excerpt from her Las Vegas show. Shooting on *Blood Freaks* commenced in 1969

In a key interchange from Satan's Sadists, *"The Freak-Out Girl" (Regina Carrol, future star of* Blood of Ghastly Horror) *discusses the meaning of life with "Acid" (Greydon Clark, future director of* Satan's Cheerleaders).

only a few months after *Sadists'* release, but when Adamson secured the services of "big name" stars J. Carrol Naish and Lon Chaney, Jr., he changed his plans in midstream. *Satan's Blood Freaks* soon became *Dracula vs. Frankenstein,* with the wheelchair-bound Naish (in his last screen role) as Dr. Frankenstein, the paunchy, sadly aged Chaney as his deaf-mute assistant, and the immortal Zandor Vorkov as Drac-

ula. In the final screen version Anchor has only a minor part and the Freak-Out Girl has become a Las Vegas lounge singer whose sister is kidnapped by Dr. Frankenstein. The picture did good business at the box office, but without the Manson connection failed to reprise the spectacular success of *Sadists.* Now, if only they had put both Dracula and Frankenstein on motorcycles. . . .

THE MOST INSUFFERABLE
KIDDIE MOVIE
EVER MADE

W̲hen a child does something extraordinary, such as cleaning up his room without provocation, getting straight A's on a report card, or changing TV channels from MTV to PBS, a parent may want to provide an appropriate cinematic reward such as The Wizard of Oz, The Muppet Movie, *or* E.T. *If, on the other hand, the kid has been a holy terror, the films in this category could be considered suitable punishment, and may well bring tearful apologies from the properly chastened youngster. One warning: Some of the movies in this Golden Turkey category are so painful to watch that local legislation may prohibit their use as tot torture. In any event, given a choice between eating brussels sprouts and viewing, say,* Pippi Longstocking, *ten out of ten normal children will opt for the Belgian vegetables over the Swedish meatball.*

AND THE NOMINEES ARE . . .

SNOW WHITE AND THE THREE STOOGES (1961)

It would be difficult to imagine a more ridiculous combination of elements in a major motion picture unless Sylvester Stallone and Steven Spielberg somehow joined forces to make *Rambo Meets E.T.* The Three Stooges are known (and, in some quarters, loved) for their anarchic, roughhouse humor, elevating eye-gouging and slap-fights to a manic martial art; Snow White, on the other hand, is the essence of sweetness and light. What possessed the executives at Twentieth Century–Fox to sink $3,000,000—a very hefty sum in the early sixties—into a project so obviously ill-conceived?

This maudlin mishmash began life as a star-making musical vehicle for Olympic figure-skater Carol Heiss, the sensation of the 1960 Winter Games. Two decades earlier Twentieth had made a bundle by churning out more than a dozen movies displaying the ice-skating abilities of a previous Olympic champion, Sonja Henie. The studio expected Miss Heiss to follow the same path to stardom, and the role of Snow White—which called for a good deal of smiling and skating and a bare minimum of acting—seemed

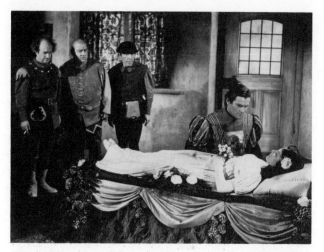

Prince Charming (Edson Strull) tries to revive the sleeping princess (Carol Heiss), while Larry, Curly Joe, and Moe fail to revive the sleeping audience for Snow White and the Three Stooges. *Larry (extreme left) displays his touching concern for Snow White, and his dedication to a new position as role model for America's children, with the cigarette displayed prominently in his right hand.*

an ideal first step. To make sure that even jaded juveniles flocked to the theaters, the producers hired those proven kid-pleasers the Three Stooges, placing their name in the title despite their small role in the film.

Whatever your personal opinion of their comic style, you can usually depend on Larry, Moe, and Curly Joe to inject some energy into the pictures in which they appear: this time, unfortunately, the boys seem stodgy, tired, and downright dull. Deploying only lame quips in place of their usual head-bashing, they seem frightened that they might offend all those well-mannered little girls in the audience by their usual bad-boy antics. Part of the problem is the script: In order to draw clear distinctions between this new movie and the fabulously successful animated Disney feature of 1938, the screenwriters offered an "update" of the classic fairy tale that turned out to be more grim than Grimm. The Stooges play kindly puppeteers who wander the countryside with Prince Charming (Edson Strull) as their adopted son, then help to bring the boy together with the lovely Snow White. Though they try to reproduce the cuddly charm of cartoon dwarves, they only succeed in competing with the interminable ice-skating sequences in terms of sheer boredom.

Three Stooges fans are by nature a masochistic lot, but very few of them have the stomach to endure this

film. In later years the veteran comics themselves reportedly looked back with regret on this idiotic outing: the "magic mirror" of audience and critical response told them that among all their films, this was the dumbest one of all. In its review of the film, *Variety* duly noted the "stubborn insipidity" of the project and added that, "all too plainly, this *Snow White* is dull grey."

SANTA CLAUS CONQUERS THE MARTIANS (1964)

In 1982 the presentation of the Golden Globe Awards stirred considerable controversy when Pia Zadora won the title of Best New Star. Astounded observers noted that Pia's performance in *Butterfly* (a wretched film about the incestuous relationship between a Nevada prospector and his daughter) drew universal scorn from critics at the time of the picture's release. The decision by the Golden Globe committee to ignore these reviews and honor the simpering sex kitten (choosing her over such worthy nominees as Kathleen Turner, Howard Rollins, Rachel Ward, and Timothy Hutton) sparked a chorus of condemnation from film fans around the world; cynics suggested that Zadora's husband, wealthy industrialist Meshulem Riklis, somehow used his untold millions to "buy" the prize for his little lady.

We object to the award for other reasons: Regardless of the quality of her performance, Pia Zadora could not plausibly present herself as a "new star." Though she and her publicists pretended that *Butterfly* marked her screen debut, she had actually played a major part in a motion picture some seventeen years before: wearing green makeup and wobbly antennae for her challenging role in *Santa Claus Conquers the Martians*.

Anyone hoping to trace the evolution of Miss Zadora's acting style must begin here. At the tender age of 8 the precocious superstar had already perfected the all-purpose pout that served her so well in future roles, though her famous golden globes had yet to appear. Moreover, the influences she absorbed on the set of *Santa Claus* determined the direction of her career for decades to come: all of the actors in this film deliver their lines in the same amateurish, stagey, declamatory style that has become the hallmark of the mature Pia Zadora.

In this film she plays the melancholy Martian lass Girmar. Her character's name, like those of all other personalities in the film, carries deep symbolic importance: *Girmar* signifies "Girl Martian," while her brother, the boy Martian, is Bomar, her mother is Momar, the king is Kimar, and so forth. The only character whose designation departs from this ingenious pattern is Dropo (Bill McCutcheon), a third-rate Pinky Lee imitator who spends so much time wiggling his hips and shaking his knees that he seems engaged in a perpetual struggle to control his bladder.

The action begins when Martian officials notice that the children of their planet (there appear to be only two of them in this ultra-low-budget effort) have lost their ability to have fun. To remedy this situation, the red planet ruler, Kimar (played by Leonard Hicks with straight-faced Shakespearean flair), orders an invasion of Earth for the purpose of kidnapping Santa Claus. The military forces of the United States rally to defend the North Pole's most famous inhabitant, unleashing some utterly irrelevant Air Force promotional footage showing various transport planes refueling in midair. All this is accompanied by stirring martial fanfares (composed by *The Gong Show*'s future musical director, Milton De-Lugg), but the Martians, with their superior technology and a killer robot ("Torg") that is represented by two cardboard boxes painted silver, overcome all opposition. Once on Mars, Santa (John Call) assembles a toy factory and manages to charm his captors; despite a conspiracy against him by a bad-guy Martian (you know he's bad because he wears a drooping mustache and resembles a green-skinned Frank Zappa), Kris Kringle succeeds in installing the brain-damaged Dropo as a Martian Santa, then returns to Earth in time for Christmas.

All this is presented on screen with the sort of heart-on-the-sleeve sentimentality usually reserved for films about cancer victims or lost dogs. Even the most dim-witted toddlers will find themselves simultaneously bored and confused by the action on screen, and irritated by the movie's thrice-repeated anthem, "Hooray for Santy Claus!" which proclaims, in part, that "He's fat 'n' round, but jumpin' Jiminey/He can climb down any chimiley!" *The Monster Times*, a publication devoted to knowledge of such things, denounced *Santa Claus Conquers the Martians* as "the worst science fiction flick ever made, bar none," though a group of young British critics recently attempted a defense of the picture. According

to their revisionist reading of the script, *Santa Claus* is an underappreciated allegory about the dangers of unbridled technology. For these scholarly savants, the Martians represent "the avatars of soulless science," Santa is a "Christlike spokesperson for the divine spirit of universal love," and the key scene comes on Mars, when Father Christmas refuses to install an assembly line for the production of toys and expresses his preference for working by hand, "the old-fashioned way."

These intriguing arguments will no doubt rage for years to come, but we suggest, meanwhile, that this film's English enthusiasts apply to Meshulem Riklis for a grant to pursue their research, in the hopes that they may cast revealing new light on this long-neglected aspect of Pia Zadora's early career.

PINOCCHIO IN OUTER SPACE (1965)

"Astro, the Flying Whale from Outer Space" makes a noble but doomed attempt to rid the world of cloying cartoon characters like "Nurtle the Twurtle from the Land of Twurtle-Dee" and our hero in Pinocchio in Outer Space.

According to producer Norm Prescott (a former Boston disc jockey), the youngsters of the "swingin' sixties" had become too sophisticated to enjoy old-time children's stories in their unadulterated form; in order to appeal to today's jaded juveniles, kiddie classics needed an up-to-date "angle." With this philosophy in mind, Prescott and his partner, Fred Ladd, hijacked the beloved Carlo Collodi story—so memorably adapted by Disney in 1940—and turned Pinocchio into an intrepid astronaut with a "hepcat" feline adviser named Mr. Groovy.

At the beginning of this animated feature our hero

is still sadly behind the times, a mere marionette living in the toy shop of his kindly creator, Geppetto. The Blue Fairy then appears to tell him that he can become a real boy by performing one conspicuous act of courage. His mission, should he choose to accept it, is to leave his Italian village far behind, take control of a rocket ship, and sail off to the stratosphere to do battle with "Astro, the Flying Whale from Outer Space." With this brilliant creation, the American producers and their bargain basement Belgian animators stole a march on the Japanese monster industry; someone at Toho Studios is probably still kicking himself, wishing that Godzilla had gotten the first crack at this flying whale from beyond the stars.

Pinocchio is aided in his challenging assignment by one Nurtle the Twurtle (who is, we are assured, no relation to "Yertle the Turtle" of the Dr. Seuss books). The voice of this alien tortoise is provided by comedy giant Arnold Stang, who also lent his talents to previous juvenile junk such as *Dondi* and *Alakazam the Great!* (both 1961). Nurtle (who unabashedly says of himself midway through the movie, "Did you ever see anything more lovable than *me*?") is actually on a special mission of his own, as "Secret Agent D-V-8 from the Land of Twurtle-Dee"; Stang's whining inflections and expressed desire to "twurtle" Pinocchio suggest that he is actually "Secret Agent De-Vi-Ate."

After meeting a talking fox called Mr. Sharp, landing on Mars and discovering sand crabs the size of dinosaurs, dropping an atom bomb to destroy the monsters, and singing the smash hit "It's a Goody-Good Morning and a Happy-Dippy-Dappy Day," Pinocchio and Nurtle finally meet up with the dreaded Astro. The flying whale, who has been ruining the U.S. space program by swatting down satellites with his giant tail, proceeds to swallow the adventurers, but they escape by aiming their rocket ship out his spout. In the climactic confrontation, Pinocchio defeats the levitating leviathan by hypnotizing him and then, in a display of goody-good happy-dippy-dappy sportsmanship, rescues the creature from the dangers of reentry as they approach Earth's atmosphere. "Astro's our enemy," he solemnly declares, "but we can't let him go up in smoke!"

By the time this cretinous cartoon finally crawls to its conclusion, the Blue Fairy has turned Pinocchio into a little boy by changing the shape of his nose, and the producers have prepared us for a possible sequel. Over a last image of Nurtle's bright-orange spaceship hurtling (or twurtling) toward distant galaxies, a spectral voice intones, "For Pinocchio, this is not the end." Maybe not, but for producers Ladd and Prescott it was: the response of America's children to *Pinocchio in Outer Space* indicated that they might have welcomed a sequel called *Pinocchio in the Toothpick Factory,* but otherwise felt relieved when the venerable marionette retired from the screen.

PIPPI LONGSTOCKING (1973)

This picture tells the story of an obnoxious little girl with breathtaking magical powers: Not only can she lift several times her own weight and make her braids stand straight out from her head, but she demonstrates a positively supernatural ability to keep her voice and her lip movements at all times out of sync. As the title song proudly proclaims:

> Pippi's world is fun
> Diddle-diddle-dee
> Pippi is unique,
> She is such an imp
> Tra-la-la-la-la
> You'll love her too! . . .

You'll also love the fact that the interminable lyrics to this song offer not a single rhyme in the course of eight stanzas, and that the words—as presented by a chorus of shouting, out-of-tune children—bear no apparent relation to the bouncy theme music to which they are attached.

While this film's problems may have been somewhat intensified by the adaptation of the Swedish original for U.S. distribution, most of the action on screen would seem equally stupid in any language. *Pippi Longstocking,* in fact, could serve as a useful corrective for those naive cinéastes who invariably associate the Swedish cinema with Ingmar Bergman and assume that all Scandinavian leading ladies resemble Greta Garbo or Liv Ullmann. In its title role, this film features an 11-year-old actress named Inger Nilsson, who may be the most homely movie star since Donald Duck. With her bubble nose, buck teeth, and coarse, dyed-orange hair, she is a dead ringer for *Mad* magazine's Alfred E. Neuman. On screen she does everything awkwardly, including walking and turning her head: even her smiles seem self-conscious and effortful.

The story, based on the popular children's books by Astrid Lindgren, describes the adventures of a

Inger Nilsson as Pippi Longstocking (left) *displays the charm and grace that made her the least welcome Swedish import since clogs.*

talkative tyke who lives alone in a picturesque village with a horse and a monkey because her sea captain father is away in the South Seas. This "staunch anti-establishment girl hero" (as she is described in the press release distributed along with the film) teaches neighborhood children disrespect for all authority, including parents, teachers, and police officers. After leading two clumsy cops on a merry chase around the town, she comments: "I think policemen are the best-est fun, next to rhubarb pie!" In addition to these witty observations, Pippi indulges in physical humor so crude it would probably embarrass the Three Stooges. One long sequence features our irrepressible heroine (someone, please repress her!) scrubbing her floor by tying brushes to her feet and skating through the kitchen; another comedic highlight shows a "grownup" tea party where Pippi teaches her friends to offend their parents by breaking the china and picking their noses in public.

The production values are every bit as bad as the social values preached by the film. When Pippi lifts a horse over her head, the effect is comparable to a back projection on the six o'clock news; the horse is surrounded by a distinct blue line that gives away the fact that this girl couldn't hold up a conversation, much less Secretariat. Ray Charles himself would be hard-pressed to miss the wires that make Pippi's "magical" braids shoot out of her freckled and hateful little head.

Equally lamentable is the dubbing, which may stand as the very worst in motion picture history. While Pippi's lips mouth some lengthy Swedish phrase akin to "Yah-dee-hoo-dee-yah-dee-hoo," a nasal American voice says merely "Yes!" or "Goody!" On other occasions the actors' mouths move furiously with no sound at all emerging from them, and lines continue long after the characters have stopped talking and walked out of camera range. Most notable of all are the instances when the system breaks down entirely: The screen shows the face of the chattering little boy, but the soundtrack uses the voice of the little girl who's supposed to be addressing him. Chief credit for these technological triumphs goes to Gordon Zahler, who is listed on the American version as dialogue director, and is best known as music coordinator for films such as *Women of the Prehistoric Planet, The Navy vs. the Night Monsters,* and *Plan Nine from Outer Space,* all duly noted elsewhere in this book.

Pippi did well enough with audiences around the world to justify the release of three later Longstockings: *Pippi Goes On Board, Pippi in the South Seas,* and, finally, *Pippi on the Run.* One can only hope that this baleful brat is still on the run from discerning children and enraged critics who had to endure her revolting motion pictures.

THE MAGIC OF LASSIE (1978)

No, Lassie doesn't perform card tricks or pull rabbits out of her hat; the "magic" in the title refers to the intangible transformation she works on everyone with whom she comes in contact. In fact, the clever collie emerges in her latest incarnation as a Spiritual Teacher and an Agent of Enlightenment who is reverentially described by her owner as "Something that came from God." Patrons may have paid to see a simple family story in the style of the old *Lassie* TV show; what they got instead was uplifting idiocy about a Doggie Deliverer.

To emphasize these religious overtones, the soundtrack score features the voices of those two bellowing born-agains, Pat and Debby Boone. Debby, in fact, plays the title role—not by donning a dog suit, but by crooning the musical voice-overs that represent Lassie's thoughts. The tunes and lyrics to these numbers are sentimental enough to make *The Sound of Music* sound like punk rock: in one memorable scene, while wandering in a forlorn mood through the estate of the bad guy who has kidnapped her, Lassie breaks into song and declares, "I'm gonna get free by and by / I'm gonna find my patch of the sky." On another occasion she pushes her evil captor (Pernell

Roberts) into his own swimming pool while tunefully informing him that "I can't be bought or sold / Love has the only hold on me."

Lassie's songs would have been more than enough, thank you, but unfortunately for the audience everyone else in the film feels a similar urge for musical self-expression. This means saccharine "show-stoppers" for such Hollywood stalwarts as Mickey Rooney (playing a cynical wrestling trainer, persuaded to "go straight" by Lassie), Alice Faye (as a kind-hearted waitress), and Jimmy Stewart (as the lovable "Gramps"). Mr. Stewart sings for the first time in a screen musical since performing Cole Porter's "Easy to Love" in *Born to Dance* back in 1936, but for this outing he hardly has Porter's witty lyrics to hide his hoarse, tuneless croaking: he opens the picture by singing, "Oh, golly gee, I love that hometown feelin' / People always say hello!" It is only the presence of Michael Sharrett, as the teary-eyed youngster who loses, then recovers this cherished dog, that spares Mr. Stewart the distinction of carrying out the movie's most embarrassing musical number. As the scintillating score slowly glug-glugs down to the very bottom of the barrel, young Sharrett sobs himself to sleep, while the soundtrack bawls out a torchy ballad:

> Lassie, my Lassie, I don't know why
> But Lassie, I can't say good-bye!
> You and me
> We're gonna be pals till we die!

As *Variety* aptly observed, the plot of the film offers "*less* substance, imagination or honest emotion than a typical half-hour episode of the long-running TV series." Jimmy Stewart owns a winery in northern California that is coveted by greedy millionaire Pernell Roberts. When the bald meanie can't take the vineyard, he steals Lassie as sour grapes. She escapes from his clutches and begins a thousand-mile journey back to her puppyhood home, while rescuing or inspiring anything fortunate enough to cross her path. Meanwhile, Michael Sharrett, as the orphan boy who loves her best, runs away from home to try to rescue his holistic hound. For a time Lassie joins a country-and-western singing group, the Mike Curb Congregation (more religious significance?), but the climax comes when a bedraggled kitten is trapped in a burning dressing room. Lassie naturally rushes into the flames, saves the kitty, and appears to perish

in the blaze, though no one makes the obvious comment about a charred hot dog. Then, miracle of miracles, in a scene strongly reminiscent of the overblown Resurrection sequence in *The Greatest Story Ever Told* (*see:* THE LEAST CLASSY USE OF CLASSICAL MUSIC IN MOVIE HISTORY), the charismatic collie comes back to life and manages to return home in time for Thanksgiving.

*Jimmy Stewart detects a tell-tale doggy odor emanating from his co-star in—and from the script for—*The Magic of Lassie.

Since *Lassie Come Home* first jerked America's tears in 1943, the persistent pooch has appeared in ten films and several hundred TV episodes. The top dog of *The Magic of Lassie* is actually the sixth collie to attempt the role on the big screen and a direct descendant of the original star. Like all her predecessors "she" is, however, nothing more than a female impersonator: according to kennel connoisseurs, the coats of male collies are far more photogenic than those of the females, so that no bona fide bitch has ever been allowed to play the part. The success of this long-running masquerade suggests that if they insist on bringing back our doggie drag queen for yet another sequel (which is unlikely, considering the latest Lassie's failure to work his/her magic at the box office), a remake of *La Cage aux Folles* with an all-collie chorus line might be the best way to appeal to contemporary sensibilities.

AND THE WINNER IS . . .

. . . *PINOCCHIO IN OUTER SPACE*

All of the nominees in this category "borrow" their main characters from classics of children's literature, but none of the others does such crude violence to the original source as *Pinocchio in Outer Space*. With its inane combination of high tech and sentimental dreck, its cloying songs and sub–Saturday morning animation, it forces even the most reluctant cynic to acknowledge the relative greatness of Walt Disney.

After watching this atrocious example of cinematic child abuse, it was hard to imagine that Collodi's beloved marionette would ever suffer greater indignities than he did here. Then, in 1976, a group of independent Las Vegas filmmakers accomplished the impossible with the release of an X-rated feature entitled *The Erotic Adventures of Pinocchio*. The plot of the film cannot be summarized here—certainly not in a chapter on kiddie movies—but suffice it to say that the ads for the film featured the provocative tag line, "IT'S NOT HIS NOSE THAT GROWS!"

The parents of America may rest assured that this is one bad movie that will never make its way to television, which remains the province of educational fare such as *He-Man* and *The A-Team*, of made-for-TV movies such as *The Harlem Globetrotters on Gilligan's Island* (1981), and of the scintillating personalities featured in our next category. . . .

As the two heroes of Pinocchio in Outer Space *appear to be searching for a lost contact lens on the surface of Mars, an enormous sand crab menaces them from behind.*

THE MOST
HUMILIATING PERFORMANCE
BY A FUTURE TV STAR

*B*efore they became cherished fixtures in millions of American homes, some of television's greatest stars pursued long and frustrating careers in motion pictures. Naturally they would like to forget about their early embarrassments, but for the sake of history—and humility—it's our duty to remind them.

AND THE NOMINEES ARE...

RAYMOND BURR IN
BRIDE OF THE GORILLA (1951)

The appearance of the future "Perry Mason" and "Ironside" in this nonsensical feature stands as eloquent proof that a struggling actor will accept absolutely any part so long as it brings him star billing. If he ever chose to do so, Raymond Burr could even claim a share of the title role in this one—not as the bride, but as the gorilla.

He begins the film as a burly plantation foreman in Central America who murders his employer out of lust for the boss's wife (Barbara Payton). To avenge this dark deed, a friendly neighborhood witch (Giselle Werbisek) afflicts Burr with a voodoo spell that turns him into a very unconvincing ape. It

is a terrible curse indeed: playing the part of a were-gorilla requires frequent on-screen transformations, as the sweating, hardworking star switches back and forth between his regular bad-guy makeup, a silly gorilla mask worn over his street clothes, and a moth-eaten head-to-toe monkey suit. No wonder this poor fellow tells his love interest: "I'm not happy here. I'm happy out there—in the jungle. The jungle's my house. The animals talk to me and I understand them. I can smell a thousand smells!"

And so can the audience, in this ridiculous romp that makes the monkeyshines in the similarly themed *Bride and the Beast* look, by comparison, like serious simian speculation (*see our next chapter:* THE LEAST CONVINCING SCIENTIFIC EXPLANATION IN MOTION PICTURE HISTORY). Lon Chaney, Jr., who plays a police detective in this film, looks even more confused than the

Raymond Burr looks in the mirror and confronts his alter ego as part of a bravura double role in Bride of the Gorilla.

rest of the cast, as if unable to comprehend why the producers gave the monster part to Burr instead of to him. At the end of the picture, when the brooding brute runs off to the wilds with Barbara Payton in his hairy arms, the cops arrive to shoot him dead and to set up Chaney's poetic closing line: "Like something that has been haunting the world for millions of years, the jungle has risen to punish him for his crime."

Three years after making *Bride of the Gorilla*, the voodoo curse that had turned Raymond Burr into an ape continued to work its evil magic on his career as he accepted another role he didn't need in a project entitled *Gorilla at Large*. This time his character might be described as "Bridegroom of the Gorilla," since he portrays a circus owner whose deranged wife (played with stunning ineptitude by Anne Bancroft) dons a gorilla suit to commit a series of murders. The next year Burr finally moved on from gorillas to associate himself with bigger game: In the American edition of the original *Godzilla* he plays a reporter named Steve Martin (a role he reprised in *Godzilla 1985*) who visits Japan in time to witness the destruction of Tokyo by everybody's favorite prehistoric lizard.

By this time he had racked up more than forty big-screen credits, most of them ominous supporting roles in which he played crooks or killers, and he actively sought a change in career. As hero of the *Perry Mason* series starting in 1957 he played the world's most famous and eloquent defense attorney, but could still say nothing for *Bride of the Gorilla*—a film that remains quite simply indefensible.

DANNY THOMAS IN
THE JAZZ SINGER (1953)

How did a nice Lebanese boy get mixed up in a movie like this?

Danny Thomas (who began life as Amos Muzyad Jahoob) plays Jerry Golding, a decorated vet with a voice (and a heart) of gold who returns from Korea eager to enter the world of show biz. This causes considerable brow-furrowing consternation to his old country papa (Eduard Franz), who is the sixth-generation cantor of the Golding clan and fully expects that his son will become the seventh. The original 1927 Al Jolson film is widely hailed as the first talkie, but Danny Thomas's bland warbling in this version makes audiences long for the days of silent actors and live organ accompaniment.

This isn't merely a remake of the Jolson original, it's also an update, so in addition to the topical Cold War references, Danny passes up "Mammy" and "Toot Toot Tootsie, Goodbye" for such modern classics as "Man on a Bus," "South Pacific Islander," and, most puzzling of all for a boy from a kosher home, "Life of a Lobster." Another surprising decision involved the casting of Peggy Lee in her first dramatic role as Thomas's love interest; she must have been wondering "Is That All There Is?" as she bounced gamely through her one-dimensional part.

Though *The New York Times* criticized the film's "unadorned and sometimes corny sentimentality,"

Cantor David Golding (Eduard Franz) takes curious pride in the fact that his only son grew up to become Lebanese-American nightclub crooner Danny Thomas; "Mama" Mildred Dunnock seems more amused than surprised in the 1952 remake of The Jazz Singer.

most reviewers dismissed it with ho-hum indifference rather than outright hostility, as if they lacked the heart to attack anything so silly and old-fashioned. In any event, just a few months after the picture's premiere, Thomas wisely abandoned his movie aspirations and launched a new television series called *Make Room for Daddy.* The program described the wholesome family life of a Lebanese-American nightclub singer cunningly called Danny Williams, and went on to become one of the decade's most popular shows.

Danny's solid success on the tube, as a fund-raiser for St. Jude's Hospital, and as Phil Donahue's father-in-law, made him a beloved American institution and placed him safely beyond derision by the time the next (and worst) *Jazz Singer* exploded onto the screen in 1980. The spectacle of Neil Diamond in blue skintight glitter moaning "Love on the Rocks" while his cantor-father, Sir Laurence Olivier, rends his robes and shrieks "I haf no zon!" brought laughter to millions and helped erase all remaining memories of Danny Thomas's earlier embarrassment.

MERV GRIFFIN IN
PHANTOM OF THE RUE MORGUE (1954)

The ads for this movie raised high expectations among America's moviegoers:

IT MAULS! IT RIPS! IT VANISHES!
A MAMMOTH, MONSTROUS MAN OR CREATURE, RISING OUT OF THE BLACK
OOZING DEPTHS BENEATH THE CITY!
NOTHING YOU'VE EVER SEEN CAN MATCH ITS RAMPAGE OF TERROR!
CAN IT BE HUMAN?!!

Can it be Merv Griffin?

Well, not exactly—Merv played only the small part of a Parisian playboy and Sorbonne psychology student named Georges Brevert who is unjustly accused of the murder of a young apache dancer. He never gets the chance to demonstrate his acting prowess by rising out of the black oozing depths beneath the city, but he does have one big scene in which he passionately pleads his innocence to the police. With eyebrows raised and lips trembling, he seems sincerely offended by the suspicions of the gendarmes; he looks as deeply wounded as if Burt Reynolds had declared a public preference for chatting with Johnny Carson.

Today all America knows Merv Griffin as Mr. Sincere, but in the movie it takes the Parisian police several hours to accept his alibi. Ultimately they track down the real killer: a lusty orangutan played by a man in a monkey suit who is even less convincing than Raymond Burr in *Bride of the Gorilla.* "This mammoth, monstrous man or creature" belongs to another future television star, Karl (*The Streets of San Francisco*) Malden, playing a mad zoologist who hypnotizes his pet to murder a pretty starlet every time he hears the chiming of church bells. The orangutan

As a Sorbonne psychology student in Phantom of the Rue Morgue, *Merv Griffin* (far left) *shows the same sort of rapt attention to a Parisian police inspector (Claude Dauphin) that he later lavished on all guests on his popular talk show.*

and Malden seem to inspire each other to greater and greater heights of overacting, and even Griffin, in his brief moments on screen, is caught up in their manic spirit. Also along for the ride are Steve Forrest as Merv's heroic psychology professor; Patricia Medina as the ape's true and tender love; Claude Dauphin as a police inspector, and the fabulous Flying Zacchinis, who, despite their billing in the credits, play a family of daring aerialists rather than a group of winged vegetables.

This ludicrous 3-D spectacular marked Hollywood's second assault on the Edgar Allan Poe classic *Murders in the Rue Morgue* and proved even less entertaining—and less faithful to the original story—than the 1932 Bela Lugosi version. For Merv, participation in the picture marked the low point of his checkered career as a Warner Brothers contract player, which included bit parts in *Cattle Town, By the Light of the Silvery Moon, The Boy from Oklahoma,* and *Three Sailors and a Girl.* His only substantial movie role came in *So This Is Love* (1953), the pallid screen biography of opera star Grace Moore, in which he plays a lovesick song-and-dance man with such gee-whiz, eye-blinking earnestness that he makes it easy to understand why co-star Kathryn Grayson chooses career over romance.

Before he ever broke into motion pictures, Griffin fluttered hearts as a popular big-band singer; later in life, of course, he dazzled America with his astonishing talent at sitting behind a desk and discussing contemporary aesthetics with Charo. Between big bands and big talk came his brief, valiant attempt at stardom in motion pictures, leaving behind as its major monument *Phantom of the Rue Morgue* and the rare opportunity of watching Merv Griffin raise his eyebrows in 3-D.

LINDA EVANS IN
BEACH BLANKET BINGO (1965)

Long before achieving her mature dignity as Krystle Carrington on Dynasty, *Linda Evans projected a less ladylike image in films such as* Beach Blanket Bingo.

Six months before she won the part of sugar-sweet Audra Barkley on *The Big Valley*, and a full fifteen years before creating the role of sugar-sweet Krystle Carrington on *Dynasty*, Linda Evans played a surfer girl named Sugar Kane in the notorious *Beach Blanket Bingo*. This fourth installment of Frankie Avalon–Annette Funicello foolishness features lovely Linda as the new kid on the strand, who temporarily turns Frankie's head before he returns to the abundant charms of Miss Funicello as Dee Dee, his steady girl. The notion that any male human being, at any time,

on any planet, could possibly choose Annette Funicello over Linda Evans might qualify as a suitable premise for science fiction, but then beach party movies have never been noted for their plausible plots.

In this film Sugar Kane is supposed to be a singing sensation on her way to the big time, so Linda Evans displays her musical talents in two songs: "He's My New Love" and "He's My Fly Boy Up in the Sky." On both occasions she does a passable job with her lip-syncing but her dancing seems absurdly inappropriate. In the midst of wildly gyrating teens she stubbornly maintains her dignity (and her rigid posture), conceding only enough to the music to turn her shoulders ever so slightly from side to side. This subtle motion is apparently enough to drive her audiences wild: poor Buster Keaton, in a sad cameo, is so inspired by one of her performances that he shakes his 70-year-old body into a grotesque approximation of the twist.

Like all of John Derek's wives (she was number three), Miss Evans looks great in a bikini, and her initial appearance provokes an enthusiastic response from the regular revelers on the beach. "Let's dig this groovy chick—c'mon, men!" says one of them, and c'mon they do, with eyes bulging and tongues hanging out. "I'd like to see her slip into something more comfortable—like my arms!" declares one of these well-honed wits, while Frankie, on the other hand, remains the perfect gentleman. "Now *there*'s a healthy girl!" he gallantly declares when he sees her for the first time.

Near the end of *Beach Blanket Bingo*, the action pauses for a moment while Frankie Avalon stares out toward the horizon and slowly croons a haunting ballad about the fleeting joys of youth:

These are the good times while we are young,
No chance untaken; no song unsung.

For Linda Evans, this movie is one chance that should have remained "untaken," while her two songs in the movie (not to mention all the other music in the film) could easily have remained unsung. From her current ladylike eminence as Krystle Carrington, she looks back on this early role as one of her youthful indiscretions, though she ought to feel grateful that she avoided the even less endurable movies still to come in the seemingly endless beach party series (*see:* THE WORST BEACH PARTY MOVIE EVER MADE).

TOM SELLECK IN
DAUGHTERS OF SATAN (1972)

Tom Selleck swears revenge on the agent who signed him to the lead role in Daughters of Satan.

Until the success of *Magnum, P.I.* made Tom Selleck one of the most wanted men in America, his acting career seemed permanently stalled. It's true that he landed an important part in a U.S. Air Force training film called *The Mental Aspects of Human Reliability*, but his roles in theatrical features proved substantially less distinguished. Remember him as a corpse in *Coma?* Or as a virile young man who applies for a job as "stud" to the 77-year-old Mae West in *Myra Breckinridge?* In the Russ Meyer extravaganza *The Seven Minutes* (1971), he impersonates a pipe-smoking pornographer, but still appears on screen for less time than is specified in the title. Even more depressing than the roles he played were big ones that got away: Steven Spielberg actually signed him to play Indiana Jones in *Raiders of the Lost Ark*, but Tom had to bow out due to *Magnum* commitments; the same conflicts prevented him from accepting the part that ultimately went to James Garner in *Victor/Victoria*.

Selleck's only starring motion picture role during the frustrating early stages of his career came in a low-budget Philippine import called *Daughters of Satan*. Designed to capitalize on the new popularity of deviltry and witchcraft in the wake of *Rosemary's Baby*, it tells the story of an art dealer in Manila (Selleck) who brings home a 400-year-old painting because one of the faces in it reminds him of his wife.

As a result of this touching gesture, poor Tom winds up simmering for nearly two hours in a rancid cauldron of satanic stupidity. It turns out that the woman in the canvas was a witch, and his wife (Barra Grant) is her reincarnation. Selleck, meanwhile, is the reincarnation of the judge who condemned her to burn, so that his wife and the other dead witches from her long-vanished coven begin pursuing him. Magnum is no doubt accustomed to women chasing him, but this gets ridiculous, especially when a devil dog named Nicodemus comes out of nowhere to join in the fun, and all of the characters begin moving wildly back and forth between the centuries.

In reviewing the film *The New York Times* generously observed: "Tom Selleck, a handsome, virile, mustachioed type, is natural in his confusion." *The Hollywood Reporter* took an understandably dim view of the property's commercial potential, suggesting that the picture "needs a strong companion piece to warrant it being taken out of the can." United Artists proceeded to ignore this sound advice and released *Daughters of Satan* in a double bill with another stinker from the Philippines, *Superbeast*, about a mad scientist who turns himself into (you guessed it) a man in a gorilla suit, but who looks considerably more comfortable in this garb than does Selleck dressed up as a Spanish conquistador.

As puzzled by *Daughters* as everyone else, the studio publicists at United Artists came up with an astonishingly imprecise ad line for the film which promised only "A THRILL DRAMA OF WITCHES AND THINGS, TO KEEP THE HORROR POT BOILING." At the same time, the exhibitors' magazine, *Boxoffice*, tried to keep the promotional pot boiling by recommending that theater owners "arrange a display of witch dummies to be burned at the stake as a lobby display (check with authorities for safety measures if a real fire is to be used)." While it's doubtful that many theater owners (except those with unusually heavy insurance policies) actually built blazes in their lobbies for the amusement of moviegoers, these fires might have served one good purpose: as handy receptacles for all prints of *Daughters of Satan*.

LARRY HAGMAN IN *SON OF BLOB* (ALTERNATE TITLE: *BEWARE! THE BLOB*) (1972)

The moviemakers who created the original *Blob* in 1958 provided their film with a deliberately ambiguous finale. As a helicopter drops the killer goo onto the frozen wastes of the North Pole and the words "The End" show up on screen, a huge question mark suddenly appears in a chilling (it's the Arctic, remember) conclusion beloved by all bad movie fans.

Amazingly enough, it took fourteen years before someone in Hollywood stepped forward to accept this obvious challenge and to unfreeze the man-eating strawberry Jell-O for a second attack on the human race. The resulting sequel—inevitably titled *Son of Blob*—defined new lows in cinematic sloppiness and left audiences longing for the sincere stupidity of the Steve McQueen original. The new film tried to combine humorous and terrifying elements in the celebrated style of *Attack of the Killer Tomatoes* but in its confusion failed either to frighten or to entertain. As one wag put it at the time of the film's release: "What they wanted was tongue-in-cheek, but what they got was finger-down-throat."

Poor Larry Hagman must have felt overwhelmed by his twin responsibilities on Son of Blob—*playing the small part of a drunken hobo at the same time he served as the film's director.*

Larry Hagman turns up in the midst of this travesty as a bearded hobo who, on the way to relieving himself, is suddenly devoured by the rampaging blob. He's only on screen for a few minutes, but his acting is so bad that he leaves an indelible impression. The future J.R. grins self-consciously at the camera, then slips into and out of his character before our very eyes. This wretched cameo would have been a serious humiliation for the veteran star, were it not overshadowed by the much greater humiliation suffered by the film's director: an ambitious but appallingly untalented novice named Larry Hagman.

This disastrous directorial debut came at an awkward moment in the actor's career. He had already enjoyed his first ephemeral taste of TV success with a co-starring role in the popular series *I Dream of Jeannie*. When the show went off the air in 1970, he tried two more series (*The Good Life* and *Here We Go Again*), but neither one caught on with the public. Though Hagman got the chance to play supporting roles in a few respectable feature films (*The Group*, *Fail Safe*, and *Up in the Cellar* with Joan Collins), he wanted to branch out in new directions. *Son of Blob* certainly offered a new direction.

Treating the project as something of a gag, and as a welcome opportunity for learning how to use a camera, Hagman helped persuade many of his pals from the world of TV to join in his fun by portraying bits of blob chow. The cast therefore includes such little-screen luminaries as Dick Van Patten, Cindy Williams, Shelley Berman, Burgess Meredith, Carol Lynley, Richard Stahl, and Godfrey Cambridge. They must have had a splendid time on the set, since the finished film looks like the home movie of a private party, where all the guests are so drunk or stoned that they have begun to look on every belch or hiccup by one of their friends as a brilliant bit of improvisatory humor. Before the insatiable S.O.B. (Son of Blob) is at long last refrozen at an ice-skating rink, there is also a good deal of incoherent social commentary; Hagman the director delivers some laughably topical touches about hippies, police brutality, drug abuse, the generation gap, and the homeless.

These are not the sorts of concerns one normally associates with J. R. Ewing of *Dallas*, and Larry Hagman, in his new status as a bona fide television superstar, seemed only too pleased to put his fatuous little film behind him. The enterprising distributors, however, had other plans. In 1982 they rereleased *Son of Blob* with the ingenious promotional line, "IT'S THE FILM THAT J.R. SHOT!" Considering the dreary quality of the product, we prefer to think of it as "The Film That Should Have Been Shot"—along with its cast, its crew, and certainly its director.

JOAN COLLINS IN
EMPIRE OF THE ANTS (1977)

Television fans who are accustomed to seeing Joan Collins swathed in diamonds and sable will be delighted to know that even when slogging through Florida swamps and battling gigantic fiberglass insects, their favorite bitch still displays the same warm, wonderful personality. "You're so terrific in the sack, it almost justifies the excessive salary I have to pay you," she snaps at one of her hapless employees. Later she purrs, "I'm *not* running a charity organization!" and bites into a stalk of celery to show she means business.

Joan Collins rebuffs the amorous advances of an inert fiberglass insect that menaces civilization in Empire of the Ants.

Despite these flashes of her fabled and familiar form, she's a long way from *Dynasty* in this one. For one thing, poor Joan wears only a single pathetic outfit in the course of an entire 90-minute film, and even the most devoted fans of polyester will quickly tire of her striped K-Mart shirt, her beige Dacron sweater, and her off-white Valley Girl gaucho skirt. Even worse, the men around her in this miserable movie wear powder-blue leisure suits, checkerboard shirts, and white shoes, instead of stylish Nolan Miller tuxedos.

Obviously, these sartorial sins prove far more frightening to Miss Collins than the enormous atomic-powered creatures that she encounters in the course of the film. These giant ants have been cleverly contrived by director Bert I. Gordon, the same man who gave the world giant rodents in *Food of the Gods,* giant teenagers in *Village of the Giants,* and a giant, bald-headed "Mr. Clean" in *The Amazing Colossal Man.* For this latest Amazing Colossal Turkey, Gordon shows us only the front third of his nylon-and-chicken-wire ants, so that stagehands can stand behind the monster heads and move them constantly up and down.

The movie explains the origins of these abominable insects by showing the U.S. Coast Guard in the act of depositing a few steel drums into the ocean; to make sure that we don't miss the point, nineteen unbearably tedious close-ups reveal the ominous label DANGER: RADIOACTIVE WASTE on the side of each barrel. When one of these kegs washes ashore on a Florida beach, a posse of ordinary ants marches up to sample the white goop that oozes out from under the lid. Needless to say, this energizing elixir instantly inspires them to grow to monstrous proportions (this is, after all, a Bert I. Gordon movie), at the same time that it equips them with psychic powers that will enable them to conquer the universe.

Now if you believe that, then Joan Collins has some Florida swampland she wants to sell you in her role as "Marilyn Fryser," a shady real estate lady promoting a bogus resort community. She takes some prospective buyers out for a cruise to inspect the property and hosts a lavish al fresco luncheon, but the picnic is ruined by the ants. They munch on a few of the most appetizing bit players, then retreat to a sugar refinery to set up a concentration camp for the indoctrination of the human race. One of the first victims of their brainwashing program is the local sheriff (Albert Salmi) who declares: "We can all do what the ants want us to do. Work for them, feed them, that's the way it should be. For the ants are superior."

How can the poor persecuted humans possibly destroy these all-knowing monsters? What deadly weapon will they use? Will they employ the neutron bomb? Nerve gas? Barry Manilow records?

If this were an episode of *Dynasty,* Joan Collins would no doubt defeat the ants by sleeping with them. But this is a Bert Gordon picture, so the resourceful victims turn to an inexpensive highway flare, taken from the glove compartment of a stolen car, and use it to set the ant queen ablaze. This seriously discourages the other insects, who throw themselves onto the spreading conflagration, saving humanity (or at least one sugar refinery) from their evil domination and saving us from watching any more of this all but unwatchable movie. Miss Collins also dies in these final flames, collapsing in a decidedly inelegant heap after the ant queen hypnotizes her with a puff of talcum powder.

With her part in this movie, Joan's career finally hit bottom after a long slide. She had already spent twenty-five years in Hollywood, turning out forty feature films of mostly mediocre quality. In her youth, her sex kitten performances on and off the screen won her the insider nickname "The English Open," but advancing age gave her the seemingly unshakable aura of a has-been. Once she turned 40 in 1973, most producers stubbornly (and blindly) refused to consider her for glamor-girl roles, so she worked instead as a character actress in movies such as *Terror from Under the House, I Don't Want to Be Born,* and of course, *Empire of the Ants.* According to her own account, she agreed to take part in this insect insanity only as a last resort: in 1976 her situation had became so bleak that she went on unemployment, signing autographs for some out-of-work fans while she waited in line to fill out the proper forms.

In 1981 *Dynasty* rescued her from these ignominious circumstances and transformed her overnight into the epitome of sophisticated glamor and sinister sex appeal. The show's popularity also allowed Bert Gordon's ant-ic *Empire* to strike back, as it became a surprise hit on videocassette some eight years after its theatrical premiere. The advertisements for this home viewing release shamelessly urged viewers to "SEE a DYNASTY of Ants Terrorize Joan Collins!" and to "SEE Joan Scream and Still Look Beautiful!" Despite these promises, the sad fact remains that Miss Collins is considerably less than her gorgeous self in this unfortunate film, and her acting is virtually nonexistent. The best that can be said about her performance is that she does manage to keep a straight face throughout the proceedings—which, under the circumstances, could pass as a major achievement.

AND THE WINNER IS...

... JOAN COLLINS IN *EMPIRE OF THE ANTS*

Miss Collins deserves the award as much for the humiliation she endured behind the scenes as for the embarrassing insipidity that shows itself on screen.

In her best-selling autobiography, *Past Imperfect,* she recalls the less than enthusiastic attitude that prevailed on the set. "It seemed a certainty that this film would guarantee none of us would ever get a job again," she writes. The picture's minuscule budget made no provision for stunt doubles, so the scenes of Marilyn Fryser swimming for her life through fetid, dangerous swamp, just a few feet away from hungry alligators, featured Joan Collins in her debut as a stuntwoman. In addition to the painful, festering sores on her legs which she acquired as a result of this adventure, Miss Collins also suffered a bloody laceration on her forehead when one of her associates accidentally slammed a car door in her face. Worst of all, her contract on *Empire* forced her to travel to the Cannes Film Festival in order to push the film, as-

sociating her name internationally and indelibly with this dreadful dog.

She should only be thankful that during her visit to France, none of the reporters asked her to elaborate on the theoretical basis for the abrupt enlarge-ment of the atomic ants in her film, otherwise she might have been required to improvise the sort of bizarre and nonsensical explanation featured in our next chapter. . . .

THE LEAST CONVINCING SCIENTIFIC EXPLANATION IN MOTION PICTURE HISTORY

AND THE NOMINEES ARE...

ELYSIA, THE VALLEY OF THE NUDE (1933)

"Father Nudist" and "Mack the Reporter" (neither of whom are further identified in the credits) discuss the benefits of clothes-free living in the pioneering 1933 "documentary" Elysia, the Valley of the Nude.

(This offbeat, exploitative docu-drama, proudly billed as "the first feature actually filmed at a nudist colony in California," purported to show "the benefits from bathing in the sun and the air." The unclothed actors allowed themselves to be identified only with nicknames.)

FATHER NUDIST: Sunshine itself is a food, and is required. All over the world, ever since mankind began, the beneficent qualities of sunshine have impressed the minds of men. In darkest Africa, all of the natives are nudists. . . . Surely, you'll admit Benjamin Franklin was civilized.

MACK THE REPORTER: Of course.

FATHER: Well, Benjamin Franklin was a nudist.

MANIAC (1934)

TITLE CRAWL: Maniacs are created by inability to adjust to the world as it is. The normal person can make such an adjustment. It is not always easy, but it is being done constantly. The person of inferior mental capacity cannot do this. He therefore creates a world in his mind which is his own idea of the world of his choice. He retreats to this world whenever the outer world becomes unbearable. This explains periods of rationalism [sic] all mental cases have. The periods of rationalism depends [sic] upon the unbearableness [sic] of the real world.

GLEN OR GLENDA (1953)

POLICE INSPECTOR (Lyle Talbot): This type of case comes to me, as well as yourself, many times during the course of one month.

PSYCHIATRIST (Timothy Farrell): The suicide?

INSPECTOR: The suicide.

PSYCHIATRIST: Most of us have our idiosyncrasies.

INSPECTOR: This fellow's was quite pronounced.

PSYCHIATRIST: Yes, but I wonder if it rated the death warrant it received. . . . Let's get our stories straight: you're referring to the suicide of the transvestite?

INSPECTOR: If that's the word you men of medical science use for a man who wears women's clothing, yes.

PSYCHIATRIST: Yes, in cold technical language that's the word. As unfriendly and as vicious as it may sound. However, in actuality, it's not an unfriendly word, nor is it vicious, when you know the people to whom it pertains. . . . Only the infinity of the depths of a man's mind can really tell this story.

ALSO FROM GLEN OR GLENDA

PSYCHIATRIST: Men's hats are so tight they cut off the blood flow to the head, thus cutting off the growth of hair. Seven out of ten men wear hats, so the advertisements say. Seven out of ten men are bald! But what about the ladies? Yes, modern woman is a hardworking individual also. But when modern woman's day of work is done, that which is designed for her home comfort, is comfort. Hats that give no obstruction to the blood flow. Hats that do not crush the hair. Interesting thought, isn't it?

BRIDE OF THE MONSTER (1955)

REPORTER (Loretta King): Okay, let's have the story on Lake Marsh and the monsters.

POLICE CHIEF (Harvey B. Dunn): Monster, monster! There are no such thing [sic] as monsters. This is the twentieth century.

REPORTER: Don't count on it!

THE GIANT CLAW (1957)

GENERAL (Morris Ankrum): Well, it's your dime, boy—what is it you want to show me?

SCIENTIST (Jeff Morrow): How to shoot that bird out of the sky!

GENERAL: Some new type of weapon?

SCIENTIST: No, with regular guns, bullets and bombs—anything you want. . . . Now, I don't care whether that bird came from outer space or Upper Saddle River, New Jersey! It's still made of flesh and blood of some sort—and vulnerable to bullets and bombs.

GENERAL: If you can get past that anti-matter energy screen!

SCIENTIST: Right! That's exactly what I think I figured out how to do. . . . Now—this is a blowup I had made of her bubble chamber photograph. The chamber was bombarded by high-speed particles. The result? Notice this hole—this gap right here. This gap is one of the most exciting and significant recent discoveries in all science . . .

GENERAL: Atoms of matter or anti-matter!

SCIENTIST: Right! Now if this thing of mine works and we can get close—real close—and bombard that bird's anti-matter energy shield with a stream of mesic atoms, I think we can destroy that shield. The bird would be defenseless then except for beak, claws, and wings. You could hit it with everything but the kitchen sink.

GENERAL: We've got the kitchen sinks to spare, son! Do you think you can do it?

SCIENTIST: I'm not sure—but it's certainly worth a try!

FRANKENSTEIN'S DAUGHTER (1958)

HUNCHBACK ASSISTANT (Wolfe Barzell): Your father and grandfather never used a *female* brain!

DR. OLIVER FRANKENSTEIN (Donald Murphy): Well, now we're aware that the female brain is conditioned to a man's world. Therefore it takes orders where the other ones didn't.

THE BRIDE AND THE BEAST (1958)

While hubby Lance Fuller looks on skeptically, psychiatrist William Justine helps Charlotte Austin explore her prior life as a gorilla in The Bride and the Beast.

PSYCHIATRIST (William Justine): Back, back to the endless reaches of time. Back, before your entry into this life as you now know it. You will speak of that life as you see it. Go on to your journey. What is your name?

LAURA (Charlotte Austin): Laura Carson.

PSYCHIATRIST: Is that all?

LAURA: Married yesterday to Dan Carson.

PSYCHIATRIST: Go on . . .

LAURA: Angora sweater—was such a beautiful thing. Soft, like kitten's fur. Felt so good on me. As if it belonged there. Felt so bad when it was gone.

PSYCHIATRIST: Dan, do you realize we've just witnessed a portion of your wife's previous existence, and her death in that previous existence? . . . Her talk about maribou, Angora, and furlike materials—there's definitely a connection between them and her dreams. I believe that it's derived from her past existence.

DAN (Lance Fuller): Aw, c'mon. You don't really believe she was a gorilla!

PSYCHIATRIST: All the evidence points to it. Her fixation for furlike materials comes from that fact.

DAN: I'm sorry, Doctor, I just don't buy any of this.

PSYCHIATRIST: Well, you have a right to your own opinion.

SHE DEMONS (1958)

MAD SCIENTIST (Rudolph Anders): It was during the course of our experimentation that we quite accidentally discovered a potential power of incomparable magnitude. The source of our radiation pointed to hot, volcanic matter.

EXPLORER (Tod Griffin): You mean lava?

SCIENTIST: Yes, precisely. The largest natural source on this earth.

EXPLORER: Why, of course! Whereas oil and coal and iron are known to exist only on the extreme crust of the earth, the entire center is a mass of boiling rock. If someone could discover a use for this lava, why, they could have a constant supply of ready-made power from now until kingdom come!

SCIENTIST: We are electronically extracting the heat from the center of the earth and converting it into useful power.

EXPLORER: Then what you're saying is, you've accomplished perpetual motion!

SCIENTIST: That is quite correct. You see, although I have succeeded in completing the most sought after dream of mankind since time immemorial, I have to keep it a close secret between myself and my creatures. I am master of my own Isle!

In She Demons, *Rudolph Anders, as master of an uncharted island somewhere off the coast of Malibu, explains his lava-powered perpetual motion machine to amazed explorers Irish McCalla and Tod Griffin, while Victor Sen Yung looks on and comments, "Holy fortune cookie!"*

PLAN NINE FROM OUTER SPACE (1959)

COLONEL EDWARDS (Tom Keene): Why is it so important that you want to contact the governments of our earth?

EROS THE ALIEN (Dudley Manlove): Because of death. *Because all of you of Earth are idiots!*

HEROIC JET PILOT (Gregory Walcott): Now you just hold on, buster!

EROS: No—you hold on! . . . Your scientists stumbled upon the atom bomb—split the atom! Then the hydrogen bomb, where you actually explode the air itself. Now you bring the total destruction of the entire universe, served by our sun. The only explosion left is the solaronite.

In Plan Nine from Outer Space, *alien commander Dudley Manlove, assisted by space cadet Joanna Lee, reveals the complexities of the solaronite bomb, while baffled Earth men (from left) Duke Moore, Gregory Walcott, and Tom Keene concentrate on the clearly visible chalk-marked X's intended to show them their places on the set.*

COLONEL: Why, there's no such thing!

EROS: Perhaps to you, but we've known it for centuries. Your scientists will stumble upon it as they have all the others. But the juvenile minds which you possess will not comprehend its strength until it's too late.

COLONEL: You're way above our heads!

EROS: The solaronite is a way to explode the actual particles of sunlight!

COLONEL: Why, that's impossible . . . a particle of sunlight can't even be seen or measured!

EROS: Can you see or measure an atom? Yet you can explode one! A ray of sunlight is made up of many atoms.

JET PILOT: So what if we do develop this solaronite bomb—we'd be even a stronger nation than now!

EROS: Stronger? You see! You see! You're stupid minds! Stupid! Stupid!

JET PILOT: That's all I'm taking from you! [He punches him.]

FURTHER INFORMATION ON SOLARONITE FROM *PLAN NINE*

COLONEL: You speak of solaronite, but just what is it?

EROS: Take a can of your gasoline. Say this can of gasoline is the sun. Now you spread a thin line of it to a ball representing the earth. Now the gasoline represents the sunlight, the sun particles. Here we saturate the ball with the gasoline—the sunlight—then we put a flame to the ball. The flame will speedily travel around the earth, back along the line of gasoline to the can—or the sun itself. It will explode this source, and spread to every place that gasoline—our sunlight—touches. Explode the sunlight here, gentlemen, you explode the universe. Explode the sunlight here and a chain reaction will occur direct to the sun itself and to all the planets that sunlight touches. To every planet in the universe.

(. . . And if a reader—or viewer—can understand all this, he or she deserves an honorary degree in theoretical physics.)

THE NAVY VS. THE NIGHT MONSTERS (1966)

NAVY NURSE (Mamie Van Doren): How did that tree get *here?*

METEOROLOGIST (Walter Sande): In plain English, it walked here . . .

NURSE: It's hard to imagine carnivorous trees that move on their own roots.

Anthony Eisley (left), *Walter Sande, Mamie Van Doren, and Philip Terry find it difficult to come to terms with the unpleasant reality of walking, man-eating trees who threaten to disrupt their scientific expedition to Antarctica in* The Navy vs. the Night Monsters.

METEOROLOGIST: Not carnivorous; omnivorous —all-devouring. He'll eat anything—even other trees.

THE ASTRO-ZOMBIES (1968)

THE HERO, "CHUCK" (Joseph Hoover): So what you're saying, Doctor, is that one man's thoughts can be transmitted to another man's brain?

DR. PETROVICH (Victor Izay): Exactly. In this way, knowledge from the minds of our top astrophysicists, aerospace medical scientists, neurosurgeons, could be combined and projected into the receiving device of a quasi-man in interplanetary space flight.

CHUCK: Quasi-man? Why, you mean a sort of a zombie?

DR. PETROVICH: Well, that's not exactly scientific terminology but it would be close to the truth.

CIA CHIEF (Wendell Corey): Well, what else would you call a man with a synthetic, electrically driven heart, a stainless steel mesh stomach, a plastic pancreas, and cellulose liver?

CHUCK: Incredible!

DR. PETROVICH: Not for a minute! And Dr. DeMarco is working on a silicon treatment of the skin which would make it impervious to *micro*-meteorites!

AND THE WINNER IS...

...THE BRIDE AND THE BEAST

This obscure exploitation flick tells the tale of a young fashion plate who discovers on her wedding night that she is less attracted to her animal-trainer husband than she is to the gorilla he keeps in his basement. While the audience asks itself "Can This Marriage Be Saved?", the groom drags his troubled spouse to a prominent psychiatrist. Under deep hypnosis she recalls numerous bits of stock footage from jungle documentaries, which the audience will also recognize with little difficulty. Eventually the brilliant doctor reaches the conclusion that this seemingly clean-cut girl experienced a previous life as a gorilla. The decisive piece of evidence that persuades him of this fact is her fascination with angora sweaters. An ordinary analyst might take this as an indication that she had lived a previous incarnation as an Angora goat—the animal that actually provides us with the precious wool—but the psychiatrist on screen knows better. At the end of the picture the young bride runs off to fulfill her "destiny," joining a family of gorillas in an African cave. She appears to be thoroughly content, though neither she nor her hosts wear sweaters of any kind.

The Bride and the Beast is nothing more than a clumsy variation of the old story of a man-in-a-monkey-suit carrying off a starlet-in-a-nightgown—a shopworn theme that had already made money for such fetching Hollywood fare as *Love Life of a Gorilla* (1937), *The Monster and the Girl* (1940), *Nabonga* (1944), *White Pongo* (1945), *Bride of the Gorilla* (1951), and many others. What made this picture even more ludicrous than its predecessors was the pseudoscientific claptrap cluttering the script and the earnest, educational tone of much of the dialogue.

In Edward D. Wood's screenplay for The Bride and the Beast, *an angora sweater inevitably arouses the primitive passions of a caged ape named Spanky—especially when he sees that it is worn by reincarnated gorilla girl Charlotte Austin.*

Knowledgeable bad movie buffs who stumble upon this curious concoction will instantly associate these elements with the work of the legendary Edward D. Wood, Jr. (1924–1978), Golden Turkey Life Achievement Award winner as the Worst Director of All Time. Though he served only as screenwriter, rather than writer-director, on *The Bride and the Beast,* the picture still bears his unmistakable imprint—as do those better-known Wood films *Glen or Glenda, Bride of the Monster,* and *Plan Nine from Outer Space,* whose enlightening scientific explanations are similarly cited above.

The Bride and the Beast is particularly important to serious students of schlock for the light it sheds on Ed Wood's lifelong devotion to angora. This fascination is most memorably expressed in his first and most intensely autobiographical film, *Glen or Glenda.* The central conflict in that picture concerns the burning desire of the transvestite hero, Glen (memorably portrayed by Wood himself under the pseudo-

nym "Daniel Davis") to borrow the fluffy sweater belonging to his fiancée, Barbara (portrayed by Wood's real-life live-in, Dolores Fuller). "I tried to keep away from these things," Glen sobs over his angora obsession. "I tried, honestly, I tried. I hadn't had a stitch of them on for nearly a week. And then I couldn't take it anymore. I had to put it on or go out of my mind!" In the film's inspiring conclusion, Barbara places her feelings for Glen above her anti-transvestite prejudices: As the music swells on the soundtrack, she nobly presents the life-giving sweater to her lover.

In a recent conversation with the authors, Dolores Fuller discussed her late friend's passion for soft, fluffy things. "He was the first transvestite I ever met," she recalled. "He told me when he was little, he dressed up one time as the Easter bunny. That was the beginning! That furry little suit made him feel so good, it gave him such a sensation, that he wanted more and more! He was hooked. When I met

Edward D. Wood, Jr. (1924–1978)

him, it was already a big part of his life. When we lived together, if he was working on a script or something, he'd have to put on one of his big fluffy angora sweaters. He said it helped him create. He adored those things!"

Producer and screenwriter Alex Gordon, another of Wood's former roommates, asserted in a 1983 article that "Eddie had a thing for angora, so our company name was briefly Angora Pictures, and every one of his scripts featured an angora sweater to be worn by the leading lady as much as possible." Charles Anderson, one of Wood's business associates and long-time friends, recalled the fabled filmmaker in similar terms: "I can't even think about Ed without thinking of angora. When they came out with those personalized license plates, he wanted to get one that said ANGORA, but somebody else had taken it first. He always loved ladies' clothes because of the softness. He used to say he had no choice about wearing them, because he was allergic to boys' clothes. He was a very sensitive guy, as you can tell from his pictures."

Canadian bad film fanatic and videocassette entrepreneur Fred Mollin is currently working on the first full-length biography of Ed Wood. In recognition of the Master's sartorial preferences, the working title for the book is *Look Back in Angora.*

But looking forward for a moment, we must now proceed to animal fur of a far less delicate and delectable variety, as we move on to our next category. . . .

THE MOST UNBEARABLE BEAR MOVIE EVER MADE

W hat is it, you might ask, about the bear? Why has he exerted such a powerful and durable hold on the human imagination?

The ancient Greeks named constellations after him (Ursa Major and Minor), North American Indians prayed to him as a hairy deity, and the Russians, many centuries ago, selected him as a national symbol. In our own time, the ubiquitous teddy bear has established himself as the world's most popular children's toy, while assorted Cubs, Bruins, and Bears regularly terrorize their opponents on every sort of athletic field. In literature our ursine friends have served as potent symbols for writers as various as Anton Chekhov, William Faulkner, and John Irving; in the world of economics, stockbrokers understandably tremble at their approach; in popular culture, folk hero bears such as Winnie-the-Pooh, Smokey, and Yogi have all won devoted followings.

Despite the bear's current prominence, his history as an entertainer has not been all honey. Beginning in the reign of Henry II (1154–1189), bearbaiting became a popular diversion in England and continued to draw crowds for nearly seven centuries. In its most common form this revolting "sport" offered the spectacle of a captive bear with one hind leg chained to a stake, fighting off the murderous attacks of a pack of hungry dogs. These bloody battles often delighted spectators for hours at a time—as did another commonly practiced form of baiting in which participants paid for the privilege of whipping a blinded bear. In 1575 Queen Elizabeth herself spent a particularly festive afternoon watching a succession of thirteen different bears exposed to an imaginative series of torments and tortures. Finally, in 1835, an Act of Parliament outlawed all forms of bearbaiting, but the callous treatment of these unfortunate beasts has persisted to the present day through the depredations of the film industry.

Numerous bear movies have appeared over the years, and nearly all of them deserve dishonorable mention. The French-Russian co-production The Talking Bear (1961, starring the immortal "Gocha the Talking Bear"), Walt Disney's Yellowstone Cubs (1963), Three Little Bruins Make Mischief (1964), Hey There, It's Yogi Bear! (1964, a big-screen spinoff from the popular TV show), Night of the Grizzly (1966), Gentle Giant (1967), Li'l Scratch (1972), Bear Island (1979), and the animated feature The Care Bears Movie (1985) might cumulatively constitute a latter-day form of bearbaiting. Such insipid features must, however, be classified as high art when compared to the six *nominees selected for this category. These films represent both contradictory extremes in the enduring image of the bear—as a friendly, adorable, and cuddly creature on the one hand, and as a vicious, bloodthirsty man-eater on the other. It is a tribute to the versatility of this noble beast that movies have celebrated both sides of his personality with similarly inane results.*

And speaking of inane results, it should be noted here that no chapter in this book has presented quite so many temptations to make cheap and predictable puns as this one. All right, we know we succumbed in the heading for this category, but from this point forward we will make a sincere effort to show restraint. No describing films as bearly endurable, or asking you to bear certain facts in mind, or talking about embearrassed stars who must grin and bear their humiliation, or screenwriters who feel a sudden need to bear their souls —all right, enough! The quality of these films is grisly enough, and having explained bearbaiting above, we will do nothing further to provide cruel and unusual punishment for the reader.

AND THE NOMINEES ARE...

THE TWO LITTLE BEARS (1961)

Eddie Albert reacts stoically to domestic tragedy when kindly forest rangers inform him that his sons have fallen under the curse of an evil witch who transformed them into The Two Little Bears.

In summarizing the plot of this bizarre and bone-headed family saga, we can hardly improve on the poker-faced prose of *Boxoffice* magazine: "The two small sons of grade school principal Eddie Albert follow some instructions given them by a gypsy and are able to turn themselves into teddy bears. As such, they create havoc and concern in town by running away from home and school to play in the woods

with a mother bear who adopts them. . . . When the kids arrive, as bears, at a hunting lodge they are captured by forest rangers and driven to the forest to live." If this isn't enough action to keep you perched at the very edge of your seat, the picture also offers a sub-par subplot about a "touching teen romance" between singing sensations Brenda ("I'm Sorry") Lee (as the bruin-boys' big sister) and Jimmy ("I Saw Mommy Kissing Santa Claus") Boyd. At the climax of the picture Eddie Albert is hauled away to a mental hospital after bragging to his neighbors that the marauding bears who have caused chaos throughout the community are actually his own talented kids, Timmy and Billy. His wife, Jane Wyatt (the mother in *Father Knows Best*), helps to win Albert's release by coaxing the cubs into displaying their transmutation for the whole town to see. Supporting players include Soupy Sales as a sympathetic cop and Nancy Kulp (Miss Jane in *The Beverly Hillbillies*) as a skeptical schoolteacher. Brenda Lee sings the sticky, goppy theme song, "Honey Bear," on camera and its strains are endlessly repeated throughout the course of the movie. Finally the music swells to a triumphal crescendo for the happily-ever-after conclusion, as the wayward boys renounce their interest in beardom and concentrate instead on developing their football skills, obviously missing their chance for the world's first double Bear Mitzvah.

The promotional lines for this picture carried the

same sense of urgency as the advertisements for Edward D. Wood's transvestite masterpiece *Glen or Glenda:* "WERE THEY TWO LITTLE BEARS . . . OR TWO LITTLE *BOYS*?" screamed the headlines. "NOT EVEN THEIR PARENTS REALLY KNEW!!!" The searing surrealistic quality of this astonishing piece of work obviously inspired an anonymous spokesman for Twentieth Century–Fox who discussed the project with *The New York Times* shortly before its release. "It will have the feeling of the immensely successful *Shaggy Dog,*" he proudly declared, "with, of all things, a faint echo of the Ionesco play *Rhinoceros.*"

Actually the studio might have argued that *The Two Little Bears* had more in common with Franz Kafka's *Metamorphosis,* but this is one cinematic cockroach that should have been stamped out at birth.

THE RUINED BRUIN (1961)

This compassionate melodrama tells the heartbreaking story of Buddy, a full-grown black grizzly who escapes from the zoo and finds it hard to adjust to the social demands of his new life as a Hollywood bachelor. Even under the best of circumstances, it's difficult to find eligible lady grizzlies in southern California, and Buddy's problems are substantially compounded when he finds himself exclusively attracted to human females. While waddling through a city park and pondering his problem, our hero spots an absurdly buxom nurse (Maureen Jansen) sitting on a bench. He immediately falls snout over claws in love with her, but in an insufferably shrill Tweetie Pie voice she emphatically spurns his efforts to begin a meaningful relationship. Having not lived in the L.A. fast lane long enough to learn the appropriately mellow adjustment to such an encounter, Buddy falls into a profound funk. In his desperation he swallows an entire bottle of male hormone pills in the hope that they will transform him into a human being, thereby improving his chances at singles bars. Unfortunately the pills do nothing to change his bearish appearance but merely serve to inflame his already considerable lust.

For the rest of this seemingly endless film, the bawdy bear pathetically pursues every girl he sees, and producer Harry Novak (perhaps best known for

Please Don't Eat My Mother, 1973) makes sure that he sees plenty. A dozen scantily clad extras bounce listlessly from scene to scene, displaying lots of bright red lipstick and unpleasant black-and-blue marks but absolutely no acting ability. At long last the featured creature crashes the annual Artists and Models Ball, where all the revelers assume he is merely a mystery guest in a clever costume—which is a highly plausible assumption, since Buddy is, in fact, played by an actor (Myron Griffin) walking around inside a bear suit so ill-fitting, moth-eaten, and unconvincing that it would have been an embarrassment even at a sixth-grade Halloween party. When the belles of the ball finally discover that what they have on their glands is an honest-to-goodness party animal, pandemonium breaks loose and the picture proceeds to its uproarious conclusion.

The producers expressed their faith in the commercial potential of *The Ruined Bruin* by spending $500 for a splashy full-color poster advertising the film's Hollywood sleaze-house run. Considering their overall production budget of less than $15,000, this seemed a surprisingly substantial investment. Though the lewd layout failed to drum up business for the film, it did generate protests from the neighbors, leading the Paris Theatre to substitute a new, more demure black and white poster with the simple, tasteful declaration: "A VERY SPECIAL PICTURE—*THE RUINED BRUIN.*" Special it was indeed, since even die-hard fans of bestiality—the presumed audience for this atrocity—felt cheated by the fact that the unfortunate Buddy never got to indulge himself in even so much as a good bear hug with one of the objects of his desire. Rerelease with an imaginative alternate title (*The Bare and the Shapely*) could do nothing to prevent the well-deserved ruin of this boorish bruin.

SANTA AND THE THREE BEARS (1970)

The political currents of the 1960s raised the consciousness of many American filmmakers. Producers and directors who had previously been content with turning out crass, commercial product suddenly committed themselves to creating enlightening message pictures. So it was that in 1970 two idealists named Tony Benedict and Barry Mahon pledged to expose on screen a gross injustice that had been all but ignored by a complacent public. The result, a social protest film for preschoolers called *Santa and the Three Bears*, revealed the discrimination which, year after shameful year, has denied bear cubs in Yellowstone Park their God-given right to enjoy Santa Claus with the rest of us.

Neo-conservatives in the audience might object that it is only an annual need to hibernate, rather than an organized conspiracy, that causes the baby bruins to miss the joys of Christmas. But the two cubs in this crude but powerful animated feature refuse to accept the idea that biology is destiny. Nikomi (the voice of Annette Ferra) and Chinook (the voice of Bobby Riha) hear stories about Kris Kringle from a kindly forest ranger (ingeniously identified as "Mr. Ranger") and resolve to postpone their hibernation until they meet the portly gentleman in red. Mama Bear (the voice of Jean Vander Pyl) is outraged at this delay ("Now you've stayed up a whole *month* past your bedtime!") and frankly blames Mr. Ranger for putting such disturbing ideas into the heads of her previously well-adjusted cubs. In an impassioned speech she demands that he make amends by impersonating Good Saint Nick to give the two cuddlies the holiday cheer they have sadly lacked until now, and he finally agrees. On Christmas Eve, however, a ferocious blizzard keeps him from the cozy cave in the heart of Yellowstone. Chinook and Nikomi are tearfully disappointed, until, in the St. Nick of time, the *real* Santa shows up with two stockings stuffed with adorable toys.

In reviewing the film after its release, *Variety* com-

In Santa and the Three Bears *the title creatures eagerly await the arrival of Kris Kringle, while viewers over the age of four seek refuge in hibernation.*

mented that despite its serious intent it turned out "sweet and saccharine enough to give the kids cavities." The adults, meanwhile, undoubtedly suffered from stomachaches. The craft behind the production proved in every way the equal of its intellectual content: the jerky, shockingly primitive animation would have embarrassed even the legendarily shameless Yogi Bear, and it is mixed pointlessly with some washed-out "live action" sequences of "Yellowstone." This footage, intended to show an old-fashioned Christmas in snowbound Wyoming, was actually shot in Dania, Florida, home of a local tourist attraction known as Pirates World, which put up most of the $200,000 needed to finance the project.

Co-producer Tony Benedict, who also wrote the screenplay and directed, treated this project as his personal crusade. He initially believed that the hour-long entertainment would work better on television than in the theaters, and it is certainly difficult to disagree with him. All three networks turned him down, Benedict recalls, "because it had no villain. It had no violence. . . . You've got to fight to give the kids something which is nonviolent, educational and entertaining. I don't understand that."

Nevertheless, he obviously understood clever marketing techniques. The picture played in scattered theaters across the country in 1970 and 1971, drawing more than a million customers and earning several million dollars in grosses. This not only helped Benedict prove his point, but opened up a new career for his co-producer, Barry Mahon. Before *Santa*, Mahon had given the world such uplifting projects as *Nudes, Inc.; White Slavery; Morals Squad; Victims of Sin; Nutty Nudes; Nude Camera; Nude Las Vegas; One Thousand Shapes of a Female;* and the unforgettable *Nudes on Tiger Beef*. It might have seemed an impressive stretch for this stalwart of adults-only films to suddenly turn his attention to *Santa and the Three Bears*, but Mahon brought to his kiddie project the same philosophy he had always applied to his work in nudies. As he told an interviewer for *Film Comment* magazine: "It's better to make the worst thing than to make nothing at all."

Despite its astonishingly low quality, *Santa and the Three Bears* helped to inspire another ambitious project: a half-hour animated film for television entitled *The Bear Who Slept Through Christmas*. These twin Cubs 'n' Christmas cartoons, along with other perennial Yuletide yuckies such as *Santa Claus Conquers the Martians*, make a persuasive case for holiday season hibernation.

GRIZZLY (1976)

A playful bear named Teddy tries in vain to look menacing for his title role in Grizzly, *a quickie rip-off shamelessly described in its own ads as "THE MOST DANGEROUS* JAWS *ON LAND!"*

A teenager goes skinny-dipping and is punished for her brazen behavior when a bloodthirsty beast suddenly appears on the scene and devours her. Several other vacationers are mauled by the crazed creature, but the greedy authorities refuse to warn the public for fear of harming the tourist trade. One heroic local peace officer refuses to accept the deception. He recruits a brilliant but obnoxious naturalist, and a crusty adventurer who owns his own craft, to help him stalk the wild thing and to destroy it if possible. The three men finally confront the monster, and after a climactic battle the oldest and most courageous of them meets his doom but manages to take the creature with him. Tourists can once again frolic in the summer sun without fear they will be chewed to tatters by an oversize killer representing nature's darker side.

Sound familiar?

It certainly should. Of all the dozens of films that attempted to duplicate the phenomenal success of Steven Spielberg's *Jaws* (1975), *Grizzly*—with a plot fully and accurately summarized above—offered the most shameless and slavish imitation. Every plot twist and every character is a blatant rip-off. In place of Roy Scheider as an intrepid sheriff, we have Christopher George as an intrepid forest ranger. In place of Richard Dreyfuss as a fast-talking marine biologist, we have Richard Jaeckel as a fast-talking naturalist. In place of Robert Shaw as the salty, eccentric, and ultimately doomed owner of the good ship *Orca,*

we have Andrew Prine as the salty, eccentric, and ultimately doomed Vietnam vet who owns a battle-worthy helicopter. In *Jaws,* you'll recall, the great white shark sinks the boat before he goes down to Davy Jones' locker, so in *Grizzly,* by God, the big bear smashes the helicopter with one swipe of its mighty paw. Even trivial details are, to use an overly polite word, borrowed. Peter Benchley, author of the novel brought to the screen so memorably by Spielberg and Company, makes a cameo appearance in *Jaws* as a television newsman. In *Grizzly,* Harvey Flaxman, co-writer of the screenplay, turns up in the course of the movie as—guess what?—a reporter.

He should, however, have played a used car salesman, since he told *The Hollywood Reporter,* with, presumably, a straight face: "We didn't get the idea from *Jaws.* . . . We wrote the script and got the idea from the newspaper story a few years back about a grizzly killing those people in their sleeping bags."

The killer grizzly heroically (if somewhat improbably) triumphs in furious blade-to-claw combat with a helicopter.

To dramatize these events, Producer "Big Ed" Montoro built an eighteen-foot-high hollow plastic bear, with room for two technicians inside the contraption to manipulate its moving parts. This mechanical marvel may have looked good on paper, but on camera it looked so hopelessly bogus that the filmmakers could use it for only a few of the big scenes. For most of the movie Montoro and director

William *(The Manitou)* Girdler rented a flesh-and-blood bear named Teddy from a roadside zoo. The promotional materials described this animal star as "trained, but untamed" (whatever that means) and suggested that viewers "will form a love-hate relationship with the bear, in spite of the fact that he maims and murders seven people." Teddy, in other words, hardly lives up to his billing as "EIGHTEEN FEET OF GUT-CRUNCHING, MAN-EATING TERROR!" but seems, rather, a good natured refugee from *Santa and the Three Bears* who would scarcely harm your pet canary let alone down a whirlybird with his bare paws. Throughout the film he seems at least as comfortable in front of the cameras as his human co-stars, though his emotional range as an actor proved distinctly limited. Teddy's one trick, apparently, involved the performance of a little dance in which he rises on his hind legs and sways adorably from side to side while waving his forearms in a parody of the hula. This, in any event, is the way he approaches each of his victims, leading one to assume that they have laughed themselves to death long before Teddy even has the chance (off camera, naturally) to munch on their limbs.

Since nothing in the movie could possibly frighten even the youngest and most impressionable members of the audience, the moviemakers tried to terrify the world with their promotional materials. In a press release distributed across the country Christopher George declared, "Let me tell you, that grizzly is more frightening than any great white shark!" Continuing the traditional shark/bear rivalry, producer Ed Montoro solemnly warned the public that "bears kill and maim more people around the world than sharks do. . . . It is a popular misconception that grizzlies are placid, fruit-and-insect-eating animals. Rather, they are foul-tempered and basically meat eaters. . . . This is one of the most dangerous animals to walk the earth—*the world's largest ground beast!*"

Oh, really?

Larger than moose? Larger than *elephants*? Or does Mr. Montoro believe that elephants don't qualify as "ground beasts" because they generally live in trees?

But never mind, since no one could argue with the size of *Grizzly*'s success. On a production budget of $680,000, it grossed more than $36,000,000 around the world. It is not known whether Teddy—having retired to his home in Lloyd Beebe's Olympic Game Farm in Sequim, Washington—ever received his fair share of the profits.

CLAWS (1977)

Just as *Grizzly* proved that it was possible to make a fortune by remaking *Jaws*, *Claws*, astonishingly enough, tried to cash in by remaking *Grizzly*. Turnabout may be fair play, but it is certainly lousy moviemaking.

This pathetic collection of deadpan clichés and out-of-focus nature footage boasts only one distinction: It is, apparently, the most ambitious feature film ever to come out of the great state of Alaska. The producer-writer-cameraman, an ex-lumberjack named Chuck D. Keen, is the leading (and only) movie mogul in the forty-ninth state, but the result of his efforts with the two (yes, two) totally obscure directors on *Claws* can only be described as half-baked Alaska. In place of the plastic dummy used in *Grizzly*, the makers of *Claws* resort in their close-up scenes to shots of the movie's overweight production manager in a borrowed bear suit. For the rest of the grizzly footage these pioneer movie men rented a beast from—yeah, you guessed it—Lloyd Beebe's Olympic Game Farm in Sequim, Washington. "Tag," the bruin used this time around, didn't dance nearly as well as his *Grizzly* counterpart, Teddy, but the shaky camera work helped to conceal the shortcomings in his performance. The laughable technical flaws in the lighting, sound, editing, and cinematography prove conclusively that Alaska is still the last frontier.

But the production values, low as they are, should take no discredit away from the acting or the script. A half dozen Hollywood veterans made the trek to the Great White North, and they stomp through their roles with a thespian style that can only be described as frozen. Jason Evers (the mad scientist from the classic *The Brain That Wouldn't Die*) plays a lumberjack who has taken his family on a wilderness camping trip. As they ride back to civilization in their pickup truck, they raise their voices and wave their arms, lustily singing:

> The bear went over the mountain,
> The bear went over the mountain,
> The bear went over the mountain . . .
> And we are going home.

A gigantic Alaskan grizzly hears their voices and is so outraged by their mangling of the last line that he not only decides to see what he could see, but resolves to eat them immediately. As a result of this attack Evers loses his left arm, and his small son winds up in a coma. Perhaps the rest of the movie is supposed to show his fevered imaginings in this semiconscious state—with more than twenty different flashbacks and flashforwards, the normal time sequence is maimed more grievously than any of the "devil bear's" victims. If you try to imagine Michelangelo Antonioni, temporarily drunk out of his skull on Moosehead beer, and attempting, on a ridiculously low budget, to render an intensely serious homage to that neglected classic *Grizzly*, then you will have some idea of the preposterous texture of this film.

Evers' best friend in the film is a Native American named Old Henry (sort of a buckskinned Alaskan version of Old Black Joe), played by Anthony Caruso of *Tarzan and the Leopard Woman* fame. In the midst of one of the remembered scenes-within-scenes, Caruso advances the theory that the killer grizzly in question is none other than Kush-Ta-Ka—the timeless Indian embodiment of evil. Their suspicions are confirmed by the state's game commissioner (played by Leon [*Son of Lassie*] Ames), who resonantly declaims: "I've got a deep gut feeling that we're dealing with something that's not natural." Certainly his dialogue seems unnatural, as he later explains that "when I come to the end of bear tracks, I like to see something standing in the last of 'em."

Jason Evers, having already sacrificed one arm to provide the Bad News Bear with an appetizer, naturally brings more passion to the situation. "It was a devil bear that did this to me! This man-eater's different," he explains to his pals. "It's like he's got a hatred, a vengeance for people. . . . That's why I'll find that stinkin' brute and kill him!" Later he addresses the bear directly while shaking his rifle in rage. "You filthy, murdering devil! I'm gonna kill ya! You bloody murdering bastard!"

Our hero fails to deliver on his promise, however, since Tag the Naughty Bear ultimately does himself in. After ravaging a frontier town, he playfully knocks over a huge gasoline storage tank, rolls around happily in the flammable fluid, and then goes out in the proverbial blaze of glory. Somehow his big immolation scene (reminiscent of a husky, hammy road company Brunhilde at the climax of *Götterdämmerung*) breaks the evil spell that had been cast on the previously mauled little boy. "Bucky's gonna be all right!" Evers' wife tearfully declares as the kid

miraculously comes out of his coma and the music swells to a triumphal crescendo.

All of this could be viewed as the most delicious sort of unintentional comedy, but the Wilderness Society wasn't laughing. Shortly before the picture's release, this conservationist organization protested to the U.S. Forest Service that "a proposed film about a marauding bear could so distort the facts about this noble animal as to build widespread opposition to its proper management and perpetuation. The grizzly bear needs all possible support to protect it and its irreplaceable wilderness habitat." The Wilderness Society need not have worried. Since *Claws* proved to be a hit only in southeast Alaska and won release in fewer than a dozen theaters in the contiguous forty-eight states, it never played a major role in shaping public opinion about the noble grizzly.

The imaginative title, however, earned special recognition. A radio station in Eugene, Oregon, sponsored a competition for listeners to come up with concepts for similarly styled *Jaws* spin-offs, and the winning entry suggested a movie called *Gnaws* about an 800-pound killer beaver. For our part, we would enjoy seeing *Paws*, about a gargantuan Norwegian elkhound that devours Hollywood, or perhaps even *Claus*—telling the horrific story of an oversize Santa who sneaks into the caves of Yellowstone Park to steal sleeping cubs to give away as teddy bears.

PROPHECY (1979)

Talia Shire is obviously appalled—either by a killer mutant bear that ravages the Maine woods or, more likely, by the sheer stupidity of her role in Prophecy.

All right, movie fans. What do you get when you mix a $12 million budget, a hot young screenwriter eager to make a profound ecological statement, a pretentious director angling for an Oscar nomination, a scenic backwoods location, a few Indian extras, some terrified campers, and a studio hoping to clean up with an old-fashioned monster movie?

What you get, in this case at least, is a huge mutant bear named Ka-Tah-Din who emerges from a polluted pond to shriek, wave his arms, and avenge himself on the despoilers of his wilderness home.

Prophecy, in short, is no ordinary bear movie, and Ka-Tah-Din is no ordinary bear. This drooling thirty-foot titan has a face that not even the most devoted Mama Bear could love—complete with slimy, pulsating purplish-orange blotches, bloodshot google eyes, and a deformed, gaping maw that bunches to one side and gives him a vague resemblance to Howard Cosell when he growls. *Time* magazine thought that Ka-Tah-Din looked like "Smokey the Bear with an advanced acne condition," while one of the characters in the film described him as "sort of a Bigfoot, only it's uglier."

This creature, in any event, has more on its mind than stealing picnic baskets. Its chief mission is to punish the greedy owners of a paper mill who have for years been dumping their industrial wastes into forest waters. As the inevitable idealistic scientist (television actor Robert Foxworth) explains to his pregnant wife (played by Rocky's old girlfriend, Talia Shire), this evil mercury pollution has caused all sorts of bizarre transformations in the Maine woods. For one thing, the local trees and mountains all seem to have grown several times their normal size so that the landscape looks far more like British Columbia (where the picture was actually filmed) than northern New England. What's more, these poisoned waters seem to have caused a deadly epidemic of overacting in all those who live within shouting distance of the paper mill. What they are all hollering about is a formula for disaster well known to anyone who has viewed other ecologically-minded monster movies, including *Godzilla vs. the Smog Monster* (1972) and *The Horror of Party Beach* (1964). According to this cherished recipe, if you take a pinch of pollution, or a tablespoon of radiation, and just add water, then—presto!—out will pop an energetic extra in an aquatic monster suit to teach us the proper respect for the grandeur of nature.

But screenwriter David Seltzer, who had scored a "mere" commercial success in his previous outing *The Omen* (1976), wanted to raise other Profound Issues of Our Time in addition to expressing his concern for the environment. As a result the avenging mutant bear's would-be snacks include an angry young Indian activist (Armand Assante) protesting the way his people have been victimized by capitalist America; a gaggle of racist and male-chauvinist lumberjacks who make insensitive comments about oppressed minorities; the utterly selfish industrial tycoon (Richard Dysart) who will stop at nothing in his lust for profit; the dedicated ghetto doctor (Foxworth) who has fled Washington, D.C., for the Maine woods because he could no longer endure the spectacle of oversize rats lunching on starving black babies; and his professional cellist wife (Shire) who, in spite of the suffering she has seen all around her, and which we have all endured in watching this movie, still summons the courage to bring a new child into the world.

Director John Frankenheimer treated all of these stereotyped characters with exaggerated respect, hoping to create the same sort of moody, hypnotic atmosphere in this silly saga of a murderous mutant bear that he had brought to his previously acclaimed films, *Birdman of Alcatraz* and *The Manchurian Candidate* (both 1962). This approach leaves him totally unable to accommodate the grotesque and humorous moments inherent in the material. In one astonishing scene Ka-Tah-Din ruthlessly attacks a group of campers in their bedrolls. One plucky young man attempts to escape by quietly standing up, holding his down sleeping bag to his chest, and hippety-hopping to safety. Before the victim can bounce off camera, a huge claw comes out of nowhere to reduce him to a shredded mess of flesh and feathers. Later, as the furry fiend suddenly shatters the surface of a deceptively tranquil lake, shaking the water from his gory locks, Robert Foxworth, while retreating to an Indian cabin, indulges in a pun so vile that not even the Medved brothers would touch it: "Let's bear-ricade this place!" he yells.

Audiences, meanwhile, yelled uncle in preview screenings staged by Paramount to promote the film. One such occasion proved so raucous that the *Los Angeles Times* filed a special report (June 13, 1979) about the audience "hissing, booing and shouting to the screen." Frankenheimer and others associated with the production, while agreeing that the gala evening had turned out to be "a disaster," blamed a small "claque who was angry that Tom Burman got the assignment for the special effects, rather than Rick Baker." Apparently Mr. Baker had attracted secret fan clubs throughout the United States, since, after the film's release, audiences across the country staged reactions identical to those at the Hollywood preview.

AND THE WINNER IS...

...PROPHECY

This picture deserves the prize because its intensely serious, "socially conscious" tone makes it even more ridiculous than its thoroughly laughable competitors. As Vincent Canby observed in *The New York Times:* "Mr. Frankenheimer treats this material with the kind of majesty usually reserved for movies about Cleopatra, Napoleon and General Patton. *Prophecy* is full of lingering lap-dissolves and elegant camera movements that suggest history is being made. Leonard Rosenman's soundtrack music is so grand it could be played at a coronation, and it's so loud that it pierces the ears and threatens the head." Ironically, our award winner might never have qualified for this category except for a fateful change in production plans. Original designs for Ka-Tah-Din called for an expensive and elaborate display of cinematic wizardry to render the sort of bizarre creature described in the script. As the owner of the paper mill declared in the movie, "It's larger than a dragon and it's got the eyes of a cat. It's an old Indian legend, and they've thrown in everything but the kitchen sink." One of the film's Indians went on to explain, "Ka-Tah-Din has awakened to protect us. He is part of all things created, and he bears the mark of each of God's creatures."

To live up to this outlandish billing, early production sketches showed a towering presence with leathery wings and a translucent body that showed throbbing organs and bodily fluids washing through various passages. As the budget mounted, however, Paramount ordered Frankenheimer to cut costs and he reluctantly abandoned these plans. One member of the special effects team told us: "We didn't have much choice at that point. Frankenheimer looked at a few different alternatives but then he said, 'Okay, we'll have to settle for sort of a skinned bear.' So we went ahead and designed a bear suit. And then, of course, we hired a guy to walk around in it. Maybe the critics didn't think it was so great, but you've got to admit: nobody ever saw another bear quite like it."

THE MOST PREPOSTEROUS ROMANTIC PAIRING IN MOVIE HISTORY

*E*veryone remembers the great romantic teams of the past, in which the chemistry between two stars seemed so natural and perfect that they appeared together in film after film. Whether it was Jeanette MacDonald and Nelson Eddy, Fred Astaire and Ginger Rogers, Spencer Tracy and Katharine Hepburn, or even Doris Day and Rock Hudson—these combinations generated their own electricity and dazzled millions of sentimental moviegoers. The late Louis B. Mayer developed a celebrated rule of thumb for making casting decisions involving two romantic leads: "You have to think if you would like to watch these two people actually making love."

Less successful attempts at romantic pairing, on the other hand, would cause even the most voyeuristic film fans to look the other way.

AND THE NOMINEES ARE . . .

RANDOLPH SCOTT AND KATE SMITH IN *HELLO, EVERYBODY!* (1933)

America's favorite 210-pound radio star plays an up-and-coming 210-pound radio star; she falls passionately in love with a heroic investigator for the Water and Power Company portrayed by long, lean, leather-faced Wild West perennial Randolph Scott.

Randolph Scott and Kate Smith

GROUCHO MARX AND CARMEN MIRANDA IN *COPACABANA* (1947)

Groucho Marx and Carmen Miranda

The "Brazilian Bombshell" is an aspiring songstress with a pineapple on her head; Groucho is an eccentric nightclub owner with a banana in his pocket. The "romantic sparks" between them cannot make up for the absence of Chico and Harpo.

RONALD REAGAN AND SHIRLEY TEMPLE IN *THAT HAGEN GIRL* (1947)

Okay, relax—the future President does *not* play a child molester; Shirley Temple was 18 at the time she made this soggy melodrama. Nevertheless, fans of perversion and incest will find plenty to cheer about when the two May-December lovebirds elope at the end of the film—despite persistent rumors from their gossipy neighbors that Shirley is actually Ronnie's illegitimate daughter. On several occasions in recent years the Chief Executive has gone "on the record" to classify *That Hagen Girl* as one of his greatest Hollywood embarrassments.

SHELLEY WINTERS AND LIBERACE IN *SOUTH SEA SINNER* (1950)

Shelley Winters and Liberace

Miss Winters, with bleached hair and feather boa, plays a sultry nightclub singer who rules a remote island with her seductive charms. Liberace is her world-weary, wisecracking piano player who conceals a burning passion for Miss Winters beneath his rough-tough macho exterior.

KATHARINE HEPBURN AND BOB HOPE IN *THE IRON PETTICOAT* (1956)

Katharine Hepburn and Bob Hope

Katharine Hepburn puts on a growlingly overdone Russian accent for her role as a man-hating Soviet air force captain; Hope impersonates a dashing, heroic American fly-boy who sweeps her off her feet during a whirlwind romance in London. This shameless *Ninotchka* rip-off earned Miss Hepburn the worst reviews of her illustrious career, with *The New York Times* describing her memorable mismatch with Ol' Ski Nose as "simply awful" and "downright embarrassing."

SOPHIA LOREN AND BURL IVES IN *DESIRE UNDER THE ELMS* (1958)

Sophia Loren and Burl Ives

The big studios of the late fifties had a difficult time selecting the right co-star for 23-year-old Italian sensation Sophia Loren. Following her unsuccessful outings with John Wayne, Cary Grant, and Frank Sinatra, Paramount turned to the one Hollywood hunk who was definitely "man enough" to handle the new star's sizzling sensuality: Burl Ives. In this solemnly misguided adaptation of Eugene O'Neill's celebrated tragedy, the bearded, barrel-bellied folksinger plays a lusty New England patriarch who woos the spicy young import in order to produce an heir for his farm. *Mama mia!*

RICHARD HARRIS AND DORIS DAY IN *CAPRICE* (1967)

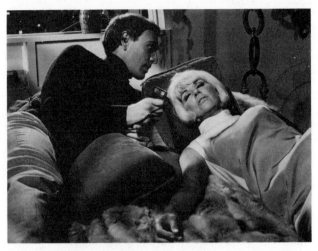

Richard Harris and Doris Day

The Man Called Horse makes charming, elegant pillow talk to that glamorous and worldly sophisticate, Doris Day. Both stars are utterly miscast in this soggy thriller about industrial espionage in the glitzy world of Parisian cosmetics, and the normally rough-and-ready Harris tries to boost the business by wearing high-visibility eye shadow in most of his scenes.

CAROL CHANNING AND JACKIE GLEASON IN *SKIDOO* (1968)

Carol Channing and Jackie Gleason

And away we go! The Great One is an aging gangster ("Tough Tony") who discovers LSD and spiritual enlightenment during a term in prison; Channing, described by Vincent Canby as "a running sight gag," plays his devoted wife who supports his efforts to escape by hosting an orgy and offering a striptease. At the grand climax to this Otto Preminger fiasco, Gleason spikes the prison soup with acid and then floats to freedom in a garbage can launched over the walls by inflated plastic bags.

Bette Davis and Ernest Borgnine

REX HARRISON AND RICHARD BURTON IN *STAIRCASE* (1969)

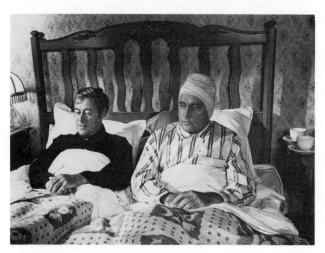

Rex Harrison and Richard Burton

After you, Alphonse; no, after you, Gaston. Richard agreed that he would do this movie only if Rex would, and Rex said he'd go ahead if Richard would, but in the last analysis they both should have stayed away. They play a bickering pair of aging gay gossips in what may have been a lark for the two British stars but turns out to be a 96-minute torment for the audience.

BETTE DAVIS AND ERNEST BORGNINE IN *BUNNY O'HARE* (1971)

As part of an egregiously inept attempt at comedy, the two former Academy Award winners play amorous oldsters who "disguise themselves" as hippies and ride a motorbike in order to rob banks.

MADELINE KAHN AND BURT REYNOLDS IN *AT LONG LAST LOVE* (1975) AND *CITY HEAT* (1984)

Madeline Kahn and Burt Reynolds (in City Heat*)*

In *At Long Last Love*, Peter Bogdanovich's epoch-making musical fiasco, Reynolds, the quintessential "good ol' boy," plays a bored, aristocratic New York millionaire, while Kahn, the rubber-faced urban comedienne, is similarly miscast as his vampy, glamorous, high society lover. The chemistry between them is as nonexistent as their musical abilities, with Burt offering "It's De-Lovely" while Madeline pleads her case in a production number of the song "Find Me a Primitive Man." Reynolds obviously filled the bill, since this ill-assorted pair appeared together once again in *City Heat*. Kahn played virtually the same part as in *At Long Last Love*—appearing as Burt's wealthy, sophisticated lady love and helping audiences understand why her man preferred the company of his co-star, Clint Eastwood.

RAQUEL WELCH AND JAMES COCO IN *THE WILD PARTY* (1975)

Raquel Welch and James Coco

In recent years the rotund, impish James Coco and the glamorous Raquel Welch have developed a common interest in diet and fitness as the authors of two best-selling books. Before penning these immortal tomes, the two future good-health gurus played doomed lovers in a slow-moving view of a fictional 1920s comedy star and his mistress, "Queenie." The on-screen affair between Jimmy and Raquel is considered such an epic event that the entire picture is narrated in rhymed verse.

DAVID BOWIE AND MARLENE DIETRICH IN *JUST A GIGOLO* (1978)

In her first film in fourteen years, Miss Dietrich plays a bawdy baroness in 1930s Germany who takes Bowie under her wing and teaches him the ropes (and chains) as a professional ladies' man. Bowie plays this disillusioned Prussian World War I veteran as if he were a Space Oddity (or sleepwalking zombie) and makes a very poor case for Dietrich, or the film's other veteran stars (Curt Jurgens, Kim Novak, David Hemmings), to be "Falling in Love Again."

GENE KELLY AND OLIVIA NEWTON-JOHN IN *XANADU* (1980)

What happens when the immortal ageless Greek muse, Terpsichore, comes down from Olympus disguised as a blonde-haired Australian roller-skater in order to reestablish contact with an over-the-hill big-band clarinetist she had inspired forty years before? What happens is that both stars disgrace themselves, with Miss Newton-John serenading her co-star with "You Made Me Love You" to which the ever-charming Mr. Kelly, smiling through his dentures, sadly comments, "I'm gettin' old, babe."

TAB HUNTER AND DIVINE IN BOTH *POLYESTER* (1981) AND *LUST IN THE DUST* (1985)

As a teenage heartthrob of the 1950s, playing opposite the likes of Natalie Wood and Debbie Reynolds, Tab Hunter never guessed that he would eventually graduate to a position in the movie business as romantic co-star to a 300-pound transvestite. In *Polyester* the inimitable Divine (whose real name is Glenn Milstead) plays suburban housewife Francine Fishpaw. Her fevered sexual fantasies come true when she/he meets her "dream man" in the person of Tab Hunter as owner of a local drive-in. In *Lust in the Dust*, Hunter is Abel (and willing), a hard-riding treasure hunter in the Old West who cannot resist the ample charms of Divine, as an aspiring saloon singer named Rosie. New projects for this dynamic duo may now be in the works, though no one expects to see them teamed for a family sitcom on network TV.

PIA ZADORA AND DESI ARNAZ, JR., IN *FAKE-OUT* (1982)

Pia Zadora, of course, is as well known for her acting ability as her other co-star Telly Savalas is for his hair. Here she plays an aspiring Las Vegas entertainer who is torn between her devotion to an aging crime boss and her growing attraction to a suave police officer, played by the son-of-Ba-Ba-Loo, Desi Arnaz, Jr. Arnaz eventually seduces her in a houseboat on Lake Mead, saving her from this painful dilemma and saving us from any more painful production numbers featuring Pia in her element at the Riviera Hotel and Country Club.

GENE WILDER AND GILDA RADNER IN *HANKY PANKY* (1982)

The fact that these two stars are married off screen doesn't make the on-screen chemistry between them any more convincing. Radner remains far better suited for comedy roles (such as her amusing turn in her husband's subsequent hit, *The Woman in Red*) than she is for parts as an elegant leading lady. Director Sidney Poitier tries to fuzz the issue, quite literally, by shooting most of her close-ups in gauzy, romantic soft focus. One can only hope that their marriage offers more excitement than this predictable "thriller" about an innocent architect drawn into international intrigue.

LUCIANO PAVAROTTI AND KATHRYN HARROLD IN *YES, GIORGIO* (1982)

Luciano Pavarotti and Kathryn Harrold

The opening credits portentously declare that "This Film Is Dedicated to Lovers Everywhere" but the two stars bear more of a resemblance to Laurel and Hardy than they do to the classy romantic teams of old. He portrays a touring opera star with a wife and family back home in Italy, while Harrold is a dedicated physician who, despite his pleas ("You must not fall in love with me!"), simply can't stop herself from tumbling into his spacious bed. The dramatic highlight of the picture concerns an enormous food fight in which the World's Greatest Tenor plants the World's Greatest Derriere in an oversize cream pie.

GRACE JONES AND ARNOLD SCHWARZENEGGER IN *CONAN THE DESTROYER* (1984)

Grace Jones and Arnold Schwarzenegger

New Wave singing sensation Grace Jones is the last word in hip, world-class body builder Arnold Schwarzenegger is the last word in hunk, and the movie they made together is the last word in junk. Jones gnashes her teeth a lot in order to play a slave, in stylish crew cut and string bikini, who is freed by the stalwart Conan. In this sorry sequel to the original *Conan the Barbarian,* she naturally falls for the big brute and fights alongside him, expressing her affection by smashing or impaling all enemies who get in their way.

SYLVESTER STALLONE AND DOLLY PARTON IN
RHINESTONE (1984)

Sylvester Stallone and Dolly Parton

Both stars are famous for their tremendous torsos, and in scene after scene, with tight T-shirts and plunging necklines, they fight the Battle of the Bulges. Parton, as a country-and-western thrush, is natural and charming as always, but Stallone works so hard to upstage her that even in their tender romantic scenes he treats her like a sparring partner. With grim intensity, he attempts a comic portrayal of a New York cabbie who is magically transformed by Miss Parton's ministrations into hillbilly superstar, but his singing at the end of the picture is just as bad as it is at the beginning. Stallone's rewrites of the script only made the situation worse, and screenwriter Phil Robinson held the producers responsible

for mishandling their strong-willed star. "If you take a non-housebroken puppy and put him in a nice house and he makes a mess on the floor, you don't blame the puppy," Robinson told the press. "He's only doing what comes naturally." In the end, Twentieth Century–Fox cleaned up Sly's mess by absorbing a $20-million loss.

AND THE WINNER IS…

… SOPHIA LOREN AND BURL IVES IN
DESIRE UNDER THE ELMS

This picture deserves the award because it places the beautiful Loren in not one but *two* absurdly implausible pairings.

Not only is she married to Big Bad Burl, who, according to the script, has already buried two wives (apparently having crushed them to death), but Sophia also begins an affair with his son—who is supposed to be such a potent and powerfully attractive figure that she cannot resist his animal magnetism. To portray this sinning stepson and to balance Miss Loren's smoldering screen presence, the producers chose none other than the awkward, twitchy Anthony Perkins—best known for his role as everybody's favorite homicidal *Psycho,* Norman Bates. In *Desire Under the Elms,* the New York *Herald Tribune* found him to be "insipid to the point of being neuter," while *Saturday Review* called him "peevish

The lack of chemistry between Sophia Loren and Burl Ives could only be topped by the anguished passion she was supposed to feel for her other co-star in Desire Under the Elms—*a badly confused Anthony Perkins.*

rather than tormented." Press accounts reported that the much heralded "hayloft scene" between Loren and Perkins provoked titters from preview audiences.

Director Delbert Mann approached the O'Neill text with great respect, but found all his good inten-

tions undermined by the bizarre casting. Advertised as "A Savage Portrait of Primitive Desires," the picture generated so little genuine sexual heat among its three stars despite all its huffing and puffing that it became known to industry insiders as "Perspire Under the Arms."

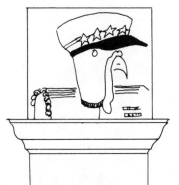

THE LEAST HEROIC BATTLEFIELD SPEECH IN HOLLYWOOD HISTORY

AND THE NOMINEES ARE...

GUNG HO! (1943)

Fighting Leathernecks, suitably inspired by Randolph Scott's uplifting words, gleefully plunge into combat in Gung Ho!

MARINE OFFICER (Randolph Scott): Ahead of you lies a hard road. You'll often have bad food and very little of that. Many times your bed will be a muddy ditch. To carry you through the rough spots before you, team-work is needed. The Chinese had a word for

it—it's "Gung ho." "Gung"—to work. "Ho" —harmony. I propose it as our motto. "Gung ho!" C'mon now, give it to me!

ASSEMBLED MARINES: Gung ho! Gung ho!

FIRST YANK INTO TOKYO (1945)

Richard Loo, as a sadistic Japanese officer, tries to put the moves on captured American nurse Barbara Hale in First Yank into Tokyo.

JAPANESE COLONEL (Richard Loo): Let us go to my study—it will be quiet there. For a while it amused me to make you believe that my American education changed my outlook on women. It did not! [He grabs her by the shoulder.]

CAPTURED AMERICAN NURSE (Barbara Hale): You Japs couldn't change! You're all alike! You ought to be put in cages!

UNTAMED WOMEN (1952)

DOWNED JET PILOT (Mikel Conrad): Boy, it's so quiet out here, you can hear the birds think!

CO-PILOT ED: It won't be for long—those jokers will be coming back.

JET PILOT: Ed, stand guard! Shoot anything with hair on it that moves!

KING RICHARD AND THE CRUSADERS (1954)

Virginia Mayo (as Lady Edith) movingly protests the warlike ways of King Richard the Lion-Hearted (George Sanders, left) and the Sultan Saladin (Rex Harrison) in King Richard and the Crusaders.

LADY EDITH (Virginia Mayo, to Richard the Lion-Hearted): War! War! That's all you think of, Dick Plantagenet! You burner! You pillager!

THE CONQUEROR (1955)

KUMLEK (Ted De Corsia, laughing derisively): Gaze upon him! Chief of the Mongols!

GENGHIS KHAN (John Wayne, in chains): I grieve.

KUMLEK: He grieves! Already the Mongol whelp whines!

GENGHIS: I grieve that I cannot salute you as I would. I am bereft of spit! . . .

KUMLEK: So be it: the slow death! Joint by joint, from the toe and fingertip upward shall you be cut to pieces. And each carrion piece, hour by hour and day by day, shall be cast to the dogs before your very eyes! Until they too shall be plucked out, as morsels for the vultures! Ah-ha-ha-ha! Away with him!

GENGHIS: You do well, Kumlek. For while I have fingers to grasp a sword, and eyes to see, your treacherous head is not safe on your shoulders—nor your daughter in her bed!

THE ALAMO (1960)

DAVY CROCKETT (John Wayne): Republic. I like the sound of the word. Means people can live free—go or come—buy or sell—be drunk or sober however they choose. Some words give ya feelin'. Republic is one of those words that makes me tight in the throat. Same tightness a man gits when his baby takes his first step—his baby first shaves—makes his first sound like a man. Some words can give ya a feelin' that makes your heart warm. Republic is one of those words.

MARINES, LET'S GO! (1961)

SERGEANT (Tom Reese): That will drive the Red buzzards back into the hills! Chatfield—stay under cover of these woods. Work your way down to that valley of Kwoy Nam, or whatever they call it. If you spot any Red goons, get back here on the double. Be careful: don't get your pants blown off! . . .

Tom Reese demonstrates the aggressive attitude toward the Korean foe that characterizes the rhetoric in Marines, Let's Go!

"PETE" (Hideo Inamura): You had him all wrong. This guy's tougher than a 50-cent steak!

GAPPA THE TRIPHIBIAN MONSTER (ALTERNATE TITLE: *MONSTER FROM A PREHISTORIC PLANET*) (1967)

The military forces of Japan face their greatest challenge when mother-and-son dinosaurs invade Tokyo in Gappa the Triphibian Monster.

TELEVISION REPORTER: The monsters are invading the city! Fortunately they're in the Negro section of town.

THE GREEN BERETS (1968)

As director and star of the Vietnam melodrama The Green Berets *(1967), John Wayne tries to explain to a war orphan named Ham Chunk—and to a skeptical public—"what this war is all about."*

GREEN BERET COLONEL (John Wayne): Ham Chunk! Always knew it could happen, didn't you?

WAR ORPHAN "HAM CHUNK" (Craig Jue, wiping away his tears): But I didn't want it to!

COLONEL: None of us did.

HAM CHUNK: Was my—was my "Peter-san" brave?

COLONEL: He was very brave. Are you going to be?

HAM CHUNK: I'll try!

COLONEL: I know you will! [The Duke pulls a green beret out of his pocket and places it on the child's head.] And I'm sure that your "Peter-san" would want you to have this.

HAM CHUNK: What will happen to me now?

COLONEL: You let me worry about that, little Green Beret! You're what this war is all about! [He takes his arm and they walk off together toward the sunset.]

WATERLOO (1970)

AIDE-DE-CAMP: Forgive me, sir. But if you took the troops into confidence they'd know what they were about.

DUKE OF WELLINGTON (Christopher Plummer): Hmmm. If I thought my hair knew what my brain was thinking I'd shave it off and wear a wig.

TIDAL WAVE (1975)

AN AIDE TO THE PRIME MINISTER (Ishiru Akiyama): The people are surrounding the palace! Shall we use guns to calm them down?

INFRA-MAN (1975)

PRINCESS DRAGON MOM (Terry Liu): Come here, creatures! I summon all of you to attend! I've opened the surface of the earth and it's time to attack.

ASSEMBLED MONSTERS: Yeah! Yeah!

PRINCESS: Enough! I've given the Earthlings an ultimatum: either they agree to be my slaves or they will be destroyed! Summon those two mutants!

BEETLE MAN: I will rip them apart with my hands!

OCTOPUS MAN: I have power the Earthlings never dreamed of! I am invincible. Do not wait, Princess: attack this instant!

SHEENA (1984)

As an honorary member of the Zambuli tribe, Sheena, Queen of the Jungle (Tanya Roberts), rallies the flagging spirits of a band of Stone Age warriors who must battle against a former American football pro who tries to rob their African home of its natural resources.

SHEENA, QUEEN OF THE JUNGLE (Tanya Roberts): Fire in my brains! It tells me I am still alive. I have not failed my people yet! . . . See! See! Even in chains we can defeat them! Turn your minds back, oh my people. Remember yourselves—a thousand, thousand moons ago! Bring your bows! Chief Harumba—ATTACK!

AND THE WINNER IS . . .

...FIRST YANK INTO TOKYO

Battlefield speeches are by nature jingoistic and intolerant, but two of the nominees listed here go above and beyond the call of duty in their bigoted extremes: *First Yank into Tokyo* and *Gappa the Triphibian Monster*. Nothing is less heroic than racism, and it is entirely fitting that these two films should be recognized in this category as the Golden Turkey winner and runner-up, respectively.

The utterly gratuitous slap at blacks in *Gappa* slipped into the film as part of the dubbing process before its release and distribution in the United States. The Japanese original reportedly presented some difficult problems for its translators: in the midst of the destruction of some rinky-dink miniatures by a pair of flying, fire-breathing reptiles, a television reporter warns the populace that "the monsters are invading our city, but so far they've only destroyed the poor section of town." Listening to these remarks, the dubbing supervisors decided they would never work with American audiences; residential patterns in the largest U.S. cities are so complex that ordinary citizens never talk about "the poor section of town." Puzzled by the challenge of finding an accurate rendering that would still make sense in idiomatic American terms, one of the translators came up with an inspiration: by dubbing in the words "Fortunately they're in the Negro section of town," the U.S. distributors hoped to explain why the gobbling gargantuas gorged themselves exclu-

Tom Neal, as an American spy who disguises himself as a Japanese officer in order to infiltrate Tokyo, manages to rouse the spirits of the enemy high command despite his thoroughly inept makeup job.

sively on shabby, rundown buildings, while appealing at the same time to what they perceived as the native prejudices of the moviegoing majority.

Fortunately the public response rebuked their calculations. During a preview screening in Chicago, the largely black audience reportedly dismantled part of the theater to show its displeasure at the offending comment. Other protests followed, so that before the movie's release on television, under the revised title *Monster from a Prehistoric Planet,* the prehistoric redneck slur had been removed.

Thanks to this timely excision, *Gappa* avoids a well-deserved Golden Turkey and the award goes instead to *First Yank into Tokyo.*

Even by the sad standards of wartime drama, the view of the enemy advanced in this yarn is pathetically primitive. The Japanese villains are not only power-hungry and treacherous, they are also possessed by an insatiable lust for "white" women, and, in a unique historical contribution, the movie suggests that the main motivation behind their attack on Pearl Harbor was a yen for American nookie. Not only does the captured American nurse suggest that all "Japs . . . ought to be put in cages" (as cited above), but at other points in the script she describes them as "slimy toads" or "fish eyes" and declares flatly that "no Jap would ever help anybody."

These comments seemed well-suited to the national mood as the struggle with Japan neared its climax, but then, much to the frustration of the RKO studios, World War II ended abruptly just four weeks before this picture's scheduled release. In the wake of the horrendous devastation of Hiroshima and Nagasaki, *First Yank into Tokyo* seemed suddenly dated, until the resourceful producers devised a clever scheme to save their property: they reshot two key sequences to include topical references to the atom bomb. In this altered, up-to-the-minute version, the WAC nurse (Barbara Hale) winds up in the same Japanese prison camp as an American scientist (Leonard Strong) who holds in his head the secret formula for the Big Bomb. This tenuous connection transformed a routine wartime melodrama into a hot (in fact, radioactive) property, with positive fallout at the box office. The studio proudly promoted its reedited movie in the *Motion Picture Herald* as "THE FIRST ENTERTAINMENT PICTURE TO FEATURE THE ATOMIC BOMB!!"

For utter tastelessness, it might seem difficult to top this cinematic exploitation of nuclear weaponry, but the extraordinary promotional gimmicks that we list in our next category make every attempt to do so. . . .

THE WORST PROMOTIONAL GIMMICK IN HOLLYWOOD HISTORY

I n general, good movies sell themselves; it's the lower-quality products that count on elaborate and imaginative publicity strategies to attract audiences. For the nominees in this category, the stupidity and tastelessness of the promotional gimmicks provide an appropriate match for the general ineptitude of the films themselves.

AND THE NOMINEES ARE...

HIRING ECCLESIASTICAL IMPERSONATORS TO DENOUNCE *MOM AND DAD* (1944)

This primitive docu-drama introduced the "shocking" facts of teenage pregnancy and venereal disease to millions of horrified Americans during World War II. With an initial production budget of $62,000, it earned back more than $40,000,000, thanks largely to grainy color footage of childbirth and the attention-getting stunts devised by its promoters. As one of them (K. Gordon "Cagey" Murray) fondly recalls, "Sometimes we'd find some old wino somewhere, dress him up to look like a streetcorner preacher, and stand him on a corner talking about the terrible evils of this movie. People would grab the handbills and head for the theater." These tactics led to bloody and well-publicized riots in New Orleans, Phoenix, and

Hamilton, Ohio, which helped give the picture its notorious reputation and its unparalleled box office appeal. Producer H. Kroger Babb (the same Hollywood hypester whose fertile mind created THE MOST TASTELESS AND IDIOTIC AD LINE IN HOLLYWOOD HISTORY, q.v.) also employed "Fearless Hygiene Commentators," who maximized his profits by selling sex manuals during intermission.

THE "PUNISHMENT POLL" FOR *MR. SARDONICUS* (1961)

Producer William *(The House on Haunted Hill)* Castle asked moviegoers in each theater to make the "ultimate choice" between two contrasting endings that had been filmed for this macabre tale of a homicidal baron (Guy Rolfe) with a deformed face. At the climax of the film, the action stopped for a "punishment poll" as the audience voted on the fate of the protagonist. By holding fluorescent "thumb-cards" either up or down, they could recommend life or death; naturally the eager crowds *always* yelled for blood and Sardonicus perished every time. That was a good thing, too, since showman Castle, supremely confident in his understanding of human nature, never actually prepared the alternate conclusion he had promised.

THE "FÜHRER LOOK-ALIKE CONTEST" FOR *HITLER* (1962)

"Sometimes, Eva, the world just doesn't understand me," sighs Adolf (Richard Basehart) to his main squeeze, Eva Braun (Maria Emo)—and the world also failed to understand the foolish and offensive promotional strategies (including a "Führer Look-alike Contest") used to sell the 1962-model Hitler.

To encourage audience identification with the Austrian *Übermensch* (as played in a whining, shrinking-violet style by Richard Basehart), the distributors urged theater owners to sponsor a look-alike contest in every town across the country. The lucky winner would win free passes to the movie, along with a shot at a part-time job that gave him the right to wear a Nazi uniform, medals, and, if needed, a false mustache. The "Exploitips" provided in *Boxoffice* magazine suggested that this suitably costumed "pseudo-Hitler" should spread the word about the film by "goosestepping in crowded areas close to theatre, or riding same on top of car or buses giving stiff-armed Nazi salute and shouting 'Heil Hitler!' " This stunt must have been particularly popular in Skokie, Illinois, and other areas heavily populated by Holocaust survivors.

THE "HORROR HORN" FOR *CHAMBER OF HORRORS* (1966)

In order to punch some life into this dreary tale about a maniac haunting a wax museum in Baltimore, producer-director Hy Averback (*Where the Boys Are '84—see:* THE WORST BEACH PARTY MOVIE EVER MADE) included the irritating noise of a "Horror Horn" at key moments on the soundtrack. This insistent "aaa-*rooo*—gahhh!" accompanies the image of a red warning light (designated the "Fear Flasher") and is supposed to alert squeamish patrons to close their eyes so they can avoid watching particularly gory scenes. In reality, the only purpose served by the Horror Horn was to awaken snoozing patrons who might otherwise have slept peacefully through the entire movie.

Neither the "Horror Horn" nor the "Fear Flasher" could make Patrick O'Neal a convincingly terrifying villain in his role as "the mad killer of Baltimore" in Chamber of Horrors.

"FREE PSYCHIATRIC CARE" FOR SENSITIVE PATRONS OF *FANGS OF THE LIVING DEAD* (1968)

Fangs of the Living Dead, starring Anita Ekberg, opened in 1968 as part of a spectacular triple bill, along with those tasty previous hits *Revenge of the Living Dead* and *Curse of the Living Dead*. The huge newspaper ads that informed the public of this important cultural event featured a photograph of a Charles Manson look-alike, along with the caption: "WARNING: This is John Austin Frazier. It has been reported that he now resides at a Mental Hospital, the result of attending our triple horror program. Because of this tragic event, we, the producers, have secured an insurance policy insuring the sanity of each and every patron. If you lose your mind as a result of viewing this explosion of terror, you will receive *free* psychiatric care or be placed *at our expense* in an asylum for the rest of your life!"

"A LIVE RAT FOR YOUR MOTHER-IN-LAW" OFFERED ALONG WITH *THE RATS ARE COMING! THE WEREWOLVES ARE HERE!* (1972)

Writer-director Andy Milligan, creator of *The Ghastly Ones* and *The Bloodthirsty Butchers*, gave the world this outrageously incompetent story of a family of werewolves in nineteenth-century England who raise man-eating rats as a hobby. To film some of the "rat attack" scenes, the moviemaker purchased hundreds of the pesky rodents, and his clever promotional gimmick provided a handy means of getting rid of them. At major showings of the film, theater managers drew ticket stubs to select lucky winners who could take home the squirmy little vermin to delight their families. For some of the low-life types attracted to this picture, however, the grand prize might only have enabled them to save money on popcorn.

"BURIAL INSURANCE" FOR *THE NIGHT OF A THOUSAND CATS* (1972)

After watching *The Rats Are Coming!*, etc., many moviegoers might welcome a few good housecats, but not the ferocious felines featured here. This Mexican import describes the adventures of an eccentric millionaire who turns his collection of tabbies into murderous beasts by training them to devour human flesh. The special effects feature a number of straight-faced actors and actresses who have obviously been smeared with cat food, and who twist and turn furiously while the featured pets politely lick it off. When one of the recalcitrant animal stars loses interest in this process and wanders out of camera range, you can see her being tossed back into the action from off screen. To make this laughable lunacy seem frightening to unwitting patrons the American distributors ran ads promising: "BURIAL INSURANCE! If you die from fright or nausea during the performance, we will give you a nice but simple funeral free of charge."

A FREE "UP-CHUCK CUP" FOR *I DISMEMBER MAMA* (1972)

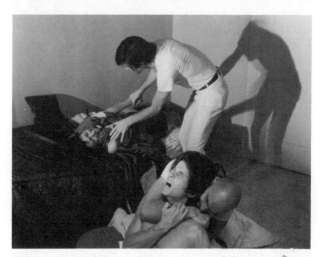

During some of the confusing action in I Dismember Mama, *the members of the cast seem to need "Up-chuck Cups" as much as the members of the audience.*

The only unusual feature of this thoroughly predictable psycho-on-the-loose saga (aside from its inventive title) was the little paper cup graciously handed to all patrons as they entered the theaters. Lettering on the side of the souvenir announced it as the "UP-CHUCK CUP: KEEP IT HANDY—It may be required on short notice during the showing of *I Dismember Mama.*" The producers obviously took greater pride in this promotional device than they did in the picture itself: the press book for the film featured two full pages touting the glories of this inspirational item. "You Gotta Believe THE UP-CHUCK CUP Will Upsurge Your Boxoffice!" the text declared. "The Cup Will Go in Many a Pocket and Purse. And Its *Message* Will Reach the Eyes and Ears of Countless Others. . . . The Exhibitor Will Be Billed At Only $3.30 Per Thousand Delivered. TAKE FULL ADVANTAGE OF ITS BOX OF-FICE POWER!" The trailer for the film certainly attempted to take full advantage of that power: it depicted stunned patrons staggering out of a Manhattan movie house, clutching their clearly labeled cups and telling a "roving reporter" that the paper goblets proved to be a much-needed accessory for the film. The director and writer for this slick bit of promotional footage on behalf of the film was a young moviemaker named Bob Clark, who later caused plenty of "upsurges" all his own by initiating the infamous *Porky's* series.

A SUMMIT MEETING BETWEEN A MOGUL, MAE WEST, AND A MUTT FOR *WON TON TON, THE DOG WHO SAVED HOLLYWOOD* (1975)

This nostalgic comedy about Hollywood's "Golden Age" featured more than two dozen veteran stars in cameo roles, but when they saw the finished film the only one who wanted to be associated with its promotion was, appropriately enough, the dog who played the title role. By the time of the movie's release, this handsome German shepherd, "Augustus von Schumacher," had secured the services of super-agent (and future producer) Allan Carr (*see:* THE WORST BEACH PARTY MOVIE EVER MADE) as his personal manager. With high hopes for the future career of his versatile new star, Carr kicked off the dog's national publicity tour with a gala celebration at Paramount Studios. Augustus presided over these proceedings from a throne on a raised dais at the center of the room, flanked by Paramount's two other "greatest stars": the 82-year-old Mae West and the 102-year-old studio founder, Adolph Zukor. These three guests of honor sat back in regal splendor in the midst of what *Variety*'s Army Archerd described as "the largest group of photographers and press this reporter has ever seen at a pre-picture bash." Augustus, by all accounts a well-trained and even-tempered pooch,

102-year-old Adolph Zukor and 82-year-old Mae West try to persuade a 4-year-old German shepherd named Augustus von Schumacher to mount his throne as the new "King of the Movies" in a promotional bash for Won Ton Ton, the Dog Who Saved Hollywood.

seemed a good deal more aware of what was going on around him than either of his elderly human colleagues. He maintained his place and his composure with admirable professionalism, but an uncontrollable physiological reaction undermined his clean-cut public image. Whenever the video cameras rolled and the lights went up, so did poor Augustus: he developed an enormous and unmistakable erection, ruining countless photographs and causing his embarrassed handlers to offer profuse apologies to the astonished multitudes.

"ALL WOMEN WEIGHING 200 POUNDS OR MORE ADMITTED FREE!" TO *CRIMINALLY INSANE* (1977)

Whoever thought that female moviemakers would automatically treat women more sympathetically on screen had obviously never seen *Criminally Insane.* With this film, producer Frances Millard proudly offered the world "another kind of monster—250 pounds of psychopathic fury!" The monster in question is a cannibalistic killer known as Fat Ethel (Priscilla Alden) who dismembers her victims with a meat cleaver. Despite the resulting snacks she enjoys on screen, she appears several pounds shy of the big 250 claimed for her in the publicity material. The producers obviously hoped to make her a cult figure, offering a free poster of "Fat Ethel and Her Bloody Cleaver" to the first hundred patrons on opening day and promising free admission to all *female* patrons who weighed at least 200 pounds. Some theater owners apparently relied on visual inspection to satisfy themselves that the eager applicants met the specified requirements; others kept scales close at hand for more scientific investigation. In any event, all men who weighed in at more than 200 and showed up at the theaters only to be denied gift passes would certainly seem to have strong grounds for a formal complaint of discrimination based on sex.

"Fat Ethel and Her Bloody Cleaver" offered all women over 200 pounds free admission to her first—and last— starring vehicle, Criminally Insane.

A "WORM-EATING DEMONSTRATION" FOR *THE WORM EATERS* (1977)

This bizarre horror film tells the story of a hermit worm breeder who turns the inhabitants of a nearby town into hideous "worm people" by sneaking a few of his creepy crawlers into hamburgers and spa-

ghetti. In reviewing the resulting mess, *Variety* dutifully reported: "Key requirement for main roles is a willingness to chomp real worms on camera. Gross closeups of the actors' mouths chewing disgusting food with live worms wriggling out of their choppers will no doubt amaze the younger patrons while striking adults as a new variant of pornography." In order to win suitable attention for this epicurean epic, the producer and director traveled along with the film and staged a series of stunts described in the

Herb Robins, director-star of The Worm Eaters, *shows off the polished technique he used in numerous "worm-eating demonstrations" across the country, designed to lure patrons into the theaters.*

press as "too outrageous to top." In Kansas City director-star Herb Robins stood in front of television cameras and hundreds of onlookers, and then proceeded to gobble down four eight-inch-long "Canadian night crawlers" while producer Ted Mikels got away with only two. Meanwhile, Howard Hall, manager of a local bar, outdid them both by consuming eight of the wriggling critters—all of which had been specially imported by the Minnesota Worm and Fly Company. This event proved such a success that the producers later staged a worm-eating contest in Las Vegas and offered free admission to anyone who ate a worm before entering the theater.

AND THE WINNER IS . . .

... WON TON TON, THE DOG WHO SAVED HOLLYWOOD

The embarrassing and untimely tumescence that afflicted the nether regions of Hollywood's newest canine star presented the dog's manager, Allan Carr, with what Carr himself later described as "one of my greatest promotional triumphs and challenges." Unless Won Ton Ton's handlers could somehow curb the hound's unhappy habit of showing an erection whenever television cameras approached him, his scheduled publicity tour might have to be nipped in the bud, or at least circumscribed. Some of the leading promotional and veterinary thinkers in Hollywood applied themselves to this problem to no avail, until Carr himself employed the expedient of a strategically placed rubber band that instantly solved the pup's public relations problem. The dog's triumphal national tour went forward as planned, though it did nothing to prevent the well-deserved box office bust of the movie it was designed to promote.

Looking back on the incident, it's unfortunate that no one recorded Mae West's comments as she sat on her throne beside a potent pup with the proverbial pistol in his pocket, but it is safe to say that she would have taken the situation in stride. The Hollywood legends in our next category, however, would have been a good deal less comfortable with the overeager actors who made such inept attempts to impersonate them. . . .

Bruce Dern and Art Carney applaud super-agent Allan Carr's ingenious achievement in helping his client, Won Ton Ton, avoid embarrassment during his first national promotional tour.

THE MOST LUDICROUS
ON-SCREEN IMPERSONATION OF A
HOLLYWOOD LEGEND

*M*any actors and actresses over the years have scored major triumphs by portraying colorful stars from Hollywood's past. Barbra Streisand, for instance, won worldwide fame—and a Best Actress Oscar—for her role as Fanny Brice in Funny Girl *(1968)*. *More recently, Kurt Russell became an overnight sensation by filling Elvis Presley's size 12 blue suede shoes in one of the highest rated television movies of all time (Elvis, 1979). Larry Parks as Al Jolson* (The Jolson Story, *1946), Susan Hayward as Lillian Roth* (I'll Cry Tomorrow, *1955), Diana Ross as Billie Holiday* (Lady Sings the Blues, *1972), Dustin Hoffman as Lenny Bruce* (Lenny, *1974), Gary Busey as Buddy Holly* (The Buddy Holly Story, *1978), and Jessica Lange as Frances Farmer* (Frances, *1982) all won Academy Award nominations in movies that purported to tell the "inside story" of big-name entertainers.*

For aspiring performers, the appeal of this sort of role is easy to understand. When they assume the identities of legendary stars, some of the glamor and magic almost inevitably rubs off on them. They can also demonstrate their thespian versatility by taking on the celebrated mannerisms of the demigods of yesteryear.

Unfortunately this same challenge has also attracted legions of inebriated would-be comedians at office parties, family reunions, and other august gatherings, who assault innocent bystanders with their lovingly crafted imitations of such luminaries as John Wayne, Marlon Brando, and Bullwinkle J. Moose. As irritating as these experiences can be, or as insufferable the ordeal of listening to your precocious 9-year-old nephew offering, for the sixth time, his famous and adorable impersonation of Mr. T, such moments are not nearly so embarrassing in the long run as the cinematic ventures celebrated in this category. Christmas party drunks will be sober in the morning and preadolescent brats will one day grow up (please God), but actors and actresses who are laughably miscast in movie biographies of world-renowned stars can never entirely escape their humiliation. For one thing, we won't let them.

The competition for this particular Golden Turkey would have been even more intense than it was had we opened the sluice gates and considered made-for-television movies. These small-screen entertainments have featured such casting masterstrokes as Loni Anderson and Arnold Schwarzenegger as Jayne Mansfield and Mickey Hargitay (respectively) in The Jayne Mansfield Story, *Tovah Feldshuh as Katharine Hepburn in* The Amazing How-

ard Hughes, Cheryl Ladd as Grace Kelly, John Gavin as Cary Grant in Sophia, and Harvey Korman and Buddy Hackett as Abbott and Costello in Bud and Lou. These impersonations may have been ludicrous and shabby, but in terms of dramatic excess and strained seriousness, they had nothing on the feature film nominees listed below.

DONALD O'CONNOR AS BUSTER KEATON IN
THE BUSTER KEATON STORY (1957)

Imagine, if you will, that you are a Hollywood producer with plans to make a screen biography of silent-era comedian Buster Keaton, whose gloomy and perpetually deadpan countenance won him the nickname "The Great Stone Face"? Whom would you pick to play this silent-era immortal in a hard-hitting film intended to face the ugly truth of Keaton's self-destructive alcoholism? How about giving the lead role to the happy-go-lucky star who is identified in Ephraim Katz's *Film Encyclopedia* as a "breezy, sprightly, eternally youthful song-and-dance comedian"? Does that sound like a good idea? If your name is Sidney Sheldon, and you are the producer, writer, and director of *The Buster Keaton Story*, it sounds like a great idea. No wonder the man went on to make a fortune as a writer of scarcely plausible fiction.

In all fairness, O'Connor did share some elements of common background with Keaton. Both men possessed outstanding acrobatic ability. What's more, O'Connor was the son of circus performers, and one of the highlights of Sheldon's imaginative script on Keaton's life featured the comedian's boyhood stint under the big top. In one of the film's dramatic highlights Buster, as a small child, must go on for his father, who has just died in a tragic circus accident. O'Connor recalled discussing this traumatic incident with Keaton himself, who had been hired as a "technical adviser" for the picture: "I asked Buster, 'What kind of circus was it?' He looked at me and said, 'I never was in a circus.' So I asked him, 'Well, how old were you when your father died?' 'Forty-five,' he said."

Keaton's presence on the set, which was publicized to the hilt by Paramount Pictures, indicated his enthusiasm for his consultant's fee—not for the ma-

terial being filmed. The studio paid him $60,000 for his services and the rights to his story, though the film and his life have few connections apart from the title. With the money he made from the project, Keaton bought the house which remained his home until his death nine years later. The notoriety associated with the movie also helped the veteran comedian make a comeback of sorts—he won bit parts in such notable films of the early sixties as *It's a Mad, Mad, Mad, Mad World* (1963), Annette Funicello's *Pajama Party* (1964), *Beach Blanket Bingo* and *How to Stuff a Wild Bikini* (both 1965, and both starring Annette and her perennial paramour, Frankie Avalon), and finally, Mr. Avalon's gripping astronaut saga, *Sergeant Deadhead* (1965). Apparently Buster Keaton, as portrayed on screen by Donald O'Connor, seemed such a lovable lightweight that studio bosses decided that the real-life Buster would make an ideal co-star for Annette and Frankie.

O'Connor's co-stars in the Keaton story, mean-

The best one could say for Donald O'Connor's attempted impersonation of Buster Keaton is that at least he selected the right sort of hat.

while, included such worthies as Peter Lorre, Jackie Coogan, Ann Blyth, and Rhonda Fleming, whose role as a "fictionalized" gold-digging siren led to a $5-million lawsuit from Buster's real-life second wife. She may have been the only one in the country who perceived realistic elements in the film.

Despite a saccharine let's-have-fun-at-the-movies ad campaign from Paramount which promised audiences "IT'S A BLUES-BUSTER!!" (not to be confused with a Blues *Brother* or a *Ghost* buster), *Newsweek* appropriately described the finished product as a "humorless humoresque." *Life* magazine, which ran a lavish photo spread promoting public interest in the picture, nonetheless warned its readers that "As a movie, *The Buster Keaton Story* is sadly lacking." The Philadelphia *Inquirer* decried the film's "embarrassing lack of warmth or interest," adding, "Donald O'Connor's aggressive personality submerges that of the deadpan comic he impersonates."

O'Connor himself candidly confessed his disappointment at the result. "It wasn't Buster's life," he recalled. "They called him a technical adviser, but they never listened to him." At the premiere, Keaton drew upon a lifetime's experience at pulling a poker face and sat in stunned silence with his third wife, Eleanor, hoping that no one would ask them what they thought of the picture. As Mrs. Keaton remembered the experience, and eloquently assessed the quality of the finished film, "My stomach turned over, it was so awful!"

JAMES BROLIN AS CLARK GABLE IN *GABLE AND LOMBARD* (1976)

Any list of the twentieth century's most romantic couples would have to include the pairing of Clark Gable and Carole Lombard. At the time of their marriage in 1939, Gable, who had just completed filming *Gone With the Wind,* was widely acknowledged as "The King of Hollywood," and Lombard had established herself not only as a gifted comedienne (*My Man Godfrey* [1936], *Nothing Sacred* [1937]) but as the movie industry's highest paid female star. The sheer physical beauty of the couple overwhelmed observers. Helen Gurley Brown, editor of *Cosmopolitan* magazine, recalls standing in a crowd as a little girl

For his role as Gable, James Brolin learned to twitch his putty ears and wrinkle his forehead in the style of the King, but frankly, audiences (and critics) didn't give a damn.

and watching the two stars at a premiere. "The spectacle of that pair was indescribably awesome. . . . They were the most glamorous vision of my life. . . . Carole and Clark could have spent months just basking in the perfection of their joint reflection." This was, as Louella Parsons declared in her own vivid and stunningly original prose, "a match made in heaven"—or at least that heaven inhabited by the spirits of gossip columnists, studio bosses, publicists, and the readers of fan magazines. The story reached its appropriately romantic conclusion in 1942, when Miss Lombard, 33 years old and at the height of her career, made a bond-selling tour of her home state of Indiana to help America's war effort. On its way back to Hollywood, her plane slammed into the side of a Nevada mountain, instantly killing all twenty-two passengers. Though Gable went on to marry twice more after her death, his friends believed that Carole remained the only one of his five wives he truly loved.

The tale of the King and his favored Consort certainly offered a wealth of material for a glamorous and sentimental film, and in the early seventies, more than a decade after Gable's death, Hollywood finally rose to the challenge. Universal Studios assigned Canadian director Sidney J. (*Lady Sings the Blues*) Furie to get the project off the ground. The veteran filmmaker felt even more strongly about this new assignment than he did about some of his earlier fine films (*Dr. Blood's Coffin*, *The Snake Woman*, *Swingers' Paradise*) and confided to the press: "I feel I was born to make this movie." The main problem he faced involved the casting for his two lead roles. Furie went first to Burt Reynolds—after all, he and Gable both had mustaches, didn't they?—but the Good Ol' Boy wisely decided to pass up the opportunity of giving America's critics a shot at comparing his acting abilities with those of Clark Gable. The movie men next brought the project to Steve McQueen and Ali MacGraw, and even offered to throw in a free blonde wig for Miss MacGraw, but these two stars, in the midst of their own off-screen *Love Story*, made a *Great Escape* from impending disaster and turned them down. Then, to everyone's surprise, wonder boy Warren Beatty agreed to accept the much-shopped Gable part, but with two conditions: first, that he be given the opportunity to rewrite the script, and second, that his character in the movie be provided with a fictitious name. Universal felt little confidence in the drawing power of a film entitled, say, *John Doe and Lombard* and so let Beatty go on to the proverbial bigger and better things. Hopelessly perplexed by the casting dilemma, the producers approached such luminaries as Valerie Perrine and Sally Kellerman for the Lombard role and talked to virtually every leading man in town, except for Woody Allen, about playing Clark Gable. At a crucial moment destiny, as they say in Hollywood, intervened: one night Sidney J. Furie took a break from his worries by watching that uplifting television entertainment, *The Sonny Bono Comedy Hour*. There, on the small screen, was a guest star from the popular *Marcus Welby* TV series: one James Brolin. According to the director's subsequent account, he knew at once that he had discovered the new King of Hollywood. Screen tests helped to confirm his instincts. "He *is* Gable," Furie told reporters. "He doesn't imitate him, but when he says a line, I find myself saying, Gawd, that's the way Gable would have said it!"

Skeptics hooted when Universal announced the choice, but Brolin quickly reassured them with his statements to the press. "They are going to put some plaster behind my ears to make them stick out a bit," he announced. With that problem happily solved, the studio went on to select Brolin's co-star: a young actress named Jill Clayburgh, who had previously portrayed a sexy Israeli soldier in that putrid paean to the pleasures of masturbation, *Portnoy's Complaint* (1972). Miss Clayburgh's own stormy live-in ro-

mance with actor Al Pacino might offer Hollywood gossips an updated urban neurotic version of the Gable and Lombard story but, other than that, it is hard to see how she qualified for the role.

Universal, which had learned about the drawing power of show business nostalgia through the phenomenal success of its celebrated "studio tour," expected a "Grand Slam" from *Gable and Lombard*. Prerelease polling of the nation's moviegoers gave further indication of a major hit. "It's a little scary," intoned one solemn executive, "perilously close to the reaction on *Jaws*." If he meant that audiences would eventually be running from the theaters in horror, he would have been close to the truth. The insipid ad campaign declared: "THEY HAD MORE THAN LOVE—THEY HAD FUN!" and then, when that failed to generate the expected box office stampede, the slogan changed to "THEY HAD MORE THAN LOVE—THEY HAD ROMANCE!", ingeniously emphasizing the dramatic contrast between love and romance. At this point the executives at Universal might as well have announced to their stockholders, "We have more than love, we have a tax writeoff." Across the country audiences stayed away in droves, and the critics attacked the movie with rare fury, or, one might say, Furie.

Before the film's release, Brolin's friend Allen Garfield (who played MGM boss Louis B. Mayer in the movie) made a loyal attempt to boost his co-star. "Most people thought Jim couldn't do it," Garfield recalled. "There was a lot of negative talk about him before he did the movie."

But that was nothing compared to the negative talk about him *after* he did the movie. If Orson Welles is right in claiming that "Every actor in his heart believes everything bad that is printed about him," then James Brolin must be suffering from a case of pathetically low self-esteem. Reviews of the film included the following representative comments about his performance:

Gable's back—in the hulking form of James Brolin—and you can have him.
—KEVIN THOMAS, *Los Angeles Times*

He looks almost alive, as mourners say of a carefully rouged corpse . . . imitation is the sincerest form of flatulence.
—RICHARD CORLISS, *New Times*

There is the abysmal performance by James Brolin as Gable, who may not have been a great actor, but who was charming, sexy and shrewd. Brolin comes out lumpish, loutish, and faintly imbecile, failing both as performer and as Gable impersonator.
—JOHN SIMON, *New York*

Mr. Brolin doesn't act. He gives an impersonation of the sort that makes you wonder if he can also do James Cagney and Edward G. Robinson.
—VINCENT CANBY, *The New York Times*

Poor James Brolin, plucked from television to play the King himself, suffers through closeups that plainly show his pinned-forward ears, sucks his pipe noisily and twitches his face muscles in an apoplectic attempt to approximate the eloquent smirks of Clark Gable.
—JACK KROLL, *Newsweek*

In all fairness to the hapless Mr. Brolin it should be noted that not even the finest and most versatile actor, not even Burt Reynolds himself, could have convincingly delivered some of the lines provided by the hilariously awful script. Screenwriter Barry Sandler, who later wrote those camp classics *Making Love* and *Crimes of Passion,* left no lily ungilded in reducing the relationship of two great Hollywood legends to what critic Judith Crist called "a 131-minute history of fornication between a department store dummy (James Brolin with putty ears) and a foul-mouthed floozy (Jill Clayburgh without her usual talent)." The most memorable spat between the two lovebirds occurs when Clark is unable to pronounce those three magic words "I love you" and Jill Clayburgh as Carole responds in the hysterically indignant style of a working-class housewife who has just been cheated by the local fish vendor. "Well, I got news for *you,* honey!! You could plant all the hair in Hollywood on your chest and it still doesn't make you a man! It makes you just what you are right now—NOTHING!!" In yet another touching and intimate scene, after the two stars are reconciled, Lombard offers her main squeeze a sentimental token of her esteem: an extra-large hand-knitted "cock-sock" to keep his Rhett Butler manhood warm during those notoriously cold Hollywood nights.

This gesture, one would think, would in itself fill any movie's reasonable quota of tastelessness, but at its conclusion *Gable and Lombard* soars to new heights and offers one of those shining, transcendent, unfor-

gettable moments that help to make the viewing of awful films so satisfying. As Gable/Brolin contemplates the charred, smoking wreckage of Carole's plane, he wipes tears from his cheeks and sniffs in agony directly toward the camera: "I *told* her she should have taken the train!"

Having achieved this sort of greatness so early in his career, what could Mr. Brolin possibly do for an encore?

With admirable courage, he crawled from the charred, smoking wreckage of *Gable and Lombard* to make another Universal fiasco the very next year. *The Car* told the chillingly plausible story of a 1977 Lincoln Continental that is possessed by the devil and begins behaving disturbingly like Bruce the Shark in *Jaws.* Brolin spends half the movie running away from this venomous vehicle, but just when he thought it was safe to go back to his suburban home, he sees that he is still being followed. Bounding up the stairs with the sweat pouring from his furrowed brow, he bursts into the master bedroom, shakes his wife by the shoulders, and bellows: "Lauren!! Lock the KIDS in their rooms! THE CAR is in the *garage*!"

Our hero proved so convincing in this role that he won the chance to play a haunted (no, not by the angry ghost of Gable) husband in the inexplicably popular spooker *The Amityville Horror* (1979). Then, at last, he settled comfortably behind the manager's desk in the glitzy television series *Hotel,* which has provided a suitable outlet for his talents.

MISTY ROWE AS MARILYN MONROE IN *GOODBYE, NORMA JEAN* (1976)

Producer-director-screenwriter Larry Buchanan (*see:* THE ROGUES' GALLERY) is best known for off-the-wall science fiction foolishness such as *Mars Needs Women* and *Zontar, The Thing from Venus* (both 1966). But this multifaceted moviemaker also has his serious side, offering the public such probing, hard-hitting dramas as *The Trial of Lee Harvey Oswald* (1964—a cockeyed "you-be-the-judge" quickie not to be confused with the 1977 TV movie of the same name), *The*

Other Side of Bonnie and Clyde (1968—a pseudodocumentary designed to capitalize on the popularity of the Arthur Penn classic and featuring narration by the one and only Burl Ives), and *Mistress of the Apes* (1981—about a sex-starved lady scientist who discovers a herd of hirsute, slope-browed "missing links" in Central Africa and finds them irresistibly attractive). He approached his biographical study of Marilyn Monroe's early years, while she still bore her original name "Norma Jean Baker," with an even deeper sense of purpose than he did these other subjects: in the promotional material for the film he claims to have "known" the great MM. (The precise nature of their relationship remains Mr. Buchanan's secret, though some film historians have speculated that he may, at one time, have even secured her autograph.) In any event, the director must somehow have learned many of the private details of her early life, since an announcement at the beginning of *Goodbye, Norma Jean* informs audiences: "THIS IS HOW SHE HAPPENED [sic]. NOT LEGEND, NOR EVEN THE WAY SHE TOLD IT. THIS IS THE WAY IT WAS."

To convey this sort of gritty realism, Mr. Bu-

Misty Rowe, in what appears to be a Halloween fright wig, displays the uncanny resemblance to Marilyn Monroe that won her the lead role in Goodbye, Norma Jean.

chanan put out feelers (you should pardon the expression) for an actress "who is vivacious without being phony." He conducted a "National Marilyn Monroe Look-alike Contest," which must have provided a good deal more fun than the finished film, and anointed one Alexis Pedersen, a 21-year-old with no prior movie experience, as the winner. Miss Pedersen's prize was, of course, the starring role in the projected blockbuster, but after one look at the script she decided that some may like it hot, but the script was a bit too hot for her; Alexis said *Goodbye, Larry Buchanan* with few regrets. The role then fell to Misty Rowe, a, shall we say, budding 19-year-old television actress who had previously played Maid Marian on the series *When Things Were Rotten* and had displayed her formidable talents as one of the haystack honeys on the ever-popular *Hee Haw*. From Buchanan's point of view, Ms. Rowe's most important qualification was the constructive attitude she brought to her role as the young Monroe. As one of her co-workers on the set admiringly observed: "Misty believes this is just a job. She doesn't care what her grandma thinks."

And a good thing, too, since the film contains six lurid rape scenes, as poor, innocent Norma Jean is tortured by her foster mother, then victimized in turn by a motorcycle cop, several fat, balding producers, a lesbian talent agent, a deranged, twitching photographer, and a drunken silver-screen swashbuckler. Even worse than these assorted indignities are the lines the lead character is forced to deliver that are intended to show her indomitable spirit.

"I am somebody—I really *am* somebody!" she declares, after winning the coveted title "Miss Whammo-Ammo," and then later in the film:

"I'm the toughest woman you've ever seen! I'm not quitting, I tell you—I'm going somewhere!!" and then, yet again:

"All my life I've been *nowhere*! Now I'm going *somewhere*!"

By the end of the movie she has won her first big screen test and assumed her new identity as "Marilyn Monroe." But to make sure that this upbeat turn of events does nothing to alter the pathetic tone of everything that we have seen so far, the audience listens to several verses of the revolting title song by Elton John sound-alike Johnny Cunningham:

She died in L.A. in a lonely room.
Nobody knew her, but they knew she died too soon.

By that time it was too late, before we began to
care.
If you can hear me now, this is my prayer.

Unfortunately *we* can hear him now, and we can
also hear Misty Rowe as she swings back and forth
inexplicably between two performance extremes.
On the one hand there is a certain high-camp charm
to her fourth-rate impression of Marilyn as the
quintessential breathy dumb blonde, but her out-of-
left-field interpretation of a savvy, hard-edged cryp-
to-feminist is not only horribly overdone but totally
irrelevant to the action on screen. "I didn't want to
imitate Marilyn; no one can," Misty told the press.
"The only time I felt weird was when I went to
Grauman's Chinese Theater to put my hands in her
prints."

She may have also felt weird when, despite its
surprising box office success, *Goodbye, Norma Jean*
failed to catapult her to big-screen stardom. *Films and
Filming* summarized the critical reaction to Ms.
Rowe's efforts: "She walks as if she'd seen a few
Marilyn Monroe films and decided to forget about
them. . . . Keen observers will recognize Dorothy
Provine rather than Marilyn in Misty Rowe's firm-
jawed features."

Ms. Rowe went on to supporting roles in *The Man
with Bogart's Face* (1980) and *National Lampoon's Class
Reunion* (1983), and also to her purely decorative
country-girl chores on *Hee Haw*. She is, as of this
writing, only 28 years old. Her sleazy work with the
irrepressible Larry Buchanan marked her feature
film debut and, as she later told *Playboy*, "We had no
lighting, poor makeup, little or no direction." Under
more favorable circumstances, she may yet find a
niche for herself in feature films, proving, despite
our skepticism, that she is indeed going *somewhere*.

Certainly, one of her colleagues on *Norma Jean* has
gone on to better things: Debra Hill, who worked as
Buchanan's script girl on the project, soon became a
producer in her own right. In this role she helped to
create thrillers such as *Halloween* (1978), *The Fog*
(1980), *Escape from New York* (1981), and *The Dead Zone*
(1984). This success, unfortunately, led her to display
a shocking disregard for her cinematic roots. "Debra
Hill, when she saw me on the street, wouldn't talk
to me," Larry Buchanan shrugs. "She is producing
fourteen-million-dollar pictures, and they're all
bombing. Apparently, it never occurred to her that,
by my side, we made a movie—*Norma Jean*—for
$130,000, and to this day, it makes money!"

ROD STEIGER AS W. C. FIELDS IN *W. C. FIELDS AND ME* (1976)

Rod Steiger has made a career out of playing some of
the world's least likable figures, from his Academy
Award–winning redneck sheriff in *In the Heat of the
Night* (1967), to *Al Capone* (1959), Jud Fry, the villain
in *Oklahoma* (1955), a crazed, bellowing Napoleon
(*Waterloo*, 1970), and Benito Mussolini *twice* (*The Last
Days of Mussolini* [1974] and *Lion of the Desert* [1981]).
Given this penchant for portraying curiously charismatic bad guys, Steiger seemed perfect for the part
of W. C. Fields. After all, all biographical accounts
make it clear that the alcoholic, misanthropic, notoriously miserly comic genius was, in his personal life,
a particularly nasty piece of work. Carlotta Monti, a
one-time starlet who became Fields' mistress and secretary for the last fourteen years of his life, nostalgi-
cally recalled just how impossible he could be in her
best-selling recollection of their life together, *W. C.
Fields and Me*. When Universal bought the rights to
this 1971 book and announced plans for a film based
on Fields' Hollywood years, Steiger leaped at the
chance to portray one of his personal heroes. "He
represented the individual in a vicious society," the
actor declared. "Fields was a street fighter. He was
one of the few men who hit this town and became
successful without kissing anyone's rear end."
Steiger later found himself haunted by "the remarkable similarities in our lives. Fields left home at
eleven; I left home at twelve. He worked delivering
ice in Philly; I worked delivering ice in Newark."
The star neglected to point out one of the other key
areas in which his life paralleled that of his subject:
Fields became famous around the world as a willing
victim of the demon rum, while Steiger has candidly
described himself in interviews as a "wino" and a
"bum."

So, with all these outstanding qualifications for the
role, what went wrong? Why did Steiger, who
dreamed of bringing home another Oscar, wind up
instead as a prime contender for the Golden Turkey?
The fault, dear readers (to paraphrase the Bard of
Avon), lies not in our star, but in our producers. The
front office at Universal worried that W. C. Fields,
especially as rendered by Rod Steiger, would turn
out to be so salty and selfish a curmudgeon that he
couldn't possibly appeal to a mass audience. Therefore, in order to make *their* Fields appropriately

Billy Barty (left) *is totally broken up by co-star Rod Steiger's W. C. Fields impressions in* W. C. Fields and Me, *a movie that never gives audiences an even break.*

cuddly and adorable, the studio bosses secured the services of screenwriter Bob Merrill, best known for penning the lyrics to the immortal 1950s hit "How Much Is That Doggie in the Window?" Given W. C. Fields' well-known feelings about doggies, in windows or anywhere else, it is intriguing to speculate on how he might have reacted to this choice, or to the sickly-sweet script that followed. To his credit, scenarist Merrill did resist the temptation of showing Fields as the proud papa of a prize-winning pooch, or the kindly coach of a Little League team, but he did come up with something nearly as cute and small as pets or kids with which his hero could establish a relationship: a lovable midget (as nauseatingly portrayed by the ubiquitous Billy Barty) who becomes Fields' "best friend." This bosom buddyship with a saccharine shorty, so convenient to the plot, was simply invented out of whole cloth, as was the touching reconciliation scene between Fields, as a tearful old man, and his estranged son. To further build sympathy for our main man, the script has him arriving in Hollywood in 1931 without a dime to his name but with the inevitable "pocketful of dreams"; in reality, Fields rode to the West Coast in a shiny new Lincoln limousine, carrying $350,000 in $1,000 bills. Never giving a dead comedian an even break, the film similarly distorts Fields' relationship with Carlotta Monti. She is portrayed by everyone's favorite *Can't Stop the Music* girl, Valerie Perrine, as an elegant angel with (you guessed it) a heart of gold who is dearly cherished by her man; in actuality, Fields expressed his deep affection for Carlotta and his profound gratitude for the many years she spent with him by leaving her the princely sum of $25 a week from his estate.

As a result of the relentlessly sentimental slant of the script, which was fully emphasized by director Arthur *(Love Story)* Hiller, Steiger on screen does violence not only to Fields' personality but to his own as well. He tries so hard to show the "warm, wonderful human being" behind the crusty exterior that he seems, at times, to be auditioning for the title role in a possible remake of the classic *Santa Claus Conquers the Martians,* and at other times comes across like the Pawnbroker with a hangover. In his confusion, the star hid behind his elaborate makeup (featuring an enormous putty nose that wobbles visibly on his face like an orange hidden inside a sweat sock) or relied on his carefully crafted Fields impersonation to try to avoid outright embarrassment. He developed that impersonation by listening to the late comic's recorded voice through headphones while he slept, and ordering all members of the film crew to avoid Fields impressions on the set. "It's so catching —everyone thinks he can do it, but it only throws me off."

Something must have thrown him off, since all his careful preparation yielded some of the worst reviews of his career. "Rod Steiger . . . has presumably kept many a cocktail party backwash in stitches with his Fields impersonation," wrote Judith Crist in the *Saturday Review.* "On screen it comes out as wearing secondhand Rich Little or potato-chip commercial—particularly since Steiger's makeup, of the death-mask-and-pancake variety, makes him look like Van Johnson decked out with a clown nose." Penelope Gilliatt in *The New Yorker* noted that Steiger's mouth looked "so immobilizingly twisted that you would think Fields began his working life after he had had a stroke." The entire enterprise, she suggested, "is best approached with a pair of tongs."

It remained for Vincent Canby in *The New York Times* to pay Steiger and his colleagues the ultimate compliment. He described *W. C. Fields and Me* as a "dreary exhibition of incompetence beside which the recent *Gable and Lombard* becomes one of the towering achievements of the world cinema."

FAYE DUNAWAY AS JOAN CRAWFORD IN *MOMMIE DEAREST* (1981)

Child abuse is not generally viewed as a surefire laugh getter; for normal people it is no more hilarious than cancer. Why, then, were so many thousands of moviegoers rolling in the aisles during *Mommie Dearest*'s climactic scene, when a bug-eyed, bellowing Joan Crawford whips her daughter viciously with a coat hanger while declaiming the immortal line: "*NO* WIRE HANGERS—EVER!!!" Most of the credit for transforming this horrific moment into a bit of irresistibly inane, unintentional comedy must go to Faye Dunaway, who seems dead set on outcamping even the real-life Joan Crawford in an unforgettably melodramatic tour de worst. In the course of two uproarious hours, she sobs, howls, clenches her fists, smashes the furniture, crosses her eyes, throws her head back, flares her nostrils, bares her fangs, grabs her breasts in despair, and stomps through her big scenes with the general air of a *sumo* wrestler trying to terrify his opponents through sheer physical presence.

Baby Christina (Mara Hobel) is thrilled with her birthday gift of a designer collection of wooden coat hangers from Mama Joan Crawford (Faye Dunaway) as "The Biggest Mother of Them All" in Mommie Dearest.

Admittedly, the part itself offered major temptations for overacting. The scandalous memoir *Mommie Dearest*, by Joan's adopted daughter, Christina, became a worldwide sensation as millions of readers shivered in voyeuristic delight at the portrait of madness and sadism behind the glamorous Crawford facade. Four confused screenwriters labored to bring forth a workable script based on this material, but wound up with a horror show that proceeds breathlessly (and pointlessly) from one atrocity to another. Joan not only beats her daughter on screen, but cuts off her curly blonde locks, steals her dolls, tries to

strangle her, bops her with a can of cleanser ("DID YOU *SCRUB* THE BATHROOM FLOOR TODAY?!!"), humiliates her in front of her friends, beats her in swimming races ("Ha! You lost AGAIN! I ALWAYS beat you!"), and even tells her to her face, "Maybe I adopted you for a little publicity!"

To create even the slightest shred of sympathy for this wretched, alcoholic, anal-retentive creature would have required enormous subtlety and great restraint from the lead actress—perhaps Anne Bancroft, originally considered for the part, could have brought it off. With a strong director keeping her in line, it's even possible that Faye Dunaway, who had been so convincing in her earlier films *(Bonnie and Clyde, Network, Chinatown)*, could have turned in an interesting performance. Unfortunately Frank Perry *(David and Lisa, Play It as It Lays)* simply stepped back and let her have her head, which should ultimately have been handed back to her on a platter. "Christina didn't understand that Joan had a wonderful life," Dunaway enigmatically informed the press. "I want to climb inside her skin."

Aided and abetted by a makeup job which, in the eyes of *Playboy* magazine, made her look like "Groucho Marx as a female impersonator," Dunaway attacked her role with all the crafty self-control of a starving tiger going after a slab of raw meat. As *Variety* reported after the film's premiere: "Dunaway does not chew scenery. Dunaway starts neatly at each corner of the set in every scene and swallows it whole, costars and all. . . . It would all be unbearable if not so badly done that scene after scene is high camp." Audiences certainly got the message. In one scene Crawford's lawyer-lover (Steve Forrest) tells her, "There's no camera in here, Joan. If you're acting, you're wasting my time." When Dunaway shrieks back at him, "I'M NOT ACTING! I'M NOT ACTING!" audiences around the country applauded their agreement.

The film concludes with poor, put-upon Christina ostentatiously getting the "last word" on her Monster Dearest, when, having been written out of her mother's will, she comes up with the idea of doing a book. It is therefore only appropriate to give Christina the last word here. When interviewed after the picture's release, she failed to see the humor in Dunaway's approach to the part. "Her portrayal was absolutely ludicrous," she said. "I've read she is saying she has been haunted by the ghost of Joan Crawford —and after seeing her performance, I can see why."

AND THE WINNER IS...

. . . FAYE DUNAWAY AS JOAN CRAWFORD IN *MOMMIE DEAREST*

The executives at Paramount Pictures knew they had a problem with *Mommie Dearest*. Preview audiences laughed and hooted when they saw it, while the critics attacked the film with the same sort of abusive frenzy that Joan Crawford reserved for little girls who dared to hang expensive dresses on wire coat hangers. The producers, whistling in the dark, might talk bravely (and fancifully) of an Oscar nomination for Faye Dunaway, but studio insiders freely admit that they expected to lose almost all of their $12-million investment.

Imagine their astonishment—and delight—when the Joanie Horror Picture Show caught on with audiences and established itself as the surprise comedy hit of 1981. As critic Jim Harwood urged the readers of *Variety*: "Do not go alone to see *Mommie Dearest*. Take a friend; take 10 friends; hijack a busload of strangers. This could be the cinematic chance of a lifetime." Many moviegoers followed his advice and boasted of watching the picture six, seven, or eight times. They memorized each delicious line ("TINA! BRING ME *THE AXE*!!!" "I'm not mad at you; I'm just mad at the dirt." "DON'T YOU EVER USE THAT TONE OF VOICE AGAIN, MISSY!" And, of course, the uplifting, "DON'T F—— WITH *ME*, FELLAS!!!") and shouted them back at the screen; they came equipped with wire hangers and cans of Dutch Boy cleanser to act out key scenes as they occurred on screen. Newspapers in several cities reported on the curious phenomenon of audience members dressed up as Joan waving coat hangers and chasing other patrons, decked out as curly-blonde Christinas, up and down the aisles as the picture rolled on. On Halloween movie buffs from San Francisco to Fire Island donned padded shoulders and severe lipstick as "Faye Dunaway as Joan Crawford" became one of the year's most popular costumes. In short, *Mommie Dearest* developed a genuine cult following.

At first the Paramount brass seemed puzzled and alarmed at the public response to a film which they had always classified as a grim and intensely serious work of art; finally, even these hardheaded executives, not noted for their sense of humor, began to hear the sound of America's moviegoers laughing all the way to the box office. To cash in on this trend, they adjusted the ad campaign for their outlaw heroine. New full-page layouts featured the catchy slogan: "No wire hangers EVER!" and urged audiences to join in the good clean family fun of *"MOMMIE DEAREST*: THE BIGGEST MOTHER OF THEM ALL." The lettering of the title even featured a little wire hanger, dangling from the final "T." This approach seemed to amuse everyone except Frank Yablans, the film's producer, who sued Paramount over their ad campaign, warning them, in effect, "DON'T MOTHER WITH ME, FELLAS!!!" In the legal documents he filed with the court he described the new ads as "obscene, vulgar, offensive, salacious"—using some of the precise words reviewers had used in hailing his cinematic masterpiece.

Faye Dunaway, at least, showed a sense of humor in the midst of the turmoil and seemed to enjoy her new-found notoriety as the focus for a rapidly emerging cult. At Dunaway-O'Neill, her fashionable boutique in Santa Monica, she constructed a colorful display featuring a poster for *Mommie Dearest* and an array of twisted wire hangers. Her popularity as the Biggest Mother of Them All helped to open new vistas for her career. In 1984 she went on to yet another triumph as the evil sorceress Selena in the fantasy hit *Supergirl*—a film in which her wild overacting was perfectly in tune with the comic book style and the wham-bam special effects.

Now that Bette Midler appears to be slowing down, we hope Miss Dunaway will help to fill the gap by learning to sing and taking her Joan Crawford act to Vegas. If she does, she'll be sure to face hordes of adoring fans, cheering her on and waving their wire hangers in tribute.

THE
WORST PERFORMANCE
AS A NAZI
MAD SCIENTIST

M *any critics have pointed to Gregory Peck's impersonation of the infamous Nazi fugitive Dr. Josef Mengele in* The Boys from Brazil *as an example of motion picture acting at its most absurdly excessive. When compared to the third-rate Third Reichers nominated in this category, however, Peck's performance is a model of dignity and restraint. For more than forty years nutty Nazis have offered movie producers their most convenient symbols of ultimate evil—and have encouraged actors to indulge themselves in on-screen orgies of teeth-gnashing, arm-waving, evil cackling, and bad German accents.*

Before Hitler even came to power, this image of the Teutonic "Mad Doctor" (so memorably advanced by Frankenstein *in all its variants) had already established itself with the moviegoing public. The all too real horrors of the Nazi era only strengthened this longstanding ethnic association and created, in the demented person of the Master-Race Man of Science with a Bizarre Plot to Conquer the World, one of the cinema's most exploitable and durable stereotypes.*

AND THE NOMINEES ARE...

BELA LUGOSI IN
BLACK DRAGONS (1942)

This wacky wartime drama offered a festive smorgasbord of paranoia, with viperous villains to suit every taste. The Black Dragons of the title are members of a Japanese secret society, decked out in shiny kimonos and satanic smiles. In order to sabotage the American war effort, they pursue a master plan more

treacherous than Pearl Harbor: They will sneak into the United States disguised as solid-citizen midwestern industrialists and use their false identities to cripple key factories and Rotary Clubs throughout the Corn Belt. In order to assist them in this Machiavellian masquerade, the "nefarious Nips" import the world-famous plastic surgeon, "Herr Doktor Melcher" (Bela Lugosi), straight from Berlin. A conflict of cultures is subtly sketched once he arrives in Tokyo to perform the surgery: his hosts greet him by bowing, while he returns their pleasantries with a hearty, heel-clicking "Heil Hitler!"

At this point armchair strategists might protest that the Axis powers could have saved themselves a good deal of trouble and plastic surgery by dispatching good ol' Aryan boys, instead of Japanese, as their undercover agents in America. This sensible expedient, however, would have put Dr. Melcher out of a job, and judging from Lugosi's sleepy demeanor in his role, the good doctor needs all the help he can get. Unlike other Hollywood Nazis, he doesn't bother to rant and rave but communicates every emotion with an all-purpose monochromatic sneer. Even when he is double-crossed by the Japanese and thrown into jail (there is no honor, you see, among the Enemies of Democracy), he manages to deliver an avuncular snicker along with his lines. "You will pay for this, you apes," he chortles, shaking his head. "You swine. The Führer will wipe you off the face of the earth."

The maniacal Melcher makes good on this threat after he manages to break loose from the Japanese hoosegow by disguising himself as a wandering Frenchman named Monsieur Cologne. To alter his appearance beyond recognition, the doctor performs plastic surgery on himself by removing the fluffy false beard he wore in his previous identity. His accent, however, remains utterly unchanged: it is neither French nor even vaguely German, but Lugosi's normal Transylvanian singsong deployed even more slowly and portentously than usual.

After his daring escape from Tokyo, Cologne/Melcher/Lugosi invades the United States and hunts down the erstwhile business tycoons, who are, you will recall, Japanese agents in disguise. As he stabs them to death one by one, this unreconstructed Hitlerite becomes a national hero in spite of himself: after he finishes his work (and dies in the process), a headline proclaims JAP SPY RING SMASHED! while an American flag waves triumphantly across the screen. One might argue that the underlying message behind the film is the noxious notion that all white people—including Nazis—must ultimately unite to defeat what the script calls "the Yellow men," except for the fact that this movie is too idiotic and inept to convey any message at all.

Ads for the picture carried a pathetic personal appeal from Bela Lugosi to his fans: "Never have I worked in a story so startling or so blood-chillingly shocking," the former Dracula declared. "See it if you dare!" One critic who accepted this dare wrote for *The Hollywood Reporter* that "any child wearing a Halloween mask of papier-mâché can cause a more instantaneous and legitimate scare. . . . When all else fails, an audience may find some slight measure of amusement in counting the entrances and exits that substitute for action in the film."

Nazi plastic surgeon Bela Lugosi tries to teach his Japanese colleagues how to "Sieg Heil" as part of an inter-Axis cultural exchange program in Black Dragons.

Bela Lugosi went on making cinematic entrances and exits for the remaining fifteen years of his life, confounding those moviegoers who believed he couldn't possibly do worse than he did with this dreadful film. In 1943 he played another Nazi madman—this time a conniving counterfeiter who presides over a New York haunted house in *The East Side Kids Meet Bela Lugosi* (also known as *Ghosts on the Loose*). Later he starred in motion pictures such as *Voodoo Man* (1944), *Return of the Ape Man* (1944), *Zombies on Broadway* (1945), *Mother Riley Meets the Vampire* (1952), and *Bela Lugosi Meets a Brooklyn Gorilla* (1952), parodying his own past successes and plumbing new depths with the carelessness of his performances. In the face of worsening drug addiction, mental illness, and marital chaos, the one-time Hungarian stage great kept working long enough to participate in his celebrated trilogy (*Glen or Glenda*, 1953; *Bride of the Monster*, 1955; and *Plan Nine from Outer Space*, 1956/1959) with director Edward D. Wood, Jr. As all bad movie buffs fondly recall, Lugosi died suddenly after shooting began on *Plan Nine* and was buried at Forest Lawn Cemetery in August of '56 in his original Dracula cape.

JACK HERMAN IN
THE YESTERDAY MACHINE (1963)

Any run-of-the-mill garden variety Nazi could find refuge in the jungles of South America, but it took "an intellectual giant and a colleague of Einstein's" to trick his enemies by setting up shop Deep in the Heart of Texas. The fugitive physicist Ernst von Hauser (Jack Herman) installs an atomic reactor in the basement of a remote farmhouse and happily pursues his time-travel experiments until he makes one crucial mistake: kidnapping a state champion baton twirler (Linda Jenkins) on the eve of a major football game.

This horrendous assault on the American Way of Life produces an appropriately energetic response from a police detective (Tim Holt), an investigative journalist (James Britton), and a nightclub singer (Ann Pellegrino) who is known as "The Girl with the Orchid Voice." These three determined anti-Fascists fight a desperate struggle against Von Hauser's evil "army" of SS men—which consists of two goons named Manfred and Wolf who repeatedly click their heels and shout "Jawohl!" to remind us that, despite their slow Texas drawls, they are supposed to be German. Also on hand to assist the diabolical doctor is an Ethiopian slave girl (Olga Powell), stolen from the court of an ancient Pharaoh by Von Hauser's nuclear-powered time machine. The sicko scientist hopes that someday this awesome device (which is represented by four art deco floor lamps that flash off and on intermittently) will retrieve Adolf Hitler from his fiery past and present him as a happy surprise to the unsuspecting present. To defeat these evil intentions, our three heroes try a little bit of everything: smashing the doc's lab equipment, firing revolvers at his storm troopers, seducing the 3,000-year-old slave girl, and even, in the case of the nightclub thrush, unleashing her "Orchid Voice" for a stirring rendition of the torchy favorite "Go On Away and Leave Me Alone" (*see:* THE WORST ROCK 'N' ROLL LYRICS IN MOVIE HISTORY). As the intrepid reporter aptly comments in the midst of this breathtakingly bad motion picture, "This is like a fantastic nightmare. I don't understand any of it."

To make *us* understand, first-time writer-director-producer Russ Marker (whose only other credit is the 1964 extravaganza *The Demon from Devil's Lake*) interrupts the action for a full ten minutes so that

"How dare *you report Adolf Hitler as a madman! He vuz a great* chee-nius!*" insists former Yiddish theater star Jack Herman to a dumbfounded American reporter (James Britton) in a scene from* The Yesterday Machine.

Professor Von Hauser can explain the operation of his time machine in excruciating detail. Late-night television viewers who happen to be spinning the dials and who stumble upon this meaty chunk of the film will assume they have accidentally tuned in a session of *Sunrise Semester* that has, for some reason, been taped by the inmates of a mental institution. Von Hauser, with chalk and blackboard, speaks with tremendous intensity about "the theory of super spectronic relativity," "the minus ray," "a silent cannon that kills with soundwaves," and other abstruse topics while his audience, the determined journalist, interrupts him periodically by declaring, "Now, let me get this straight . . ." or, "I'm afraid you lost me, Doctor . . ."

He certainly has lost us, except when he expostulates on more familiar political topics:

> REPORTER: There's one thing that puzzles me, Herr Doktor: why a man of your brilliance should identify himself with that fanatical madman?
>
> VON HAUSER (Taken aback): How *dare* you report Adolf Hitler as a madman! He vuz a great *chee*-nius, ahead of hiss time. The vorld, in its ignorance, vuz not ready to accept him!
>
> REPORTER: The world did not accept him because he was a lunatic. . . . You call a man who was responsible for the mass murder of millions a great man, a genius? . . .

VON HAUSER (Waving his arms): Vott do you know in your stupid, pesty little mind?! . . . Ach, you Americans are such an egotistical und arrogant lot! How proud und superior you felt venn you strutted through the ruined streets of our city . . . but that is only temporary, my Yankee friend! [He cackles with joy.] Soon Hitler vill return! [He shakes his fist at the camera.] Ve vill rewrite history! Und der Third Reich vill endure . . . not for a thousand years, or a hundred thousand years . . . but *forever*! [Looking to the heavens and breathing heavily] The rest of the vorld vill fall at our feet—und ve vill rule for all ETERNITY!!

It would be impossible to enumerate all the grotesque details of the shtick employed by Jack Herman in delivering this material: he raises his eyebrows à la Groucho, clicks his dentures, licks his lips, giggles with insane abandon, closes his eyes in ecstasy, clenches and unclenches his fists, and flaps his arms at his sides like a frustrated chicken trying to take flight. Considering the course of his career, it's easy to understand why the aging thespian pulled out all the stops in his performance: though he had played small parts in other Texas productions such as *Beyond the Time Barrier* and *Zontar, The Thing from Venus,* his casting as Professor Von Hauser gave Herman his first (and last) shot at a starring role. Ironically enough, he prepared for this "chance of a lifetime" part as a Prussian putz with a decade of devoted work in New York's Yiddish Theater. After moving to Texas, he served as a drama coach at Bishop College—a small black liberal arts school just outside Dallas. Between takes on the set of *The Yesterday Machine* he used to entertain the crew by reciting soliloquys from *Richard III* and *King Lear.* After his acting career fizzled definitively, he managed to earn a living by presenting warmup speeches to service clubs and trade conventions throughout the southern United States. His co-workers remember him fondly as "quite a character," "one hell of an actor," and "a crazy perfectionist," and they all mourned his passing in 1968.

DANA ANDREWS IN
THE FROZEN DEAD (1967)

Dana Andrews is best known for playing clean-cut, all-American GI's in movies such as *The Purple Heart*

In The Frozen Dead, *Dr. Joseph Norberg (Dana Andrews,* left) *proudly displays the detached talking head resulting from his pioneering medical experiments.*

(1944), *A Walk in the Sun* (1945), and *The Best Years of Our Lives* (1946). Seeing him turn up suddenly in *The Frozen Dead* as a fanatical Nazi is a bit like encountering Bela Lugosi in the role of Jesus Christ (which Lugosi played in his early days in Hungary before coming to Hollywood—*see:* THE ROGUES' GALLERY). In this movie Andrews takes the role of "Dr. Joseph Norberg," who is described in the screenplay as "an expert in repairing vital organs." This sounds like a promising premise for a pornographic fantasy, but in this context it makes no sense whatever. The plot concerns 1,500 high Nazi officials who have been frozen in "suspended animation" in gigantic meat lockers hidden in various caves throughout Europe. At the beginning of the picture Dr. Norberg receives orders from a Wehrmacht general (Karel Stepanek) to begin the defrosting process. "I've waited twenty years for this, and it's cost the Party a lot of money," declares the Aryan officer, "but the stakes are tremendous—and worth every penny!" We can only assume that he means *stakes* and not *steaks,* since Norberg tries to revivify the Nazi elite rather than proceeding to barbecue them.

In any event, his scientific efforts are interrupted when two touring coeds turn up at his London laboratory for a surprise visit. Their rudeness in arriving unexpectedly is suitably punished by Andrews' lumpish, sniveling assistant, "Essen" (Alan Tilvern). This inept Peter Lorre imitator kidnaps one of the girls and delivers her for strangulation to the Mad Doctor's even madder brother (Edward Fox), who is part of the collection of crazies imprisoned in the basement of the lab for experimental purposes.

The plot then makes a bizarre bow to those two 1963 severed-head spectaculars *The Brain That Wouldn't Die* and *They Saved Hitler's Brain,* as the detached noggin of the dead girl assumes a life of its own under a high-tech electrified hair dryer and develops far-reaching telepathic powers. "That head vill destroy us all!" exclaims Essen, drooling and breathing heavily, causing his boss, Dana Andrews, to bark back: "You're a blundering fool, Essen. . . . Go to your room!" In the grand finale Essen's chilling prophecy is vindicated: the heinous head hypnotizes a row of severed arms that happen to be hanging on a coat rack on the wall. These loose limbs proceed to strangle Norberg and the Nazi general, making a subtle but effective case for the importance of arms control.

In presenting his own version of a Fascist physician, Dana Andrews tries to win sympathy by emphasizing his character's nostalgia for those golden moments of World War II. He sighs and turns misty eyes toward the horizon while offering comments such as "It's just not like it was in the old days" and "I'm just as good a Nazi as I was twenty-five years ago!" He delivers his lines so slowly and tentatively that it's hard to know whether he is struggling to remember his dialogue or else embarrassed about his own decidedly intermittent attempts to lend a German flavor to his speech. As *The New York Times* commented in its review, he "grapples with a guttural accent manfully, professionally and sadly."

Despite the decline in his career evidenced by his participation in this film (and in the execrable *Hot Rods to Hell* the same year) Dana Andrews remained a popular and prominent member of the Hollywood community. His work as vice-president of the Screen Actors Guild, and as an outspoken and effective member of Alcoholics Anonymous, won him many admirers. In the early sixties he launched a national campaign in association with Hedda Hopper to ban nudity in all major films. The success of their crusade can be measured today by a visit to a theater or drive-in near you.

JAN MURRAY IN
A MAN CALLED DAGGER (1967)

No man of Jan Murray's protean talents could be permanently satisfied with a career as a nightclub comic and television game-show host. Inevitably, he felt the need to make important dramatic statements in motion pictures and so arranged the necessary adjustments in his life. He sacrificed more than $500,000 in Las Vegas bookings, sold his New York home, and moved his family to the West Coast, bragging to a *Los Angeles Times* reporter shortly after his arrival, "I've done various roles since I've been here. . . . I've done straight roles. I've been a heavy. In *A Man Called Dagger* I play a Nazi war criminal. . . . For the first time in my life I'm something other than Jan Murray!"

He is also something other than a convincing Nazi. His performance stands as living proof of the wisdom in the old adage: You can take the boy out of the Bronx, but you can't take the Bronx out of the boy. Though Murray makes a feeble attempt at reproducing Germanic inflections, he can't conceal the unmistakable New York flavor in that grating, Borscht Belt waiter's voice. Watching his energetic efforts in this ridiculous role, one has to conclude that Murray could have played absolutely anything else—including a Viking sea captain—more persuasively than he portrays the crippled scientist and former concentration camp Kommandant in this film. The problem is physical as well as cultural: "Rudolph Koffman" is supposed to be a twisted wreck of a man in the best *Dr. Strangelove* tradition,

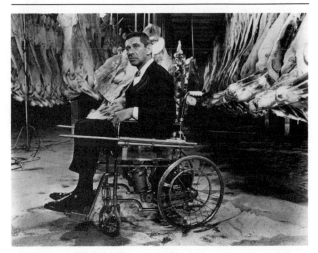

Former game-show host Jan Murray plots to take over the world from his bloody headquarters in a meat-packing plant, where he specializes in installing remote-control radio transmitters in the teeth of his unsuspecting victims. Meanwhile, the producers of A Man Called Dagger *themselves became unsuspecting victims of a lighting crew that took insufficient care to conceal its equipment—still plainly visible at the left of this still.*

confined to a wheelchair from which he operates a variety of deadly gadgets. Mr. Murray, on the other hand, looks as fit and tanned as a country club golf pro, and when he tries to grimace he manages only a smirk. In discussing the film, the comic recalls that when he first approached producer Lewis M. Horowitz about playing the Nazi killer the idea seemed absolutely absurd. "Jan, I've admired you for years," Horowitz told him. "But there's no part in here for a comic. Besides, you're too young to play the villain." The producer should have trusted this instinctive reaction, but instead found himself swayed by Murray's pleas that he was older than he looked and by photographs of his grandchildren.

In the finished film Murray's character harbors the dream of every red-blooded Nazi boy: to take over the world and facilitate a comeback for "Mr. H." To advance these objectives, he owns and operates a gigantic meat-packing plant where the steaks are even more tremendous than they were for Dana Andrews in *The Frozen Dead*. And talk about beefy: the cunning crackpot's girlfriend Ingrid (Sue Ann Langdon) operates a "beauty farm" from which she recruits unsuspecting starlets to participate in his experiments—including the installation of tiny radio receivers in their teeth that force them to follow Koffman's orders. In the nick of time two courageous secret agents (Paul Mantee and Terry Moore) butcher the cleaver-wielding Kommandant in his own freezer locker. In the grizzly conclusion Murray is hoisted on one of his own meat hooks, surrounded by slabs of beef that are no more lively or kosher than his performance.

VERONICA LAKE IN
FLESH FEAST (1970)

In 1941 Paramount Pictures launched a major new star in the movie *I Wanted Wings*. With her slow, husky voice and cascading waves of blonde hair, Veronica Lake achieved instant fame as "The Girl with the Peek-a-Boo Bang." Her distinctive hairstyle inspired such widespread imitation during World War II that the federal government officially requested that she change it; too many young women in munitions factories were suffering accidents when their long hair became entangled in the machines.

Veronica Lake in her glory days, some twenty-five years before she took the role of a German mad scientist in Flesh Feast.

Whether it was the shift in the way she wore her locks, or a change in public taste, by the end of the 1940s her career had gone into a sharp decline.

In 1951 she filed a bankruptcy petition and left Hollywood for parts unknown. Neither the press nor her former movie associates learned of her activities until the *New York Post* "discovered" her in 1962, waiting on tables in a Manhattan restaurant and living at a $7-a-night hotel. Following a flurry of publicity concerning the former star's sad circumstances, she won additional headlines with arrests for public drunkenness. At this point it seemed hard to imagine how the one-time glamor queen could possibly sink any lower. Then she answered that question by making *Flesh Feast*.

Miss Lake co-stars in this movie (which she also co-produced) along with a bargain basement Hitler and a few dozen maggots. She plays the part of "Dr. Elaine Frederick," a brilliant scientist recently released from an insane asylum, whose German background is only revealed in the picture's grand climax. Like all the other whacked-out wizards in this category, she spends most of her time in a basement laboratory, continuing research begun at a concentration camp during the Third Reich. Her especially appetizing experiments offer the promise of "eternal youth" to those hardy souls who allow a small swarm of maggots to crawl over their faces, devouring, then replacing the tired flesh. This sort of beauty secret might never make it at the Golden Door, but Miss Lake tells one of her Nazi colleagues (Phil Philbin) that she has developed a deep personal attachment to her little lab assistants:

> VERONICA LAKE: You know I've been working for years—developing, breeding, and conditioning these maggots. It's a special breed of Calipara. . . . The colors of the spectrum lights affect the larvae in much the same way changes in climate affect us. They feed on human flesh.
>
> PHIL PHILBIN: Why must it be human flesh? Why not animal?
>
> VERONICA: I haven't got time to explain it to you now.

She's pressed for time because she's about to face the greatest challenge of her career: restoring the youth of an unidentified "Commander" who plans to launch a "world revolution" from his hideaway in South America. When the dotty doctor straps Mr. Big onto her lab table, she discovers, of course, that he's none other than Adolf Hitler—or at least a nervous bit player (Otto Schlesinger) wearing a cheap rubber Hitler mask. In the conversation that follows, Miss Lake reveals the dark secret of her past: Her own mother died as a "human guinea pig" in previous maggot experiments and she holds the Number One Nazi personally responsible. With the Führer tightly bound (but unfortunately not gagged) she sadistically applies the pesky little critters to his face. In earlier scenes of the movie a few genuine maggots make an impressive appearance, but in this sequence a bowl of Rice Krispies is conveniently substituted. "This one is for democracy!" Miss Lake proudly declaims as she tosses a bit of cereal at his face.

> ADOLF: Are you *insane*? I had nuzzing to do viz it! It vuz Eichmann—und Goebbels.
>
> VERONICA: No, it was you—only you! Doctors! Butchers and maniacs! Remember, der Führer—this is all in the interest of medical science. . . . What's the matter? Don't you like my little maggots? Oh well, I understand. *Mother* didn't like them either! Heil *Hitler*!

This salute, reverberating over a close-up of the rice flecks on the Hitler mask, provides a conclusion for this revolting excuse for a motion picture. No

explanation is provided as to why Veronica's beloved "little maggots"—which are supposed to have such wonderful therapeutic effects—are suddenly turned into crawly killers; at no point do we hear their mistress yelling "sic 'em!" or otherwise altering their instructions.

Given the quality of the screenplay, not even the world's most accomplished actress at the absolute top of her form could have possibly escaped humiliation in this vehicle. Veronica Lake, on the other hand, had never been a particularly gifted actress even in her glory days, and by the time she participated in *Flesh Feast* she was far, far from the top of her form. On screen she looks far older than her 48 years, with badly stained teeth, twisted jaw, and curled, Listerine-yellow hair. The best that can be said for her performance is that she at least spares us an attempt at a German accent. She concentrates instead on the "emotional content" of her role, punching up words for no apparent reason, declaiming her lines with consistent fervor but not the faintest indication that she knows what they mean.

The finished film proved so hopeless that it sat on the shelf for three years before its release, timed to coincide with the publication of Miss Lake's autobiography. As part of her recollections, she offered a series of surprising comments on *Flesh Feast*, her last film. In addition to her acknowledged roles as star and co-producer, the one-time Girl with the Peek-a-Boo Bang insisted in print that she also should have been credited as the director. "Some of the footage is very good and imaginative. . . . It was designed to turn your knuckles white, set your heart pounding, and cause your girl friend to cuddle up close in sheer terror," she wrote of the film. "We had a lot of fun shooting the movie."

With this comment, Miss Lake takes her place as the only human being in the history of the world who ever found any aspect of this dreadful film in the least bit enjoyable.

DYANNE THORNE IN
ILSA, SHE WOLF OF THE SS (1974)

Ads for *Ilsa* promised us "THE MOST DREADED NAZI OF THEM ALL!" If they had described her instead as "the most bedded" they would have been more accurate. As scientific director of the Third

Reich's Medical Camp Number Nine, she abuses the women prisoners by day, the male prisoners by night, and all viewers of this movie for 95 minutes of excruciating stupidity. Former burlesque queen Dyanne Thorne plays the title role, and her outlandishly inflated breasts (whose 44-inch dimensions are duly celebrated in all promotional materials) suggest that the main purpose of her evil research has been perfecting the techniques of silicone implantation.

With these ingredients, the moviemakers might have treated this project most productively as an exercise in high (concentration) camp, but instead they try for a tone of compassionate solemnity. The movie begins with a personal message from producer Herman Traeger, which helpfully explains that "What you are about to see is based on documented fact." While admitting that "some liberties" have been taken for the sake of dramatic impact, he insists that "these medical atrocities are historically accurate." This clearly commendable sense of social responsibility leads the moviemakers to depict all of Ilsa's activities in detail as she sterilizes the most attractive women for future use in "Wehrmacht field brothels" and uses cattle prods to conduct "pain threshold" experiments on the others. The men, predictably, have a more interesting time of it: Our demented dominatrix selects a different candidate for her bedroom each night, and then, if he fails to satisfy her monumental lusts, he is castrated (without anesthetic) the next morning.

Dyanne Thorne may look like a fun-loving party girl, but she is actually supposed to be a dedicated scientist as Ilsa, She Wolf of the SS. *"Berlin laughs at my theory," she sneers, "but soon I vill give zem documented proof and zey vill laugh no more!"*

Needless to say, the only inmate who can please this petunia turns out to be a clean-cut American GI (Greg Knoph) and Ilsa instantly falls in love. After numerous plot twists and turns (and screams and squirms), he challenges her to prove that she can take pain as well as she can dish it out, and Ilsa, the sort of fun-loving fräulein who will try anything once, happily binds herself to her bed. This gives the pathetic prisoners a chance to murder all the guards and make their escape, but before they can go far they are squished by Nazi tanks. Clearly on a roll, these armored vehicles proceed to the camp itself, where they crush Ilsa (who is still tied to her bed) and all evidence of her atrocities. This cunning cover-up happily allows the film's producers to throw up their hands with puzzled expressions when pressed for documentation of their "historically accurate" presentation.

Though Vincent Canby of *The New York Times* described *Ilsa* as "the worst soft-core sex-and-violence film of the decade—and the funniest," for many viewers it will be impossible to laugh while watching it. The historical record of the actual "medical experiments" conducted by Dr. Josef Mengele and other Nazi scientists remains so hideous that even the most fanciful and foolish film references to these realities leave a disturbing aftertaste.

Dyanne Thorne's acting, on the other hand, is an occasion for uncontroversial and unbridled hilarity. She boasted to a reporter for the *Los Angeles Herald Examiner* that in addition to her extensive Las Vegas experience, she studied for a master's degree in anthropology at UCLA and pursued acting instruction under Lee Strasberg and Stella Adler. To remind us of these credentials, she presents Ilsa, She Wolf of the SS, as if she were a tragic heroine out of Eugene O'Neill or Tennessee Williams. "Mr. Strasberg trained me," she told the press, "and when you're well trained at something and have a smathering [sic] of experience you can do anything." She certainly appears to be *capable* of anything in this film, and spends so much time snarling at the camera that she threatens at any moment to lunge out and bite one of her co-stars.

Sadly enough, this film proved itself such a potent crowd-pleaser that two years later its director (Don Edmonds) teamed again with Miss Thorne for the eagerly awaited sequel. In *Ilsa, Harem Keeper of the Oil Sheiks* our anti-heroine faces new challenges in the present-day Middle East. She is so remarkably well-preserved after thirty years (and after her unfortunate encounter with a tank at the end of the last film) that one can only assume she has discovered Veronica Lake's astonishing maggot treatment for eternal youth. Ads for the new film promised: "ILSA'S BACK! MORE SADISTIC THAN EVER! TWICE AS MUCH WOMAN TO HATE!" By the time Dyanne Thorne made the last of her sadomasochistic money makers *(Wanda the Wicked Warden)* in 1979 her age (47) had at long last caught up with her bust size. She returned to Las Vegas, to pursue, no doubt, her studies in comparative anthropology, while making lucrative appearances in various novelty acts and revues.

AND THE WINNER IS . . .

. . . VERONICA LAKE IN
FLESH FEAST

With a grateful nod at the enthusiastic efforts of all the other contenders—in particular, Jack Herman—Miss Lake wins the award as the most hopelessly muddled and miscast mad scientist of them all. The incredibly inept technical details of the film help to emphasize her confusion: despite spending more than $20,000 on film stock alone, this 35-millimeter full-color presentation looks as if it were edited with a garden shears. Reaction shots—in some of which Miss Lake looks as if she is posing for a passport photo or a police mugshot—appear in the most unlikely places and help to reduce what little coherence the picture might otherwise possess.

As she recalls in her memoirs, *Flesh Feast* originated under the puzzling title *Time Is Terror,* through the initiative of her roommate and long-time "confidante," Yanka Mann. The house in Miami that Veronica shared with this eccentric Bulgarian actress and twenty-nine cats could have easily passed as a mad doctor's laboratory. "Yanka and I were cat lovers," the former star recalled. "I mean *really* cat lovers. You needed a gas mask when you walked in the door. All the furniture was torn to shreds and none of the cats had been toilet trained." In addition to these frolicsome felines, Yanka had befriended the operators of an industrial film production house who had always dreamed of making a theatrical feature. When she mentioned the availability of her friend, Veronica Lake, the aspiring producers saw the famous name as an instant passport to the big time.

Another actress would have treated this opportunity as a chance for a major comeback, but Veronica refused to alter the established patterns of her life. Her co-workers on the picture remembered that she always showed up on the set several hours late, and shooting seldom began before 3 P.M. During her big scenes Miss Lake seemed bored and preoccupied; like most viewers and critics who have watched this picture since its release, she had no understanding of what it was supposed to be about.

After finishing work on *Flesh Feast* in 1967, she went on to appear in dinner theater, to work on her autobiography, *Veronica,* and to run away to England when she became convinced the FBI had tapped her phone. The 52-year-old star died of hepatitis in 1973. She maintained till the end a philosophical attitude toward *Flesh Feast* and all the other disappointments and embarrassments of her later years. "I've reached a point in my life where it's the little things that count. I'm no longer interested in doing what's expected of me," she wrote. "I was always a rebel and

probably would have got much further had I changed my attitude. But when you think about it, I got pretty far without changing attitudes. I'm happier with that."

Dr. Karl Schumann (Phil Philbin) reassures his troubled colleague, Veronica Lake, that he still has faith that her "maggot treatments" will guarantee eternal youth for one very special patient in Flesh Feast.

THE LEAST CLASSY USE OF CLASSICAL MUSIC IN MOVIE HISTORY

Literally hundreds of movie soundtracks have borrowed from the works of great compos-ers in order to set the right mood or lend an air of dignity and sophistication to the action on screen. On occasion these matches of music and the movies have proven truly memorable; films such as Brief Encounter *(Rachmaninoff's Second Piano Concerto),* 2001 *(Richard Strauss's* Also Sprach Zarathustra*),* Death in Venice *(Mahler's Fifth Sym-phony),* Apocalypse Now *(Wagner's* Ride of the Valkyries*),* Ordinary People *(the Pachelbel* Kanon*), and even* 10 *(Ravel's* Bolero*) come to mind as particularly prominent examples. On occasion the clever use of a great piece of music in a film will dramatically increase its popularity; for years Mozart's Piano Concerto Number 21 has been known to many listeners as the* Elvira Madigan Concerto, *after the 1967 Swedish movie that used its second movement so effectively as a lyrical background score. It is difficult to imagine, however, that any of the nominees listed below could ever have enhanced the appreciation of the musical selections that they borrowed and abused: no one, for instance, has ever referred to the Shostakovich Fifth as "The* Brain Eaters *Symphony." The motion pictures described below prove conclusively that the use of classical music is in no way a guarantee of class.*

AND THE NOMINEES ARE...

MANIAC (1934)

This crudely shot and hilariously overacted oddity depicts the macabre adventures of a crazed lab assist-ant (Bill Woods) who murders his mad scientist boss in order to take over his sadistic transplant experi- ments. The dramatic highlight of the picture shows the title character plucking out the eye of a scream-ing, tortured cat and swallowing it whole while in-forming the audience, "Why, it's not unlike an oyster or a grape, ah-ha-ha-ha!" The main theme music for the picture is stolen from the last movement of Tchaikovsky's Symphony Number 6. The popular nickname of this sorrowful masterpiece (*Pathetique*) makes it seem almost appropriate as accompaniment to such a pathetic mess.

MARIHUANA, THE WEED WITH ROOTS IN HELL (1936)

This 1936 educational offering showed its serious intentions by using the heroic strains of Beethoven's Egmont Overture as its theme music.

Ludwig van Beethoven wrote his Egmont Overture to honor the memory of a courageous sixteenth-century statesman who became a martyr in the Dutch struggle for independence against the Spanish. Even without this background knowledge, it would be difficult to conceive of a more incongruous use for Beethoven's stirring, heroic score than as background for giggling, drug-crazed orgies, or as accompaniment to several scenes in which "Tony the Pusher" (Harley Wood) sells packets of the "killer weed" to his unsuspecting victims. In this primitive, pioneering anti-drug exploitation epic, marijuana (or "marihuana," as it is consistently spelled here) proves more potent than PCP and more deadly than heroin. It causes its users to take off their clothes (if they happen to be female), impregnate one another, abandon themselves to screaming fits, kidnap babies, hallucinate about talking ghosts, steal to support their "marihuana habit," and ultimately kill themselves with overdoses. Perhaps the producers of this "public-service" film (the same fine people who brought us *Maniac*) could blame the devastating

effects of this soul-destroying drug for their repeated and unforgivable misuse of some of Beethoven's noblest music.

THE LOVES OF BEETHOVEN (1936)

All of Beethoven's biographers have focused on his problems in developing relationships with women; sadly enough, the great composer never experienced sex in his life except in the company of prostitutes. Such inconvenient facts, however, failed to dissuade the French producers of this film from portraying the gloomy genius as an ooo-la-la master of *l'amour* in the classic Champs-Elysées mold. Historical purists who carped about the departures from reality in *Amadeus* had obviously never sampled this outrageously inaccurate and sugary concoction. Director Abel Gance (best known for his monumental silent-screen biography of Napoleon) concentrated on Beethoven's farcical difficulties in trying to juggle two pretty mistresses simultaneously. In the course of its 150 minutes, the movie not only misrepresents Beethoven's life, but also manages to trash his music. In one astonishing scene, as the great composer (Harry Baur) flirts shamelessly with a seductive chambermaid, the door bursts open and one of his mistresses suddenly walks in. As a close-up of his face shows his consternation and embarrassment, the soundtrack belches up a resounding "duh-duh-duh-*dum*!", reducing the well-known "Fate Knocking at the Door" theme from the Fifth Symphony to the level of situation comedy.

In the utterly misleading French fantasy The Loves of Beethoven, *Harry Baur as the title composer spends more time worrying about his complicated amours than he does writing music.*

RIDIN' THE CHEROKEE TRAIL (1941)

It's true that Tex Ritter won fame as a star of the Grand Ole Opry, but that didn't mean he was equipped to handle the demands of Giuseppe Verdi. Nevertheless, in the course of his adventures in *Ridin' the Cherokee Trail*, our hero offers his own distinctive version of a celebrated aria from *Rigoletto*.

While Ridin' the Cherokee Trail, *Tex Ritter (right) forces an Italian interloper in the Wild West to concede that cowboy music is superior to Verdi.*

The hero and his faithful pony, White Flash, have been taken prisoner by a nefarious, scheming Italian Fascist who mercilessly "subjects" them to numerous recordings of the immortal tenor Enrico Caruso. As he plays the record of Caruso singing *"La donna è mobile"* he taunts Ritter (and, by implication, America itself) by sneering, "You-a hear? An' do you hav-a any *cowboy* songs as good as dees?" Rushing forward to defend liberty and the flag, "America's Most Beloved Cowboy" puffs up his chest and declares that what Caruso is singing *is*, in actuality, a cowboy song. Picking up a guitar, he proceeds to provide the villainous foreigner with the "original" lyrics to Verdi's classic melody:

> Ol' Pete the bandit-o
> Robbed the ran-chero . . .

FIRE MAIDENS FROM OUTER SPACE (1956)

The "Polovetsian Dances" from Alexander Borodin's opera *Prince Igor* are noted for their lush, exotic romanticism. The producers of *Fire Maidens from Outer Space* (*see:* THE MOST PRIMITIVE MALE CHAUVINIST FANTASY IN MOVIE HISTORY) naturally reasoned that they could provide action for this music even more lush and exotic than Borodin's original tale of medieval Russia. As a result, the familiar strains of this haunting music (which also served as the basis for the hit tune "Stranger in Paradise" in the musical *Kismet*) assist the scantily clad inhabitants of the thirteenth moon of Jupiter in seducing a crew of visiting earthly astronauts and recruiting them for battle against the dreaded "Creature of Horror" and for repopulating their "reconstituted Atlantis." Their choppy version of the Borodin, meanwhile, appears to have been taken directly from an ancient and badly scratched record; at one point the soundtrack preserves the unmistakable sound of a needle dropping clumsily onto the disc.

THE BRAIN EATERS (1958)

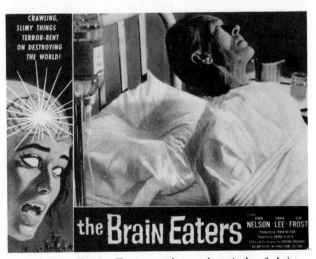

Just as The Brain Eaters *suck out the minds of their helpless victims, so too the producers of this film "borrow"—without credit—numerous classics of twentieth-century music for their pretentious patchwork background score.*

The music of Dmitri Shostakovich is without question intense and dramatic, and in the course of a long career this distinguished Soviet composer wrote scores for more than a dozen films. It is highly unlikely, however, that Shostakovich, who passed away in 1975, saw *The Brain Eaters* at the time of its release, or else he probably would have dropped dead some seventeen years before he did. His music—in particular, his Fifth Symphony—has been pirated shamelessly, and grinds away on the soundtrack through most of this idiotic excursion. The plot describes an invasion of earth by fuzzy little bedroom slippers with wiggling pipe-cleaner antennae. The creatures look cute as they shuffle along the floor, but they have developed a nasty habit of boring holes into human heads and sucking out the brains. Everyone naturally assumes that the visitors have arrived from outer space, but in a surprise twist we discover that they have actually emerged from the center of the earth and that, despite their deceptively youthful appearance, they are more than 200 million years old. At the end of the picture (by which time we may feel 200 million years old) one of earth's determined defenders proudly declares *"Nothing* could have lived through that!"—which is certainly true if the creatures in question happened to love music.

THE GREATEST STORY EVER TOLD (1965)

For his $20-million epic account of the life of Jesus, producer-director George Stevens commissioned a lavish score by veteran Hollywood composer Alfred Newman. Stevens used most of this music in the finished film, but for some reason felt that the exultant strains that Newman had specifically written for the raising of Lazarus and for the big Resurrection scene failed to measure up. Instead the moviemaker wanted Handel's Hallelujah Chorus, and so arranged for the music to come roaring at us from out of absolutely nowhere, suddenly blasting viewers out of their seats and, presumably, helping blast Lazarus out of his tomb. "More of *The Messiah* is heard after Christ rises on the third day," observed Brendan Gill in *The New Yorker*, "but by then it seems a sort of musical comedy reprise, and I wouldn't have been surprised if the soundtrack had favored us with a stanza or two of 'Oh, What a Beautiful Mornin'.'" Several of Stevens' associates had warned him against using Handel's overly familiar music in such an obvious and ham-fisted way, but the legendary director refused to listen to them. "This movie," he reportedly announced to his colleagues, "will make Handel immortal."

PROPHECY (1979)

This tale of a murderous mutant bear (*see:* THE MOST UNBEARABLE BEAR MOVIE EVER MADE) begins with a search party making its way through the Maine woods to investigate mysterious goings-on. In short order they are chewed and clawed to death by the ravening beast; director John Frankenheimer then cuts to early morning, and a long, lingering look at each one of the mutilated corpses. This gruesome and seemingly endless sequence is inexplicably accompanied by the lush, dreamy second movement of Brahms' Fourth Symphony. Considering this wretched perversion of beautiful music, it is small wonder that, a few scenes later, the heroine (played by Talia Shire) wants to quit her job as cellist in a symphony orchestra.

CRIMES OF PASSION (1984)

Kathleen Turner conducts Dvořák's "New World" Symphony while Anthony Perkins savors the aroma of her feet in Ken Russell's unspeakable stinker, Crimes of Passion.

There are certainly worse films than Ken Russell's *Crimes of Passion,* but it is difficult to imagine a more thoroughly unpleasant moviegoing experience. Kathleen Turner plays a stylish young industrial designer who spends all her free time as a skid-row streetwalker and manages to attract the attention of a deranged derelict preacher (Anthony Perkins, who else?) who tries to murder her with a gigantic steel dildo. In the meantime, Miss Turner (as "China Blue") entertains a nauseating variety of kinky customers in her filthy neon-lit hotel room, giving director Russell the chance to express his distaste for sexuality in all its forms and for life in general. To the despair of even the most casual music lovers, all of this is played out over a background of Antonín Dvořák's magnificent New World Symphony. The well-loved themes have been mercilessly jazzed up in lame renditions for synthesizer, but they are all there, and none of the symphony's four movements escapes contamination. A few critics suggested that the music had been chosen deliberately to emphasize the "new world" of contemporary sexuality, or perhaps to advertise the fact that "New World Pictures" claimed responsibility for this atrocity.

AND THE WINNER IS . . .

. . . THE BRAIN EATERS

None of the pictures listed above used classical music as extensively—or incompetently—as this soporific sci-fi thriller. In addition to the first movement from the Shostakovich Fifth Symphony—which, note for note, provides the movie with its endlessly repeated main theme—the same composer's First and Tenth symphonies have also been brutally ransacked, with

big undigested chunks of music ripped, bleeding, from their context and plunked down at irrelevant moments in the soundtrack. As if this weren't enough, the producers also attacked Shostakovich's Soviet colleague Sergei Prokofiev (1891–1953), snatching moments from his Seventh Symphony, his ballets *Romeo and Juliet* and *Cinderella*, and his celebrated score to the great Eisenstein film *Alexander Nevsky* (1938). Then, entirely out of left field, they invaded Richard Wagner's *Tristan und Isolde* for various orchestral interludes. All of this "borrowing" is accomplished with an absolute maximum of clumsiness: the different pieces bump up against one another with no transitions or breaks and with all their jagged edges showing; then, after running for a while, the music is suddenly cut off in the middle of a phrase.

It's hard to believe that anyone would want to take credit for this abysmally awkward display, but the name "Tom Jonson" proudly appears on film as the man solely responsible for its music. Shostakovich, Prokofiev, and Wagner are never mentioned in the credits, nor do their names appear in the official "Music Cue Sheet" filed with ASCAP (The American Society of Composers, Authors and Publishers) at the time of the movie's release. Our curiosity led us to secure a copy of this astonishing document, which lists twenty-nine pieces of "original" music composed especially for the film. In each case a title has been appended to correspond to the action on film, and "Tom Jonson" is listed as sole composer. And so, through the magic of mendacity, the Prelude to Act III of Wagner's *Tristan* becomes "Up the Hatch" by Tom Jonson, while Prokofiev's "Romeo and Juliet Before Parting" is miraculously transformed into Tom Jonson's haunting "Attack of a Parasite."

Little is known about the resourceful Mr. Jonson. His name never turned up on another motion picture, and the music house in Woburn, Massachusetts, which is officially listed as publisher of his original "compositions" has a disconnected telephone number.

Giving him the benefit of every doubt, perhaps this mysterious man of music felt he was doing his patriotic duty by stealing so flagrantly from foreign composers—especially a contemporary Commie like Dmitri Shostakovich. Even if he could have gotten formal permission to use his music, why give credit to one of *them*. In fact, back in the dark Cold War years of 1958, Mr. Jonson may have believed that by robbing two Russkie composers to enrich the texture of *The Brain Eaters,* he was actually striking a mighty blow for the American Way of Life . . . a way of life most beautifully and memorably extolled, perhaps, by the idyllic musical films celebrated in our next category. . . .

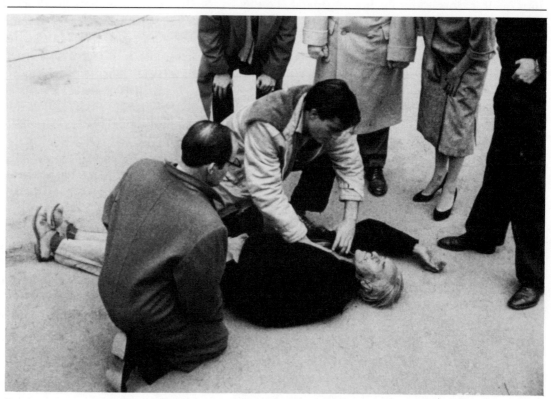

No, that's not Dmitri Shostakovich who's passed out in shock at the way his music's been abused—it's just another on-screen snack (Saul Bronson) for The Brain Eaters.

THE WORST
BEACH PARTY MOVIE
EVER MADE

*I*n *1960 MGM celebrated the beginning of an exciting new decade by releasing* Where
the Boys Are, *a harmless fantasy about the mating rituals of migratory college
students who flock to the beaches of Fort Lauderdale, Florida, every spring. Despite a ho-hum
reaction from critics and most other adults, the picture became a smash hit with America's
teens and inspired a major new Hollywood trend. During the next few years all the major
studios, and a host of independent producers, cashed in on the pubescent public's seemingly
insatiable appetite for sun, surf, bikinis, bonfires, and rancid rock 'n' roll.*

*Most people today remember only the best-known products of this formula—including
such classics as* Gidget Goes Hawaiian *(1961) and* Beach Blanket Bingo *(1965). There
were, however, more than a hundred of these films, cranked out with incredible speed (and
breathtaking carelessness) during the brief heyday of this distinctive art form in the golden
years between 1962 and 1966. With titles ranging from* It's a Bikini World *to* Beach
Party Italian Style, *these cloying comedies presented a strangely sanitized view of adolescent reality. The romantic leads (including, of course, those perennial beach buddies Frankie
Avalon and Annette Funicello) engaged in nothing more steamy than light kissing and
volleyball while the audience enjoyed an excuse for watching whole squadrons of starlets
exposing their bodies in a socially acceptable setting. The best of the surf-and-suntan cinema
offered an appealingly empty-headed sort of innocence—the worst of them displayed a
lead-footed clumsiness in pursuit of their obviously exploitative ends that rendered them all
but unendurable. This is particularly true of those Frankie-come-lately attempts to revive
the dead trend which turned up in the jaded eighties and which are duly noted below.*

*Historians might argue that the one cultural development which actually got the beach
ball rolling in the first place—and which has sustained it on the big screen over the years
—was the popularization of the skimpy two-piece bathing suit known as the bikini. This
controversial garment took its name from the Bikini Atoll in the South Pacific, site of a
well-publicized series of United States atomic tests in 1946. The designer of the new
swimwear, Louis Reard, seemed to be suggesting that his product would produce a reaction*

on the world's beaches resembling the detonation of an atomic device. In any event, it seemed a fatefully appropriate designation for an article of clothing destined to figure so prominently in several of Hollywood's most memorable cinematic bombs.

AND THE NOMINEES ARE...

THE HORROR OF PARTY BEACH (1964)

"COME ON IN, THE RADIATION'S FINE!": The dreaded atomic zombie-monster rears its ugly head in The Horror of Party Beach.

Oh, sure, it's easy to belittle *The Horror of Party Beach.* In his book *Danse Macabre,* best-selling novelist Stephen King dismisses it as "an abysmal little wet fart of a picture." Many others, including critics for the *Monthly Film Bulletin,* the New York *Herald Tribune,* and the fan magazine *Monster Times,* have classified it as one of the most incompetent horror films ever made, while we ourselves included it in our 1978 book, *The Fifty Worst Films of All Time.*

But now, more than twenty years after Twentieth Century–Fox first unleashed its *Horror* on an unsuspecting world, the time has come, we believe, for a sober second look and a thorough reappraisal. Having endured at least a dozen screenings of this film, we have come, at last, to appreciate some of the deeper themes and higher purposes beneath its occasionally amateurish facade.

The plot of this misunderstood masterpiece is easily summarized. The camera discovers human skulls lying in a shipwreck at the bottom of the sea. In the same vicinity, a steel drum instructively marked RADIOACTIVE WASTE leaks its poisons into the ocean. Before our eyes, the pollutants combine with the skeletal remains to form monsters in hideous rubber suits, with light bulbs for eyes, mouths bulging with sausages, and several layers of stiff and leafy scales that give them a resemblance to ambulatory artichokes. These creatures invade a dreary strip of the Connecticut coast exclusively inhabited by cretinous rejects from Broadway chorus lines who are foolishly pretending to be beach-partying teenagers. After several gruesome murders Dr. Gavin, the friendly neighborhood "scientist" and father of the uncrowned queen of these perpetually gyrating revelers, discovers an ingenious means of defeating the sea zombies and Saving Humanity. In the grand finale the good doctor and his associates toss sodium pellets on the two marauders from the ocean depths, who obligingly ignite like a pair of Fourth of July sparklers. Then, according to the official synopsis provided by the studio: "A pall of smoke lingers for a while over the scene—and then that too is gone— Exhausted but triumphant, the little group returns to town."

This strange story may seem simple at first glance, but sensitive viewers will surely discern the resonance in the deceptively slender plot materials that have allowed *The Horror* to achieve the status of an international cult film. To director-producer Del (*I Eat Your Skin*) Tenney and screenwriter Richard (*Psychomania*) Hilliard the monsters are far more than radioactive zombies—they are persuasive and deeply disturbing symbols of the unrestrained adolescent lust that had, by 1964, begun to threaten America's youth. On the surface, perhaps, they may be creatures from the ocean floor but in a deeper sense they are *monsters from the id*—emerging from the primal ooze to disturb the playful, libidinous entertainments of the golden youth on Party Beach. The cluster of hot dogs that protrudes so memorably from the mouth of each beast, and which has puzzled so many prior students of this film, makes perfect sense in the context of this overall interpretation. The swollen sausages perfectly express the crude, singleminded desires of these creatures, and, in filling their mouths, have even deprived them of the fundamentally humanizing power of speech. Significantly, these dreaded killers walk in a strange crouch throughout the film and stand fully erect only at those moments when they are slaughtering a beach bunny.

A careful consideration of these seemingly random killings reveals a punishing, puritanical pattern to the monsters' mayhem. The first victim is Tina (Marilyn Clarke), companion to Hank (John Scott), the first surfer/scientist in the history of beach party films and lab assistant to the saintly Dr. Gavin. Hank and the doctor (Allan Laurel) clearly represent the superego and the struggle within each of us to contain our rampaging hormones. We hear Hank pleading with his girlfriend to "grow up" and abandon the "Wigglin'-and-a-Wobblin'" practiced by the Party Beach regulars and celebrated (in the song of that name) by the lusty rock 'n' rollers the Del Aires. Tragically, Tina ignores his sound advice, repairs to her old haunts by the seashore, and performs a sizzling striptease for a group of dangerously aroused bikers. To cool off after this frenzied display, the panting girl jumps into the ocean—where an atomic horror suddenly rears its head and proceeds to tear her to shreds. An artful close-up focuses on one shapely leg, horribly covered with dripping red nail polish—summarizing, with one searing image, the fundamental message of the picture.

This notion of the deadly consequences of unrestrained sexuality is hammered home with relentless force. Each murder is immediately preceded by some scene of abandon or innuendo, and the contrapuntal structure of the film, in which the twin themes of orgiastic adolescence and avenging sea beasts are artfully woven together, form a fugue of overwhelming weight in the celebrated slumber party scene. Here, seven saucy wenches from a local sorority gather at midnight to sing folk songs and to await a visit from a group of naughty fraternity boys. At the very moment of the expected raid, one of the giggling girls tells her colleagues, "I smell something awful . . . I hope they don't throw fish again like they did last year!" These ironic words give way to a brutal sequence of pillage and plunder, with the monsters

Some of the carefree teenagers of Stamford, Connecticut, perform a new dance craze called the Zombie Stomp just moments before they are attacked by murderous mutants from beneath the sea.

bringing death and destruction in place of the anticipated sensual delights of the frat boys. The spectacle is hardly subtle, but it overwhelms the viewer with its naive power.

The personality of Eulabelle (as formidably portrayed by Eulabelle Moore) is, of course, an inextricable element in the grand scheme of the film. Some film historians have criticized this characterization as an offensive racist stereotype, citing her position as Dr. Gavin's black maid, her embarrassing attempts to provide comic relief through dialect humor, and her overall role as an overweight, latter-day Stephanie Fetchit. In one typical interchange Dr. Gavin shows the deep affection behind their master/servant relationship. "You better go to bed, Eulabelle," he declares. "Did you lock up?" She responds enthusiastically: "Locked—double-locked, *an'* triple-locked! Ain't no monsters gonna git in here tonight—no, *suh*!!" But this dusky earth mother is something more than a two-dimensional Aunt Jemima—while all the other characters are at a loss to explain the origins of the creatures from the sea, Eulabelle offers her own intriguing theory. "It's duh Voo-Doo, I tells ya! . . . It's duh Voo-Doo! Dat's what it is! It's duh

Voo-Doo, all right!" In a sense, her role within the symbolic landscape of the film is consistent with the role of black characters in much classic American literature of the nineteenth century and the timeless image of these mysteriously potent figures within our national unconscious. Professor Leslie Fiedler and other literary critics have described the notion that blacks are somehow in touch with the elements, with nature, and with their own sexuality in a way that can only be envied by troubled representatives of the majority culture. Eulabelle, located in the unlikely environs of Party Beach, seems destined to play this role of high priestess, or oracle, and to reveal the deeper, organic mysteries beneath the superficial confusion in the plot. It is hardly a coincidence that it is Eulabelle, with her deep, instinctive wisdom, who ultimately reveals the secret that provides the key to vanquishing the monsters, and to thereby ending the neurotic association of libidinous indulgence and bloody dismemberment. At a key moment in Dr. Gavin's laboratory she accidentally spills a beaker of sodium over a severed monster paw and watches as it goes up in flame. Though she tries to apologize ("Oh, Doctah Gavin, I'se sorry! Oh, Lawdy, Lawdy!"), the brilliant scientist immediately sees the potential in her inadvertent discovery. "Sodium! Plain old sodium!" he exclaims. "There's the answer we've been searching for!" It is this common element ("plain old sodium") in its humility that combines with Eulabelle and her homespun nobility to provide deliverance for humanity.

Not to be confused with the aforementioned murderous mutants from beneath the sea, the red-hot "big beat" band, the Del Aires, contributes its swingin' sounds to the ongoing festivities at Party Beach.

This motion picture, in other words, is bursting with ideas and imagination as director Tenney strains against the normal conventions of the beach party movie and tries his best to expand the expressive horizons of the form. While most examples of the genre are full of bright colors and simpleminded "feel good" music, the prevailing atmosphere in *The Horror of Party Beach* is appropriately moody and somber. The teenagers in the film never come to the beach to dance, except, it would seem, on gloomy or overcast days—or else these scenes have been lit and shot so incompetently that they only appear hazy. In any event, the dim, grainy, black and white look of this film seems to emphasize that the beach at Stamford, Connecticut (where the action took place), is indeed a long way from the celebrated shores of Malibu and Santa Monica.

Moreover, the Del Aires, who provide the haunting music in the film, are hardly the smiling and tanned Aryan surf jockeys found in most beach pictures. These four troubadours are dedicated musicians in striped shirts, poets who hide their serious intentions behind a facade of gooniness and feature a leader who looks as if he may grow up to become Elvis Costello. Their work—in particular the unforgettable theme song of the picture, "The Zombie Stomp"—provides just the right touch of eerie foreboding, combined with a desperate but clearly doomed attempt to return to the innocent and playful joys of youth, as they wail to the audience:

> Baby, baby, don't you *care*?
> Something here lookin' kinda weird.
> Honey, I'm no Frankenstein.
> Oh, yeah, baby, really I feel fine.

To emphasize the contributions of the Del Aires, Twentieth Century–Fox billed *The Horror of Party Beach* as "The First Horror Monster Musical!"—a marketing mistake that may have played a role in preventing critics from giving the picture the serious consideration it so richly deserved. In his review for *The New York Times*, Eugene Archer declared that "the question in *The Horror of Party Beach* is which is more horrible—the monsters or the rock 'n' roll?" while *Newsweek* suggested that "musical numbers by the Del Aires push this Twentieth Century–Fox release over the bottom as the worst movie of the last twelve months."

This cool response must have been profoundly discouraging to that underappreciated *auteur*, Del Tenney; following release of *The Horror*, this former off-

Broadway actor directed no further feature films. Those who wish to study the evolution of his unique style will have to content themselves with his beach party masterpiece and two prior efforts: a stylish thriller called *The Curse of the Living Corpse* (1963, starring his wife, actress Margo Hartman, and a young actor named Roy Scheider in the title role) and the unreleased zombie musical extravaganza, *Voodoo Bloodbath*. In 1971, more than seven years after completing *Voodoo*, Tenney finally managed to sell it to the aptly named producer Jerry Gross, who retitled it *I Eat Your Skin* and released it as part of a popular double bill along with his own magnum opus, *I Drink Your Blood*.

By that time Tenney had already returned to his first love—the stage—and served as a director of several regional theaters in New England. At last report, he had left the Del Aires, Dr. Gavin, and the sausage-mouthed monsters far behind him and was working as artistic director of the Eugene O'Neill Theater Center in New York City. He has, alas, no current plans to return to the world of motion pictures.

HOW TO STUFF A WILD BIKINI (1965)

A dozen muscular surfers make their way toward the water with boards under their arms and dazzling smiles pasted on their faces when, lo and behold, they spot a leopard-skin bikini magically suspended in midair.

With his chin dropping down to his tanned chest in order to register astonishment, "Bonehead" (played by Jody McCrea, son of Hollywood veteran Joel McCrea) comments to his similarly stunned colleagues, "Man, dig that *wild* bikini!"

The response to his observation gives the film its title and its theme. "Yeah," quoth Johnny (John Ashley), "but it ain't nuthin' . . . without the stuffin'!"

The rest of the California cretins react to this provocation by placing their hands on their knees, wiggling their heads from side to side, and singing directly to the camera.

> Take a girl that's lovely as can be,
> Any girl will do as long as she's
> A thirty-six—
> Twenty-two—
> Thirty-six—
> That's how you . . .
> *Stuff* a wild bi—kee—eee—neee!

John Ashley (with guitar) *tries to charm* Playboy Playmate Jo Collins *by singing her the title song from* How to Stuff a Wild Bikini.

This opening musical number eloquently conveys the unique flavor of this insipid sequel-to-a-sequel-to-a-sequel-to-a-sequel. Hailed by Bosley Crowther of *The New York Times* as "the worst film of the last two and maybe the next two years," *Wild Bikini* proved to be the grand finale in a history-making series of beach party movies from American International Pictures. The fun (and the profits) began with the original *Beach Party* in 1963, then continued with such distinguished titles as *Muscle Beach Party* (1964), *Bikini Beach* (1964), and the ever-popular *Beach Blanket Bingo* (1965). Each of these films starred singing sensation Frankie Avalon and grown-up Mickey Mouse Clubber Annette Funicello as Frankie and Dee Dee, a pair of young lovebirds who spend all their time walking back and forth across the shining sands in modest bathing suits, "roasting weenies" in seaside barbecues, waxing surfboards, fending off the advances of various male and female interlopers, and singing some of the silliest love songs ever composed.

What makes *How to Stuff a Wild Bikini* even worse than its putrid predecessors is the dispirited approach of the two stars. By 1965 Frankie Avalon had begun to nurse professional aspirations that made him a bit too big for his bathing britches. He played lead roles in five feature films that year—including Bob Hope's *I'll Take Sweden* and the title part in the heavily promoted "astro-nut" comedy *Sergeant Deadhead*—and it seemed he had a chance to break through to mainstream stardom. In any event, he didn't want to spend the rest of his career cavorting in a bathing suit in front of unconvincing process shots of the Pacific as the aging consort to a Mouseketeer. Frankie accepted this final beach party role only with great reluctance, and his curious credit at the end of the picture reflected the awkward situation. After all the other actors have been identified, the titles on the screen finally get around to identifying the star: "The Producers Wish to Extend a Special Thanks to Frankie Avalon as Frankie—Watch for *Sergeant Deadhead*!"

Despite this elaborate gesture of appreciation, Avalon made himself available for only a few hours of filming, and he appears for a grand total of seven minutes in the finished picture. The plot is designed to account for his absence: Frankie is supposedly in Tahiti on navy reserve duty, while Dee Dee waits for him back at the beach party. Frankie is naturally concerned that while the cool cat is away, the Mouseketeer may play; in fact, given the sophisticated sensuality of the beach party series, she might even hold hands with another boy! To prevent such a calamitous occurrence, he meets with a Tahitian witch doctor named Bwana-Chickie-Baby, played by the 70-year-old Buster Keaton in a straw hat and a grass skirt. The good doctor casts a spell that allows Avalon's "spirit" to take the form of a molting pelican who flies across the ocean to serve as chaperone to the desirous Dee Dee. The appearance of this enchanted bird back in California allows us to sense Frankie's presence even when he's nowhere to be seen.

Annette, meanwhile, suffers a very different sort of problem: We see altogether too *much* of her. By the time she showed up for work on *How to Stuff a Wild Bikini* she was more than five months pregnant with her first child. Perhaps American International should have considered retitling the picture *How to Stuff a Wild Maternity Dress*, but instead director William Asher (of television's *Bewitched* series) did his best to conceal his star's delicate condition. Miss Funicello is usually shown only from the waist up, and she wears spacious, flowing, and appropriately matronly bathing suits that bear about as much relationship to a bikini as does Barnum and Bailey's Big Top to a one-man pup tent. Her performance is, in a word, regal: for most of the movie she sits in solitary splendor on a beach blanket while her carefree friends dance and caper around her. Despite her fabled musical abilities, Annette solos in only one song, "The Perfect Boy." She is, of course, seated on the sand in a floral muumuu and backed up by a wiggling chorus of bathing beauties as she soulfully intones:

ANNETTE: The perfect boy doesn't have to be a Hercules!

CHORUS: Her-cu-leees!

ANNETTE: The perfect boy doesn't have to be Euripides!

CHORUS: 'Rip-pi-deees! . . .

The thought that these squealing surfer girls have been nursing a secret fantasy of going out with Euripides is only one of many curious notions advanced by this film.

Annette Funicello used flouncy muumuus and circles of adoring extras to conceal her increasingly obvious pregnancy during the shooting of How to Stuff a Wild Bikini.

Another is the idea that all the men in the plot will look beyond the surface charms of the four *Playboy* Playmates and other Beach Blanket Bimbos who participate in the seaside revels, and will concentrate instead on the irresistible "inner beauty" locked within Annette's bulky body. Mickey Rooney, for instance, plays an advertising executive named Peachy Keene who plans to anoint Annette as the winner of a promotional competition for the most beautiful girl in America. But before our pregnant princess can claim the crown, she must first win a cross-country motorcycle race sponsored by the ad agency. If this sounds confusing here, it is even harder to follow the convoluted developments in the film itself, because, as the producers boasted in their promotional materials: "For the first time a 'beach' film is full of the songs and music which tells [sic] the story instead of using the musical numbers as mere fill-ins or interludes." These tuneful bits of narration come from diverse sources, including highlighted performances by Harvey Lembeck (as the biker chieftain, Eric von Zipper), Mickey Rooney, Brian Donlevy (as advertising tycoon Big Deal MacPherson), Dwayne *(Dobie Gillis)* Hickman, and the Kingsmen, the short-lived group responsible for making America's youth listen v-e-r-y closely to "Louie Louie." These various contributions add up to what Howard Thompson of *The New York Times* considers "*the* worst musical score since 1925 (the year before sound movies)."

The producers tried to top this achievement a year later with a last-gasp effort at reviving their fading formula. By this time Frankie Avalon refused to provide even seven minutes of his time, and Annette was busy with her baby, so they had to rely on other stars to populate their party, including Tommy Kirk, Nancy Sinatra, Deborah Walley, Francis X. Bushman, Basil Rathbone, Boris Karloff, and George Barrows (who played Ro-Man in the immortal *Robot Monster*) as "Monstro the Gorilla." The ungainly vehicle meant to accommodate these diverse talents went through a dizzying change of titles, from its initial designation as *Beach Party in a Haunted House,* to *Pajama Party in the Haunted House,* to *Slumber Party in a Haunted House,* to *Slumber Party in Horror House,* to *Bikini Party in a Haunted House,* to *Ghost in the Glass Bikini,* to its final designation as *The Ghost in the Invisible Bikini.*

It might have been a better idea to stick with one of the interim titles, since the picture provided something of a slumber party for its audiences. In any event, the merrymakers on the beach seemed to be suddenly engulfed in a tidal wave of public indifference, as patient moviegoers, after suffering through this last foolish film and the even greater indignities of *Wild Bikini,* at long last turned around and told the producers to stuff it.

THE BEACH GIRLS AND THE MONSTER (ALTERNATE TITLES: *MONSTER FROM THE SURF* AND *SURF TERROR*) (1965)

Moviegoers of ripe enough age will surely remember Jon Hall: he won fame as a primitive loinclothed hunk in some two dozen South Seas, Arabian Nights, and Darkest Africa movies. This native-born son of exotic Fresno, California, is perhaps best known as Dorothy Lamour's island consort in John Ford's *The Hurricane* (1937), or as the heroic lead in the popular 1950s television series *Ramar of the Jungle.* As a sort of male equivalent of Yvonne De Carlo or Maria Montez, Hall starred in such other notable projects as *South of Pago Pago* (1940), *Aloma of the South Seas* (1941), *White Savage* (1943), *Cobra Woman* (1944), *The Invisible Man's Revenge* (1944), *San Diego, I Love You* (1944), and *Zamba* (1949).

Unfortunately, while accumulating these credits the redoubtable star also accumulated a good deal of excess body weight, and by the mid-fifties he had to hang up his loincloth for good. With no acting work to occupy his time, he pursued his hobbies and became known in the motion picture community as something of a lovable eccentric. No one in Hollywood knew more about camera equipment or tinkered with it more passionately; in his later years he invented a complex lens and printing process that were adapted by NASA for filming the space shuttle. In his home in the Hollywood Hills, Hall put together a personal collection of camera, sound, and lighting gear so advanced that on several occasions major studios paid handsomely for the privilege of using it.

These technical treasures led to Hall's last starring role, and his only venture as a director. In 1964 independent producers Ed Janis and Mark Lipsky (the founder of the Reddi Wip Whipped Cream Corporation) approached the aging nature boy and asked to borrow his motion picture equipment. Instead of offering Hall a straight rental agreement, or a year's supply of Reddi Wip, the twin tycoons proposed that he take a percentage of the profits in their "can't miss" project. The veteran star listened attentively and then startled the ambitious moguls with a counterproposal: they could use all of his various lights and cameras if they gave him a chance to direct the picture himself and to play the leading role. Considering Hall's lack of directorial experience and his paunchy, puffy physical condition, the producers knew they were taking a risk by agreeing to his demands, but the appealing prospect of all that free motion picture equipment persuaded them to make the deal.

The idea of making a spectacular comeback as a director-star filled Hall with such unbounded enthusiasm that he overlooked the obvious flaws in the script that came to him along with the project. Written by Joan Gardner, a former production assistant for the kiddie TV show *Kukla, Fran and Ollie* and the wife of co-producer Ed Janis, the story showed the unmistakable influence of the seminal surf-and-splatter saga *The Horror of Party Beach.* Once again a mysterious creature with a sweet tooth for bathing beauties emerges from the waves to interrupt the orgiastic revels of a group of wildly dancing teenagers. This time, however, the pathetically low budget allows us to see only one monster, instead of the two zombies who stalk the Connecticut shore in the previous film. To explain this economy move, Joan Gardner gives her plot a startling twist—at the end of the picture we learn that the weirdo from the deep is only an oceanographer dressed in a seaweed suit. As the last tragic lines explain to the audience, he has undertaken the masquerade and launched his murderous rampage in order to save his son from the baleful influence of the local surfers.

This central role of the scientist/surf monster is of course played by Jon Hall. In full battle regalia, with a dripping kelp shawl, gaping maw, and pointed headpiece, he's supposed to look terrifying, but as Kevin Thomas commented in the *Los Angeles Times,* "He's about as scary as one of those rubber baby toys that squeak when you squeeze them." When he's not dressed to kill, Hall walks around in a smoking jacket belted tight around his considerable girth and mutters over the deterioration of his on-screen domestic situation. His heartless-but-buxom second wife (former showgirl Sue Casey) flirts with every surfer on the beach and tells Hall "the honeymoon's over." His grown son (Arnold Lessing) turns away from the family oceanography business and coldly rejects his father's values. "There's more to life than test tubes and fish!" he passionately declares in one key scene. "I'm gonna surf on the beach in Waikiki—and enjoy it! Man, life goes too fast!"

Is it any wonder that the professor begins to feel a powerful resentment toward the beach party set? When he talks to the local sheriff about the scientific background to the monster murders, he illogically holds the surfers responsible. "Strange," says the peace officer. "I always thought them to be a nice bunch of kids trying to find themselves."

"Hah!" Hall explodes. "They'll find themselves in your jail one day! They contribute absolutely nothing to a decent society."

The professor, on the other hand, contributes all sorts of erudite observations, commenting on the

Exhausted after their fabulous night together beside the pounding surf, a thrill-seeking beach bunny (Margo Sweet) relaxes in the big green arms of director-star Jon Hall during a romantic moment from The Beach Girls and the Monster.

traces of the killer creature, "It looks exactly like the South American fantigua fish—a deadly man-eater. . . . It's not the *claw* print of any fish in *this* area!" The entire concept of fish with claws obviously constitutes a major oceanographic breakthrough.

Even with all the tedious speeches, Hall wound up with barely sixty minutes of usable footage after he had finished shooting the original script. This called for some creative padding so that distributors would accept the film as a feature, and conveniently enough the director-star owned an extensive library of stock footage that could be adapted for this purpose. Halfway into the film a crippled former surfer (Walker Edmiston) comes up to the oceanographer's son with a reel of film under his arm. "Come on," he says, "hit the lights! Wait till you see these films—the surf's great!" The audience is then subjected to a series of grainy, black and white surfing clips which run, without interruption for dialogue or narration of any kind, for a full seven and a half minutes on screen. The only accompaniment to this perfectly pedestrian footage is some perfectly pedestrian "surf music" for bongos and electric guitar, composed by that well-known creative powerhouse Frank Sinatra, Jr.

Fortunately Mr. Sinatra, Jr., resisted the temptation of singing on the soundtrack, but Walker Edmiston, co-star of the film and the voice of "Cecil the Seasick Sea Serpent" on the *Beany and Cecil* cartoon series, rushes in to fill the gap. In a robust but off-key baritone reminiscent of Burt Reynolds in *The Best Little Whorehouse in Texas,* he croons the touching, folksy ballad "Monster in the Surf" while his friends huddle around a beachside bonfire:

> There's a monster in the surf—
> Yeah, yeah, yeah!
> There's a monster in the surf—
> Yeah, yeah, yeah!
> Everybody's sleeping,
> Monster comes a-creeping,
> Yeah, yeah, yeah!
> Yeah, yeah, yeah!

The song *is* strangely catchy, in the style of a particularly insipid advertising jingle, but it hardly justifies the hysterical hyperbole used in the ads for the film:

"PLUCKED FROM TODAY'S BEAT! THE GO! GO! GO! GENERATION! ITS KICKS, ITS DRAGS, ITS TUMULT AND SONG!"

In the midst of all the tumult and song we are meant to shed a tear for the tragic oceanographer, who is ultimately exposed as the alter ego of the creature. When one of his victims tears off his monster mask, Hall steals an MG convertible which has been conveniently waiting for him in a beach parking lot with the keys in the ignition. With his eyebrows madly twitching, but still wearing his monster suit from the neck down, he drives at top speed into Malibu Canyon. The sheriff's deputies are after

As part of the fun and frolic in The Beach Girls and the Monster, *the musical talents of teen idol Arnold Lessing send a bevy of astonishingly glamorous beach bunnies into a frenzy of self-expression.*

him now: the charge of impersonating a radioactive fish-zombie is a serious offense. "We've got to stop him, Sheriff," comments the professor's wayward son. "I think he's gone mad!" He does, at last, go quite literally around the bend, driving off the edge of a cliff and plunging to his fiery doom. The only problem with this spectacular finish is that Hall used some of his stock footage to show the car going over the side, and the boxy sedan depicted is at least ten years older and five feet longer than the MG convertible that he has been driving during the chase.

This climactic crash proved sadly prophetic for the fate of the film and the comeback attempt of its star. Despite a gala premiere in a drive-in in Bakersfield, California, and several attempts at alternate titles (*Surf Terror* and *Monster from the Surf*), *The Beach Girls and the Monster* disappeared beneath the waves after a disastrous three-week run. As the Hollywood *Citizen-News* declared in its representative review, "Reading the telephone directory would probably prove more entertaining and exciting and suspenseful and satisfying and psychologically rewarding than does this production."

Jon Hall never again directed or appeared in a feature film. In the fourteen years remaining to him, he continued to dream of a comeback; just a few months before his death the 66-year-old actor confessed to a reporter that he had long been hoping for the right movie or television role but "the part just never came." On December 13, 1979, after undergoing a series of chemotherapy treatments for what had been diagnosed as terminal cancer, he put an end to his pain with a self-inflicted gunshot wound. The newspaper obituaries all featured photos of Hall in his glory days, wearing the inevitable sarong, and stressed his achievements as a camera designer while graciously omitting any mention whatever of his final infamous film.

SURF II (1984)

It is a familiar movie convention that a single bump on the head can lead to all sorts of embarrassment, causing people to lose their memories, change personalities, or fall in love. In the case of aspiring director Randall Badat, however, a real-life knock on the noggin led to even more disastrous consequences: It inspired him to make the motion picture *Surf II*. In an interview with the *Los Angeles Times,* he explained the origins of the film in dramatic terms: "I was swimming and got hit on the head with a surfboard. I went to a party filled with pain killers and got tired of explaining what really happened, so I started talking nonsense." A few days later he used this nonsense as the basis for a movie treatment that made a feeble attempt to satirize the beach party hits of yesteryear.

The plot concerns the evil machinations of a high school nerd named Menlo Schwartzer (Eddie Deezen) who has been consistently victimized by a group of arrogant surfers. After they spike his Coca-Cola with female hormones, causing him to sprout a pair of embarrassingly small and shapeless breasts, Menlo retreats to a laboratory on the ocean floor to plot his revenge. There he develops a secret formula for "Buzz Cola," a concoction that seems to be composed of equal parts NutraSweet and motor oil, and which turns wholesome lunk-headed surfers into pasty-white lunk-headed punk surf zombies. After recruiting an "army" of these surf zombies (which, for this ultra-low-budget excursion, means about eight of them), he feels ready to humiliate the beach boys at his high school by beating them at the up-coming Surf Competition. Eric Stolz, who later won respectability for his touching performance as Rocky Dennis in *Mask,* plays the all-American boy who must defend his school's honor and the flower of southern California womanhood against the depredations of the menacing Menlo and his New Wave riders. In the utterly jumbled finale the good guys destroy the insidious underwater lab, humiliate perverted adults (including unemployed actors Cleavon Little, Carol Wayne, Lyle Waggoner, and Ruth Buzzi, who have already humiliated themselves plenty), and win the celebrated Surf Off.

Along the way first-time director-screenwriter Badat bombards the audience with a relentless series of painfully unfunny gags that make the films in the *Porky's* series seem by comparison as dry and sophisticated as Restoration comedy. Most of the humor focuses on either bare drooping breasts or blubbery male behinds, and before the end of the film we see an overabundance of both. All the characters have been give yuk-yuk clever names, including the two bumbling cops, "Officer Underwear" and "Chief Boyardie." Each of these personalities gets a chance for the thrust-and-parry of sparkling repartee, including

lines such as "Kids, if I need any sh—t out of you, I'll squeeze your heads!" In one climactic scene a good-guy surfer challenges one of the punk zombies to a garbage-eating contest, in which they consume broken glass, rotten fish, seaweed, and dead sea gulls, all nicely spiced with an exquisite sauce of bird droppings. By the end of the picture, of course, the audience feels as if it has just lost a garbage-eating contest. As *Boxoffice* magazine reported, "This movie would probably be considered lowbrow even by Cheech and Chong." *The Hollywood Reporter* saw it as "a bummer for all," while the *Los Angeles Herald Examiner* aptly described it as "crass and dumb and ugly. . . . Rock-bottom bad."

This sort of critical response did nothing to dim the optimistic expectations of producer George G. Braunstein, who declared, "I'm sure *Surf II* will make more money than the original—because there wasn't one." As if the garbage-eating scene weren't enough to win this picture its own dingy little niche in cinema history, this film must also be remembered as the only sequel in Hollywood history to appear without a predecessor. Fortunately for moviegoers everywhere, there was no *Surf I,* and considering the disappointing box office performance of this film it is unlikely that anyone will rush in to fill that gap. The misleading title of *Surf II* constitutes an "in joke" on the part of the producer and director which, lame as it is, remains the most amusing aspect of the production.

WHERE THE BOYS ARE '84 (1984)

If anyone should be qualified to know *Where the Boys Are,* it would be impresario/producer/Beautiful Person Allan Carr.

The alchemist who turned garbage into gold with *Grease* (1978), then turned gold (in the form of lavish production budgets) into cinematic and box office garbage with *Can't Stop the Music* (1980) and *Grease II* (1982), felt confident that be could work yet another magical transformation by remaking the granddaddy of all beach party movies.

The original 1960 *Where the Boys Are* made stars out of Paula Prentiss, Connie Francis, George Hamilton, and Jim Hutton, so naturally Carr approached Prentiss, Francis, and Hamilton to make cameo appearances in his new film. He would also have ap-

Lynn-Holly (Ice Castles) Johnson and Wendy (Fantasy Island) Schaal refine their lovemaking techniques on an inflatable dummy named Dave, who just may have been the brains behind Where the Boys Are '84.

proached Hutton, but, inconveniently enough, the personable leading man had died in 1979, so our merry mogul tried to sign his son, Academy Award winner Timothy Hutton. After a few months of well-publicized offers and conversations, each of these established stars, including young Hutton, wisely turned down producer Carr's attempts to proposition them. In the end the closest he could come to the cast of the original film was hiring George Hamilton's ex-wife, Alana Stewart, for a supporting role as a Florida socialite in the remake.

In addition to the famous title, designed to produce knowing smiles all the way from West Hollywood to Fire Island, Carr borrowed the basic premise of the ageless classic: Four college girls visit the famous fleshpots of Fort Lauderdale during spring break and encounter a series of amusing and romantic adventures. In the original the featured coeds came across as innocent and incurably good-natured; the very worst anyone could say about them is that they were "boy crazy." In the remake the best anyone could say about the featured femmes is that they are sex crazy, and the worst is that they are sleazy, jaded, self-indulgent tramps. They deliver lines such as "Look at the buns on that one!" or "I want to meet some total bonehead with the most gorgeous bod you've ever seen" or "I'll turn his mind to guacamole —I'm talking Conan the Barbarian!" or "All you need to bring to Fort Lauderdale is your diaphragm and a bikini." Unfortunately the girls disregard their own sage advice and, in addition to their bathing suits and contraceptives, they arrive in the Sunshine

State complete with an inflatable "Party Doll" named Dave which they use to practice their lovemaking. In an absolutely nauseating sequence one of the girls bites this man-shaped beach ball in an inconvenient spot and causes him to deflate like a burst balloon.

Such puerile and prurient antics could never have been particularly entertaining, but if performed by a group of fresh-faced, firm-bodied young starlets they might have at least been endurable. Yet for reasons known only to himself, Allan Carr cast as his coed cuties four long-in-the-tooth leading ladies who look at times as if they could have *daughters* of college age. Lynn-Holly Johnson (the blind ice skater in the 1978 weepie *Ice Castles*) leaves her goody-two-shoes image far behind for her role as the most sexually insatiable of this well-traveled quartet, while Lisa Hartman *(Knots Landing)* and Wendy Schaal *(Fantasy Island)* demonstrate their suitability for continued television work. It is the final member of the fab four, however, who suffers the greatest embarrassment. Lorna Luft, the daughter of Judy Garland and half-sister of Liza Minnelli, was 31 when she took this role as a college sophomore, but considering her insipid behavior on screen it's not hard to believe that she's been flunking all her classes for the last twelve years.

Producer Allan Carr discovered Russell Todd, star of Where the Boys Are '84, *while visiting his hairdresser; the girls in the movie (from left: Lynn-Holly Johnson, Lisa Hartman, Wendy Schaal, and a stand-in for the unfortunate Lorna Luft) ogle him while visiting the Fort Lauderdale beach.*

The most spectacular of her stupidities involves her utterly implausible entry in a "Hot Bod" contest which provides the picture with its climactic sequence; poor Miss Luft would have fared far better in a Cellulite Festival. When she grabs second place and wins enough money to bail one of her wayward pals out of jail, it is obvious that the contest has been rigged, though no one would suspect that she's bribed the judges by granting her sexual favors. Like all the other males in Allan Carr's fantasy Fort Lauderdale, the cuddly collegians who evaluate the beachside beauties have something more on their minds than mere girls. In fact, the promotional materials released with the film boasted that the primary male lead, high-fashion model Russell Todd, was discovered by Allan Carr when the producer saw his photograph at a hairstyling salon. Judging from Todd's limp and listless performance, Carr would have done just as well casting his hairstylist.

While Carr busied himself arranging a spectacular debut-night "Beach Party" at New York City's ultra-fashionable Studio 54, the film's director, Hy Averback (*I Love You Alice B. Toklas*) rushed into print to defend the picture against its critics. He denied that his intentions had been in any way "exploitative" and insisted that the film should be praised for its courage and integrity. "*Where the Boys Are* attempts to capture the *real* spirit of Ft. Lauderdale during spring break," he declared. "There are some sexual scenes, sure, but that's realistic and natural—like driving cars."

What was driving Carr, meanwhile, came out in an article in *Esquire* magazine. After spending several days watching the producer in his natural habitat on location in Florida, reporter Richard M. Levine described an afternoon in which the ebullient impresario swept through a mansion, trailed by his underlings, to prepare the way for the filming of a show-stopping party scene. While his associates dutifully took notes, Carr showed his respectful and affectionate attitude toward women by demanding the display of fourteen bare breasts. These specific instructions on set decoration ("I want four of them hanging out those bay windows behind the wet bar, and two over by the fireplace and two more on the couch") demonstrated his exemplary concern for every detail of the production. The *Esquire* article went on to describe the peripatetic producer as "Auntie Mame played by Divine . . . dressed in a colorfully striped caftan, he looks something like a beach ball wearing aviator glasses." Perhaps this re-

semblance helps to explain his intense personal feeling for the beach party format.

His loving attempt to revive—and update—the surfside spectacles of the sixties opened in 1,300 theaters across the country in April 1984. To make sure that millions of Americans flocked to this cinematic celebration, Carr departed on a national publicity tour that gave him the chance to talk about his work on numerous radio and television talk shows. In all interviews he anticipated negative reviews but bragged that, in view of the low ($6,000,000) production budget, he couldn't possibly fail to make a box office killing.

As it happened, Carr's predictions ended up half right: The reviews of *Boys* were indeed terrible. More than a dozen critics placed it on their "10 Worst of the Year" lists—a great honor in a fiercely competitive twelve-month period that saw the release of such other memorable stinkers as *Rhinestone, Sheena, Bolero, Hard to Hold, Conan the Destroyer,* and *Cannonball Run II.* On the business side, however, Carr's optimism proved utterly unfounded: *Where the Boys Are* turned out to be Where the Moviegoers Weren't. Its tepid audience appeal may have generated enough business to barely pay its production, promotion, and distribution costs, but it hardly turned out to be the "money machine" its producer so confidently expected.

With this third feature film disappointment in a row, Carr might well have retired as a producer to pursue a promising new career as a celebrity caterer, except for his other notable project of 1984: the Broadway presentation of the transvestite toe-tapper *La Cage aux Folles.* The spectacular commercial and critical success of this musical version of the popular French film farce has ensured Allan Carr's long-term survival as a major power in the world of show business and we have little doubt that, in the years ahead, he will continue as always to astonish and entertain us.

AND THE WINNER IS . . .

... THE HORROR
OF PARTY BEACH

Despite the embarrassing notices that greeted its release, this picture developed a cult following almost immediately. The cult grew year by year as insomniacs and other unfortunates marveled at the film's splendor on television Late Late Shows throughout the nation. This dedicated group of bad film fanatics, jealous of the exhaustive attention lavished on other classic clunkers such as *Robot Monster* (1953), *Plan Nine from Outer Space* (1959), and *The Creeping Terror* (1964), have lobbied long and hard to win similar respect for *The Horror of Party Beach*.

The release on videocassette of Del Tenney's most important statement has formidably bolstered their case. No matter how many times you watch this film, each additional viewing reveals new layers of incompetence.

The music stopped long ago on the solemn sands of Party Beach; the piercing tones of the Del Aires no longer skim over the cold gray sea. The dancing youths who once populated this Edenic corner of our planet are middle-aged now, their once glorious flesh running, no doubt, to flab and wrinkles. The monsters themselves have gone the way of rotting fish, and Eulabelle has been declared unconstitutional by several decisions of the United States Supreme Court.

Still, to this day, the magic remains—so that *The Horror* easily overcomes its very worthy competitors in this hotly contested category and stands as a deathless example of the very heights of cinematic stupidity. In seeking to explain its hypnotic and mystical appeal to two and a half decades of moviegoers we come, face to face, with a terrifying but unavoidable conclusion: it's the Voo-doo, we tell you. It's the Voo-doo.

Perhaps the same sort of malign spiritual force came into play to punish the nominees in our next category, for taking not only the name but also the voice of the Lord in vain. . . .

Two of the starlets in The Horror of Party Beach
*worry that an uninvited guest could ruin their carefully
planned slumber party.*

THE LEAST UPLIFTING
CONVERSATION WITH GOD
IN MOTION PICTURE HISTORY

AND THE NOMINEES ARE...

GOD IS MY CO-PILOT (1945)

Fighter pilot Dennis Morgan and Chaplain "Big Mike" (Alan Hale, Sr.) receive encouragement from Above on the eve of a major battle in God Is My Co-Pilot.

GENERAL (Raymond Massey): We're going to blast her industrial centers until she screams for peace! . . . We're going to bomb the Japs on the Fourth of July!

PILOT (Dennis Morgan, turning quietly to his chaplain): But I've never killed a man before, Big Mike!

CHAPLAIN "BIG MIKE" (Alan Hale, Sr.): You're confused, Scotty.

PILOT: I've been lost before, but somehow I've always gotten through!

BIG MIKE: What do you call that "Somehow"? [Clouds separate and a heavenly choir is heard.] Believe!! . . .

PILOT: Dear God: I never asked for anything before, but this is a mission I've worked on for years! If it be Your will, let me go with them—just this one time!

BIG MIKE: Yes, more things have been brought about by prayer than this world dreams of!

THE NEXT VOICE YOU HEAR (1950)

Nancy Davis (later known as Nancy Reagan) and James Whitmore listen to the Voice of the Lord on the radio in The Next Voice You Hear, *a movie described by Hedda Hopper, in a characteristic fit of exaggeration, as "The Worst Picture of All Time."*

(The Lord addresses the masses through an international radio hookup; apparently television in 1950 remained too unreliable to suit His purposes.)

THE VOICE (No, not Mr. Sinatra): I have spoken to you these few days to ask you to count your blessings. You are like children going to school. You have forgotten some of your lessons. I ask you to do your homework for tomorrow! . . . This is God speaking! And a lot of people who don't believe will say, "If it's really God, why doesn't he perform some miracles?"

JOE (James Whitmore): Miracles?

MARY (Nancy Davis): Like what kind of miracles, Joe? What would He do?

JOE: Come on now, none of that. What's there to be scared of? You know it can't be—it can't be—God!

RED PLANET MARS
(ALTERNATE TITLE:
MIRACLE FROM MARS) (1952)

SPACE SCIENTIST (Andrea King): What *is* the message, Chris?

ELECTRONICS EXPERT (Peter Graves): "You have been given knowledge and have used it for destruction. Seven lifetimes ago you were told to love goodness and hate evil. Why have you denied The Truth?"

SCIENTIST: The Sermon on the Mount—on Mars!!!

God, speaking from His headquarters on Mars, uses an oscillograph to send the Sermon on the Mount to Earth scientists Walter Sande, Peter Graves, and Andrea King in an inspiring moment from Red Planet Mars.

JUBILEE TRAIL (1954)

"WIDOW WOMAN" (Joan Leslie): Florinda, what are you sitting there for?

SALOON SINGER (Vera Hruba Ralston): That stupid brute! That big lumbering ox! He gave me this—an icon, he calls it! He gave it to me so I feel like a fool and act like one. I hope his ship sinks and the whales eat him!

WIDOW: Florinda, I've never seen you like this before.

SINGER: You'll never see me like this again. Leave me alone! [Her friend departs, while Vera Hruba looks heavenward and organ music plays in the background.] Dear God: this is my first prayer. So don't expect too much. I'll just say what's on my mind. First, I didn't mean it about the ship sinking or about the whales. I don't know whether I want the handsome brute to come back here or not, so I guess I'll leave it up to You. But let him be happy—the way he is now—as long as he lives. Florinda.

SINCERELY YOURS (1955)

CRIPPLED BOY (Richard Eyer): . . . And dear God, one more thing. I know You got lots on Your mind. Maybe I shouldn't be reminding You, but—You know I missed football season last year. I kinda thought You'd help me this year. So far—well, I missed the first two games. I guess You've just been too busy . . .

WORLD-FAMOUS PIANIST (Liberace): It makes me wonder—wonder about God. A God who hasn't time. Hasn't time to help anyone who needs Him!

SOLOMON AND SHEBA (1959)

After destroying the temple with lightning as punishment for a badly choreographed orgy, God tells King Solomon (Yul Brynner) and a properly repentant Queen of Sheba (Gina Lollobrigida) that all is forgiven in Solomon and Sheba.

QUEEN OF SHEBA (Gina Lollobrigida, after being stoned by intolerant Hebrews): For Thine is the Power and the Glory—Forever!

GOD (As a wind blows open the curtains of the temple): Because thou didst call upon My name in thy dark hour, I have heard thee. Return therefore unto thine own land and keep the covenant thou didst make with Me. . . .

KING SOLOMON (Yul Brynner): If this be Thy will, O God, I submit to Thy judgment. May Thou watch between us while we are apart, one from the other.

HEBREW SOLDIER: Shout unto God, all the Earth! Sing praises unto the glory of His name! Sing praises unto the Lord, O Israel!

DONDI (1961)

WAR ORPHAN "DONDI" (David Kory, kneeling in prayer beside his bed): I wish You make them let me stay in America, Mr. Big Buddy. Please!

NIGHTCLUB SINGER (Patti Page, with tears in her eyes): Dondi's talking with the most influential Friend of all!

KING OF KINGS (1961)

"Your face looks familiar," says a Roman guard to Jesus Christ (Jeffrey Hunter) in King of Kings.

PRISON GUARD (Ron Randell): Who are you? Where do you come from?

JESUS CHRIST (Jeffrey Hunter): My name is Jesus. I come from Nazareth.

GUARD: Nazareth? I've not been there for many years. Yet your face is familiar.

JESUS: You once came to Our house and spoke to My Mother.

GUARD: The house of the carpenter—oh yes.

THE GREATEST STORY EVER TOLD (1965)

JESUS CHRIST (Max Von Sydow): What is your name, my friend?

JAMES THE YOUNGER (Michael Anderson, Jr.): James. Little James. They call me "Little" because I'm the youngest. What's yours?

JESUS: Jesus.

JAMES: Ah, that's a good name!

JESUS: Thank you!

Ida Lupino pleads for divine aid in fending off an attack by killer earthworms and giant rats in Food of the Gods.

JOHNNY GOT HIS GUN (1971)

JESUS CHRIST (Donald Sutherland): Since your real life is a greater nightmare than your dreams, it would be cruel to pretend that anyone could help you. What you need is a miracle.

JOHNNY (Timothy Bottoms): No, not a miracle —just tell me what is real and that the way I am now is just a dream!

JESUS: Perhaps it would be better for you to go away now. You're a very unlucky young man and sometimes it rubs off.

JOHNNY: I'll go—just tell me one thing: Are You and I really here together or is this a dream too?

JESUS: It's a dream.

IN SEARCH OF HISTORIC JESUS (1980)

JESUS CHRIST (John Rubinstein): The Kingdom of Heaven is at hand!

GOD (Mark Peter Richman, in an echo chamber, his voice swelling with pride): You *are* My Beloved Son, and in You, I am *very* proud . . . You've done well, My Son. You've set an Example for all to follow. But Your great mission has only just begun!

CRIMES OF PASSION (1984)

STREETCORNER PREACHER (Anthony Perkins): Forgive me, Lord, I speak not in vain, but this little bitch provokes me so!

FOOD OF THE GODS (1976)

MRS. SKINNER (Ida Lupino): O God, help us! Forgive me for doing bad things—I swear I won't sin again if You just return my husband to me . . . I won't never sin again, never! Only don't let no rats eat us! Please God!

AND THE WINNER IS . . .

. . . *IN SEARCH OF HISTORIC JESUS*

Critic Leonard Maltin appropriately suggests that this film should have been retitled *In Search of Morons Who Will Believe Anything.* This picture provides interviews with various "experts," shots of lightning bolts and clouds parting, some pseudoscientific evidence about the Shroud of Turin, views of biblical landscapes, and plenty of portentous questions from narrator Brad Crandall, whose stentorian voice suggests that he is advertising a household laundry product on television. *"Was* Jesus the son of man—*or* the Son of God?" he asks, and then, "Did He *really* work miracles? Did He actually visit North America in His youth? Did He really *exist?"* The movie then seems to answer this last question in the negative by casting the curly-headed television star John Rubinstein in the title role. This hip Healer wanders from one miracle to another, pausing only long enough for more interruptions from the narrator and for a few intimate Father-and-Son conversations with the disembodied voice of bit player Mark Peter Richman. In the course of these idiotic interchanges Richman sounds like a smug, self-satisfied papa publicly congratulating his overachieving Son on the occasion of his bar mitzvah.

Sunn Classic Films, the Salt Lake City production company that foisted *Historic Jesus* on a puzzled public, specializes in speculative pseudodocumentaries about mysterious phenomena. The most mysterious phenomenon of all is why people pay good money to see these movies. *In Search of Noah's Ark,* a 1977 quickie that spent 95 out-of-focus minutes showing an investigative team seeking (but never finding) the biblical boat, brought in a whopping $24 million at the box office. Other subjects covered by Sunn Films include prehistoric visits by helpful aliens (*The Outer Space Connection,* 1975); spoon-bending, mind-reading, and demonic possession (*The Amazing World of Psychic Phenomena,* 1975); the Loch Ness sea serpent and the Abominable Snowman (*The Mysterious Monsters!,* 1976); an effectively concealed nineteenth-century assassination plot (*The Lincoln Conspiracy,* 1977); and the "well-known" incident in which the U.S.

Air Force confiscated flying saucers from another galaxy (*Hangar 18,* 1980).

As for future projects, we suggest a hard-hitting investigation of whether William Shakespeare actually wrote his own plays, a probe of the deep mystery surrounding the dubbed voice of Muki the Wonder Hound in the classic film *Dog of Norway* (1948), a consideration of the possible "faked death" of martial arts star Bruce Lee, an exploration of the alligator colonies in the sewers of New York City, and most important of all, we eagerly await that can't-miss crowd pleaser, *In Search of Historic Elvis.*

John Rubinstein, as "the Historic Jesus," has a heart-to-heart chat with His Dad in a dramatic highlight from the religious schlocku-drama In Search of Historic Jesus.

THE
MOST PRIMITIVE
MALE CHAUVINIST FANTASY
IN MOVIE HISTORY

*O**ne of the most common themes in folklore is the legend of a far-off land inhabited exclusively by unspoiled, beautiful females. The appeal of this notion is obvious: it allows men to fantasize about situations in which even the most ordinary among them would be greeted as conquering heroes. As often as not, the women in these sagas are fierce and formidable warriors—like the Greek Amazons or the Norse Valkyries—who battle men with fury and effectiveness until they are overcome by the power of love and happily lay down their spears. This idea of transforming tough, competitive women into swooning idiots through the sheer mystic force of male potency is sure to inspire 15-year-olds of all ages.*

It took Hollywood a surprisingly long time to discover the commercial potential of mobs of man-hungry, scantily clad fighting females, but once the trend began in the early 1950s it proved all but unstoppable. The movie industry created more than two hundred of these lusty lost worlds, offering primitive tribes of strutting starlets with beehive hairdos, false eyelashes, and bathing suits, who populate the remote fastnesses of jungle Africa, the moon, the South Seas, and the planet Venus.

Like most fantasies, these inane excursions served a deeper purpose in addition to their dubious entertainment value. Sociologists characterize the period following World War II as an era of sweeping "counterrevolution" in terms of the balance between the sexes. The GI's who came marching home after the war faced the disturbing reality of tens of millions of American women who had been pushed into the work force during their absence; for these returning vets, part of the return to "normal" peacetime life involved dragging their women back to the secure comforts of hearth and home. This struggle is obviously reflected in the big-screen tales of strong-willed women who have been forced to get along without men, but who gladly give up all silly notions of independence the moment that a torn T-shirt beefcake star comes along to show them what they've been missing. After a few steamy kisses even the most ferocious amazons gladly trade in their iron bras for aprons and baby carriages.

Whatever one's opinion of the underlying ideology of these films, the outrageously awful quality of nearly all of them makes them prime Golden Turkey contenders. With an obvious embarrassment of riches, or at least a richness of embarrassments, we could hardly limit the choices in this category to the usual number of nominees. Instead we've provided an overview of the mind-numbing and many-splendored ways in which moviemakers over the years indulged their prefeminist fantasies.

AND THE NOMINEES ARE...

PREHISTORIC WOMEN (1950)

The Prehistoric Women *celebrate their group wedding with a dance of jubilation—choreographed, like all other numbers in the film, by future dance-great Bella Lewitzky in a prehistoric stage of her career.*

After a few shots of "primeval nature" (actually, the grounds of the Department of Water and Power in Whittier, California), the roving camera discovers half a dozen bathing beauties in heavy makeup, carefully sculpted perms, and animal skins. While these clumsy cuties form a circle, wiggling their hips and shaking papier-mâché clubs toward the heavens, a narrator solemnly intones: "Under the spell of the full moon, Tigri and the women of her tribe dance restlessly, *savagely,* impelled by a feeling of frustration, not knowing why." Maybe these cave girls can't understand their predicament, but the audience certainly can: Having been kept by their man-hating mothers from all forms of masculine companionship up to this point, the tribal teenagers are now definitely ready for a night on the town. Since none of

the prehistoric women share the sexual preferences of modern-day tennis stars, this means attacking a nearby tribe, kidnapping their menfolk, and holding them prisoner in their treetop penthouses as "love slaves."

To make sure that we follow every absorbing detail of this plot, the producers provide an unseen narrator whose kindly comments and breathless "scientific" observations call to mind the eager explanations in Walt Disney nature films. Like the best sort of U.N. interpreter, he also provides simultaneous translation of the grunts and belches of the actors on screen. In one thrilling scene Engor (Allan Nixon), the muscular captive of tribal queen Tigri (Laurette Luez), argues with her over their division of household tasks. "Gee-nay! Elko! Lee-to!" he boldly declares, before the narrator explains, "He has asked her, 'If she is so wise and superior, why doesn't she see if *she* can move the rock?'"

Eventually Engor uses his "higher intelligence" to prevail in this battle between the sexes. Right before our eyes he invents fire and then goes on to develop the world's first barbecue, back rub, razor, and shaving cream. He is such a clever Cro-Magnon, in fact, that one gets the feeling he may at any moment discover the wheel, the alphabet, and the Cuisinart. When he and his male-bonded buddies successfully defend their lady captors from a backlot pterodactyl and a marauding, drooling giant (played by eight-foot-three Icelandic circus performer Johann Peturrson, who appears to be grievously mentally impaired), the girls give up their feminist aspirations. The narrator chortles as he describes this "happy" ending in memorable terms: "And so the tables are turned. The dominant male is happy and contented. Women wait on him as though he were a king. The once proud, fiery leader of the tribe meekly obeys. ... And so in those distant days, even as today, the

The entire cast of Prehistoric Women *reacts to the sudden appearance of a rubber pterodactyl in a dazzling display of ensemble acting.*

eternal battle for supremacy between woman and man was solved, not through the clout and the glove [?], but through romance."

Original plans for the film called for this inspiring speech to accompany a final fade-out in which the lovers wander off together into the woods. Unfortunately the censors in the Production Office contended that this might lead impressionable young viewers to the horrifying conclusion that some of our honored neolithic ancestors may actually have engaged in premarital sex. In handling these bureaucratic objections, producer Albert J. Cohen resisted the temptation to write in a new role for an Anglican priest, and instead devised an appropriately primitive "marriage ceremonial" in which all four of the fur-clad couples scratch their wrists and mingle blood before engaging in hanky-panky.

Despite such compromises with public taste, the moviemakers felt they had made an important statement about man's origins and the proper relationship between the sexes. Producer A. J. Cohen proudly told the press that his movie would be "50 per cent accurate, scientifically."

Apparently recognizing these noble intentions, French director and film scholar Alain Resnais *(Last Year at Marienbad, Hiroshima Mon Amour)* planted his tongue firmly in his Gallic cheek and included *Prehistoric Women* on his public list of the ten best motion pictures of the year. The L.A. *Daily News,* on the other hand, described it more appropriately as "one of the worst movies ever made . . . people laugh uproariously all through it."

UNTAMED WOMEN (1952)

Like most aboriginal islanders who have been discovered in Hollywood's anthropological research over the years, the Stone Age sweeties in *Untamed Women* sport shaved legs, tweezed eyebrows, and a great deal of fire-engine-red lipstick. What makes this tribe unique, however, is its use of language. These may be Untamed Women, but they use very civilized English. In place of the crude oogah-boogah of other caveman capers, these lost-world ladies speak an archaic form of the language full of "thou's," "ye's," and "what ho's!" This makes perfect sense in the context of the script, since these South Seas natives are all identified as "Druids" (that's right, *Druids*) whose ancestors left England centuries before. Whether these ancient voyagers made their way to the South Pacific by building a prehistoric version of the Panama Canal, or else made the long trek across the entire Eurasian land mass and then swam the rest of the way, is one of the movie's intriguing unanswered questions.

In any event, the tranquility of their quaint existence is irrevocably shattered when the four-man crew of an American bomber, shot down by the Japanese at the height of World War II, washes up on shore. The chief Druid and high priestess of the island cult—a haughty honey with the exotic name Sandra (Doris Merrick)—takes a shine to the stranded fly-boys and offers them a chance to prove themselves and to save their lives. She releases them

Two ancient British Druids, who have somehow made their way to a remote corner of the South Pacific, fight for the attention of stranded American pilot Morgan Jones in Untamed Women.

in the dreaded "Valley of the Monsters," where our heroes find themselves badly superimposed over stock footage of dinosaurs, smoking volcanoes, and giant armadillos—all borrowed from that ubiquitous classic *One Million B.C.*

The macho Americans escape just in time to help the hometown girls defend themselves against an attack by the "Hairy Men" of a neighboring island—the same antisocial brutes who killed off the Druid menfolk some years back. Naturally one of the local volcanoes selects the climactic point in the ensuing battle as the perfect moment to blow its top, and all the principals perish in an avalanche of still more stock footage. Only one of the visiting Americans (Mikel Conrad) remains alive to tell the tale to his skeptical doctor (Lyle Talbot) while recuperating in a military hospital.

Untamed Women (promoted with the poetic ad line "SAVAGE BEAUTIES WHO FEARED NO ANIMAL YET FELL BEFORE THE TOUCH OF MEN") made its debut as the companion feature to another piece of quality cinema, the self-explanatory *Bela Lugosi Meets a Brooklyn Gorilla.* The tepid public response to this fascinating double bill proved that the public cared little about Bela Lugosi, untamed women, or Brooklyn gorillas; a pity, since a sequel entitled *Bela Lugosi Meets an Untamed Brooklyn Women's Gorilla* might have been a real treat.

MESA OF LOST WOMEN (1953)

This picture has absolutely everything: a race of buxom "Spider Women" with long fingernails and filmy nightgowns; their bespectacled mad scientist creator (Jackie Coogan) in his underground Mexican lab; the heroic pilot (Bob Knapp) who crash-lands his plane dangerously close to this den of iniquity; a Chinese philosopher named Wu (played by Samuel Wu) who delivers innumerable profound observations ("There is a day to be born and a day to die"); a millionaire adventurer (Nico Lek) and his golddigger girlfriend (Mary Hill); an eight-foot-high spider puppet; "the world's foremost organal [sic?] therapist" (Harmon Stevens) who escapes from an insane asylum to try to save humanity from the Kiss of the Spider Women; and half a dozen killer midgets who must have wandered over by mistake from the set of *The Terror of Tiny Town.*

Mad scientist Jackie Coogan warns another stranded pilot (Robert Knapp this time) to keep his grubby hands off the delectable Spider Women in Mesa of Lost Women.

As if this weren't enough to delight even the most masochistic moviegoer, *Mesa* also provides a musical score that is considered by many connoisseurs the very worst ever composed for a motion picture. It features endless repetitions of the same annoying flamenco phrase as rendered by a single Spanish guitar and a tinkly café piano, reminding us at every turn that the moviemakers couldn't afford more than two instruments. Hoyt S. Curtin, the prodigiously gifted composer and performer who created this surefire headache producer, later gained a measure of professional success as musical director of the caveman cartoon series *The Flintstones.*

The "mesa" of the title is supposed to be a remote plateau that rises six hundred feet from the floor of the desert. Though it is never shown on screen in even so much as a single establishing shot, the characters describe it poetically on several occasions. "It's stuck up in the air like an island in the sky!" declares our pilot protagonist as he stares in wonderment toward the horizon. Later he stumbles onto the hideaway where the evil Dr. Aranya conducts his notorious experiments. "Aranya?" our hero helpfully declares when he is first introduced to the villain. "Why, that's Spanish for 'spider'!"

True to his name, the dirty doc has selected a dozen incredibly wooden and klutzy starlets to inject them with tarantula serum that produces "all the savagery of true arachnids." With these new qualities, Aranya believes he has finally created "an indestructible insect, a female creature that may someday control the world." To show the seriousness of their intentions the girls walk through their parts with sealed lips and blank expressions, holding their arms out to their sides and making clicking insect noises whenever they appear. They have also been trained to perform mincing "spider dances" for the sombreroed patrons at the local cantina, though the most deadly side effect of the doctor's dread serum appears to be the terrible taste in negligees it has induced in all its victims.

This film is so wretchedly incompetent in each of its details (camera work, editing, costumes, special effects, you name it) that it represents a nadir for all concerned—but most particularly for Jackie Coogan. As a child star of the silent era, he became a top box office draw with movies like *Oliver Twist*, *Peck's Bad Boy*, and Charlie Chaplin's *The Kid*, but by the time he reached puberty the Kid had hit the skids. With his role as Dr. Aranya he definitely scraped the bottom of the barrel, and so tried to hide behind a shoe-polish beard, an oversize wart, and thick, opaque glasses. Coogan delivers his lines in a timid, self-absorbed monotone as if presenting a public service reading of the U.S. Constitution, and he remains at all times perfectly oblivious to the other actors on screen. He seems, in short, even more eager than his captives to escape the Mesa of the Spider Women, and once he did so, he managed to stage a minor comeback. By the end of the decade he had won work in such distinguished projects as *High School Confidential* (1958) and *Sex Kittens Go to College* (1960), as well as earning a continuing role as the beloved Uncle Fester in the *Addams Family* TV show.

Spider Woman Dolores Fuller shows why no man can possibly resist the charms of the seductive female zombies of Mesa of Lost Women.

CAT WOMEN OF THE MOON (1953)

Sonny Tufts (with his mouth open, center) *leads a crew of intrepid astronauts in battling a giant lunar spider before they encounter the devastating appeal of the fabled* Cat Women of the Moon.

This early 3-D release offers an eloquent argument for outer space spay-neuter clinics.

The "Cat Women" of the title are supposed to be advanced but heartless creatures who killed off the males of their race thousands of years ago. According to the script, the moon men gulped down too much oxygen from the precious lunar atmosphere, so the feline femmes had to practice "planned genocide" to remove them.

In this indiscriminate slaughter, they not only rid themselves of truck drivers and construction workers, but they also must have killed off the interior decorators, since the underground palace of their queen is arranged in a bizarre hodgepodge of conflicting styles that would give the editors of *Architectural Digest* an instant headache. These premises, the focal point of "2 million years of lunar civilization," feature African tribal masks and Arabian scimitars on the walls, Japanese bonsai trees and Romanesque columns in the corners, a shrine with a gold Buddha in the center of the room, and a giant spider puppet —the same one, it would appear, that was used in *Mesa of Lost Women*—as a house pet.

No one ever explains this astonishingly eclectic taste, or why the girls are known as Cat Women in the first place. It's true that they wear black leotards and rhinestone collars and slink around a lot, but when they greet the visiting American spacepersons they seem to resemble California sorority girls hosting a reception for new pledges in which the punch has been heavily spiked with Valium. "I know it's been a *long* journey," says their leader, Alpha (Carol Brewster, of *Untamed Women*). "Welcome to the moon! This is my second-in-command, Beta, and this is Lambda."

Before long, the moon maidens fall head over paw for the beefy Earth men, and who can blame them, when the captain of the lunar expedition turns out to be the inimitable Sonny Tufts? The former "Male Sensation of 1944" had already begun his long decline toward world recognition as a nonacting cult favorite, and in the course of *Cat Women* he waged a losing struggle to remember his lines. Fortunately Douglas Fowley, who is listed in the credits as "Dialogue Director," appears on screen as one of Tuft's co-stars and manages to stand next to the fumbling matinee idol to provide needed prompting during many of his big scenes. In one noteworthy exchange Commander Sonny tries to explain one of the scientific mysteries uncovered by the expedition:

> TUFTS: Well, the magnetic field on the dark side could exert a gravitational pull, and, uh . . .
>
> FOWLEY: . . . And that means that this is a natural decompression chamber, doesn't it, sir?

In addition to the passionate interaction between the conniving Cat Women and the unsuspecting Earthlings, there is also a sizzling subplot involving the second-in-command space jockey, Victor Jory, and the token female in the intrepid crew, Marie

The Cat Women bare their claws, threatening the visiting Earth men with certain death.

Windsor. As Sonny Tufts aptly observes in the midst of these entanglements, "You know, there must be something to this moon and romance stuff." Jory, who is best known for his supporting roles in *Gone With the Wind* and *The Miracle Worker*, treated his rare shot as a romantic lead in *Cat Women* as if it were the chance of a lifetime. When he finally reveals his obsession with Miss Windsor (*see:* THE MOST AWKWARD ON-SCREEN MARRIAGE PROPOSAL) he shouts the lines at the top of his voice. "Look, Helen, I have a very high regard for you," he roars, with his hands on her shoulders. "You're smart, you have courage, and— YOU'RE *ALL* WOMAN!"

She certainly is, and she demonstrates her femininity when, after a rough landing on the dark side of the moon, her first move is to grab her compact and repair the damage to her mascara. Apparently the moviemakers shared the philosophy of one of their fictional astronauts, who tells a smitten Cat Woman, "You're too smart for me, baby. I like 'em stupid!"

For those filmgoers who also like 'em stupid, *Cat Women of the Moon* provides an endlessly entertaining excursion to the very bottom of the lunar litter box. It has earned a devoted following among bad film fanatics to rival the cult that surrounds Astor Pictures' other 1953 outer space adventure—the immortal *Robot Monster*. Both films reached the public with the same ad line, "YOU'VE NEVER SEEN ANYTHING LIKE IT!!"

Five years later the studio released yet another moon-creatures-versus-Earthlings extravaganza to which this boast could not possibly apply. When moviegoers went to see *Missile to the Moon*, they knew they most definitely *had* seen something *very much* like it, since the picture amounted to nothing more than a ridiculously reverential remake of *Cat Women of the Moon.* To most of us, the notion that *Cat Women* required a remake would seem about as sensible as the thought that World War II deserved an encore, but the production chiefs at Astor refused to let their feeble feline fantasy rest in peace. *Missile to the Moon* used a new cast and slightly upgraded costumes and special effects to tell the same inane story. The moon maidens this time wear gold lamé bathing suits instead of black leotards, and they are portrayed exclusively by "International Beauty Contest Winners" (including Miss New Hampshire, Miss Illinois, and the dynamic Miss Yugoslavia), but they still use the same names, with our old pals Alpha, Beta, and the ever-popular Lambda back for one more run at the visiting Earth men. The film also displays the same enlightened attitude toward women so memorably advanced in the original. "Don't think, honey," an astronaut tells one of the mincing moonettes. "Just be beautiful!"

FIRE MAIDENS FROM OUTER SPACE (1956)

Anthony Dexter and his fellow astronauts decide to make love, not war, with Susan Shaw and her fellow Fire Maidens from Outer Space.

The action begins when a mixed crew of British and American astronauts blast off on a voyage of "friendly scientific exploration" to the thirteenth moon of Jupiter. One can only admire the courage of these stalwarts who depart for distant worlds without space suits, helmets, oxygen tanks, or special equipment of any kind; even when they leave their spaceship (which is briefly represented by some World War II stock footage showing a German V-II

rocket in flight) they are wearing the standard khaki summer uniforms of the British Army. They do, however, enjoy up-to-date timekeeping equipment courtesy of the Longines Company, which appears to have made some sort of special arrangement with the producers. The large clock that decorates the cabin of the spaceship proudly displays the Longines name in big letters and, just before takeoff, Captain Blair (Anthony Dexter) asks his crew: "Do *all* of you have your *Longines* space watches? Good. Set them!"

Right on time, our space jockeys reach their destination, and it should go without saying that they discover an advanced civilization of man-starved females in skimpy costumes eagerly awaiting their arrival. In fact, the sales slogan used to promote this film after its release ("WORLD OF WOMEN SEEKING MALE PARTNERS TO CARRY ON RACE!") sounded like an ad from the Interplanetary Personals. Fortunately our astronauts manage to rise to the occasion, as one of them sagely observes upon first contact with these exotic creatures, "Why, it's a woman!" to which his chivalrous colleague responds, "You can say that again—with all the necessary ingredients!"

What makes these otherworldly wenches unique is their affiliation with the "ancient culture" of Atlantis. How the Lost Continent made its way to the thirteenth moon of Jupiter is anybody's guess, but the script does explain why the sensuous Fire Maidens survived the well-advertised destruction that befell their legendary homeland back on Earth: These dancing dollies are actually the "imperishable granddaughters of Aphrodite." To make clear their Olympian origins, the barefoot beauties pay homage to a garish wall-hanging that shows the goddess dressed in the same low-cut white mini-dress, with a Greek design along the hemline, that they all wear. This sacred relic, resembling the black velvet images of Elvis that decorate many American homes, inspires them to perform the fabled "Dance of Desire" for the astonished Earthlings. This, however, is an English sci-fi travesty, so the well-bred ladies perform, not to the crude beat of rock 'n' roll or even to the sinuous snap of a cha-cha-cha, but rather to the lilting strains of orchestral Orientalia (*see:* THE LEAST CLASSY USE OF CLASSICAL MUSIC IN MOVIE HISTORY). With admirable British restraint they prance around cardboard pillars, burning torches, and plaster garden statuary, waving their arms like swimmers and turning their faces, openmouthed, toward the ceiling.

The Fire Maidens show how they earned their name as they uphold the traditions of the Lost Continent of Atlantis on a remote moon of Jupiter by burning their homecoming queen in a horrifying human sacrifice.

These revels not only impress the visiting missile men but also arouse the dreaded "Creature of Horror," who lives behind a bush outside "The New Atlantis." This incredibly minimal monster is nothing more than a skinny fellow in a black turtleneck and spandex pants who wears a papier-mâché mask that suggests an unfortunately advanced case of acne. To terrify his victims he staggers as he walks and displays impressive lung power in repeatedly bellowing the single word "ROAR!"

In order to appease this evil spirit and to punish one of their sisters (Susan Shaw) for her untoward intimacy with the earth men, the giggling girls decide to offer her as a human sacrifice. They convene a lively toga party in which the guest of honor is chained to an altar with ropes of pearls while flames leap up from a barbecue pit behind her. The Creature then makes an unscheduled entrance, undeterred by the blazing revolvers of the intrepid astronauts. "Bullets bounce off him!" one of them helpfully observes. "For Pete's sake, throw a gas grenade!" The resulting puff of smoke topples the monster into the fire pit (with a last pathetic "ROAR!") and provides the superbly satisfying conclusion. Released from the altar, actress Susan Shaw (who, before her movie career, bore the melodious moniker "Patsy Sloots") tells her cohorts: "I go with my beloved to Earth. But I shall return!"

Despite this perfect setup for a sequel, neither the lead character nor the other Fire Maidens ever returned to the screen. For writer-director Cy Roth, the remarkably low quality of his most ambitious project also meant the end of the line; his name never

again appeared on the big screen, though there is speculation that he secured a job with the Longines Company.

QUEEN OF OUTER SPACE (1958)

Despite the title, this is *not* a vehicle for Liberace in which "the people's pianist," fresh from his triumph in 1955's *Sincerely Yours,* wins new fans in the far reaches of the galaxy. It is, rather, a cockeyed vision of the American space program (set in that far-in-the-future year of 1985) in which four astronauts make a disastrous wrong turn on their way to an orbiting space platform and end up crash-landing on the surface of Venus.

The boys can hardly be blamed for their poor navigation; as the pipe-smoking professor who accompanies the expedition (Paul Birch) gravely explains, it was actually a mysterious "energy ray" that blew them some twenty-five million miles off course. He uses the same rigorous scientific approach to explain the surprises that await them after they land. In elementary astronomy we all learned that the planet Venus is enveloped by an impenetrable cloud cover, with an atmosphere of poisonous gases and a surface temperature that reaches 700 degrees. The Venus of *Queen of Outer Space,* however, proves far more hospitable, with temperature, atmosphere, and sky resembling a balmy day in Malibu. How can a brilliant scientist explain this discrepancy? "Well," shrugs the professor, "it appears all things are possible in space."

There must be a planet somewhere in the Milky Way on which the women all weigh three hundred pounds, with stumpy limbs, thinning-hair heads, and black moles covering their faces—but Venus isn't it. Instead the voluptuous inhabitants of "The Female Planet" (as it is described in the ads for the film) wear elaborate coiffures, stylish cocktail dresses, spiky high heels, and a great deal of costume jewelry. They also carry deadly ray guns that look like power drills, and use them to capture the visitors from Earth as "specimens" for their queen.

Even before her frosty greeting to the members of this expedition, Her Highness (Laurie Mitchell) had established a formidable reputation as a man-hater. Long ago she arrested all the males on Venus and shipped them off to "a nearby satellite." What, you may ask, led her to such a drastic step? Still smarting from a nasty divorce? Hoping to achieve a higher level of feminist consciousness? Furious over watching too many male-made movies about distant planets full of nubile, man-hungry females?

There are, to be sure, always plenty of good reasons to send your menfolk packing, but what actually sealed the fate of the good ol' boys of Venus was their tacky mistake in starting an atomic war that left many of their women with serious complexion problems. The queen herself, for instance, wears a silvery mask to hide the fact that her face, in this DeLuxe color Cinemascope presentation, resembles a pepperoni pizza studded with rhinestones. The other members of her "planetary council" are similarly afflicted and wear stylish party masks that bring back memories of the old panel from *What's My Line?*

To go along with the game-show atmosphere, we now meet, as our special mystery guest, "the most brilliant scientist on Venus"—played by none other than Zsa Zsa Gabor. Her Hungarian accent has survived the journey to outer space remarkably intact, though she is obviously ill-suited for life on a planet

Zsa Zsa Gabor displays the heavenly style that made her, by the end of the movie, Queen of Outer Space.

without even one viable marriage prospect. As Zsa Zsa declares to a few of her pals, who, like her, are miraculously unscarred by the radiation poisoning: "Vimmen cannot be happy vizout man!" This shattering scientific discovery leads her to plot a rebellion to overthrow the evil queen, release the earth men, and make the planet safe for truth, justice, and alimony.

The malevolent monarch, meanwhile, recognizes the sad fact that men don't make passes at girls with radiation splashes, so she decides to take matters into her own hands. No, not that way; what she does is to select a particularly hunky example of earthly manhood and order him to her boudoir. As she seduces him, this undone astronaut (played by Eric Fleming, best known as the trail boss on the *Rawhide* television show) utters the film's one great imperishable line: "You are not only a queen—you are a woman!"

Despite his relief at discovering that she is not, after all, a transvestite, Fleming rips off her mask, exposing the royal wretch in all her hideous vulnerability. Zsa Zsa then uses the mask to impersonate the queen, and since the girls of Venus are noted for their beauty rather than their brains, none of them notice that their ruler has suddenly developed a heavy Hungarian accent. It's a good thing, too, because Her Highness had already revved up the dreaded "Beta Disintegrator" as part of her scheme to blow up the planet Earth, and it uses the same fearfully effective energy rays that drew the American rocket boys to Venus in the first place.

In a heart-pounding climax Zsa Zsa turns off the machine in the nick of time and declares a new regime to the polite cheers of her subjects. Naturally the astronauts want to repair their spacecraft and return home as soon as possible, but they graciously consent to a year's shore leave on Venus to help the locals in their determined efforts to repopulate the planet.

For Miss Gabor, *Queen of Outer Space* marked the pinnacle of a career more noted for its off-screen escapades and talk-show appearances than for its cinematic contributions. Her achievement here even exceeds her unforgettable performance as *The Girl in the Kremlin* (1957), in which she plays twin sisters who help Stalin (as portrayed by Maurice Manson) rise from his grave, undergo plastic surgery, and find a new life as a playboy in Greece.

In addition to the presence of the beloved Miss Hungary of 1936, *Queen of Outer Space* featured one more well-known name: Ben Hecht, the brilliant screenwriter who helped create *The Front Page, Scarface, Gunga Din,* and some seventy other films, is credited as coming up with the original story. Hecht's biographers, however, insist that "he contributed nothing to the film" but merely allowed the producers to use his prestigious name in return for a substantial cash payment. Others associated with the production recall that Hecht does in fact deserve credit for the concept of the film, but that he dreamed it up as part of an impromptu cocktail party monologue meant to illustrate the latest trends in trash. According to these accounts, Hecht felt more surprised than anyone else when some of those who had been present on this lively occasion took his satiric notion to Allied Artists and made a deal for a picture called *Queen of the Universe*. Eventually the studio scaled down the title to the more modest form in which it is known to the ages, but Hecht's credit, much to his embarrassment, remained associated with the project as it moved along. The veteran scenarist passed away in 1964, but his name lives on today in connection with some of the best, and one of the worst, moments in the history of motion pictures.

WILD WOMEN OF WONGO (1958)

It's possible to appreciate *Wild Women of Wongo* on many levels: as a plea for enlightened eugenics, a stirring yarn of South Seas islands adventure, an ambitious re-creation of pagan fertility rites, a prehistoric precursor to the beach party movies of the sixties, a dramatization of the eternal confrontation between woman and alligator, and a showcase for the last word in leopard-skin bathing suits.

For once, the featured females actually live in a civilization with a full compliment of male inhabitants; the problem for the Wongos is that the men of their tribe are all hopeless nerds ("brutes" as they are described by the sympathetic narrator) who are obviously unsuitable for dating. Meanwhile, in the village of Goona, "many days march to the south," all the men are smiling, broad-shouldered disciples of Jack LaLanne while the women look like veteran potato pickers from a Ukrainian collective farm.

Some sort of exchange program is obviously in order, and it commences when Engor (Johnny

The Wild Women of Wongo *rebel against the "Brute Men" of their tribe in a civilization so backward that they don't know enough to move the car and trailer (upper left) out of camera range.*

Walsh), the crown prince of Goona, visits Wongo for the first time. The local lovelies are deeply stirred by his appearance: never before have they seen a man with a shaved chest or so much pomade on his hair. What's more, they know he's a good guy because he wears an immaculate white loincloth, while all the hometown hulks are dressed in grays and browns.

The men of Wongo are jealous of all the attention aroused by the strapping stranger, and so plan to execute him in the morning. Before they can perform the dirty deed, the redheaded "spitfire" Omoo (Jean Hawkshaw) takes the prisoner into the bushes out behind her grass hut and performs a dirty deed of her own. Turning him loose at the break of day, she then faces the wrath of her father, the king of Wongo. To punish his headstrong child, and to discipline the other girls who aided in Engor's escape, the king orders the women of the tribe (all nine of them) to seek atonement at the "Temple of the Dragon God."

The women make their way to this awesome structure, which resembles the eighteenth hole of a particularly gaudy miniature golf course. The pivotal role of the high priestess is played by Zuni Dyer, a Miami waitress with a long face, waist-length black hair, and a thick Bronx accent, making her movie debut. "Maidens o' Wongo!" she whines to the assembled multitude as she scowls at the camera. "Duh Dragon God is angry! Dance! Dea-ay-ance!" At her command, the Wild Women begin gyrating wildly, like poorly coordinated beach girls taking their first lesson in the watusi, or debutantes at a masquerade charity ball trying to dramatize the plight of epileptics. As the soundtrack punches out great gobs of mock Stravinsky, they hold their arms straight out in front of them, lean back from the hips, and wiggle their shoulders furiously.

Jean Hawkshaw piously touches her head to the ground and leads the other Wild Women of Wongo *in solemn worship of their fearsome Dragon God.*

Having appeased the priestess with these exertions, the girls take a dip in a river near the temple, only to discover that the Dragon God still holds a grudge against them. This dippy deity—nothing more than an elderly alligator rented from a nearby animal park—shows his displeasure by waddling toward the ladies as they run from the water in terror. The heroic Omoo, however, remains behind to battle the invader as the moviemakers treat us to a full three minutes of their struggle. To facilitate the filming, the alligator had been drugged into unconsciousness, and poor Miss Hawkshaw is forced to shake the pathetic beast wildly from side to side to make him look as if he is awake.

With this ordeal behind them, the maidens of Wongo return to their home village—a handful of patently plastic grass huts planted incongruously on a narrow strip of beach—to find that their menfolk have disappeared. As Omoo declares with passionate intensity: "We do not want to *live,* and to grow *old,* and to *die,* without *men*!! Wongo is ended. Tomorrow we leave Wongo—we'll go south!"

As the attentive viewer (or reader) surely recalls, south is the direction of Goona—home of beauteous body-builders. The women of Wongo kidnap these preening peacocks by trapping them in nets and then drag them away to the Temple of the Dragon God. Meanwhile, the men of Wongo—who had been away on a brief hunting or bowling expedition—follow

their femmes to Goona. They never catch up with the celebrated Wild Women, but they do meet the native Goona gals and discover that they have much in common—particularly in terms of physical unattractiveness. These additional couples also make their way to the temple, and the picture concludes with a mass wedding ceremony even more bizarre than the well-publicized Madison Square Garden events staged by Reverend Moon.

An investigation into the story behind this most unusual motion picture confirmed our suspicions that cinema professionals had nothing to do with it. The director, James L. Wolcott, was a frustrated accountant taking his first halting steps as a filmmaker, and playing every nuance of the script with flat-footed, deadpan earnestness. "We all worried about him and wanted to protect him," recalled one of Wolcott's co-workers on the picture. "He seemed so vulnerable and helpless. He was actually the kind of guy who didn't know enough to come in out of the rain."

Wolcott's cast displayed the same innocent approach. The embarrassed actors kept their arms at their sides at all times, as if standing at attention; even the most emotional lines are delivered without gestures. To play the "Brute Men of Wongo," the director recruited half a dozen middle-aged members of the Coral Gables Police Department. He also hired several key players from the University of Miami football team to play the men of Goona, and supplemented their ranks with a few flamingly flamboyant Miami Beach musclemen. Only one member of this ill-assorted company went on to work regularly in motion pictures: Ed Fury, who portrayed "Gahbo of Goona," continued his career as the star of several Italian Hercules movies and spaghetti westerns. The name "Adrienne Bourbeau" also appears on the credits, leading some film historians to speculate that Adrienne *Bar*beau, star of television's *Maude* and wife of director John Carpenter, actually made her movie debut as "Wana of Wongo." Miss Barbeau, however, emphatically denies that she participated in the film, and the fact that she would have been only 13 in the year it was made—if one believes the birthdate listed in her official biography—gives her position credibility.

Another famous figure connected with the production made no effort to obscure his association. The playwright Tennessee Williams, vacationing in South Florida during the two-week shooting schedule, had been introduced to one of the body-beautiful men of Goona and hoped to advance their relationship. One afternoon he visited the set and watched the production in progress as he waited impatiently for his friend to finish his scenes and join him for their scheduled dinner date. The presence of one of America's leading dramatists caused great excitement among cast and crew, but before any graduate students rush off to propose a project drawing parallels between *Night of the Iguana* and *Wild Women of Wongo,* they should take careful note that Williams' role remained entirely passive. According to eyewitnesses, he tried to watch politely as the nervous cast ran through its lines, but dozed off almost immediately and slept soundly for several hours. Many present-day viewers of this film will be tempted to react in precisely the same way.

SLAVE GIRLS OF THE WHITE RHINOCEROS (1967)

In a civilization dominated by sadistic brunettes, all blondes (whether bleached or natural) become the helpless Slave Girls of the White Rhinoceros.

The ads for this British bilge pulled out all the stops in their efforts to grab attention. "A KINGDOM OF WOMEN WHERE MEN ARE CHAINED AND TORTURED AS SLAVES!!!" they screamed. "A SAVAGE WORLD WITH MEN AT THE MERCY OF *WOMEN* IN POWER!"

Now, wait just a minute here. If this movie actually serves up the "Slave Girls" promised by the title, how can it be that *women* are in power? The picture

clearly deals in bondage of some sort, but who's in charge, and who are the victims?

The ultimate victims, of course, are those moviegoers who actually paid money to witness this nonsense under any of its alternate titles, as *Slave Girls of the White Rhinoceros, Slave Girls,* or *Prehistoric Women* (not to be confused with the classic *Prehistoric Women* released seventeen years before and discussed above).

If the various titles and the contradictory ad lines make for a confused situation, just wait till you try to digest the preposterous plot. A Great White Hunter (Michael Latimer) follows a wounded leopard into the underbrush of equatorial Africa. Hot on the trail, he passes the ominous image of a pale-faced rhino carved into a tree trunk. His native guides refuse to go further, but our foolhardy hero plunges ahead, only to find himself mystically transported to the timeless stomping grounds of the legendary white rhinoceros.

The big beast presides over a topsy-turvy lost world in which women are in charge, and in which they exploit some of their fellow females as slave girls. The only way to tell which women are on top is, believe it or not, by examining their hair color. The Kulnaka, a tribe of brunette, Caucasian amazons in fur bikinis, decide that a bevy of nearby blondes have even less business in darkest Africa than they do, so they enslave all fair-haired females and offer them as occasional sacrifices to the rhinoceros god.

It's too bad that Michael Latimer plays a hunter rather than a hairdresser; had he arrived in rhinoceros land with a few packages of hair dye, he could have undermined the entire basis of their civilization. In any event, he promptly falls in love with one of the blonde slave girls (Edina Ronay) and so has no trouble resisting the advances of the evil queen of the brunettes, played by Martine Beswick. Ms. Beswick, former plaything of 007 in two James Bond movies, and future star of *The Happy Hooker Goes to Hollywood,* wears a bone headdress and spends most of her time snapping her whip or taking bubble baths in a hollowed-out jungle log.

When the visiting hunter refuses to make love to this neolithic dominatrix, she condemns him to a nearby concentration camp, where he is chained together with the other males of the tribe. This sad lot of unshaven and broken-down wretches is thoroughly intimidated by Queen Martine and her buxom bodyguards, but the newcomer in their midst manages to stir their flagging manhood. Building a coalition between the blokes and the blondes, the hunter launches a revolution just in time to save his beloved from her fate as a human sacrifice to the "Devils of Darkness"—members of a nearby tribe, portrayed by a group of deeply embarrassed West Indian blacks wearing gorilla skins. In the midst of the climactic battle, a white rhinoceros comes roaring out of nowhere, strolls around the set for a few moments while the extras scream in terror, and then impales the evil queen on his enormous horn.

In Slave Girls of the White Rhinoceros, *the Great White Hunter (Michael Latimer) enjoys a lavish feast to strengthen him for his role as the chosen love toy to the evil Queen of the Brunettes, Martine Beswick.*

The symbolism in all this is consistent with the scheme that has been set up throughout the movie. Apparently, producer-director Michael Carreras couldn't get over the stupid old joke about the rhino as a horny beast, and so works endless variations on this clever theme. Every time Martine Beswick appears on screen she caresses either a rhinoceros tusk or some other obvious symbol. There are other undercurrents that attempt to give "meaning" to this lunacy: obviously, Carreras intended the "tragic" conflict between blondes and brunettes in the film as a heavy-handed commentary on the futility of racism. Why, then, did he introduce a few black actors in the most degrading possible circumstances?

The solemn approach of most of the actors raises other questions about the director's intentions. All of the prehistoric damsels, the dark and the fair alike, speak in the "veddy, veddy" refined tones of the British upper crust. When Martine Beswick first meets

Michael Latimer, as she is emerging from one of her innumerable baths, she cleverly observes, "You look different. You *are* different. Do you speak our language?" Not only does he speak their language; it sounds as if he attended the same schools.

Other lines in the movie ("A heavy heart does not make the feet light!" or "Kill him! He no longer amuses me.") have delighted bad movie buffs, as have the technical details of the production. The claustrophobic set features enough potted palms to resemble a cut-rate nursery, and the crudely painted cloth backdrops bear a remarkable resemblance to crudely painted cloth backdrops. Though a sense of humor on the part of the producers (Hammer Films, specialists in thinly veiled sadomasochistic schlock) is never apparent on screen, Martine Beswick maintains fond memories of the atmosphere during the shoot. "We giggled a lot on the set," she recalls. "It was probably the silliest film ever made."

VOYAGE TO THE PLANET OF PREHISTORIC WOMEN (1968)

The story behind this amazingly inept opus is far more intriguing than the feeble plot that unfolds on screen.

In 1962 a Leningrad studio called Popular Science Films released a diverting fantasy called *Planeta Burg (Planet of Storms)*. It told the inspiring story of two heroic cosmonauts who crash-land on the surface of Venus with their giant robot and struggle to survive in this desolate, inhospitable world until a rescue party of their comrades manages to reach them. The only life forms they encounter during their adventure are primitive water creatures and a giant pterodactyl, who, like the other special effects, is exceptionally well done. The acting is horrendously wooden, to be sure, and the action is painfully slow by American standards, but the entire production stands as a competent example of Soviet sci-fi and its declared purpose of "education for the masses."

At first glance this sober, stolid 73-minute piece of celluloid would hardly seem to be a hot, exploitable property, but somehow *Planeta Burg* made the long journey to the film markets of the West in three colorful incarnations.

First came a straightforward, dubbed British release with the enticing new title *Cosmonauts on Venus.*

Then came the veteran "B" movie producer-director Roger Corman, who, during one of his trips to England, happened to see the film and convinced himself of its spectacular commercial potential. For a minimal sum, he snapped up the U.S. rights for American International Pictures, then returned home and commissioned director Curtis Harrington to shoot some new material to "spice up" the Soviet original. The result, released as *Voyage to the Prehistoric Planet* (1965), featured a few brief scenes of Basil Rathbone and Faith Domergue as would-be rescuers who never quite make contact with their Russian counterparts.

This first cut-and-paste job proved successful enough so that producer Corman resolved to recycle his Russian treasure one more time. Three years after giving the world *Voyage to the Prehistoric Planet,* he came up with the concept for a new film inventively entitled *Voyage to the Planet of Prehistoric Women.* To supervise this latest cannibalization of the aging Soviet special effects, Corman turned to his 27-year-old second-unit director from *The Wild Angels,* an ambitious newcomer named Peter Bogdanovich.

Working under the pseudonym "Derek Thomas," Bogdanovich came up with a script cunningly adjusted for domestic sensibilities. While Russian audiences might actually enjoy the spectacle of two spacemen and a robot trudging through dust and lava on a deserted planet, Bogdanovich knew that red-blooded American moviegoers would never stand for an expedition to Venus that failed to turn up a civilization of bathing beauties.

The budding director therefore recruited a dozen actresses and models, lavished nearly $500 on costumes and props, rented a single soundless Arriflex camera, and hit the beach at Malibu for one week of shooting. To save money, his wife, Polly Platt (who later won fame as production designer for films such as *Paper Moon* and *Terms of Endearment*), created "outer space" bikinis for the cast made entirely out of string and seashells. These costumes offered both visual and economic advantages, but they also entailed conceptual problems when it came time to cut together the new scenes with the material from the Russian original. Why would the girls of Venus be running along the sand or splashing in the surf like extraterrestrial beach bunnies at the same time that the visitors from earth remained dressed in their stodgy Soviet space suits? The script answers this

question by describing these wholesome California girls as "Gill Women" who have developed certain fishy qualities that enable them to breathe the noxious atmosphere of Venus. To explain the fact that they never talk to one another (after all, Bogdanovich had no sound equipment on location) he equips these creatures with mysterious telepathic powers; their inner thoughts are expressed as narration on the soundtrack, but their lips never move, and their expressions never change, on the screen.

The Gill Women may boast advanced extrasensory faculties, but everything else about them (and about the poorly lit, horribly photographed scenes in which they appear) is primitive. As it turns out, they worship a giant pterodactyl—which offers an ingenious context for the scene from the original in which the cosmonauts shoot down the big bird. Naturally the death of "the Great God Ptera" provokes a crisis among the participants in the Venus beach party, and, after providing a solemn burial at sea, they elect the Soviet robot (affectionately dubbed "Robot John" in the American version) as their new deity.

The comely queen who leads the shell maidens through these thrilling transformations is none other than Mamie Van Doren, who, after triumphal roles in *High School Confidential* (1958) and *Sex Kittens Go to College* (1960), was now nearing the end of her distinguished career. "It was the worst period of my life," she recalls today. "When the sixties came along, they brought the feminist movement. Feminists started the natural, no-bra look. I admired that, but that's what put me out of business." As if to support her point, the production manager on *Voyage* remembers that "our biggest problem on that picture was trying to find seashells that were big enough to handle Mamie." To add to the difficulties, Miss Van Doren developed a morbid fear of sharks and worried that the killer beasts might leap out of the water and attack her on the sand during one of her big scenes. To avert this danger, she ordered her husband, former major-league pitcher Bo Belinsky, to stand just out of camera range with a rifle at the ready.

Hoping to make full use of Mamie and her charms, Bogdanovich wanted to show a touching love affair between his charismatic star and one of the visiting earth men (Vladimir Yemelianov). Unfortunately he faced a most formidable obstacle in depicting the development of their relationship: Though he cut freely back and forth between the old and the new footage, there was no way to show the Russian actors and the American girls on screen at the same time. In order to overcome this problem, he resorted once more to the amazing powers of telepathy. Although they never actually see each other, the two lovebirds communicate their passion through voices on the soundtrack. Bogdanovich himself dubbed the role of the infatuated cosmonaut. "We had to leave, but I'm going back soon," he intones at the picture's conclusion. "Maybe someday I'll find her. Maybe I'll die trying."

Despite this pledge of eternal devotion, the eager *auteur* soon forgot about Queen Mamie and moved on to other things. He wrote and directed the thriller *Targets* later in 1968, and in the years that followed he of course shaped many major hits (*The Last Picture Show; What's Up, Doc?; Paper Moon; Mask*) and misses (*Daisy Miller, At Long Last Love, Nickelodeon*).

Voyage to the Planet of Prehistoric Women seldom receives the attention it deserves as his feature film debut, partially because of the confusion surrounding its title. It's all too easy to mistake it for *Voyage to a Prehistoric Planet*, or even *Women of the Prehistoric Planet* (1965), a Realart production starring John Agar that had no connection whatever to the Soviet source. To make matters worse, *Women of the Prehistoric Planet* was also known as *Prehistoric Planet Women*, not to be confused with either the original *Prehistoric Women* (1950) or the latter-day, British *Prehistoric Women* (1967), which, of course, is better known as *Slave Girls of the White Rhinoceros* or simply *Slave Girls.* . . . If you're still reading at this point and have not yet thrown up your hands in desperation, then you certainly deserve to see those long-awaited magic words . . .

AND THE WINNER IS . . .

. . . *MESA OF LOST WOMEN*

All of the nominees in this category are so thoroughly inept and reprehensible that selecting just one of them as the Golden Turkey Award winner has been a difficult challenge. We finally turned to *Mesa of Lost Women* not because it offers the most *sexist* vision of the bunch, but because it is the most *primitive* of all these Male Chauvinist Fantasies—primitive in terms of the sheer incompetence involved in its production.

The moviemakers behind it can hardly be criticized for lack of ambition. Part of the fascination of this film is the gap between its complex artistic intentions (with flashbacks within flashbacks, biblical quotations, the arty guitar soundtrack, and the monumentally pretentious narration), and the shoddiness of the pathetic production values.

At the very beginning of the picture the sonorous voice of veteran actor Lyle Talbot narrates a sequence of shots showing "The Great Mexican Desert." "Strange!" he declares. "The monstrous assurance of this race of puny bipeds with overblown egos! The creature who calls himself man. He believes he owns the Earth! In the continuing war for survival between man and the hexapods only an utter fool would bet against the insect. Let a man or woman venture from the well-beaten path of civilization, let him cross the threshold of the limited intellect . . . and he encounters amazing, wondrous things! The unknown—and the terrible!"

For the knowledgeable bad movie buff the distinctive cadence in this narration, and the fact that it is delivered by Lyle Talbot, suggest the shaping hand of the legendary writer-director, the late Edward D. Wood, Jr., Golden Turkey Life Achievement Award winner as Worst Director of All Time (*see:* THE LEAST CONVINCING SCIENTIFIC EXPLANATION IN MOTION PICTURE HISTORY).

Though Wood's name appears nowhere in the credits, his loyal fans have contended for years that he must have been associated in some way with the production. In the same way that devoted "Marlovians" argue that their man Christopher Marlowe actually wrote the plays of Shakespeare, so the legions of Wood devotees have assembled an impressive array of evidential bits to support their case concerning *Mesa:*

- Wasn't Lyle Talbot, narrator of the film, also a star of Wood's mess-terpieces *Plan Nine from Outer Space, Jail Bait,* and *Glen or Glenda?*
- Didn't Dolores Fuller, who plays one of the Spider Women in *Mesa,* share a house with Wood for years, as well as playing his fiancée in his autobiographical epic on transvestitism, *Glen or Glenda?*
- Isn't Mona McKinnon, another of the Spider Women here, best known as the romantic lead in *Plan Nine from Outer Space?*
- And most persuasive of all, didn't Ed Wood borrow the outrageously irritating flamenco score from *Mesa* and use it note for note in his own film *Jail Bait,* which was released two years later?

These clues, along with the stylistic similarities between this remarkably wretched film and all of Wood's mature work, make an intriguing case. Some scholars have even suggested that the name "Herbert Tevos," which is listed in the credits as the writer and co-director, is actually a pseudonym for the Master. After all, the Tevos name never again appeared on a motion picture, and little or nothing is known about the man.

We will freely confess that we wanted to please the Woodies of this world, and make a contribution to film history, by announcing here our sober and considered conclusion that Wood himself participated in some way in this production. Alas, our investigation points entirely in the other direction.

We have now spoken with eleven individuals who participated in the making of this movie more than thirty years ago, including actors, technicians, script supervisors, executives, the widow and son of co-director Ron Ormond, and Wood's former live-in, Dolores Fuller. *None* of these people recalled Wood's presence on the set or suggested that he had any hand in creating this motion picture. This would seem to offer decisive evidence against Wood's association with the movie, since the flamboyant filmmaker—known as a pioneering transvestite to all his friends and associates—was not the sort of man who could easily be ignored.

What's more, several of the actors had specific recollections of the mysterious "Herbert Tevos." "He was a mad Hungarian with a thick accent," remembers George Barrows, who played "George," the male nurse in *Mesa,* and later won screen immor-

tality as "Ro-Man the Monster" in *Robot Monster.* "It was very difficult to work for him. He was high-strung, sort of on the edge. He was a complete amateur, who'd never even picked up a camera before. And he'd put all his savings into this thing! He ran around the set thinking he was Von Stroheim, but the fact was he didn't know a damn thing about the movie business."

After three weeks of shooting and thousands of feet of film, the unfortunate Mr. Tevos proved incapable of completing his project, and Howco International, the distribution company which had already purchased the rights, decided to shelve the entire venture.

A year later the experienced exploitation director Ron Ormond *(Yes Sir, Mr. Bones; King of the Bullwhip; Outlaw Women; Untamed Mistress)* purchased the Tevos footage and brought the picture back from the dead. He contacted all the members of the previous cast and asked them to reassemble in order to shoot some entirely new material. Dean Reisner, who went on from his bit part in *Mesa* to a successful career as a screenwriter (of *Play Misty for Me* and *Dirty Harry,* among other films), candidly recalls: "I thought he was crazy. I didn't understand what he was doing. But it meant work for me and I was glad to do it. Fortunately I was drunk half the time anyway."

After another two weeks of shooting, Ormond retired to the editing room to weave together his new scenes with the existing Tevos material. Along the way he changed the original title from *Tarantula* to *Wild Girls of the Mesa,* then to *The Lost Women,* then to the happy compromise, *Mesa of Lost Women.*

Ron Ormond died in 1981, just a few months before a new generation of moviegoers discovered his controversial film, and *Mesa* established itself as a cult favorite of various "Worst Movies" festivals. His widow, June Ormond, is puzzled by this phenomenon. "I remember that picture, sure I do! The women all looked like they were wearing mops on their heads. It was terrible. Ron tried to save it, but there wasn't much he could do. It's definitely not representative of his work. Frankly, I don't understand why people are so interested in that film. In my opinion, it's one of the worst movies ever made."

As the narrator of Mesa of Lost Women *asks the audience, "How would you like to be kissed by a girl like this?" the "Tarantula Girl" (Tandra Quinn) attempts to sink her fingernails into Allan Nixon, fresh from his triumphal role as "Engor" in* Prehistoric Women.

THE MOST RIDICULOUS COWBOY HERO IN HOLLYWOOD HISTORY

The American movie industry has churned out more than ten thousand westerns over the years, most of them cheapie formula pictures with white-hatted heroes who are all but interchangeable.

Occasionally a moviemaker rides onto the scene whose talent allows him to gallop free of the thundering herd; John Ford and Howard Hawks come to mind as directors whose personal visions made all the venerable conventions seem fresh and vital.

Lesser lights also tried to inject new life into the overly familiar horse opera format, but they often looked for silly shortcuts in order to do so. Their desperate attempts to win public attention with "novelty" westerns provided a few memorable mixtures of sagebrush and stupidity and created some ridiculously offbeat heroes along the way.

AND THE NOMINEES ARE...

A PISTOL-PACKING CHIMPANZEE IN *THE LITTLE COVERED WAGON* (1933)

Hi-yo, Bonzo, and away!

Come with us now to those thrilling days of yester-year, when, at the height of the Great Depression, producer-director Sig Neufeld offered a big surprise to cowboy fans who thought they had seen everything. As *The Little Covered Wagon* rattled onto the scene, even the most jaded moviegoers felt compelled to take deep breaths and doff their ten-gallon hats to the edifying spectacle of the world's very first western adventure with an all-chimpanzee cast.

Before Neufeld, no moviemaker had the vision or courage to depict the little-known but important role played by these simian sod-busters in the opening of the Great West. In this inspiring motion picture the plucky primates all wear big, floppy hats and bright bandanas while facing such grim challenges as finding a way to keep their baggy pants and heavy holsters from falling down around their little knees.

With The Little Covered Wagon, *Sig Neufeld gave the world a western with a difference: a stirring horse opera with an all-chimpanzee cast. In later years his brother Sam Newfield tried to top this achievement by directing innovative sagebrush sagas with an all-midget cast* (The Terror of Tiny Town) *and an "all-colored cast"* (Harlem Rides the Range).

The picture presents all the most familiar western stereotypes: the saloon singer, the world-weary bartender, the local Mexican ("Senor Tamale") in a big sombrero, the inscrutable Indian chief, the black-hatted bad guy, the poor but honest rancher, his lovely and virtuous daughter, and the straight-shooting young buck who stands up for all that's right and true.

The problem is that to human eyes, these clever chimps look very much alike. To compound the confusion, the voices all seem to have been dubbed by the same person (could it have been Neufeld himself?) so that even this crude and rudimentary plot becomes as enigmatic as a play by Pirandello.

The story begins with a single covered wagon "crossing the Great Divide, along the Oregon Trail." A daddy chimp holds the reins of the two miniature donkeys that haul his rig. In our first taste of the stirring action to come, we see a long, loving close-up of the contemplative creature slowly chewing a plug of tobacco, drooling the dark brown juice down the side of its mouth, and then spitting it out onto the Oregon Trail. The local "Injuns" are, apparently, so disgusted by this tasteless act of ecological irresponsibility that the befeathered Chimp Chief leads his braves in an attack on the fur-skinned intruders. What the credits describe as "an entire Indian tribe"

—namely, three mounted monkeys—descends on the solitary wagon. As the battle rages, two other chimps cringe and hug each other in the back of the beleaguered vehicle. It slowly becomes clear that they are supposed to be mother and child, since the voice on the soundtrack turns suddenly high-pitched and squeaky.

After an artful fade to black, Neufeld shows the aftermath of the simian savagery: a weeping chimp wails in despair under the smoking wreckage of the ruined wagon. As he sits there puling on the prairie, a frontier scout saunters onto the scene and promises to adopt the boy as the son he never had. This is tremendously confusing, since the "helpless child" is actually somewhat larger than the "old-timer" who becomes his benefactor; they are all but indistinguishable as they waddle off, hand in hand, into the sunset.

Through the magic of movies, twenty years pass in an instant—though we are left to draw that conclusion ourselves without even the assistance of an explanatory crawl. The only hint that two decades have elapsed comes from the fact that the frontier scout is suddenly wearing a false gray beard and his adopted son has donned an oversize white cowboy hat. We also know that the boy, "Handsome Dan," has attained drinking age, since he now makes his way to the local saloon, where a gunslinging bully tries to humiliate him. "There's a guy here named Handsome Dan," the rough-tough stranger declares. "I'm gonna make a *monkey* outa him!" After this one feeble attempt at humor, the movie plays the rest of its action absolutely straight, making it seem far longer than its 25-minute running time.

The chimps themselves can hardly be blamed if the finished film turned out to be considerably less fun than the proverbial barrel of monkeys. Handsome Dan in particular turns in a convincing performance; aside from one embarrassing lapse when he tries to eat his playing cards before throwing them down on the poker table, he is a relaxed and likable western star. He even manages to generate some raw animal chemistry for an intimate interlude with his gal, "Nellie Darling." After presenting her with a beautiful bouquet of roses, he plants a big blubbery kiss directly on her lips—despite the fact that a blonde Phyllis Diller fright wig renders his supposed love interest easily the least appealing ape in the cast.

Whatever this picture's shortcomings in terms of

makeup, costume design, continuity, plot, camera work, and other production details, one can only admire Sig Neufeld's way with his actors: it could not have been easy to persuade chimpanzees to ride ponies and burros, shoot off pistols with big puffs of smoke, drink beer, whittle sticks of wood, smoke cigarettes, play the piano, and say grace before eating.

The dozen versatile stars who appeared in *The Little Covered Wagon* prepared for their moment of glory through their work as part of an august circus and vaudeville entourage known as Bud Barsky's Chimps. They lived together in the same suburban home with Mr. Barsky, an eccentric entrepreneur who reportedly raised them as his "very own children." After many years on the fringes of Hollywood, Mr. Barsky (who used to tell his friends, "The chimps are my life!") finally hit it big with Neufeld's wild, wild western. The success of *Wagon* spawned six sequels featuring Barsky's troupe in various costumes and situations and helped pave the way for such future primate production sagas as *Greystoke* and *Planet of the Apes*.

A RANGE-RIDING, ROBOT-BATTLING RADIO STATION OWNER IN *RADIO RANCH* (1935)

Cowboy newcomer Gene Autry is more than a little out of place in the underground civilization of Murania, which he discovers beneath his combination cattle spread and broadcasting station as part of the oddball adventure in Radio Ranch.

No western in movie history has thrown together a more bewildering jumble of incongruous elements than this one—featuring the spectacular adventures of a dude cowboy named Gene who operates a radio station on his ranch and personally croons out the prairie ballads that make his programs popular. In addition to his beef and his broadcasts, our busy hero also operates a radium mine on the premises, which is coveted by the evil Professor Beetson (Frank Glendon) and his gang of crooks.

The action begins when the baddies arrive by airplane and, after a blazing gun battle, leave Gene for dead. When the professor and his greedy cohorts begin looting the radium deposits, they accidentally stumble upon the entrance to the futuristic city of Murania, a center-of-the-earth civilization far in advance of our own. Angered by the intrusion, the Muranians dispatch a raiding party to the surface of the earth, featuring soldiers who wear Scottish kilts, gas masks, pineapple-shaped helmets, and flowing capes. Since this is a western, they also ride some pretty ponies hell-bent for leather, like a posse of outer space Ku Klux Klansmen. Meanwhile, our hero has recovered from his gunshot wounds in time to make it back to the ranch for his regular weekly program, on which he warbles "Uncle Noah's Ark."

Shortly thereafter, the "Thunder Riders" from the center of the earth take him prisoner—showing little appreciation for singing cowboys. They also capture Gene's pals, Betsy and Franky, two kiddie bronc busters who perform daredevil feats on their specially trained ponies. Down, down, down they all go . . . traveling in an elevator 25,000 feet below the surface of the radium mine. Once esconced in beautiful downtown Murania, they are held prisoner by a squadron of incredibly advanced robots who look like gingerbread men wrapped in aluminum foil with broad-brimmed silver top hats. Fortunately these mechanistic marvels enjoy a good song as much as the next fellow; they graciously allow Gene to return to the ranch just in time for his next scheduled broadcast and a performance of the lilting frontier favorite, "Moon-Eye View of the World."

Meanwhile, back in Murania, our hero, his stunt-riding junior sidekicks, and the ruthless radium poachers have all been drawn into the complex cross currents of local politics. Prince Argo (Wheeler Oakman), the scheming prime minister, is plotting a rebellion of slaves and robots to seize the throne from Queen Tika (Dorothy Christy). Gene naturally allies himself with the forces of law and order, and the pretty blonde queen, battling the killer robots with his six-guns and his formidable fists. To aid in the battle, two more of his cowpoke pals (Smiley Burnette and William Moore) arrive in Murania disguised as robots, but their efforts cannot turn the tide. Technology triumphs, temporarily at least, and the brave broadcaster perishes in a blinding explosion.

The movie, however, is only half finished at this point, so the queen's scientists bring Gene back from the dead using the well-known healing powers of radium (just check that one with the Nuclear Regulatory Commission). After several more gunfights, chase scenes, and musical interludes from the ranch to soothe the bewildered audience, the hero rescues his two comical sidekicks (the ones dressed as robots, remember), as well as the two stunt-riding children, just moments before the underground city goes up in flames. Queen Tika decides to die on her throne during the tragic meltdown, rather than escaping to the surface and listening to more cowboy ballads from Radio Ranch, while Gene takes the magic elevator back to the real world and delivers the conniving Professor Beetson to the local sheriff.

In its original incarnation, this sprawling story filled twelve episodes of a Saturday afternoon serial called *The Phantom Empire.* The concoction proved so popular with juvenile moviegoers that producer Nat Levine, boss of notorious Mascot Pictures, edited the material down to a 71-minute feature with the spiffy new title *Radio Ranch.*

The most astonishing aspect of this altogether astonishing motion picture was its role in creating a shining new sagebrush star.

The hero of the piece, Gene, was, of course, none other than Gene Autry, a 27-year-old Texas yodeler then under contract to Mascot Pictures at a salary of $100 a week. Before grabbing the lead in *Radio Ranch,* he had played only bit parts in two Ken Maynard features, *Mystery Mountain* and *In Old Santa Fe.* Maynard, at the time Hollywood's most popular cowboy, had also been slated for the starring role in *Phantom Empire/Radio Ranch,* but his temperamental behavior on the set persuaded Nat Levine to substitute the unknown Autry at the last moment.

Despite the ridiculous plot, and the silly space suits Autry had to wear during some of the Murania sequences, his talent shone through. After all, he had the chance to interrupt the action on innumerable

occasions to sing his original songs, including his first million-seller, "Silver-Haired Daddy of Mine."

He went on from *Radio Ranch* to make dozens of successful horse operas for Republic Pictures, to host his own very popular show on network radio, and to write and perform more than two hundred hit songs. He remains the only cowboy star ever to be listed (1938–1942) among the top ten Hollywood box office attractions. Today he is a multimillionaire who owns a baseball team, oil wells, a music publishing house, a flying school, a television chain, *and* his own radio station—though the broadcasting tower is *not* located on his ranch.

A GUITAR-STRUMMING MIDGET ON A SHETLAND PONY IN *THE TERROR OF TINY TOWN* (1938)

No one ever accused Billy Curtis, star of this classic shoot-'em-up, of riding tall in the saddle: he stood only 48 inches in cowboy boots, though the gigantic, snow-white ten-gallon—or at least ten-pint—hat he wore throughout the picture may well have added a full foot to his height. Even without the headgear, Curtis managed to tower over his on-camera adversaries, since the bad guys, the good guys, and some sixty assorted singing, dancing bystanders were all part of what the distributors proudly proclaimed as "THE VERY FIRST *ALL-MIDGET* CAST EVER ASSEMBLED FOR A MOTION PICTURE!"

This bizarre and unsettling cinematic experience originated with Jed Buell, a former theater manager from Denver, and a well-established specialist in producing musical westerns. After creating more than thirty of these ultra-low-budget sagebrush sing-alongs, the crafty Coloradan became bored with the form and began searching for a new "angle" to exploit. He found it by recruiting "little people" from around the world to join an acting ensemble known as Jed Buell's Midgets and dressing them all in adorable kiddie cowboy suits. To direct what he eagerly described as "a rootin' tootin' shootin' drama of the great outdoors," Buell hired the versatile Sam Newfield, who, in the course of his extraordinary twenty-five-year career, somehow managed to direct ninety-three horse operas (including *Roaring Lead, Bar Z Badmen, Thundering Gunslingers,* and other similar titles far too numerous to mention). In addition to *Tiny*

Town, the hardworking director lovingly crafted thirteen other musical westerns in 1938 alone. Moreover, Newfield's background made him specially qualified to work with very short cowboys: five years before, his older brother, Sig Neufeld, put a dozen hard-ridin' chimps through their paces as producer-director of *The Little Covered Wagon*.

To make sure that *The Terror of Tiny Town* stood out below the crowd, Newfield and Buell found an unusually tall, bow-tied announcer to "introduce" the picture. In the painfully patronizing pre-titles sequence, he smiles down at the two lead midgets, who barely come up to his knees, and promises the audience "a soul-stirring drama, a searing saga of the sagebrush." This is our last view of a full-sized human being, and for the next 63 minutes we watch the cutesy cast riding back and forth in one confusing sequence after another. None of it makes any sense. In the opening scene a bitesize blacksmith hammers away at the hoof of a full-grown horse; later the peewee pardners ride fragile-looking ponies that seem too small even for them.

In this context the normal cowboy clichés are supposed to sound humorous: on several occasions the villain orders his henchmen to "Hit leather" or "Beat it, boys!" (making the proceedings sound even more perverted than they are), while the hero describes his tiny steed as a "hoss." The problem is that the novelty wears thin almost immediately and, instead of viewing the cast as a group of clever sideshow performers, you see them only as a posse of incredibly inept actors with unusually squeaky voices.

Our hero, "Buck Larson," has to struggle to stay aboard his munchkin mount; on several occasions we

watch him wrestling desperately against the neck of his pony while the ornery li'l critter, with a mind of its own, lunges in the opposite direction. This is only the first of many indignities endured by the aspiring star, Billy Curtis, since his skill as a horseman, and his height, are exceeded only by his musical abilities. In one tuneful romantic encounter he rides out to a sylvan rendezvous with his light o' love, Yvonne Moray, who is Tiny Town's answer to Jeanette MacDonald. As he dismounts from his pony and produces a huge guitar to serenade her, she remains seated firmly in the saddle, clutching her picnic basket and listening rapturously. His hand twitches absentmindedly across the face of his instrument, but for safety's sake stays at all times at least six inches away from the guitar strings. Nevertheless, Mr. Curtis gamely tries to smile while moving his mouth to fit the utterly alien tenor voice that turns up on the soundtrack. While one might reasonably expect a presentation of that beloved western ballad "Gnome on the Range," what we actually get is a touching love song entitled "Down on the Sunset Trail":

> Some cowboys are so lo-o-o-nely,
> Sad as the ki-yote's wail,
> But I am n-e-e-ver lo-o-o-nely
> When you and I hit the trail . . .

Despite such awkward moments, Billy Curtis acquits himself far more honorably than do his colleagues in the cast, including his co-star "Little Billy," an undersize (but overacting) Edward G. Robinson imitator who plays the villainous title role of the local "Terror." Our hero defeats the bantam baddie's claim-jumping schemes and ultimately uses a stick of dynamite to blow him to itty-bitty pieces, without once varying the smile of suave self-assurance that shines forth from his handsome face. His oozing charm helped make *Tiny Town* a surprise hit across the country and started Billy Curtis on the road to stardom.

The year after his triumph in the Wild West, the miniature matinee idol won the plum part of the "Lord High Mayor" who welcomes Dorothy to Munchkin Land in *The Wizard of Oz*. He went on to play "bit parts" for directors Frank Capra, Alfred Hitchcock, Cecil B. DeMille, and others nearly as prestigious as Sam Newfield. He also played the pale-faced pygmy chieftain "Macumba" in the classic adventure *Jungle Moon Men* (1955), and appeared as Clint Eastwood's sidekick in *High Plains Drifter*

(1973). Along the way Mr. Curtis married six times, including one well-publicized union with a towering showgirl named Lois de Fee who was reported to be six feet eight inches tall. As Mr. Curtis told an interviewer, with admirable understatement, "All of my wives have been big girls."

Billy Curtis has, without question, enjoyed a long and colorful career, but he looks back on his pivotal role in *The Terror of Tiny Town* with little more than a shrug of the shoulders. "We rode Shetland ponies, of course, and whenever a little guy ran into the saloon, the doors would swing shut *over* his head. Other than that," he insists, "it was the same as any western."

A BLUES-SINGING "BRONZE BUCKAROO" IN *HARLEM RIDES THE RANGE* (1939)

Following his surprising success with *The Terror of Tiny Town*, producer Jed Buell hit upon the inspired idea that black people could be every bit as cute and quaint as midgets. Working once again with the redoubtable director Sam Newfield, he gave the world *Harlem on the Prairie*, billed as "The World's First Outdoor Action Adventure with an All-Negro Cast." The picture drew large and enthusiastic audiences, particularly in the more than four hundred movie houses across the country that catered primarily to black audiences. In an era of strict segregation and Jim Crow laws, when southern blacks in particular found themselves barred from mainstream theaters, they welcomed the chance to cheer for their very own "colored cowpokes" in the security of their own picture palaces.

The saddest aspect of this phenomenon was the offensively racist content and pathetically low quality of the western films offered up to this eager market. After *Harlem on the Prairie* (1938) came *Bronze Buckaroo* (also '38), and then two more films in 1939, *Harlem Rides the Range* and *Two-Gun Man from Harlem*.

All four pictures featured the same stalwart saddle-jockey, a six-foot-four former jazz singer named Herb Jeffrey. Billed as "Bob Blake, the Happy Cowboy," Jeffrey performed minstrel show musical numbers while backed up by groups such as the Four Black Birds and the Four Tones. To accommodate the ethnic market, the producers felt that Jeffrey

should yodel something more flavorful than the bland ballads offered by his white counterpart, Gene Autry: when he rides into view for the first time in his first film, astride a magnificent white steed called Stardusk, he manfully belts out "Way down upon duh Swanee Ri-buh . . ."

In each of Jeffrey's "Happy Cowboy" songfests he comes across as a sort of "Shuffalong Cassidy," but *Harlem Rides the Range* stands out as the least competent of the lot. In one memorable scene the good guys and the villains shoot at one another for a full five minutes from hiding places behind rocks that are no more than ten feet apart. In another sequence Jeffrey battles the claim-jumping villain (Lucius Brooks) with his fists, but he is so polite that he stops all blows several inches away from his co-star's chin.

The plot concerns a radium mine (shades of *Radio Ranch*!) owned by the pretty heroine, Artie Young, and coveted by the dastardly Brooks. Jeffrey, the "Bronze Buckaroo," rides to the poor girl's rescue, aided by his pudgy and slap-happy sidekick, Dusty

(Rollie Hardin), who provides feeble comic relief when, in several instances, he can't tell the difference between human "vittles" and dog food. The action grinds to a screeching halt in dead center of the 60-minute saga so the Four Tones can pour heart and soul into a slow, harmonized version of "Home, Home on duh Range!" To tell the good guys from the bad guys, white hats and black hats are hardly necessary; in this racist rubbish, skin tone alone does the job. Jeffrey, son of an Irish mother and an Italian/Ethiopian father, is the pale-faced hero, while the meanies are all several shades darker.

After completing *Two-Gun Man from Harlem*, Jeffrey rode off into the sunset, hung up his six-shooters for good, changed his name to "Jeffries," and resumed his jazz career. He sang with Earl Hines, Duke Ellington, and other greats; his 1940 rendition of "Flamingo," backed by Ellington on the Victor label, became an international hit and a recognized classic. Today, at age 70, the affable entertainer still slays 'em at club dates around the country and remembers his movie days with bemused affection. Despite the wretched substance of the films, he offers no apologies for his participation. On the occasion of his election to the Black Filmmakers Hall of Fame, he offered a touching explanation of his motivation. "One time we were playing the Cotton Club in Cincinnati," he said. "It was a hot night and we were taking a break out in the alley behind the club to cool off. Some children were playing cowboys out there, a group of black and white children. As they went running through the alley, we noticed one little fella about seven or so. He was chasing after the other kids and crying. I asked him what he was crying about and he said, 'They said I can't be Tom Mix 'cause Tom Mix is white'.... I thought it was a shame that black children didn't have a black cowboy figure to relate to."

A NAZI-HUNTING COWBOY VENTRILOQUIST (AND HIS DUMMY, "ELMER") IN *TEXAS TO BATAAN* (1943)

Many western heroes developed close relationships with their sidekicks—the Lone Ranger and Tonto, Cisco and Pancho, Roy Rogers and Dale Evans, and

When Max "Alibi" Terhune rode the range, he always brought along his loyal sidekick—the ventriloquist's dummy, Elmer.

James Stewart and Richard Widmark in the John Ford classic *Two Rode Together*. None of these saddle pals, however, enjoyed a more durable and intimate bond than Max "Alibi" Terhune and his wisecracking buddy, Elmer. In more than fifty films together they proved all but inseparable—in fact, Elmer, a pug-nosed, poker-faced wooden dummy in an over-size Stetson hat who looked like Texas's answer to Howdy Doody, never left his master's lap. With all due respect to Stewart and Widmark, these two *really* rode together.

The partnership between the perennial co-stars displayed greater complexity than one might have expected; over the years the ubiquitous Elmer proved to be far more than a mere wood chip off the old block. The burly Terhune, a former vaudeville magician and sideshow ventriloquist from Franklin, Indiana, usually portrayed a slow-witted, lovable, and unmistakably punch-drunk cowpuncher with saddle sores on his brain. Elmer, on the other hand, had a sharp tongue and a cynical sense of humor. On more than one occasion the junior partner picked up a six-gun with his spindly little arms to bail his boss out of trouble. The bone-headed repartee between "Alibi" Terhune and his alter ego provided the only vaguely amusing moments in many a dreary melodrama.

These bickering but bonded buckaroos first rode to fame in 1936 as members of Republic Pictures' celebrated ensemble The Three Mesquiteers—counting as only one Mesquiteer between the two of them.

In this context they participated in a series of low-budget, high-profit oaters with a number of co-stars, including a rising young actor named John Wayne. In 1939 a salary dispute with the Republic brass caused Terhune and Elmer to ride off into the sunset in pursuit of better pay. They found a new home at Monogram Studios and became part of a freshly constituted band of "legendary" heroes known as the Range Busters.

This hard-riding, camera-mugging cowboy ensemble became an overnight sensation; during their brief three-year heyday the Busters sauntered through an impressive total of twenty-four motion pictures. Their innocent adventures might have gone on forever, except for the fact that World War II headed them off at the pass. With American GI's fighting and dying in the far corners of the globe, the simpleminded struggles of the Range Busters against rustlers, claim jumpers, and conniving bankers suddenly seemed less compelling.

To overcome this problem, "the boys" made some desperate and thoroughly ludicrous attempts at topicality in their later films. *Cowboy Commandos* (1943) gave them the chance to break up an evil cabal of Nazi saboteurs, led by a Texas saloon owner with the suspicious name "Werner" (who is played by an actor with the even more suspicious name "Bud Buster"). The picture also offered a stirring patriotic anthem called "I'm Gonna Get That Fuehrer Sure as Shootin' " while warning audiences of the swastika-toting, Heil-Hitlering animals that everyone knew to be so prevalent in the American West of 1943.

Texas to Bataan makes a similar attempt to enlist America's rough-riding darlings in the struggle against fascism, but it is still, after all, a Range Busters movie so it inevitably begins with a love song to a horse. While Alibi Terhune strums his guitar in accompaniment, and Elmer looks on, blinking his eyes, their "pod'ner" John "Dusty" King tries to kiss his snow-white steed and sings a ballad that he composed himself:

> Me and my pony,
> We love to go to town,
> And watch the people
> As they stand around.
>
> Me and my pony,
> We love to herd the strays,
> And when our work is through
> We love to hit the hay!

To cool off after this sizzling sequence, the boys adjourn to a pistol range for target practice using portraits of Hitler and Mussolini. While the three flesh-and-blood cowboys blast away, Elmer hollers his encouragement. "Let 'em have it!" he squawks. "Knock 'em bowlegged! Do it again! Massacre 'em! Yippee!" After perfecting their skills as sharpshooters, they are ready to deal with a new threat to the American Way of Life: The cook and houseboy at the ranch where they work is actually a Japanese spy. He works closely with a city slicker Nazi secret agent named Herr Muller (Guy Kingsford) on a plan to "dynamite America's vital harbors." It is typical of the fiendishly clever Axis mentality that this plan to disrupt Allied shipping has been hatched in the dry, dusty heart of the Texas plains. In any event, "Cookie" (Escolastico Baucin) is exposed as a traitor when he receives several letters with a Tokyo postmark. Range Buster "Dusty" finds the fatal evidence and brings it to the owner of the ranch.

"Why, he *told* me he was a Filipino boy!" the old man protests.

"He fooled you," says Dusty. "He's a *Jap!*"

As if this weren't excitement enough, the U.S. Cavalry in the Philippines suddenly decides it needs four hundred horses from Texas. To insure safe and prompt delivery of this vital national resource, the army contacts the Magnificent Three and a Half. (Who ya gonna call? Range Busters!) They sail to Asia via steamer-class stock footage and, in an outrageously tacky trading post set left over from one of Monogram's jungle pictures, they listen to a native trio singing "Home on the Range" in Tagalog, which Elmer snidely describes as "Doubletalk!" In the middle of this serenade the Busters spot Herr Muller and Cookie, who, having escaped from the ranch and somehow made their way to the Philippines, just happened to walk in for a drink. "Let's corral them Texas style," Dusty suggests, and a battle royal ensues. At the climactic moment it's the littlest Range Buster who saves the day. While the bad guys point guns at our temporarily defeated heroes, Max warns that Elmer is outside and waiting to get a jump on them. He then throws the dummy's voice over to the far side of the room, startling his adversaries and turning the tide of battle.

In the final scene Elmer once again rides proudly on his master's lap as all of the Range Busters gallop toward the horizon. While the ranch owner and his pretty daughter (Dorothy Manners) wave grateful good-byes, he comments, "This time I hope they'll ride all the way to Tokyo!"

With the release of this patriotic pastiche, our boys approached the end of their long and dusty trail. Max Terhune went on to play small parts in another dozen motion pictures—including George Stevens' *Giant*—but producers generally called him for "comic relief" rather than allowing him to show his stuff as a heroic, range-riding ventriloquist. Elmer, meanwhile, had permanently retired from the screen, though he continued to receive loving and respectful treatment from Max and his family.

"Alibi" Terhune died at age 82 in 1973, but, according to one of his long-time associates, Elmer lives on in an attic "just outside of Hollywood," ready, at a moment's notice, to hit the comeback trail.

A BLIND GUNFIGHTER (WITH A SEEING-EYE HORSE) IN *BLINDMAN* (1971)

In 1971 producer-star Tony Anthony provided even the most seasoned cowboy fans with a thrill they had never experienced before as he blazed his way onto the screen playing the world's first (and only) blind gunfighter in Blindman.

Blindman is no bluff: it is a gritty, intense, hyperviolent spaghetti western with serious existential pretensions.

The hero is a filthy, battered drifter who talks to himself almost constantly. Under his enormous brown hat, he wears a twisted expression and keeps his eyes slightly crossed at all times to indicate his affliction. Refusing to allow a small matter such as his blindness to stand in the way of a rewarding career, he works as a hired gun for a variety of equal opportunity employers.

The movie opens with an establishing shot of the Great American Desert (which, in this picture, is actually southern Spain). A riderless horse makes its way slowly across the burning sands. It appears to be utterly alone, until, with a dramatic flourish, it moves its rear end to reveal a pathetic, sightless figure staggering along behind and clutching its tail. This may seem a primitive form of guidance, but the horse, "Boss" (appearing this time without the E Street Band), displays sensitivity and smarts that would put any German shepherd—or even Mr. Ed—to shame. Through various whinnies, shakes of the head, and timely nudges, the miraculous steed not only tells the Blindman what to do but shows him where to shoot. Other than that, our hero relies upon his uncanny sense of hearing, mystical intuition, and a Winchester rifle which he uses like a red and white cane to pick his way through a hostile saloon.

A group of girl-hungry Texas miners are so impressed by his optimism in the face of adversity that they hire the gutsy gunman to protect a shipment of fifty mail order brides who are due to arrive from the East. Since the ads for the movie describe these female extras as "50 of the World's Most Beautiful Women," the husbands-to-be like the idea of a blind bodyguard who won't be distracted by the visual charms of his charges.

Unfortunately the same cannot be said for a pair of Mexican bandit brothers who are understandably aroused by the sight of all those *muchachas* on the hoof. They attack the convoy, humiliate the Blindman, and kidnap the girls for a South of the Border brothel that combines all the most charming elements of a Nazi concentration camp and the women's prison in *Chained Heat* (*see:* THE MOST EMBARRASSING NUDE SCENE IN HOLLYWOOD HISTORY). For the duration of the picture our blind buckaroo works to avenge himself on the baddies and their unspeakable sister, "Sweet Mama" (Magda Konopka), who owns the Worst Little Whorehouse in Mexico. The producers provide a happy ending of sorts when the senior bandito (Lloyd Batista) is sadistically blinded by a fat and fun-loving Mexican general (Raf Baldassare); Sweet Mama is stripped and tied to a tree; and the younger villain is humiliated when the credits reveal him to be Ringo Starr. The former Beatle would have been well-advised to get back to where he once belonged; he looks scruffy and bored, as always, and gets no chance to display either musical or comedic talents before the sightless sharpshooter blows him away. Though our hero thoroughly enjoys the sweet taste of vengeance (with all the appropriate biblical eye-for-an-eye symbolism) he still fails to deliver the fifty soiled doves to their Texas destination, setting the stage for an expected sequel.

The guiding light behind this madness is one Anthony Anthony, of Clarksburg, West Virginia, a former stage actor who made his mark (under the name Tony Anthony) as star of the popular Italian westerns *A Stranger in Town* (1967), *The Stranger Returns* (1968), and *The Silent Stranger* (1975). He originated the concept for *Blindman*, co-wrote the script, co-produced the movie, and played the title role. "He's not your typical gunslinger," he recalls today with an absolutely straight face. "He's more of an existential hero, or really whatever you want to make of him. The point of the film is its simplicity. I never wanted to be a superhero; I felt audiences could relate to me as someone in the street." Apparently Mr. Anthony forgot that not everyone in the street carries a white cane and a tin cup.

Blindman stumbled into theaters around the world at a time when European westerns had reached their peak of popularity. As Mr. Anthony remembers the situation, "They were making so many of these movies that it was almost scary. There were about four hundred a year out of France, Germany, and Italy by the end of the sixties. You could go into some Spanish villages at the time and you'd see signs to keep one film company out of the way of another one."

In this crowded field the novel notion of a visionless vaquero with a spiritually enlightened horse helped distinguish Anthony's adventure from all its competitors. Despite universally negative reviews ("An outstandingly unpleasant film," sniffed the British publication *Films and Filming*) and disappointing business in the United States, *Blindman*, which cost only $1.3 million to produce, pulled more than $15 million in box office receipts from theaters around the world. In Karachi, Pakistan, for instance, it emerged as such a phenomenal hit that it played to consistently packed houses in the same theater for six months. The producers unleashed the film for its third worldwide release in 1985 while Anthony threw up his hands and smiled. "It's unbelievable," he declares. "New generations are seeing the picture all the time. It's like an animal that won't die."

AND THE WINNER IS...

...BLINDMAN

While the other cowboys in this category approached their movie chores with appropriately whimsical attitudes, Tony Anthony reached for mystical profundity in his role as the Blindman. When he mutters to himself or offers vulgar asides to the audience, his comments on the action show even greater philosophical depth than those of Elmer the Range Buster. "When a woman's got you by the short hairs," he intones, "you're dead," or, "To have no eyes means to be half a man . . . to have no eyes and no money . . . that's a bitch!"

In real life Mr. Anthony has both eyes and money, but so far, despite many offers, he has resisted the temptation of making a sequel. Instead he has concentrated his efforts on two successful 3-D schlockbusters, *Comin' At Ya* (1981) and *Treasure of the Four Crowns* (1983), on which he worked as both producer and star.

Supporters of the Hire the Handicapped campaign might still get the chance to enjoy a *Return of the Blindman* project at some point in the future but only, Mr. Anthony told us, under one condition. "They would have to do it without those damn contact lenses for my eyes. I hated those things, I mean

I couldn't stand it. They were supposed to make my eyes look fluorescent blue, like I was really blind, and by the end of the picture I almost was. They rubbed against my eyes, and the sun got in there, and it was agony. My brother was on the set to put numbing solution in my eyes. I never suffered so much in my life. But in the end," he sighed, "I guess it was worth it."

THE MOST SHAMELESSLY (AND TASTELESSLY) DERIVATIVE TITLE FOR A PORNOGRAPHIC FILM

X-rated features are deservedly notorious for their wretched production values and their unabashed exploitation of women—not to mention men, boys, pets, vegetables, and various household implements. On occasion these feeble fantasies try to hide their shortcomings with titles (and free publicity) adapted from much-heralded Hollywood hits. In substance, these feckless flicks bore no resemblance to their mainstream models, but each of the "high concept" titles no doubt managed to lure a few extra raincoat-clad fans into the theaters, hoping, in vain, for something new and different.

AND THE NOMINEES ARE...

MY BARE LADY (1963)

SEX FAMILY ROBINSON (1968)

ONE MILLION A.C./D.C. (1969)

PRAY FOR ROSEMARY'S BEAVER (1969)
We await announcement of the inevitable sequel, *Leave it to Rosemary's Beaver.*

FLESH GORDON (1972)

LUST HORIZONS (1974)

THE SEXORCIST (1974)

NAUGHTY NETWORK (1977)
This tribute to the Academy Award–winning Faye Dunaway–Peter Finch vehicle describes a struggling television network that tries for a comeback by offering exclusively X-rated fare to its viewers, including the smash-hit daytime drama *Genital Hospital.*

THE PINK LAGOON (1981)

EVERY WHICH WAY SHE CAN (1981)

THE FRENCH LIEUTENANT'S BOYS (1982)

BEYOND THE VALLEY OF THE ULTRA MILK MAIDS (1983)

ON GOLDEN BLONDE (1983)

FLESHDANCE (1984)

FLASHPANTS (1984)

FIRST TIMES AT CHERRY HIGH (1984)

SPERMS OF ENDEARMENT (1984)

SISTER DEAREST (1985)

E.T.: THE EXTRA TESTICLE (1985)

ROMANCING THE BONE (1985)

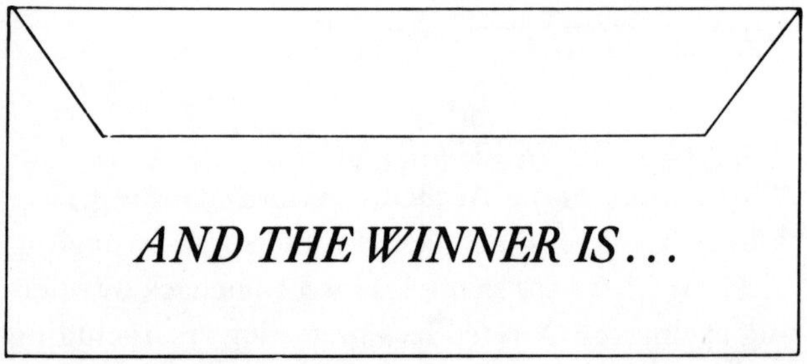

BEYOND THE VALLEY OF THE ULTRA MILKMAIDS

Talk about derivative titles . . .

In the beginning there was Jacqueline Susann's *Valley of the Dolls* (1967), a terrible film, to be sure, but at least a vaguely respectable one. Then came the sleazy pseudosequel, *Beyond the Valley of the Dolls* (1970), directed by the incomparable Russ Meyer from the witty screenplay he co-authored with film critic Roger Ebert. Meanwhile, back at the raunch, Meyer scored major hits with his softcore spectaculars *Vixen* (1968) and *Supervixens* (1975). In 1979 this inventive *auteur* managed another filmic first when he succeeded in ripping off three of his own films at the same time with the title of his latest project: *Beneath the Valley of the Ultravixens*.

As if determined to top that extraordinary achievement, the producers of *Beyond the Valley of the Ultra Milkmaids* managed to evoke echoes of all the films noted above, in an absolutely disgusting motion picture that had nothing whatever to do with Russ Meyer, vixens, dolls, valleys, Jacqueline Susann, *or* Roger Ebert. While making fun of motherhood (and apple pie), the moviemakers further insulted their audience with some sour, out-of-tune musical interludes which, had they been accompanied by lyrics of suitable stupidity, might have helped them qualify for our next category. . . .

AND THE WINNER IS . . .

THE WORST
ROCK 'N' ROLL LYRICS
IN MOVIE HISTORY

AND THE NOMINEES ARE...

"STRANGE PURSUIT" FROM
THE HIDEOUS SUN DEMON (1959)

The Hideous Sun Demon *(Robert Clarke,* center*) engages in the "Strange Pursuit" of feminine companionship that is lyrically described by a torchy song presented in a piano bar.*

Robert Clarke, who also produced and directed this hideously incompetent horror movie, plays an atomic scientist who, after being contaminated by

radiation, is forced to wear an ill-fitting lizard-monster suit whenever the sun comes out. Before this transformation takes place, he meets the love of his life (Nan Peterson) in a cocktail lounge and is hypnotized by her haunting serenade:

> Strange pursuit,
> The pursuit of love,
> Is a strange, compelling desire.
> When you're not there
> You're not mine to hold
> And I want the joy your lips inspire.
> My heart is there,
> You know I care,
> Will you take my love or throw it away?

"VICKIE" FROM *EEGAH!* (1962)

Before he does battle with a prehistoric giant (Richard Kiel) in the desert near Palm Springs, California, a high school band leader (Arch Hall, Jr.) tries to arouse the jealousy of his teen queen girlfriend (Marilyn Manning) by singing her a song about another girl. As she listens, she passes the time by doing the backstroke in a country club swimming pool, without getting a drop of water on her beehive hairdo.

> Vickie, oh Vickie, I'm so alone!
> Would you just talk to me or
> call me on the phone?
> Would you give one last chance
> to a fo-oo-oo-oo-ool?
> Vickie, oh Vickie, Vickie, you are my love!

"THE MIGHTY SONS OF HERCULES" FROM *THE MOLE MEN VS. THE SON OF HERCULES* (1962)

This stirring, hard-driving title song proved such a hit with fans of Italian muscleman sagas that producer Joseph E. Levine recycled it for subsequent use in some of his other releases, including *The Terror of Rome Against the Son of Hercules*, *Medusa Against the Son of Hercules*, and *The Devil of the Desert Against the Son of Hercules*.

> The Mighty Sons of Hercules
> Thundered through the years.
> These men of steel could never feel
> The pulse of a coward's heels. [???]

"TO HAVE AND TO HOLD" FROM *MARS INVADES PUERTO RICO* (ALTERNATE TITLE: *FRANKENSTEIN MEETS THE SPACE MONSTER*) (1965)

A sexpot princess from Mars (Marilyn Hanold) and her bald-headed dwarf assistant, the appropriately named Dr. Nadir (Lou Cutell), come to Earth to replenish the "breeding stock" of their planet. Since they want only the finest examples of feminine pul-

chritude, they concentrate on nabbing a bevy of Puerto Rican bathing beauties from a poolside party. Who can protect the Earth girls from this menace? Only a robot astronaut named Frank, who suffers an injury to his face that makes him "Frankenstein" of the alternate title. Before the climactic title bout between this good-guy monster and an intergalactic gorilla named Mull (no relation to Martin), Frank's space scientist handlers pause to fall in love. With the future of the universe hanging in the balance, this wholesome couple (James Karen and Nancy Marshall) takes a motorbike tour of scenic San Juan, enjoying the sights while the sweet sounds of twanging guitars and harmonized falsettos pay tribute to their grand passion:

> To love and adore
> You, tell you what's more
> You're everything,
> Breath of spring,
> Ho! Ho! Ho!

While aliens attack the Earth in Mars Invades Puerto Rico *to kidnap terrestrial bathing beauties, the soundtrack offers sentimental fare such as "To Have and to Hold."*

"GO ON AWAY AND LEAVE ME ALONE" FROM *THE YESTERDAY MACHINE* (1963)

In The Yesterday Machine, *Tim Holt dramatizes the featured ballad, "Go On Away and Leave Me Alone."*

On the evening she learns that her drum majorette sister has been abducted by an evil German physicist (Jack Herman—*see:* THE WORST PERFORMANCE AS A NAZI MAD SCIENTIST) nightclub singer Ann Pellegrino manages to go on with her show, but the searing, hard-edged selection she belts out to her audience shows her profound hurt and pain:

> Go on away and leave me alone. . .
> I don't care whether I live or I die.
> Why is it everything happens to *me*
> And my dreams all explode in my face?

city as they conduct their grudge match. A smiling nightclub singer (Kipp Hamilton) provides this song as a romantic interlude; the green gargantua reacts to her musical talents by smashing his hand through the ceiling, lifting her to his mouth, and eating her in a single gulp.

> If I had a hidden microphone inside of
> My heart I would turn the power on.
> It would amplify my love for you.
> But the words get stuck in my throat!

A green gargantua battles his orange colleague for the attention of glamorous lounge singer Kipp Hamilton.

"STUCK IN MY THROAT" FROM *WAR OF THE GARGANTUAS* (1967)

American scientist Russ Tamblyn journeys to Tokyo to save Japanese civilization from two battling giant gorillas, one green, the other orange, who smash the

"FIRST LOVE" FROM *THE PIRATE MOVIE* (1982)

When Universal Studios announced plans for a film version of the hit Broadway production of *The Pirates of Penzance,* Australian record producer David Joseph came up with an idea for some piracy of his own. Grabbing Gilbert and Sullivan's public domain

Teen sex symbols Christopher Atkins and Kristy McNichol celebrate their "First Love" in The Pirate Movie—*the biggest bomb ever developed in Australia, unless the Aussies unexpectedly decide to acquire a nuclear capacity.*

score, hiring teen heartthrobs Kristy McNichol and Christopher *(Blue Lagoon)* Atkins, Joseph rushed to finish this insipid and insufferable travesty so it would reach theaters several months ahead of the more publicized Linda Ronstadt–Rex Smith version. In the process, he created the most expensive ($9 million) Australian film made up to that time—and one of the very worst. The producer and his writers considered W. S. Gilbert's classic lyrics "outdated" and so not only attempted to rewrite his well-known words, but also added four utterly incongruous "mellow rock" originals to be sung by McNichol and Atkins. The two stars warble "First Love" as they approach each other, in soft focus and slow motion, on a lonely beach:

> Some kind of miracle brought you here
> Just when I had given up hoping.
> From the moment when you first appeared
> I could feel my whole life opening.

AND THE WINNER IS...

...MARS INVADES PUERTO RICO

This altogether incoherent insanity from Alan V. Iselin, executive producer of *The Horror of Party Beach* (which features some horrendous rock lyrics of its own—*see:* THE WORST BEACH PARTY MOVIE EVER MADE), wins the award because it delivers a double dose of musical incompetence from two different sources. In addition to the nominated song "To Have and to Hold" (written and performed by those dynamic hard rockers, The Distant Cousins), the soundtrack to *Mars* also offers "That's the Way It's Got to Be" by a sensitive, introspective group appropriately known as The Poets. This second song pleased the producers so thoroughly that they used it twice in the film: in the opening sequence as American astronauts pile into their spaceship, and as background for the harrowing sequence in which the Martians invade the earth. In neither instance is there even the slightest connection between the song's lyrics and the furious action on screen:

> You may live by me today,
> Then tomorrow go away,
> There will be no tears from me,
> That's the way it's got to be.
>
> But for now let's live and we may find
> That our love could be the lasting kind.
> Love may be like summer's rain,
> Quickly come then gone again,
> It may last eternally,
> That's the way it's got to be.

Copyright © 1965 by ABKCO Music, Inc.

"Mull the Space Monster," who battles Frank, the scarred but good-hearted earth robot, to decide the future of the universe in Mars Invades Puerto Rico (*also known as* Frankenstein Meets the Space Monster).

The bald dwarf Dr. Nadir and the nefarious Princess Marcuzan watch in despair as the heroes defeat their plans for world domination. As The Poets sing so eloquently on the soundtrack, "That's the Way It's Got to Be."

The use of this song enhances the general air of confusion and decadence that pervades the film, with a flamboyant cast that seems to take lip-smacking delight in its own overacting, and a ridiculously un- convincing simian monster from outer space, which, silly as it is, could not quite qualify as one of the honored nominees in our final category . . . .

THE MOST LAUGHABLE CONCEPT FOR AN OUTER SPACE INVADER

AND THE NOMINEES ARE . . .

A MONSTER TV SET FROM THE FUTURE IN *THE TWONKY* (1953)

If this harebrained morality play had been made in the 1970s, the terrifying "Twonky" of the title might well have been a television set from Japan that invaded America with superior technology and low prices. Instead the featured creature here is a boxy 1953 Admiral, with menacing rabbit ears and tiny legs that carry it awkwardly from place to place. The chief victim of this telepathic telly, philosophy professor Kerry West (Hans Conried), realizes only belatedly that the home entertainment center his wife has purchased "on the installment plan" has been possessed by the spirit of a demonic robot from a distant civilization in the future. This mad machine proceeds to take over Conried's life, following him from room to room, lighting his cigarettes, doing the dishes, and, worst of all, or so the script informs us, "denying his God-given right to be wrong."

This clunky machine, manipulated by wires so visible they would embarrass the Flying Nun, is supposed to be an incredibly powerful and intelligent

Hans Conried is locked in mortal combat with a killer TV set in The Twonky.

machine, but in the end it proves no match for the wily Hans Conried; he eventually destroys his tormentor in an automobile accident. At the time of its theatrical release, *The Twonky* suffered from poor reception, presumably leaving earthlings safe from sequels about invading Water Piks from the future. In reviewing the movie, *Variety* described it as "unbelievably bad" and commented that it "bears no resemblance to motion picture entertainment other than being on film."

ROBOT GORILLAS FROM THE MOON IN *ROBOT MONSTER* (1953)

This celebrated 3-D fantasy presents a race of killer robots dressed in gorilla suits and deep-sea diving helmets who invade the earth and slaughter all of humanity, except for six very bad actors. We actually meet only two of the dreaded invaders—the sensitive, conflicted "Ro-Man" and his unfeeling, martinet boss back on the moon, "Great Guidance"—and both parts are played by the same versatile actor, George Barrows. He won the pivotal role because he owned his very own moth-eaten gorilla costume and offered an unbeatable bargain to master director Phil Tucker, who couldn't afford the cost of renting a robot suit. As Tucker recalled the careful planning behind the film, "I thought, 'I know George will work for me for nothing. I'll get a diving helmet, put it on him, and it'll work!'"

The first problem with this scheme involved Barrows' courageous attempts to deliver his lines, including several intense, dramatic soliloquys dramatizing Ro-Man's inner turmoil in choosing between his love for an earth girl and his sense of higher duty. With a stocking over his face to hide his features, and a papier-mâché diving helmet on top of that, the words came out so hopelessly muffled that Tucker could use none of it. The director hired another actor (a veteran Shakespearean named John Brown) to dub in the lines later, but his delivery is comically ill-matched with Barrows' broad, expressive gestures.

And speaking of broad, Barrows weighed 240 pounds at the time he reported for duty, which made him look like a particularly paunchy primate inside his gorilla suit. "The shoot took a week, and it was hot the whole time," he recalls. "Maybe ninety degrees, maybe more. And I was wearing my suit and

In Robot Monster *everybody's favorite bloodthirsty robot from the moon comes to Earth in gorilla suit and diving helmet to menace two of the last surviving humans, George Nader and Claudia Barrett.*

all the other equipment, so believe me, it was a difficult show. Especially the time when that screwball director ordered this incredibly long shot of me walking up the hill, carrying the girl in my arms—well, you better believe, I was sweating up a storm. But, like they say, that's show business!"

A HUGE, FIRE-BREATHING ARMADILLO IN *GIGANTIS THE FIRE MONSTER* (1955)

In Japanese science fiction movies it's impossible to tell the monsters from one another without a scorecard. Gigantis, the star of this film, is none other than our old friend Godzilla in the second of his sixteen screen appearances. He performs this time under an alias because Warner Brothers, which bought the rights to dub and distribute the film in America, refused to pay the extra money to use the golden Godzilla name.

Godzilla, appearing here under the nom de monster "Gigantis," defends Osaka against the depredations of a giant armadillo named Angurus.

Our hero's opponent in this outing is a 220-foot-long armadillo with a spiky back named Angurus. In the time-honored tradition, Angurus and Gigantis (né Godzilla) thrash around endlessly like a pair of determined *sumo* wrestlers, flattening pagodas and skyscrapers without pausing to interrupt their struggle. In the end a squadron of heroic Japanese jet jockeys fly a daring bombing raid to unleash an avalanche that helps Big G win his grudge match. When one of the fly-boys (Mindru Chiaki) returns home and wins warm praise from his sweetie for his bravery, he sheepishly shrugs off her compliments with the eloquent declaration, "Aw, banana oil!"

A KILLER CUCUMBER FROM VENUS IN *IT CONQUERED THE WORLD* (1956)

This megalomaniac vegetable lands on earth, establishes its headquarters in a cave, and proceeds to subjugate an Arizona town with the help of little rubber bats that bite their victims into submission. Also assisting in this noble project is a Benedict Arnold Earth scientist (played by spaghetti western immortal Lee Van Cleef) who believes that the Big Green from Venus will establish a blessed era of world peace and crispy fresh pickles. His wife (Beverly Garland) knows better, and confronts the vicious veggie in its lair. "I hate your living guts. . . .

You're ugly!" she screams as she fires her rifle at the visitor from Venus. "You think you're going to make a slave of the world. Go on, try your intellect on me!" With an invitation like that from a blonde sweater girl like Beverly Garland, the cunning cuke comes rolling out of its cave on furniture casters, while sharp-eyed moviegoers enjoy a good view of the gentleman who is pushing the creature from behind. *Variety* sagely suggested that producer-director Roger Corman (making only the second science fiction film of his long and distinguished career) "would have been wiser to suggest the creature, rather than constructing the awesome-looking and clumsy rubberized horror. It inspires more titters than terror."

Beverly Garland has to concentrate all her formidable intellectual powers in order to outsmart a giant cucumber from Venus in Roger Corman's It Conquered the World.

The same could definitely be said of the watermelon monster in the wretched remake of *It Conquered the World*, Larry Buchanan's *Zontar, The Thing from Venus* (1966). Anthony (*Mars Needs Women*) Houston plays the Lee Van Cleef role, and John Agar is the good-guy scientist who tries to stop him.

AN EXTRATERRESTRIAL TURKEY IN *THE GIANT CLAW* (1957)

Mara Corday and Jeff Morrow courageously resist the enormous talons of a man-eating turkey from deep space in The Giant Claw.

"It's a bird!" declares brilliant young scientist Jeff Morrow. "A bird as big as a battleship!"

This squawking invader comes to earth from deep space with a profound primal need to nest atop the Empire State Building. Why, you may ask, doesn't the U.S. Air Force protect the terrified city by sending up its jet fighters for a spectacular turkey shoot? Because, the men of science inform us, the avian alien comes conveniently equipped with an invisible "bubble chamber" force field that shields it from harm. It also travels with visible marionette wires, stiff flapping wings, google eyes, and an impressive collection of tail feathers.

The actors in this Sam Katzman spectacular (Morrow, Morris Ankrum, and former *Playboy* Playmate Mara Corday as a brilliant mathematician) react with exaggerated horror every time they hear the creature's telltale cackle. Jeff Morrow, who battled more formidable outer space invaders in some half dozen other sci-fi features of the fifties, recalled: "We shot the film before we ever got a look at this monster that was supposed to be so terrifying. The producers promised us the special effects would be first class. The director—Fred Sears—just told us, 'All right, now you see the bird up there, and you're scared to death! Use your imagination.' But the first time we actually got to see it was the night of the premiere. The audi-

ence couldn't stop laughing. We were up there on screen looking like idiots, treating this silly buzzard like it was the scariest thing in the world. We felt cheated, that's for sure, but they told us afterward that they just ran out of money. They couldn't afford anything except this stupid puppet. But it was just terrible. I was never so embarrassed in my entire life."

Though critics have variously described the behemoth bird as a vulture, an eagle, and a dodo, we naturally prefer to think of it as a turkey. Certainly this film's box office performance supported that classification. To most moviegoers *The Giant Claw* proved no more horrifying than *Sesame Street*'s Big Bird, who recently made his feature film debut in *Follow That Bird*.

A GIGANTIC KILLER SQUIRREL IN *VARAN THE UNBELIEVABLE* (1958)

Varan the Unbelievable, the world's largest and nastiest flying squirrel, destroys every toy tank and toy helicopter he can get his claws on and inevitably squashes the city of Tokyo.

The careless experiments of Japanese scientists arouse the concern of an otherworldly ecological activist. To protest their attempts to use electricity to turn salt water into soda, Varan arises from the bottom of a lake to decimate the countryside around oft-abused Tokyo. Crown-International, desperate to extend the running time for U.S. distribution, added a subplot in which an American G.I. played by Myron *(Panther Girl of the Kongo, Jungle Moon Men, Claws)* Healey and his prettily ailing Japanese wife (Tsuruko Kobayashi) mobilize a joint effort by American and Nipponese forces to beat back the ravaging rodent. Some observers have commented on Varan's reptilian qualities, but the bulk of critical opinion accepts him as a huge flying squirrel. Now, if this shrieking airborne critter could only find himself a talking moose sidekick, perhaps he could someday qualify for his own TV cartoon series. . . .

A KILLER CATTLE SKULL FROM A DISTANT GALAXY IN
SHIP OF MONSTERS (1959)

This picture rivals *The Wrestling Women vs. the Aztec Mummy* (1965) as the worst movie ever made in Mexico. In fact, it features one of the celebrated Wrestling Women, Lorena Velasquez, as a princess from Venus who invades the earth along with her partner, Anna Bertha Lepe (a former Miss Mexico). You can tell that these space girls represent an advanced civilization because they wear stylish one-piece bathing suits, fishnet stockings, and the highest heels available anywhere in the Milky Way. The purpose of their mission is to kidnap an ideal male specimen to bring back to the "planet of women" for breeding purposes. With this goal in mind, they naturally aim their rocket ship at the great city of Chihuahua, home of the hemisphere's most irresistible Latin lovers.

The specific lover they select is the ever-popular "Pipporo," a well-known singing cowboy in more than a dozen Mexican films. With his slick, carefully oiled black hair and a pencil-thin mustache, this South of the Border Gene Autry looks like a cross between Ernie Kovacs and Cantinflas, and sings four songs from the saddle while accompanied by an off-screen accordion. He naturally refuses to leave his home in Ol' Mexico for the trip to Venus, which

forces the man-hungry *muchachas* to turn loose the four monsters they have brought along to terrify the Earthlings.

The most notable of these pathetic creatures is an insidious talking skeleton named Zok who repeatedly comments "Haw! Haw! Haw!" at the foibles of the Earth men. In an attempt to make this Halloween gag look exotic and frightening, the producers took an ordinary human skeleton and attached the skull of a steer—the same sort of relic you see bleaching by the side of the road in any desert of the Southwest. The head of the monster wiggles up and down slightly as it talks—thanks to a prominently displayed string attached to its jaw—but other than that the creature is totally immobile. When it chases its Earth prey, it must be carried by one of its "intergalactic monster" colleagues, "Tagual, the Beetle-Man."

In the end the heroic Pipporo, aided by his 8-year-old sidekick, Joey, and a turncoat Venutian robot named Tor, defeats all four monsters using a slingshot, matches, and his trusty hunting knife. Presumably Zok, the formidable Skeleton Monster, is still rotting somewhere alongside the highway outside the city of Chihuahua, where he would hardly be noticed by passing tourists.

A MAN-EATING CARPET FROM OUTER SPACE IN
THE CREEPING TERROR (1964)

The action of *The Creeping Terror* consists entirely of the title monster devouring a series of unsuspecting citizens, including a mother and her baby, a girl who wears a bikini for a picnic in the woods, all the patrons of the local lovers' lane, a folksinger and his followers, a platoon of the United States Army (all six of them), a prom-full of twisting teenagers, and one grotesquely fat fisherman. Oddly enough, these victims never run away from danger; if they did the slow-moving, intergalactic rug (with the feet of the prop masters propelling it clearly visible at the bottom of the screen) would never catch up with them. What's more, these selected snacks provide friendly assistance above and beyond the call of duty when it comes to cooperating with the monster who is trying to swallow them. In most cases they struggle energetically to crawl into its gaping mouth, until the

A look of sheer terror on the faces of two fun-loving "teenagers" as The Creeping Terror *invades a high school prom and asks for a dance.*

stagehands inside (who were actually students from Glendale College) manage to yank them through.

The confused sexuality of the Creeping Terror has puzzled a full generation of scholars since the film's release. On the one hand, the gas mask hoses that dangle from its forehead become engorged whenever it digests a comely starlet; on the other, the deadly yawning chasm at the very center of its being suggests the dark, primordial fear of the enveloping power of the female.

In view of the sex-obsessed nature of this creature, it seems only appropriate that the paralyzed earth people should try to protect themselves by summoning "the world's leading authority on space emissions." Dr. Bradford (William Thourlby, who doubled as the movie's producer) arrives from England and works closely with the heroic sheriff, Martin (played by "Vic Savage," who is actually the movie's director, Art J. Nelson), to solve the riddle of the crawling, slithering invader and its cardboard spaceship. Eventually they kill this threat to humanity with the timely toss of a hand grenade and discover that the carnivorous carpet is actually a "mobile laboratory" which, according to the omnipresent narrator (Larry Burrel), "consumes human beings in order to analyze them chemically, undoubtedly to detect weaknesses in the human species."

Any future visitor from outer space searching for examples of human weakness need look no further than this film.

A FIFTY-FOOT-HIGH RUBBER CHICKEN FROM "UP THERE" IN *THE X FROM OUTER SPACE* (1967)

Why did the chicken cross the galaxy? To destroy Tokyo, of course. A Japanese "explorer rocket" returns from a mission to the far reaches of space bearing a mysterious organism as part of its cargo. This itty-bitty blob quickly matures into "the X," a gigantic chicken dinosaur that wobbles around on its spindly little hind legs, flaps its wings at its sides, and crows with a voice like a hippopotamus in heat. To distinguish himself from other East Asian monsters, Our Boy X belches out deadly steel spears instead of breathing ordinary old fire, and crushes some of the shoddiest toy trucks ever seen in a monster movie. The world is in peril until the cunning counterattack, led by those stalwarts Eiji Okada (star of *Hiroshima Mon Amour*) and Shinichi Yanagisawa (star of nothing else that we know of), in a simpleminded soufflé that definitely lays an egg.

DON'T COOK TONIGHT, CALL CHICKEN DELIGHT: A piece of interplanetary poultry devours a battleship in The X from Outer Space.

A GIANT KILLER EYEBALL IN *VOYAGE INTO SPACE* (1968)

"The Emperor Guillotine," ruler of the evil planet "Gargoyle," is a cackling baddie in a green mask, silver pajamas, and a bathrobe, who invades the earth with a score of scaries. These heinous henchmen include a monster starfish, a killer octopus, and a gigantic doglike creature who swallows an entire train as if it were a Milk Bone.

When these creatures fail to subjugate humanity, the emperor calls on his *beast de resistance:* a detached eyeball the size of Grand Central Station. This lumbering monstrosity has neither arms nor legs and doesn't do much of anything except blink occasionally. Nevertheless, the evil eye uses the power of hypnosis to conquer beautiful downtown Kyoto—its telepathic powers cause cars to float through the air and plunge to their doom.

Japan looks to be in big trouble once again, until a brave band of commandos, known as the Unicorns and dressed in the national colors of red and white, arrives on the scene. These saviors include a handsome teenager named Jerry Mano (no relation to Gerry Mander), a "world-famous scientist," an adorable little girl in pigtails, and the leader of the group, an unusual 8-year-old named Johnny Seiko (Akio Tito). Ordinarily one might not expect this insufferable brat, who combines the pudgy face and grave demeanor of an East Asian Gary Coleman, to overcome the formidable Emperor Guillotine and his preternatural peeper, but Johnny uses his wristwatch (a Seiko, no doubt) to control the movements of his best pal, known simply as Giant Robot. This flying mechanical marvel proceeds to battle the oversize oculus until Johnny, shouting into his watch, orders a knockout blow. "Giant Robot!" he commands. "*Mega-punch!*" His faithful friend obliges, and the Gargoyle Eye explodes into a shower of fireworks.

In the end the robot runs a kamikaze mission to a distant star to destroy the emperor himself, reducing each of the Unicorns to tears as the narrator solemnly intones: "Giant Robot sacrificed himself to save the earth from the terrible Guillotine. But who knows—when Johnny needs him again, perhaps—like a miracle—he will come back out of the sky."

Don't hold your breath—*Voyage into Space,* adapted from a popular Japanese television show, never generated enough interest to inspire the expected sequel.

MOLDY COTTAGE CHEESE FROM BEYOND THE STARS IN *THE GREEN SLIME* (1969)

A one-eyed moldy cottage cheese creature from the Great Beyond quarrels with an Earthling astronaut over the interior decoration scheme for a U.S. spaceship in The Green Slime.

Some of the worst American actors (Robert Horton and Richard Jaeckel) meet some of the worst Japanese special effects in this multinational fiasco released by MGM. The deadly slime of the title is represented by several two-legged cyclops monsters with foam rubber bodies that look as if they have been assembled by melting a pile of green golf balls together, or perhaps covered by a huge scoop of four-week-old cottage cheese. The slime creatures could kill normal victims by causing them to die laughing, but to overcome the humorless dunderheads on board the space station "Gamma III," the monsters make use of serpentine tentacles that flash intermittently (like neon beer signs) to remind us they are electrified.

The fun begins when a killer asteroid heads straight toward Earth and threatens to inspire a terrible new disaster movie. Under orders from the U.S. government, our intrepid adventurers blast off to intercept this hurtling rock and investigate its surface. In the process they pick up a small drop of what looks like ordinary mint jelly, but which promptly transforms itself into the hissing slime monster. The arrival of this uninvited guest on the space station interrupts Captain Jaeckel and his second-in-command, Horton, who have been having a great time fighting each other over the ample va-va-voom charms of Italian bombshell Luciana Paluzzi, who is hilariously miscast as the all-American science whiz "Dr. Lisa Benson." Faced with this dire threat to civilization as we know it, she quickly applies her superior intellect and reaches the conclusion that instead of killing the monster, bullets only cause it to multiply. Before long, Gamma III suffers a formidable infestation problem, which proves so tedious for the authorities back on Earth (not to mention the audience) that they blow up the entire spacecraft and end the movie.

The peril faced by the astronauts on screen paled beside the deadly challenge encountered by the publicists back at the studio: They couldn't decide whether the word "slime" denoted singular or plural. Some ads proclaimed that "The Green Slime Are Coming!" while others, appearing at the same time, proclaimed that "The Green Slime Is Here!!!" The promotional material from MGM promised "a hair-raising story of fiendish creatures . . . a spell-binding science fiction horror drama" but the *Los Angeles Times* discovered "one of the funniest made-in-Japan science fiction monster movies ever!" Director Kinji Fukasaku went on from his triumph with these culinary creatures to direct the adventures of a group of friendly walnuts from another galaxy in the memorable *Message from Space* (1978) for United Artists.

AND THE WINNER IS . . .

. . . THE CREEPING TERROR

In the hands of competent filmmakers, some of the ludicrous concepts for outer space invaders described above might have beaten the odds and turned into respectable movie monsters. With the right sort of special effects magic, it's conceivable that gorilla robots, gigantic turkeys, killer eyeballs, and man-eating flying squirrels could have intrigued, or at least entertained, some undemanding moviegoers. Even the idea of an oversize cucumber from Venus possesses, if nothing else, an undeniable Freudian resonance.

But a deadly *carpet* from beyond the stars? Not even the fabled technical wizards of George Lucas's Industrial Light and Magic operation could ever redeem such a hopelessly dull and unimaginative notion. *The Creeping Terror* wins the award on the strength of a basic concept so flat-footed and so unshakable in its stupidity that it makes the mad, go-for-broke flamboyance of *Robot Monster* and *The Giant Claw* seem admirable by comparison.

Though the action on screen provides plenty of laughs for bad movie fanciers around the world, the true story of how the *Terror* first crept into our consciousness offers far more in the way of action and ingenuity than anything in the script.

Art J. Nelson—the man behind the monster—first made his way to Hollywood in the mid-1950s. "He was the kind of guy you could never forget," recalls *Creeping Terror* co-writer Alan Silliphant. "He used to wear dark glasses, flashy white suits, pink shirts, and elevator shoes. He drove around in used Cadillacs, a different one every few months. His proudest possession was his gold-rimmed business card that used to say he was the president of 'Metropolitan International Productions,' whatever that was. He put up a good front, but for all I know he was sleeping in his car."

The background of this motivated mogul remains an item of dispute. Some of his associates remember him as a full-blooded Cherokee Indian from a reservation in Oklahoma; hence the name "Vic Savage," one of his many aliases, and the designation he used as an actor in the lead role of "Deputy Martin" in *The Creeping Terror.* Others claim that Nelson actually hailed from Bridgeport, Connecticut, while screenwriter Silliphant insists that the aspiring entrepreneur came from the Chicago area. "The one thing you could be sure of was that this guy knew

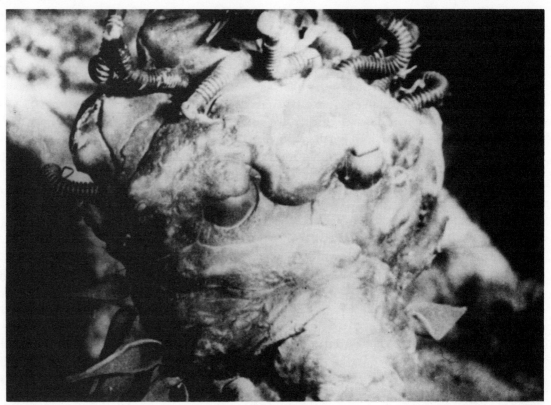

A rare close-up of a most unusual monster: Art Nelson's Creeping Terror.

how to talk and he knew how to sell and he had a very vivid imagination."

These gifts enabled Nelson to convince a surprising number of Californians of his credentials as one of America's leading moviemakers. He had, in fact, written, directed, and starred in an ultra-low-budget teenage gangster exploitation flick called *Street Fighter,* using one of his other aliases, "Arthur J. White." The only review of the picture appeared in the *Motion Picture Herald* shortly after its very limited release in 1959 and praised Nelson/White/Savage for his "deft sure touches" and "promising production talent." One can only assume that he made multiple copies of this charitable critique and handed them out along with his snazzy business cards as he laid the groundwork for *The Creeping Terror.*

In any event, he managed to take the sleepy town of Glendale, California, by storm. "What a great line he had!" remembers Dr. Frederick Kopp, who wrote the *Terror*'s avant-garde musical score. "He kept saying he was going to make the greatest, the *biggest* monster movie ever made."

The eager *auteur* made the same proposal to each of his potential "investors": If they put up money to

help him mount his monster, they would not only share in the fabulous and all but assured profits, but would win the chance to participate in the production. According to records later filed with the Superior Court of the State of California, Dr. Kopp, a music teacher with ambitions as a classical composer, shelled out $6,000 for the privilege of writing the score. Jack King paid $2,500 for the small but pivotal role of the portly "Gramps," while it cost William Thourlby, a male model (who later won fame as wardrobe consultant to President Richard Nixon) some $16,000 for his star turn as the heroic scientist, "Dr. Bradford." Sculptor Jon Lackey, who designed the rapacious rug monster according to Nelson's specifications, remembered that "the whole thing just kept rolling along. Everybody he talked to wanted to get a part in that motion picture. One of the reasons that the poor monster had to gobble up so many victims is that most of those victims were paying good money to act in the film. Nelson wasn't in a position to say no so he just had to keep feeding that darn thing."

To make these and other adjustments in the script, Nelson worked closely with his untried screen-

Star and co-producer William Thourlby tries to crawl away from The Creeping Terror; *in real life he found it even more difficult to escape the aftermath of this troubled production.*

writer. "I was all of eighteen at the time," Alan Silliphant laughs. "I didn't know the first thing about movies, but I knew I wanted to be a writer." His half-brother, Stirling Silliphant (who went on to script such important motion pictures as *In the Heat of the Night, The Poseidon Adventure,* and *The Swarm*), had already established himself in the entertainment industry, and Alan dreamed of following in his footsteps. "One day Art Nelson introduced himself to me. He told me he was going to give me my big break and he took out a thick roll of bills and started flashing them. I stood there with my mouth open. Then he handed me two hundred dollars in cash and told me to go write about this monster. I was so excited that I finished in three days, and Nelson thought it was the greatest script since *Gone With the Wind.*"

Despite these creative triumphs, the preproduction arrangements dragged on for months. "When I look back, it was very much like the Mel Brooks movie *The Producers,*" says Silliphant. "This guy had collected a great deal of money from the people in Glendale so that it didn't matter what he knew—or didn't know—about moviemaking. He had a big project and he had to go ahead with it."

When shooting began, Nelson rose to the occasion. "He was definitely trying his best," says Ken Savage (no relation to Nelson's alter ego, Vic Savage), who played a minor part in the film. "He was very intense, very excited, trying to do everything himself. I thought he cared a lot about how it turned out. One time he wanted a crazy overhead shot to show the point of view of the monster. That meant climbing to the top of this gigantic tree that must have been forty feet high. Nobody would go up there because it was just obviously dangerous and insane. So Nelson climbed up himself and got the shot. I remember thinking to myself, 'I wouldn't do that for a million dollars. But this guy is really dedicated!' "

He further demonstrated that dedication by asking his lady love to play the female lead in the picture. This mysterious young actress employed nearly as many aliases as Nelson himself, and appears in the various lawsuits surrounding the picture as "Shannon O'Neil," "Shannon Ripley," "Shannon Boltress," and "Mrs. A. J. Nelson." The legal documents also describe her as a minor—which seems to confirm the recollection of two participants that she was a teenage runaway at the time of the picture.

Whatever her name or her life situation, no one could doubt her physical charms. On screen she projected a combination of innocence and sensuality that foreshadowed Brooke Shields at 16. Had she associated herself with another director—and traveling companion—she might well have made a career for herself in Hollywood.

While displaying her face and figure to full advantage, *The Creeping Terror* did nothing to demonstrate the effectiveness of her line reading, or that of any of the other featured players: to cut costs, Nelson shot the entire project without sound. "The plan was that we would mouth our lines, and then we'd come back later and dub in the words," recalls co-star and co-producer William Thourlby. "But by the time that S.O.B. finally got around to it, I think he had lost the script and anyway it was impossible to get everyone together again. So we had to settle for a narrator doing all the goddamn parts. It was horrible, just horrible!"

He can say that again. In the final version of the picture, Larry Burrel, veteran of numerous driver training films, delivers great gobs of undigested narration while the actors offer irrelevant and occasionally contradictory gestures on the screen. At the climax of the action, for instance, the narrator smoothly intones:

"The sergeant, a shaken man, returned babbling about what had happened. Colonel Caldwell, realizing the full danger of the situation, decided he had only one means left to stop the monster: grenades. Now Dr. Bradford made a drastic move. Acting on his superior authority, he forbade Caldwell to destroy [sic] the creature. The colonel, more concerned with saving human lives than advancing science, told Bradford to go to hell."

In another vein, this omnipresent commentator offers philosophical reflections on some of the eternal issues in human existence. During one poetic interlude, Deputy Martin (Art J. Nelson/White/Vic Savage) and his new bride, Brett (Shannon O'Neil/Ripley/Boltress/Nelson), invite their friend Barney (Norman Boone) for dinner. "Barney and Martin had been virtual buddies for years," the narrator helpfully explains, "but now that Martin was settling down for marriage they were slowly drifting apart. Barney naturally was still dating all the girls in town and couldn't understand why Brett and Martin didn't hang around with him more than they did. He couldn't comprehend that married life

In order to raise money for the Creeping Terror *project, enterprising producer-director Art J. Nelson unveils his magnificent monster to astonished crowds on Hollywood Boulevard several weeks before production begins.*

brought with it not only new problems, but also the necessary togetherness of the husband and wife. . . . Since time began, this change in relationships has probably happened to *all* buddies in similar circumstances. Life has its way of making boys grow up and with marriage, Martin's time had come. His life was now Brett, a life that he thoroughly enjoyed."

Nelson, on the other hand, discovered that editing a motion picture was *not* a life that *he* thoroughly enjoyed, and so before the movie could finally be prepared for release, its creator vanished without a trace. Needless to say, his various associates tried to track him down but they met with no success; in the face of a flurry of lawsuits launched against him and a Superior Court ruling that he had "been guilty of fraud and deceit," his whereabouts remained unknown.

In recent years the emergence of *The Creeping Terror* as a perennial favorite at Worst Film Festivals and on videocassette has generated intense new efforts to locate the enigmatic artiste, but Mr. Nelson remains as elusive as ever. Alan Silliphant, who survived his experience on the picture and went on to direct the softcore 3-D smash hit *The Stewardesses* (1971), believes that "he is probably selling hotdogs somewhere—maybe Miami Beach. I can see him now—telling all the old ladies that he used to be a famous producer in Hollywood." William Thourlby, who wrote the 1978 best seller *You Are What You Wear,* maintains a less benign vision of Art J. Nelson's fate. "Nobody knows where he is. Nobody. If he were still alive, I expect he would have turned up by now. But my guess is that he left this world a long time ago. I wouldn't be at all surprised if they found him one day—underneath the Brooklyn Bridge, in twenty feet of dirty water, with his feet attached to a big block of concrete."

THE ROGUES' GALLERY:
Who's Who
in the World of
Bad Movies

*T*his last section of Son of Golden Turkey Awards *celebrates the unsung heroes and heroines who have made it all possible: the directors, producers, writers, stars, and assorted others who helped create Hollywood's most wonderfully wretched motion pictures. A few of the names and faces in this lineup will look familiar, but our list also includes many obscure visionaries whose work has never before been described in print.*

The compilation of this sort of dishonor roll is inevitably a subjective process, and we know there are those who will disagree with our decisions. Some may feel offended that they are included in an index of incompetence; others, whose names do not appear, will be disappointed that they have been ignored. Rather than protesting individual choices, we hope that the reader will accept the Rogues' Gallery for what it is: a good-faith effort to show the broad range of personalities who have helped to bring entertainingly awful movies into the world. By noting a moviemaker as part of this august assemblage, we do not suggest that his or her work is exclusively idiotic: many of these people have created worthy and even distinguished films in addition to their Golden Turkeys.

After watching one of the feckless films featured in our book, many viewers ask themselves, "What kind of person would make a movie like this?" The Rogues' Gallery is intended as a generalized answer to that question, and as overdue recognition of those who have made important contributions to the world of bad movies.

BEVERLY "WOODSIE" AADLAND
Blonde teenage starlet of late fifties; made screen debut at age 6 in industrial film called *Story of Nylon;* became Errol Flynn's mistress at the end of his life; co-starred with him in his dreadful last film, *Cuban Rebel Girls* (1959), when she was 17; subsequently worked in nightclubs, married a car dealer, and retired to Van Nuys, California.

WILLIE AAMES
Cute-so, chunko, curly-headed heartthrob to millions of prepubescent girls; star of television's *Swiss Family Robinson, Eight Is Enough,* and *Charles in Charge;* contributed two memorably awful movies to date: the Israeli-Canadian *Blue Lagoon* rip-off, *Paradise* (1982), and the high school psychic-powers fantasy, *Zapped!* (1983).

ACQUANETTA

Exotic jungle girl of the forties and fifties; *see:* THE MOST LUDICROUS PROFESSIONAL NAME IN MOVIE HISTORY.

AL ADAMSON

Director Al Adamson (open shirt) *shows the breezy, sleazy style that characterizes all of his pictures as he tries to motivate the cast of* The Mean Mothers.

Amazingly inept director of sixties monster movies and seventies sexploitation sagas; son of Australian cowboy star Art Mix (also known as Denver Dixon); married to sleaze star and nightclub singer REGINA CARROL. His films include *Psycho-a-Go-Go* (1963); *Blood of Dracula's Castle* (1967); *Dracula vs. Frankenstein* (1969); *Satan's Sadists* (1969—*see:* THE WORST BIKER MOVIE OF ALL TIME); *Horror of the Blood Monsters* (1970); *Uncle Tom's Cabin* (1972; *see:* THE MOST IDIOTIC AD LINES IN HOLLYWOOD HISTORY); *The Mean Mothers* (1973); *The Naughty Stewardesses* (1973); *Blazing Stewardesses* (1974); *I Spit on Your Corpse* (1974); *Black Samurai* (1974); and many others.

JOHN AGAR

Bland, lifeless leading man of fifties and sixties; best known for his brief marriage to Shirley Temple (1946–1949) and his well-publicized arrests for drunk driving. Major film discredits include *The Mole People* (1956); *Daughter of Dr. Jekyll* (1957); *Attack of the Puppet People* (1958); *Jet Attack* (1958); *The Brain from Planet Arous* (1958); *Journey to the Seventh Planet* (1962); *Women of the Prehistoric Planet* (1965); *Curse of the Swamp Creature* (1966); and *Zontar, The Thing from Venus* (1966). Retired from screen in late sixties to pursue career as cotton candy magnate, but made comeback playing the mayor of New York City in Dino De Laurentiis's *King Kong* (1976), and with small parts in the X-rated *How's Your Love Life?* (1977) and *The Amazing Mr. No Legs* (1978).

IRWIN ALLEN

Producer-director-screenwriter known as the Master of Disaster; he himself summarizes his philosophy by stating, "As long as there are disasters, there will be disaster pictures. People like to watch tragedy. And why shouldn't they sit on plush theater seats and watch in comfort?" His two major successes (*The Poseidon Adventure* [1972] and *The Towering Inferno* [1974]) are easily overshadowed by a long series of amusingly inane and overblown failures, including *The Story of Mankind* (1957—featuring Harpo Marx as Sir Isaac Newton); *The Big Circus* (1959); *Five Weeks in a Balloon* (1962); *Viva Knievel!* (1977); *The Swarm* (1978); *Beyond the Poseidon Adventure* (1979); *When Time Ran Out* (1980).

SAMUEL Z. ARKOFF

Cigar-chomping mini-mogul of the fifties, sixties, and seventies, and master of the low-budget exploitation flick; self-described "farm boy" and "country lawyer" from Iowa who founded American International Pictures (with his partner, James H. Nicholson) in 1955; produced more than five hundred films, with special emphasis on the "beach party" series, motorcycle sagas, low-budget monster movies, and bargain basement Japanese imports with slapdash American dubbing. Arkoff retired from A.I.P. in 1979 to found the *new* A.I.P. (*Arkoff* International Pictures), where he has continued his dedicated service to cinematic art with idealistic offerings such as *Up the Creek* (1984) and *Hellhole* (1985).

JOHN ASHLEY

Smooth-talking star of A.I.P. pictures of the fifties and sixties who later made his way to the Philippines, where he produced a series of twelve even less distinguished films; made screen debut in John Wayne's *The Conqueror* (1955); currently producer of television's hit series *The A-Team*. Credits include *Drag Strip Girl* (1957); *Frankenstein's Daughter* (1958); *High School Caesar* (1960); *Beach Party* (1963); *Muscle Beach Party* (1964); *Bikini Beach* (1964); *Beach Blanket Bingo* (1965); *How to Stuff a Wild Bikini* (1965); *The Eye Creatures* (1965); *Brides of Blood* (1968); *The Mad Doctor of Blood Island* (1969); *Beast of Blood* (1970); *Beyond Atlantis* (1973); and many more.

OVIDIO ASSONITIS

Italian producer-director who occasionally works under the pseudonym "Oliver Hellman"; best known for *Beyond the Door* (1974—an *Exorcist* rip-off about a young woman who vomits spaghetti sauce); *Tentacles* (1977—about a green octopus that eats San Diego); and *The Visitor* (1980—featuring Shelley Winters, John Huston, and killer pigeons from outer space).

FRANKIE AVALON

FRANKIE GOES TO HOLLYWOOD: The Amazing Mr. Avalon is ready, as always, to hit the beach in a publicity shot from the mid-sixties.

Surprising male sex symbol of the early sixties and popular recording star; broke into show business as 9-year-old trumpet prodigy in South Philadelphia; played a dramatic role as John Wayne's protégé in *The Alamo* (1960). Other roles include five A.I.P. "beach party" movies with Annette Funicello, plus *Voyage to the Bottom of the Sea* (1961); *Panic in the Year Zero!* (1962); *Drums of Africa* (1963); *Sergeant Deadhead* (1965—in title role); *Dr. Goldfoot and the Bikini Machine* (1965); *The Million Eyes of Su-Muru* (1967); Otto Preminger's *Skidoo* (1968); *Horror House* (1970); and others. Parodied his earlier success with an amusing cameo in *Grease* (1978).

H. KROGER BABB

One of Hollywood's most flamboyant promoters and producers, who described himself as "America's Fearless Showman"; president of Hygienic Productions; *see:* THE MOST IDIOTIC AD LINES IN HOLLYWOOD HISTORY and THE WORST PROMOTIONAL GIMMICK IN HOLLYWOOD HISTORY.

THE BAND FAMILY

Independent filmmakers, under the company banner "Empire International." Father Albert most often directs their pictures, while son Charles produces and son

Richard composes the musical scores; they seem engaged in a one-family crusade to prove that trashy horror films of the seventies and eighties *can*, despite popular skepticism, turn out to be as outrageously tacky as the trashy horror films of the fifties and sixties. Their major projects include *Little Cigars* (1973); *Crash!, End of the World, Mansion of the Doomed* (all 1977); *Dracula's Dog, Laserblast* (both 1978); *Tourist Trap* (1979—with Tanya Roberts); *Parasite* (1982); *Metalstorm: The Destruction of Jared-Syn* and *Dungeonmaster* (both 1983); *Ghoulies* (1985 —*not* to be confused with Steven Spielberg's *Goonies*); plus *Laserblast II, Troll, Zone Troopers,* and *Terror Vision* (all—God help us—forthcoming).

JOE "BRICK" BARDO

Billed as a "Rock Hudson look-alike," he acted in numerous exploitation movies of the fifties and sixties, including PHIL TUCKER's *Dance Hall Racket* (1955—with Lenny Bruce); RAY DENNIS STECKLER's *The Thrill Killers* (1964); and *The Lemon Grove Kids Meet the Green Grasshopper and the Vampire Lady from Outer Space* (1965). More recently working as cinematographer and distributor of adult films.

GEORGE BARROWS

George Barrows, whose self-assembled gorilla suit won him parts as an ape in more than three hundred movies and television shows, including the title role in the fabled Robot Monster.

Two-hundred-twenty-pound Bronx-born "gorilla suit man" and bit player; assembled his own gorilla suit in 1947, using the hair of yaks and human beings, along with molded leather; wore that $800 suit in more than three hundred movies and television shows, playing a gorilla in films such as *Robot Monster* (1953—*see:* THE MOST LAUGHABLE CONCEPT FOR AN OUTER SPACE INVADER); *Gorilla at Large* (1954); *The Ghost in the Invisible Bikini* (1966); and *Hillbillies in a Haunted House* (1967). Also played occasional "straight" (non-gorilla) roles in *Mesa of Lost Women* (1953—*see:* THE MOST PRIMITIVE MALE CHAUVINIST FANTASY IN MOVIE HISTORY); *Frankenstein's Daughter* (1958); *Hot Rods to Hell* (1967); and many others.

WILLIAM ("ONE SHOT") BEAUDINE
Hardworking director, noted for bringing in his films on time and on budget, regardless of quality; enjoyed greatest success as director of silents, and continued to insist on exaggerated, silent style of acting in more than 150 talkies; directed more than 70 episodes of *Lassie* television series near the end of his long career (he died in 1970). His most important bad films include *Ghosts on the Loose* (1943); *Voodoo Man* (1944); *Mom and Dad* (1944 —*see:* THE WORST PROMOTIONAL GIMMICK IN HOLLYWOOD HISTORY); *The Prince of Peace* (1948—*see:* THE MOST IDIOTIC AD LINES IN HOLLYWOOD HISTORY); *Bela Lugosi Meets a Brooklyn Gorilla* (1952); *Billy the Kid vs. Dracula* and *Jesse James Meets Frankenstein's Daughter* (both 1966). His son, William Beaudine, Jr., has served as production manager for numerous low-budget features, co-producer of *The Magic of Lassie*, and as a board member of the Directors Guild of America.

STEPHEN BOYD
Beefy, befuddled leading man, best known as Messala in *Ben-Hur* (1959), a role that won him an Oscar nomination. *The New York Times* commented that "Mr. Boyd probably never should become involved in any predicament that he can't get out of by swinging a broadsword from a speeding chariot". Concerning his astonishing performance in *The Oscar* (1966), *Time* magazine wrote that "his portrait of a sneaky, sniveling contender at the Oscar countdown should be shown exclusively in theatres that have doctors and nurses stationed in the lobby to attend viewers who laugh themselves sick." His most notable turkeys include *Jumbo* (1962); *The Poppy Is Also a Flower* (1966); *The Oscar* (1966—*see:* THE MOST AWKWARD ON-SCREEN MARRIAGE PROPOSAL); *The Caper of the Golden Bulls* (1967); *Shalako* (1968); *Slaves* (1969); *Kill! Kill! Kill!* (1971); *Potato Fritz* (1976). Died in 1977.

DAVID BRADLEY

Temperamental director David Bradley, who describes himself as "the Low-Budget Orson Welles," proudly contemplates his most celebrated creation: the "monster head" from They Saved Hitler's Brain.

Wildly eccentric "artistic" director who has described himself as "the Low-Budget Orson Welles"; made his first films at Northwestern University School of Speech, including versions of *Peer Gynt* (1941) and *Julius Caesar* (1949), both starring fellow-student Charlton Heston; came to Hollywood in 1950 and won contract with MGM. His films include *Talk About a Stranger* (1952—a melodrama about a dead dog with George Murphy and Nancy Davis); *Drag Strip Riot* (1958); *Twelve to the Moon* (1960); and his final film and masterpiece, *They Saved Hitler's Brain* (1963). Since the mid-sixties he has concentrated his efforts on assembling one of the world's largest collections of silent cinema and taught film history intermittently at UCLA.

BRONSON CANYON
A one-time rock quarry in the Hollywood Hills that has served as location for more than 1,000 low-budget western and sci-fi films, including Gene Autry's *Radio Ranch* (1935—*see:* THE MOST RIDICULOUS COWBOY HERO IN HOLLYWOOD HISTORY); *Robot Monster* (1953); *It Conquered the World* (1956—*see:* THE MOST LAUGHABLE CONCEPT FOR AN OUTER SPACE INVADER); *Invasion of the Star Creatures* (1962); and DAVID BRADLEY's *They Saved Hitler's Brain* (1963).

LARRY ("BUCK") BUCHANAN

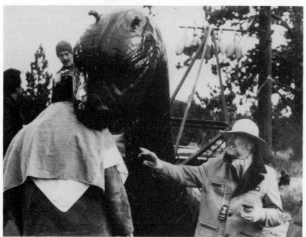

That irrepressible Texan, Larry Buchanan, enjoys himself, as usual, while giving acting instructions to The Loch Ness Horror.

Charming, tall-in-the-saddle Texan who, as producer-director, has worked hard to realize his vision of Dallas as the "Bad Movie Capital of the World"; has made films since age 11, and gained nothing over the years in terms of polish and sophistication; particularly noted for utterly incompetent editing, zipper-back monsters, and ill-considered subject matter, with a specialty in even more terrible remakes of other people's terrible sci-fi originals; most celebrated achievement his immortal 1966 trilogy: *Mars Needs Women* (remake of *Pajama Party*); *Curse of the Swamp Creature* (remake of *Voodoo Woman*); and *Zontar, The Thing from Venus* (remake of *It Conquered the World*). Other titles: *Naughty Dallas* (1964); *The Eye Creatures* (1965—remake of *Invasion of the Saucer Men*); *Creature of Destruction* (1967—remake of *The She Creature*); *It's Alive!* (1968); *Goodbye, Norma Jean* (1976, remake of Marilyn Monroe's life—*see:* THE MOST LUDICROUS ON-SCREEN IMPERSONATION OF A HOLLYWOOD LEGEND); *Mistress of the Apes* (1981). Currently working on major science fiction project, tentatively entitled *The Grand Hotel in Outer Space*.

RENÉ CARDONA

The most consistently awful producer-director in the history of Mexican cinema; creator of the popular monster-battlers *Las Luchadoras* (The Wrestling Women). Films include *The Wrestling Women vs. the Murdering Robot* (1965); *The Wrestling Women vs. the Aztec Mummy* (1965); *The Panther Women vs. the Wrestling Women* (1966); *Night of the Bloody Apes* (1968); *The Night of a Thousand Cats* (1972—*see:* THE WORST PROMOTIONAL GIMMICK IN HOLLYWOOD HISTORY). Father of director René Cardona, Jr., for whom he has produced *Survive!* (1977) and *Tintorera, Tiger Shark* (1977).

ALLAN CARR

Ebullient producer of glittery schlock, and former press agent; broke into feature films in 1977 by dubbing René Cardona, Jr.'s *Survive!* into English and releasing it successfully in U.S.; shattered box office records with *Grease* (1978), then shattered his own career with lumbering losers such as *Can't Stop the Music* (1980), *Grease II* (1982), and *Where the Boys Are '84* (1984—*see:* THE WORST BEACH PARTY MOVIE EVER MADE). Well known for his lavish parties and elaborate publicity gimmicks (*see:* THE WORST PROMOTIONAL GIMMICK IN HOLLYWOOD HISTORY for a description of his contribution to *Won Ton Ton: The Dog Who Saved Hollywood* [1975]). Produced *La Cage aux Folles* on Broadway with great success, and is currently at work on the musical feature film version.

JOHN CARRADINE

Veteran character actor with hawklike face and stentorian voice; has appeared in well over four hundred films since 1930, including some fine achievements, along with an impressive array of Grade Z stinkers, such as *Captive Wild Women* (1943); *Revenge of the Zombies* (1943); *Return of the Ape Man* (1944); *Sex Kittens Go to College* (1960); *Invasion of the Animal People* (1962); *The Wizard of Mars* (1964); *Munster Go Home!* (1966); *Billy the Kid vs. Dracula* (1966); *Hell's Bloody Devils* (1967); *The Astro-Zombies* (1968); *Myra Breckinridge* (1970); *Is This Trip Really Necessary?* (1970; is this list really necessary?); *Portnoy's Complaint* (1972—as the Voice of God); Joyce Jillson's *Superchick* (1973); *Satan's Cheerleaders* (1977); *Nocturna, Granddaughter of Dracula* (1979); *Vampire Hookers* (1979); and *The Boogey Man* (1980). At age 79 in 1985, he was still working; father of talented actors David, Keith, and Robert Carradine.

REGINA CARROL

Regina Carrol, in a publicity still from The Creature's Revenge, *demonstrates the sultry appeal that made her a cult symbol in the 1960s.*

Buxom blonde bombshell and nightclub singer in sixties biker and horror movies; former waitress, real name Regina Gelfan; married to bottom-of-the-barrel director AL ADAMSON, who has made all her movies, including *Dracula vs. Frankenstein* (1969); *The Female Bunch* (1969); *Blood of Ghastly Horror* (1971); *Angels' Wild Women* (1972); *Blazing Stewardesses* (1974); and many more.

WILLIAM CASTLE

Hollywood's "Mr. Gimmick"; producer-director of campy horror films; broke into show business with a Broadway part in 1929 by falsely presenting himself as Sam Goldwyn's nephew; once said "I have modeled my career on P.T. Barnum"; noted less for his movies than for his promotional stunts, which have included insuring moviegoers with Lloyds of London against death by fright while watching *Macabre* (1958); a rubber skeleton dropping from the ceiling during *The House on Haunted Hill* (1959); theater seats wired for mild electric shocks to inspire viewers of *The Tingler* (1959); "a punishment poll" asking the audience to decide the fate of *Mr. Sardonicus* (1961—*see:* THE WORST PROMOTIONAL GIMMICK IN HOLLYWOOD HISTORY); and free cardboard axes for all who paid to see *Strait-Jacket* (1964). Died in 1977.

HERMAN J. COHEN

Diminutive, tough-talking producer-director, concentrating on tasteless, sloppily made exploitation pictures, such as *I Was a Teenage Werewolf* and *I Was a Teenage Frankenstein* (both 1957); *Horrors of the Black Museum* (1959); *Konga* (1961—an English King Kong rip-off where the big ape meets Big Ben); *Trog* (1970—Joan Crawford's last feature film); *Today We Kill, Tomorrow We Die* (1970); *Crocodile* (1979); *Watch Me When I Kill* (1983).

CRISWELL

Self-important, flamboyant TV psychic of the fifties who appeared as himself in three remarkable EDWARD D. WOOD, JR., films: *Plan Nine from Outer Space* (1959); *Night of the Ghouls* (1959); and *Orgy of the Dead* (1965). Son of an Indiana undertaker, he began life as Jerrond Charles Criswell King; publicly predicted that U.S. would fight World War III by 1975, and the Supreme Court would include only female justices by 1976, and that all women of St. Louis, Missouri, would turn bald in 1983. After his death in 1982, his long-time manager boasted: "It's been proven that Criswell's predictions were 87 percent correct, most of the time."

BO DEREK

Bo Derek writhes in agony over the critical response to Tarzan the Ape Man.

Actress, producer, nude model; made movie debut in *Fantasies* (1974), a dreadful film about the search for the perfect bathtub (featuring the immortal line "I have bosoms"); next appeared in a bit(e) part, when *Orca, the Killer Whale* chewed off her shapely leg; became a star with her part in *10* (1979) and several photographic spreads in *Playboy*; is also credited as producer in the hilariously misguided movies she made with her husband, JOHN DEREK: *Tarzan the Ape Man* (1981) and *Bolero* (1984).

JOHN DEREK

John Derek, as a young romantic lead in The Adventures of Hajji Baba, *delivers the eloquent line "I may carry the instruments of a barber, but I have the desires of a prince!"*

Veteran actor, director; born Derek Harris; under contract with David O. Selznick at age 17 in 1943; played parts in several reputable projects (*The Ten Command-*

ments, *All the Kings Men, Exodus)*, but also starred in two terrible "Arabian Nights" follies: *The Adventures of Hajji Baba* (1954) and *The Life and Loves of Omar Khayyam* (1957); retired as an actor in 1968 to concentrate on still photography and learning the craft of directing. He once described himself as "an abrasive, opinionated weirdo . . . who looks for women who recognize that I am God"; among those he found are his actress-wives Ursula Andress, Linda Evans (*see:* THE MOST HUMILIATING PERFORMANCE BY A FUTURE TV STAR), and Bo DEREK; for the current Mrs. D. he directed *Tarzan* and *Bolero*, two impossibly pretentious softcore spectaculars that surely stand among the worst motion pictures of the decade so far.

DWAIN ESPER

Producer-director of "hard-hitting" topical melodramas of the thirties, which he wrote with his wife, Hildegarde Stadie; titles include *Maniac* (1934—*see:* THE LEAST CONVINCING SCIENTIFIC EXPLANATION IN MOTION PICTURE HISTORY); *Marihuana, Weed with Roots in Hell* (1936 —*see:* THE LEAST CLASSY USE OF CLASSICAL MUSIC IN MOVIE HISTORY); *How to Undress in Front of Your Husband* (1935); and *Narcotics Racket* (1936).

RICHARD FLEISCHER

Versatile director; son of animator Max Fleischer; under contract with RKO in late forties. He has been responsible for several fine films (*20,000 Leagues Under the Sea* [1954], *Compulsion* [1959], and others), but in the later stages of his career he has churned out a long list of lifeless losers, including *Che!* (1969); *Tora! Tora! Tora!* (1970); *The Don Is Dead* (1973); *Mr. Majestyk* (1974); *Mandingo* (1975); *The Incredible Sarah* (1976); *Ashanti* (1979); *The Jazz Singer* (1980); *Amityville 3-D* (1984); *Conan the Destroyer* (1984); *Red Sonja* (1985).

JESUS ("JESSE") FRANCO

Prolific Spanish director working principally in West Germany, emphasizing slow, sadistic ultra-sleazy sexploitation pictures, such as *Attack of the Robots* (1962); *The Diabolical Doctor Z* (1966); *Succubus* (1968); *Night of the Blood Monster* (1970); *Barbed Wire Dolls* (1972); and *Wanda the Wicked Warden* (1979).

DOLORES FULLER

Long-faced blonde starlet of early fifties with a slow, grating voice; best known as the long-time live-in of legendary director EDWARD D. WOOD, JR.; retired from films by 1960 to work in the music business, briefly managing Tanya Tucker and writing several songs for Elvis, including "Rock-a-Hula Baby." Her major screen

credits include *Mesa of Lost Women* (1953—*see:* THE MOST PRIMITIVE MALE CHAUVINIST FANTASY IN HOLLYWOOD HISTORY) and three films for WOOD: *Glen or Glenda* (1953); *Jail Bait* (1955); and *Bride of the Monster* (1955).

GODZILLA

Godzilla climbs into the ring to take on an American rival in the third of his sixteen films, King Kong vs. Godzilla.

Japan's biggest star; this fire-breathing dinosaur lived peacefully for millions of years at the bottom of the sea; then in 1954 nuclear radiation drove him to the surface and impelled him to destroy Tokyo in his debut role, *Godzilla, King of the Monsters;* since then he has appeared in fifteen other films, changing, in mid-career, from a scourge of humanity to a defender of civilization who protects Japan against the depredations of alien cockroaches (*Godzilla on Monster Island,* 1971), an enormous man-eating cocker spaniel (*Godzilla vs. the Bionic Monster,* 1974), and a mechanized replica of himself (*The Terror of Godzilla,* 1975). Known as "Gojira" in his homeland; the name is derived from the Japanese word for whale ("kojira"), and was borrowed from a nickname that had been applied to a grotesquely overweight janitor at Toho Studios. Godzilla's son, Minya, has appeared alongside in four of his father's films.

MENAHEM GOLAN

High-flying Israeli producer-director and, more recently, an ambitious tycoon in U.S.; after twenty years of phenomenal success in Israel, he and his cousin, Yoram Globus, took over Cannon Films in 1979, concentrating since that time on shabby, exasperating, and exploitative quickies, including *The Hospital Massacre* (1982); *The Last American Virgin* (1982); Lou Ferrigno's *Hercules* (1983); *Ninja III: The Domination* (1984); *Breakin' II: Electric Boogaloo* (1985); *Death Wish III* (1985); *Rappin'*

(1985); *Ben, Bonzo and Big Bad Joe* (1986). Two of producer Golan's rare big-budget efforts (the $20-million *Sahara* [1984, with Brooke Shields] and the $25-million *Lifeforce* [1985]) have proven two of his biggest turkeys, critically and financially.

BERT I. GORDON

Resilient producer-director known as Hollywood's "Mr. BIG," because of both his initials and his choice of subject matter: *King Dinosaur* (1955); *Cyclops* (1957); *Beginning of the End* (1957—about huge grasshoppers); *The Amazing Colossal Man* (1957); *War of the Colossal Beast* (1958); *Attack of the Puppet People* (1958); *Village of the Giants* (1965); *Food of the Gods* (1976—about gigantic monster rats); and *Empire of the Ants* (1977).

TOM GRAEFF

Producer- director- writer- editor- cameraman- star *and* music coordinator of that $14,000 landmark of pompous incompetence, *Teenagers from Outer Space* (1959), which was presented by Warner Brothers with the proud declaration, "The Lowest Budgeted Picture Ever Released by a Major Studio"; hailed by *Variety* as "inescapably inept," while *The Hollywood Reporter* wrote that "Tom Graeff's production constantly struggles to overcome the disadvantage of his own bad direction which, in turn, is gravely handicapped by a script written by himself." In 1972, hoping to revive his permanently stalled movie career, he legally changed his name to "Jesus Christ II" and took occasional ads in *Variety* in hopes of selling his screenplay ideas.

HUGO HAAS

Director-star Hugo Haas with his perennial protégée, Cleo Moore, in the gut-wrenching melodrama Strange Fascination.

Burly Czechoslovakian actor, writer, and director; in Hollywood after 1937, specializing in earnest, insanely overdone melodramas in which he plays sensitive, middle-aged men humiliated by young temptresses invariably played by his perennial star, CLEO MOORE. Titles include *Strange Fascination* (1952); *One Girl's Confession* (1953); *The Other Woman* (1954); ten more. He died in 1968.

ARCH HALL, SR.

Arch Hall, Sr. (with pompon, left), and Arch Hall, Jr. (with guitar), discuss a scene from Wild Guitar *with rising young director Ray Dennis Steckler (who is separately listed in* THE ROGUES' GALLERY*). With them is former stripper Virginia Broderick, who played a minor role in this typical Fairway-International production.*

Affable, enterprising writer-producer; also director (under the name "Nicholas Merriwether") and actor (under the name "William Watters"); created Fairway-International Productions and filmed *The Choppers* (1961); *Wild Guitar* (1962); *Eegah!* (1962); *The Sadist* (1963); *What's Up Front?* (1964); *Deadwood '76* (1965); *The Nasty Rabbit* (1965—alternate title: *Spies-a-Go-Go*). Co-writer of cult classic *The Corpse Grinders* (1971). Died in 1980.

ARCH HALL, JR.

Teenage star and tone-deaf "singing sensation" in nearly all of his father's films, most notably *Eegah!* (1962 —*see:* THE WORST ROCK 'N' ROLL LYRICS IN MOVIE HISTORY) and *Wild Guitar* (1962); decorated veteran of Vietnam War who is currently employed as a pilot for a private airline in California.

ALLISON HAYES

Statuesque, hard-edged leading lady, best known for sci-fi roles, including *The Unearthly, The Undead, The*

Disembodied, and *The Zombies of Mora Tau* (all 1957); *Attack of the Fifty-Foot Woman* (1958—title role); *The Crawling Hand* (1963); *The Hypnotic Eye* (1960).

INOSHIRO HONDA

Attack of the Mushroom People *(also known as* Matango, The Fungus of Terror*) represented a characteristic achievement for Inoshiro Honda, "King of Japanese Monster Movies."*

"The Uncrowned King of Japanese Monster Movies," and Toho Studios' most wildly imaginative director; creator of *Godzilla, King of the Monsters* (1954); *Varan the Unbelievable* (1958—see: THE MOST LAUGHABLE CONCEPT FOR AN OUTER SPACE INVADER); *Mothra* (1962—about a huge killer moth); *Gorath* (1963—about a giant man-eating walrus); *Attack of the Mushroom People* (1963—alternate title: *Matango, The Fungus of Terror*); *Godzilla vs. the Thing* (1964); *Dagora the Space Monster* (1964—about a gigantic jellyfish from outer space); *Frankenstein Conquers the World* (1964); *Ghidrah the Three-Headed Monster* (1965); *Monster Zero* (1966—in which GODZILLA travels to outer space); *War of the Gargantuas* (1967); *Destroy All Monsters* (1968); *King Kong Escapes* (1968); *Godzilla's Revenge* (1969); *Latitude Zero* (1969—featuring a flying lion); *Yog, Monster from Space* (1970—about an octopus from beyond the stars).

TOR JOHNSON

Enormous, hulking, bald actor whose limited command of English drew him to a series of offbeat roles as a mute, drooling, openmouthed monster; former professional wrestler who used the mat name "The Swedish Angel." Appeared in three films directed by his "drinking buddy" EDWARD D. WOOD, JR.: *Bride of the Monster* (1955); *Plan Nine from Outer Space* (1959—in a rare speaking part); and *Night of the Ghouls* (1959). Also played in *The Black Sleep* (1956); *The Unearthly* (1957—in which he speaks a single line, "Time for go to sleep"); *The Beast of Yucca Flats* (1961—as a mute Russian scientist).

J.D. KENDIS

Producer-distributor of pioneering sexploitation films of the thirties and forties which usually came disguised as part of a "moral crusade" for the enlightenment of the public; these noble, selfless titles include *Polygamy* (1934—also known as *Illegal Wives* for audiences with limited vocabularies); *Maiden and the Monster* (1935); *White Slave Traffic* (1936—also known as *Love Mart*); *Jungle Virgin, Jaws of the Jungle,* and *Crusades Against the Rackets* (all 1937); *Bowanga, Bowanga* (1938); *Dance of the Blonde Slave's Revenge* (1939); and then, in the forties, the deluge: *Nite Club Girls; Escort Girls; Call Girls; Main Street Girls; Hoodlum Girls; Girls in Hell; Girls of the Underworld; Girl with an Itch; Pindown Girl; Guerilla Girl; Nature Girl; Girl Fever; A Night at the Zomba Club; Unclad Cuties; Exposé of the Nudist Racket; Why Nudism?;* and *Take Off Your Clothes and Live!*

MANUEL KING

Twelve-year-old Manuel King was known as the world's youngest (and lumpiest) animal trainer when he appeared in Batmen of Africa. *His co-stars included Clyde Beatty, Jr., and future cowboy hero Ray "Crash" Corrigan in a gorilla suit.*

Plump, diapered jungle boy of the thirties, billed as "The World's Youngest Wild Animal Trainer"; may have been good with animals, but not so great with dialogue; after twelve episodes of the dreadful serial *Batmen of Africa* (alternate title: *Darkest Africa*) he retired permanently from the screen, to help his father, W.A. King, on his wild animal farm in Brownsville, Texas.

JOI LANSING

Busty blonde bombshell and sleepwalking actress; born Joyce Wasmandorff in 1935; named "Miss Armed Forces Day of the World" in 1967; star of *Hot Cars*

(1956); *Hillbillies in a Haunted House* (1967—where she sings three duets with the unforgettable Ferlin Husky); and her last film, *Bigfoot* (1969—in which she is carried away and tied to a stake by the primitive beast).

LASH LA RUE

Whip-cracking cowboy star whose career is described in detail under THE MOST LUDICROUS PROFESSIONAL NAME IN MOVIE HISTORY.

HERSCHELL GORDON LEWIS

"The Godfather of Gore"; a former college professor and Ph.D. in English who worked in advertising before settling down to direct pioneering splatter movies such as *Blood Feast* (1964); *Two Thousand Maniacs* (1964); *She-Devils on Wheels* (1964); *Color Me Blood Red* (1965); *The Gore-Gore Girls* (1972—with Henny Youngman); and more than thirty additional titles. Arrested in 1974 for running a bogus abortion referral business; currently employed as an expert lecturer on direct mail marketing, while laying plans for *Blood Feast II*.

BELA LUGOSI

Youthful actor-director Edward D. Wood, Jr., discusses a key scene in Glen or Glenda *with the movie's star, Bela Lugosi.*

Best known for his genuinely chilling performances in horror films beginning with *Dracula* (1931), Hollywood's "Aristocrat of Evil" also appeared in dozens of wretched and one-dimensional entertainments; began his career as matinee idol in legitimate theater in Hungary, winning fame for his portrayal of Jesus Christ in *King of Kings*; came to U.S. in 1921 and played Dracula on stage before his most famous movie role. His self-destructive and eccentric personal life, as well as an inability to say no to any script, no matter how inane, led to his major embarrassments, including *Murder by

Television (1935); *The Phantom Creeps* (1939); *The Devil Bat* (1940); *Spooks Run Wild* (1941—with the Bowery Boys); *Black Dragons* (1942—*see:* THE WORST PERFORMANCE AS A NAZI MAD SCIENTIST); *Zombies on Broadway* (1945); *Bela Lugosi Meets a Brooklyn Gorilla* (1952); and, shortly before his death in 1956, three classic films for EDWARD D. WOOD, JR.

MONA McKINNON

Leading lady of the fifties who delivered all of her lines in a flat, drab, uninflected, hypnotized style; may be the only star in history who could scream in a monotone; appeared as model of the queen's wardrobe on fifty-five episodes of *Queen for a Day* television show; sang, danced, gargled, and kissed her husband in a popular mouthwash commercial; appeared on the big screen in *Mesa of Lost Women* (1953); EDWARD D. WOOD JR.'s *Jail Bait* (1955); *Teenage Thunder* (1958); *Unwed Mother* (1958); and *Plan Nine from Outer Space* (1959). Married a manufacturer of refrigerator parts and retired from the screen to raise her family.

DUDLEY MANLOVE

Dudley Manlove (left) *played a deeply troubled robot in the neglected futuristic masterpiece* Creation of the Humanoids.

Colorful character actor and radio voice; born Dudley Manlove (believe it or not) in Oakland, California; former professional violinist and vaudeville hoofer; his resonant, singsong voice gave him a successful radio career, and he worked as an announcer for the NBC network; recorded popular commercials for Lux Soap and Scott Tissue; concentrated on films and television after 1955 with forlorn hope of winning work as a romantic lead; major credits include *Sing, Boy, Sing* (1958); *Plan Nine from Outer Space* (1959); *Creation of the Humanoids* (1962).

JAYNE MANSFIELD

Breathy, busty Marilyn Monroe imitator who, in terms of acting ability, made MM look like Meryl Streep; married to Hungarian muscleman Mickey Hargitay, with whom she co-starred in *The Loves of Hercules* (1960). Starred in such worthy fare as *The Female Jungle* (1955 —as a nymphomaniac); *Playgirl After Dark* (1960—as a stripper); *Dog Eat Dog* and *Primitive Love* (both 1964); *The Fat Spy* and *Las Vegas Hillbillies* (both 1966). Died in New Orleans car crash, along with her cherished Chihuahua, in 1967; subject of posthumous documentary, *The Wild Wild World of Jayne Mansfield* (1968), using footage of her European travels accompanied by "beyond the grave" first-person narration ("I think it's absolutely great being a star") in her "own" very inimitable voice.

DR. TOM MASON

Successful chiropractor in Orange County, California, and surprise star of low-budget horror films; stood in for Bela Lugosi in *Plan Nine from Outer Space* following the star's unexpected death; also appeared as a "foster ghost," along with his "big-boned" wife, Margaret Mason, in EDWARD D. WOOD JR.'s *Night of the Ghouls* (1959). Died of a stroke in 1981.

TED ("T.V.") MIKELS

Bearded, nonconformist director and cinematographer, responsible for unbearably boring so-called "shockers," including *The Black Klansman* (1966); *The Astro-Zombies, Up Your Teddy Bear,* and *The Girl in Gold Boots* (all 1968); *The Corpse Grinders* (1971—which cost $18,000 to make and grossed $15,000,000); *The Doll Squad* (1973); and the ever-popular *Blood Orgy of the She-Devils* (1973). Currently planning a serious film version of the medieval classic *Beowulf.*

MARIA MONTEZ

High priestess of high camp, star of exotic fantasies in which the luridly colored sets and costumes are no more convincing than her incomparably atrocious acting; daughter of a Spanish diplomat; worked as New York model before winning contract with Universal in 1941; unflattering weight gain helped send her career into decline; died at age 31 in her bathtub under mysterious circumstances. Major bad films include *White Savage* (1943); *Ali Baba and the Forty Thieves* and *Cobra*

The grande dame of "B" picture costume dramas: the many-splendored Maria Montez as the Cobra Woman.

Woman (both 1944—in double role as evil queen of Cobra Island and her good sister); *Sudan* (1945); *Siren of Atlantis* (1948); *The Pirate's Revenge* (1951).

CLEO MOORE

Plump beauty queen from the Old South and star of seven conspicuously corny films under Master of Melodrama HUGO HAAS; titles include *Women's Prison* (1955) and *Hold Back Tomorrow* (1955—as a suicidal prostitute); known as "Hollywood's Canary Yellow Blonde"; retired from films at age 27, ran unsuccessfully for lieutenant governor of Louisiana, then settled down as Inglewood, California, housewife before her death from a heart attack at age 43.

GEORGE NADER

Leading man with slick hair, mighty muscles, and "aw shucks" next-door neighbor appeal; strong of body yet weak of voice, making wooden appearances in films such as *Robot Monster* and *The Sins of Jezebel* (both 1953); *Congo Crossing* (1956); *The Million Eyes of Su-Muru* (1967 —with Frankie Avalon and Klaus Kinski); *House of 1,000 Dolls* (1967); moved to Europe in late sixties and made popular German language spy thrillers; later returned to Hollywood to focus his energy on writing "philosophically oriented" science fiction novels.

HAL NEEDHAM

Former stunt man and Good Ol' Boy director, with special interest in car crash movies; once told an interviewer, "I can teach you everything you need to know about directing in five minutes"; hit box office paydirt with *Smokey and the Bandit* (1977), *Smokey and the Bandit II* (1980), and *Cannonball Run* (1981), all featuring his good buddy Burt Reynolds; then went on a losing streak with *Megaforce* (1982); the unspeakably awful *Stroker Ace* (1983); and the $30-million turkey *Cannonball Run II* (1984).

ART J. NELSON
Native American from Oklahoma with a primitive touch as a director; ever-elusive creator of the classic *The Creeping Terror* (1964); his controversial career—and his numerous aliases—are described in detail under THE MOST LAUGHABLE CONCEPT FOR AN OUTER SPACE INVADER. Current whereabouts unknown.

WYOTT ORDUNG
Yes, that's his real name; he's a screenwriter specializing in intensely personal, off-the-wall science fiction oddities; a decorated World War II combat veteran, he describes himself as "a professional psychic and a Master of Esoteric Science." His script credits include *Robot Monster* (1953); *Monster from the Ocean Floor* (1954—he also directed and starred); *Phantom from Ten Thousand Leagues* (1955); *First Man into Space* (1959—not his autobiography); *Women of the Prehistoric Planet* (1965). Also served as assistant director on *The Navy vs. the Night Monsters* (1966).

RON ORMOND
Fun-loving director of ridiculous westerns and other cheapies; former vaudeville magician from South Carolina; directed twelve features with "King of the Bullwhip" Lash La Rue (*see:* THE MOST LUDICROUS PROFESSIONAL NAME IN MOVIE HISTORY). Several of his films have been hailed among all-time worsts; concerning *The Dalton Gang* (1949) *The New York Times* wrote, "Watch out for turkeys like this one. Ptomaine poisoning you know," while the same august newspaper described Ormond's *Outlaw Women* (1952) as "probably the worst motion picture to run at a first-run house this year." His other most important titles include *Yes Sir, Mr. Bones* (1951); *Square Dance Jubilee* (1952); *Mesa of Lost Women* (1953—*see:* THE MOST PRIMITIVE MALE CHAUVINIST FANTASY IN MOVIE HISTORY); *Untamed Mistress* (1960); *The Girl from Tobacco Row* (1966); *White Lightnin' Road* (1967); and *The Exotic Ones* (1968—in which marijuana-crazed monsters mangle strippers in New Orleans). In later years made his home in Nashville, Tennessee, became a born-again Christian, and concentrated on religious and inspirational films until his death in 1981.

EARL OWENSBY
The number one movie magnate of Shelby, North Carolina; owner of his own studio, E.O. Corporation, with its own elaborately equipped, 111-acre back lot; writes, directs, and stars in his own clumsy, violent, painfully predictable features; son of a mountain bootlegger, he made his first million as a salesman of pneumatic tools; promoted as "A Confederate Clint Eastwood." His twenty movies include *Frank Challenge: Manhunter* (1973); *Death Driver* (1975); *Buckstone County Prison* (1977); *Wolfman—A Lycanthrope* (1978); *Living Legend* (1980); and *Rottweiler!* (1982—a 3-D feature about a man-eating dog).

STEVE PEACE
Ambitious maverick producer, co-founder of Four Square Productions in San Diego, California; in mid-seventies he saw the terrifying potential in household vegetables and crusaded to make *Attack of the Killer Tomatoes,* for which he drew co-producer and co-writer credits; as a result of this stunning achievement, he won election to the California State Assembly at age 28 and is considered a rising star in the Democratic party.

VERA HRUBA RALSTON
Embarrassingly bad "B" movie star of the forties and fifties; former Czechoslovakian figure skater who won the crown as "Queen of Republic Studios" after she became the mistress of the company's king, studio chief executive Herbert Yates. Her husky voice and stubbornly imperfect mastery of English made her lines difficult to understand; her performances indicated she herself never understood them. Among her forty films: *Lake Placid Serenade* (1944); *Angel of the Amazon* (1948); *Hoodlum Empire* (1952); *Jubilee Trail* (1954); *Timberjack* (1955).

STEVE REEVES
Bearded muscleman hero of countless Italian sword-and-sandstorm epics; former Mr. America and Mr. Universe; made movie debut playing a policeman in EDWARD D. WOOD JR.'s *Jail Bait* (1955). Titles include *Hercules* (1957); *Hercules Unchained, The White Warrior,* and *Goliath and the Barbarians* (all 1959); *Sandokan the Great* (1964); *A Long Ride from Hell* (1968).

TANYA ROBERTS
In the words of critic Sheila Benson: "Tanya Roberts is the best news Pia Zadora's had since she learned she was going to be a mother"; poker-faced Bronx-born beauty who brings Method-acting intensity to even the most ridiculous roles; former star of TV's *Charlie's Angels;* according to studio press material, she crusaded for the part of *Sheena* (1984—*see:* THE LEAST HEROIC BATTLEFIELD SPEECH IN HOLLYWOOD HISTORY) by telling casting

directors, "If you don't let me try out for this part I'll kill myself!"; also appeared in *Tourist Trap* (1978—where she is stabbed in the head by Chuck Connors); *The Beastmaster* (1982—as a sensitive slave girl); and as a screaming bimbo in the James Bond film *A View to a Kill* (1985).

GORDON SCOTT

Gordon Scott successfully wrestles a bearskin rug into submission in Duel of the Titans (1962), *one of his many muscleman roles.*

Muscular, perpetually puzzled star of slow-moving outdoor adventures; real name Gordon M. Werschkul; former lifeguard, fireman, and cowboy; made six Tarzan films in the fifties, plus *Samson and the Seven Miracles of the World* and *Goliath and the Vampires* (both 1961); *Gladiator of Rome* (1962); and *Conquest of Mycene* (1964).

CHARLES SELLIER

Dynamic head (1974–1980) of Sunn Classic Films in Salt Lake City, Utah, where he specialized in "enlightening and educational" projects such as *In Search of Historic Jesus* (1980—*see:* THE LEAST UPLIFTING CONVERSATION WITH GOD IN MOTION PICTURE HISTORY). "We make positive movies," Sellier declares. "The hero always tells the truth, works hard, and therefore always wins." The producer has applied that philosophy to several projects on his own since leaving Sunn, including *The Boogens* (1982—about killer footballs with fangs who invade Colorado) and also the controversial *Silent Night, Deadly Night* (1984—about a psycho dressed as Santa who strangles his victims with Christmas lights).

RAY DENNIS STECKLER

Incurably optimistic, unstoppable dynamo who has provided employment for countless friends and family members in his ultra-low-budget improvisations, in-

cluding *The Incredibly Strange Creatures Who Stopped Living and Became Mixed-Up Zombies* (1964); *Rat Pfink a Boo Boo* (1964); and *Body Fever* (1972). Often serves as producer-director-writer-cinematographer and on-set coffee brewer, while also starring under the screen name "Cash Flagg" (*see:* THE MOST LUDICROUS PROFESSIONAL NAME IN MOVIE HISTORY for a more complete view of his career); married for many years to Carolyn Brandt, star of seven of his films; broke into films as a protégé of the beloved schlockmeister ARCH HALL, SR.; currently at work on "an action picture about a female Rambo" tentatively entitled *The Survivalist*.

LYLE TALBOT

Terminally bland character actor who has appeared in more than two hundred low-budget features; best known as the jovial neighbor on the *Ozzie and Harriet* television program, but often played heavies on the big screen; characterized by his relaxed, careless, what-the-heck approach to all his roles, including *Page Miss Glory* (1935); *Trapped by Television* (1936); *Torture Ship* (1939); *Are These Our Parents?* (1944); *Atom Man vs. Superman* (1950); *Untamed Women* (1952); EDWARD D. WOOD JR.'s *Glen or Glenda* (1953) and *Jail Bait* (1955); *Trader Tom of the China Seas* (1954); *Plan Nine from Outer Space* (1959—as U.S. Air Force general-in-chief); in recent years made guest appearances on *The Love Boat* and *Charlie's Angels*.

DEL TENNEY

Offbeat artistic director noted for brooding atmosphere and profound symbolism he brought to movies like *Curse of the Living Corpse* (1964), *I Eat Your Skin* (1964), and his masterpiece, *The Horror of Party Beach* (1964—*see:* THE WORST BEACH PARTY MOVIE EVER MADE for a more complete description of his career and analysis of his challenging cinematic style). Broke into pictures as assistant director on *The Orgy at Lil's Place* (1963); currently working as stage director.

WILLIAM C. THOMPSON

Gained fame as Hollywood's only "blind cinematographer"; actually blind in only one eye, though critics often complained that he might as well have been sightless in both; Canadian director of photography on more than a hundred out-of-focus features, including several films celebrated as among the worst of all time. Credits include DWAIN ESPER's *Maniac* (1934); *Project Moonbase* (1953); *The Astounding She-Monster* (1958); and six major films for EDWARD D. WOOD, JR.: *Glen or Glenda* (1953); *Jail Bait* (1955); *Bride of the Monster* (1955); *Plan Nine from Outer Space* and *Night of the Ghouls* (both 1959); and *The Sinister Urge* (1961).

PHIL TUCKER

Intense, enigmatic individualist who directed one of history's most grotesquely grandiose science fiction movies, *Robot Monster* (1953). Tall, grizzled, charismatic cowboy and Marine Corps veteran who broke into pictures directing installments in the *After Midnight* series for GEORGE WEISS; collaborated with his friend, Lenny Bruce, on the expressionistic burlesque film *Dance Hall Racket* (1955); emotional problems following disastrous premiere of *Robot Monster* led to his temporary retirement from films (and from the world), but he returned in triumph with *Cape Canaveral Monsters* (1960) and *Space Jockey* (1963); worked as post-production supervisor for *King Kong* (1976) and *Orca the Killer Whale* (1977), and as editor on *The Nude Bomb* (1980) and *Charlie Chan and the Curse of the Dragon Queen* (1981); most recent work as a director includes his as-yet-unreleased "sex comedy" *Hollywood Fever* (1980) and the motorcycle documentary *Star Spangled Bummer.*

VAMPIRA

Vampira, TV horror hostess, erstwhile movie star, and one-time girlfriend of James Dean, poses for a late-fifties Halloween promotion.

Curvaceous "ghoul girl" of the fifties; real name Maila Nurmi; grew up in Astoria, Oregon; won popularity on Los Angeles TV, beginning in 1954, as host for late-night screenings of horror movies; dated James Dean for several months at the end of his life; best known for her movie roles in *Plan Nine from Outer Space* (1959) and *Sex Kittens Go to College* (1960); launched a new career in 1984 as a New Wave performance artist under the name "Helen Heaven."

MAMIE VAN DOREN

As a prime example of Untamed Youth *(in the movie of the same name), Mamie Van Doren entertains her fellow prisoners with a stirring rendition of "Jiggle and Wiggle and Wriggle and Rock."*

If JAYNE MANSFIELD could be described as an unconvincing imitator of Marilyn Monroe (see above), then Van Doren can only be perceived as an even worse imitator of Mansfield; native of Rowena, South Dakota; worked as secretary, then big-band singer, before making her way into low-budget Hollywood features; brought great sincerity and exaggerated emotion to her roles as daring "rebel girls"; major turkeys include *Running Wild* (1955); *Untamed Youth* (1957); *High School Confidential* (1958); *Guns, Girls and Gangsters* (1959); *The Private Lives of Adam and Eve* and *College Confidential* (both 1960); *The Navy vs. the Night Monsters* (1966—*see:* THE LEAST CONVINCING SCIENTIFIC EXPLANATION IN MOTION PICTURE HISTORY); and *Voyage to the Planet of Prehistoric Women* (1968—*see:* THE MOST PRIMITIVE MALE CHAUVINIST FANTASY IN MOVIE HISTORY). Recently recorded several albums of "song stylings" and is planning a movie comeback.

HAROLD P. WARREN

Fast-talking producer-director-screenwriter-star from El Paso, Texas; made his living as a fertilizer salesman and, true to his profession, managed to persuade thousands of locals to buy shares in his "spectacular" new motion picture, *Manos, The Hands of Fate* (1966); in finished film, not only are microphones and stagehands regularly in view, but even the clapper board makes an uncredited cameo appearance; the failure of the hopelessly amateurish piece of Texas gothic made Warren the laughingstock of El Paso and doomed his next project, *Wild Desert Bikers;* moved to Phoenix ahead of his creditors, where he is currently working as a packager of tax shelters.

JERRY WARREN

Enterprising importer; as "director-producer" specializes in purchasing bottom-of-the-barrel movies from abroad (Mexico, Germany, Chile, Italy, Lapland) then dubbing them, shooting a few primitive new American scenes, and releasing them in U.S.; these titles include *Man Beast* (1955); *Face of the Screaming Werewolf* (1959); *Creature of the Walking Dead* (1960); *Invasion of the Animal People* (1962); *Attack of the Mayan Mummy* (1963); *Curse of the Stone Hand* (1965). In addition to these contributions to international understanding, has also created some homegrown product, including *Teenage Zombies* (1957); *The Incredible Petrified World* (1959); *She Was a Hippy Vampire* (1966); and *Frankenstein Island* (1981).

GEORGE WEISS

High-strung owner-operator of New York–based Screen Classics Productions; responsible for the celebrated *After Midnight* burlesque series (*Bagdad After Midnight; Paris After Midnight; Hollywood After Midnight; New York After Midnight; Tijuana After Midnight;* and so forth); branched out to produce many other important bad films: *Love Life of a Gorilla* (1937); *White Slaves of Chinatown* (1938), *Test Tube Babies* (1953); *Glen or Glenda* (1953); *Olga's Massage Parlor* (1954); *Olga's Dance Hall Girls* (1955); *Dance Hall Racket* (1955); *Love Captive in Greenwich Village* (1955); and the feminist classic *All Women are Bad* (1956).

EDWARD D. WOOD, JR.

Golden Turkey Life Achievement Award Winner as Worst Director of All Time; son of a mail clerk, born in Poughkeepsie, New York, October 10, 1924; enlisted in Marine Corps, 1942; wounded in combat in the Pacific; returned to the U.S., joined traveling carnival, and made his way to California; wrote, produced, and directed a stage play in Burbank, California, entitled *The Casual Company,* but it proved unsuccessful; first film released in 1953: *Glen or Glenda,* with Wood in dual title role (*see:* THE LEAST CONVINCING SCIENTIFIC EXPLANATION IN MOTION PICTURE HISTORY); wrote and directed seven more iconoclastic films during the next nineteen years; applied himself with boundless energy and optimism to process of filmmaking, despite dismal results; regularly employed his faithful friends and "drinking buddies" as part of the Wood Stock Company, including BELA

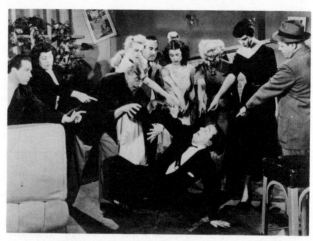

A CONTROVERSIAL DIRECTOR CONFRONTS HIS CRITICS: Edward D. Wood, Jr., in the expressionistic dream sequence from Glen or Glenda, *the autobiographical transvestite epic in which he played the dual title role.*

LUGOSI, LYLE TALBOT, TOR JOHNSON, DOLORES FULLER, MONA MCKINNON, Tom Keene, Paul Marco, Conrad Brooks, Kenne Duncan, Duke Moore, and CRISWELL. When his pictures failed to win the wide audience he craved, he slipped into work as a pornographic novelist in 1970s, exploiting his own lifelong preference for wearing women's clothes; novel titles include *Diary of a Transvestite Hooker, Killer in Drag, Death of a Transvestite, Naked Bones;* battled alcoholism and creditors at end of his life, but still dreamed of making powerful motion picture statements; died while watching a televised football game on December 10, 1978; has developed enthusiastic cult following after publication of *Golden Turkey Awards* in 1980; scholarship and documentation on his life and works currently coordinated by Edward D. Wood, Jr., Film Appreciation Society, 2265 Westwood Blvd., Suite B150, Los Angeles, California 90064.

His credits:

—as writer-director: *Glen or Glenda* (1953); *Jail Bait* (1955); *Bride of the Monster* (1955); *Plan Nine from Outer Space* (1959); *Night of the Ghouls* (1959); *The Sinister Urge* (1961); *Take It Out in Trade* (1971); and *Necromania* (1972).

—as screenwriter only: *The Violent Years* (1956); *The Bride and the Beast* (1958); *Shotgun Wedding* (1963); *Orgy of the Dead* (1965); *Fugitive Girls* (1971).

PIA ZADORA

Perennially aspiring actress, nightclub singer, and sex kitten; born Pia Schipani in New York City; movie debut at age 8 in *Santa Claus Conquers the Martians* (1964 —*see:* THE MOST INSUFFERABLE KIDDIE MOVIE EVER MADE); from age 17 on, intimately connected with her future husband, Meshulem Riklis, who has been described as

Pia Zadora portrayed an ambitious screenwriter who suffers a nervous breakdown in The Lonely Lady; *somehow, even after this draining role, the aspiring star found the inner strength to continue with her career.*

the sixth wealthiest man in the world; he has financed all her recent films in an energetic effort to make her a star, featuring his beloved in splashy, sleazy soap operas in which she invariably portrays a "smoldering" seductress; novelist Truman Capote, however, wrote of her

"limp dirty hair that drapes the sides of a long face with mouselike eyes and fat cheeks." Her major titles include *Butterfly* (1981); *Fake-Out* (1982—*see:* THE MOST PREPOSTEROUS ROMANTIC PAIRING IN MOVIE HISTORY); *The Lonely Lady* (1983); *Voyage of the Rock Aliens* (1985—retitled *When the Rain Begins to Fall*).

AL ZIMBALIST

Brusque, hard-driving producer of fifties monster movies; tried to encourage confusion between himself and Sam Zimbalist of MGM (no relation), who was producer of *Ben-Hur;* has reacted with threats and lawsuits when critics have ridiculed his preposterous pictures, including *Watusi* (1959—*see:* THE MOST AWKWARD ON-SCREEN MARRIAGE PROPOSAL); *Cat Women of the Moon* (1953 —*see:* THE MOST PRIMITIVE MALE CHAUVINIST FANTASY IN MOVIE HISTORY); *Robot Monster* (1953—*see:* THE MOST LAUGHABLE CONCEPT FOR AN OUTER SPACE INVADER); *Monster from Green Hell* (1957); and *Young Dillinger* (1965, starring Beverly Hills—*see:* THE MOST LUDICROUS PROFESSIONAL NAME IN MOVIE HISTORY). We eagerly await the response of Mr. Zimbalist—or his lawyers—to this book.

JUNIOR

THANK YOU, THANK YOU

No awards ceremony would be complete without a few tearful words of appreciation to all the "little people" who toiled behind the scenes. It is therefore only appropriate that we conclude Son of Golden Turkey Awards *by acknowledging our unadvertised accomplices on the project, including:*

Diane Medved, PhD, who knowingly married into our manic menagerie, and who provided live-in clinical psychology services for the two authors during the duration of the project. Needless to say, she also provided endless stores of inspiration, comfort and entertainment. According to recent reports, she is writing a new book (her fourth) describing the psychopathology of bad movie addiction.

Kevin Allman, free-lance journalist and New Wave boy wonder, who found time in his increasingly busy schedule to serve, once again, as our tireless researcher. Kevin's invaluable assistance on four different projects during the last seven years has earned him the title of "Honorary Medved Brother" —whether he wants it or not.

And speaking of Medved brothers, there are actually four of us, not just two. Michael is the oldest of the clan, Harry the youngest. In between these two extremes stands the imposing figure of Jonathan Medved, who, despite his demanding life as one of Israel's up-and-coming high tech tycoons, helped to

conceive the categories for this book and provided humor and insight for many of the chapters. Our other brother, Ben Medved, is a psychology graduate student in northern California who helped research the chapter on THE MOST EMBARRASSING NUDE SCENE IN HOLLYWOOD HISTORY.

Many others provided useful suggestions and information or made available to us rare photographs, periodicals, films, and videotapes. These helpful souls and institutions included Bruce Akiyama, Jeff Stein, Michael "Psychotronic" Weldon, Ray Dennis Steckler, Richard Foos, Kathy Dougherty, Charles Higham, Bennett Yellin, Paul Clemens, Larry Buchanan, June Ormond, Tracy Terhune, Scot Holton, Ernie Santilli, Kenneth Turan, Jim Jewell, Stan Neufeld, Simon Rattle, George Barrows, Gary Myer, Fred Mollin, Don Nagel, the late Dick Toborg, Michel Levesque, the Museum of Modern Art, Sir Kalby Bundle, the UCLA Film Archives, Russ Marker, Jeff Sillifant, Ross Barnard, Herbert D. Schimmel, Jon Lackey, Bob Martin, Karen Machande, Eddie Brandt and his "Saturday Matinee," Randy Simon, Eric Caidin of Hollywood Book and Poster, Jeff Barry, David Bradley, Dave Lewis, J. Watson Garman, John Davies, Judd Magilnick, Michael Mann, Harry Green, and Sol Genuth.

Special thanks, as always, to our agents, Richard and Arthur Pine, who first suggested this project; and to our editor at Villard Books, Peter Gethers, who commissioned this work and helped to guide it to its final form.

Our parents deserve their own recognition: David Medved contributed the loyal ability to laugh uproariously at any line we would write, no matter how inane it happened to be, while Ronnie Medved instructed Harry in her own unique system of filing and organization.

We should also express our gratitude to the dedicated research staff at the Margaret Herrick Library of the Academy of Motion Picture Arts and Sciences in Beverly Hills. In addition to their assistance in investigating many of the movies in this book, they also helped answer a question that has haunted us for years: How did the turkey, an honorable and useful bird, come to be associated with wretched and rejected motion pictures? We learned that this strange colloquial usage actually originated during the heyday of vaudeville at the turn of the century. It seems that theaters used to offer shows on Thanksgiving day, but few Americans abandoned their festive holiday tables in order to attend. Thanksgiving, or "Turkey Night," became notorious as the worst occasion of the entire year in terms of box office receipts. Consequently, impresarios assigned their bottom-of-the-barrel talent to play these dreaded engagements, and referred to the hapless entertainers as "Turkey Acts," or, later, simply as "Turkeys." By the mid-1920s, the term had been carried over to the motion picture business.

Finally, and most importantly, we must thank our faithful readers, so many of whom have written to us over the years, and who have provided scores of useful suggestions that have found their way into the pages of this book. Until recently, we tried to answer each of these letters individually, but the steadily increasing flow of mail (we've received well over five thousand cards and letters to date) made this continued special handling impossible. Nevertheless, we continue to feel a strong personal connection to all those who have written to us or who happen to have read our books. As we explained in the introduction, this project marks our final literary statement on the subject of bad movies, but we maintain undimmed affection for those who have come to share our peculiar passion. Anyone who has sat through *Mesa of Lost Women* or *The Creeping Terror* cannot seem to us a total stranger; shared adversity forges a powerful bond, and the fellowship of bad film fanatics is formidable indeed.

ABOUT THE AUTHORS

HARRY MEDVED, 24, is, with his brother Michael, the co-author of four books on motion pictures. In frequent television appearances and as host of "Worst Film Festivals" in North America, Europe, and Australia, he has emerged as the world's leading authority on bad movies. In 1981 he served as chief researcher on Paramount's feature film *It Came From Hollywood*—starring Dan Aykroyd, Cheech and Chong, and John Candy. He recently completed his BA in film production at UCLA and hopes for a career as an editor and as a director of his own Golden Turkeys.

In addition to collaborating with his brother on movie books, MICHAEL MEDVED, 36, is the author of nonfiction bestsellers about the sixties generation, the White House staff, and the practice of medicine. An honors graduate of Yale, he prepared for his work on Golden Turkey Awards by serving three years as a professional speechwriter for a variety of prominent politicians. As a screenwriter, he worked on three major studio projects and a network miniseries. Since the fall of 1985, he has served as co-host of *Sneak Previews*, the popular movie review show on PBS.